Asian Anthropology

Asian Anthropology raises important questions regarding the nature of anthropology, and particularly the production and consumption of anthropological knowledge in Asia. Instead of assuming a universal standard or trajectory for the development of anthropology in Asia, the contributors to this volume begin with the appropriate premise that anthropologies in different Asian countries have developed and continue to develop according to their own internal dynamics.

With chapters written by an international group of experts in the field, *Asian Anthropology* will be a useful teaching tool and a fascinating resource for scholars working in Asian anthropology.

Jan van Bremen is Professor at the Centre for Japanese and Korean Studies in Leiden University.

Eyal Ben-Ari is Professor of Anthropology at The Hebrew University of Jerusalem.

Syed Farid Alatas is Associate Professor at the Department of Sociology, National University of Singapore.

Anthropology of Asia series
Edited by Shaun Malarney
International Christian University, Japan

Asia today is one of the most dynamic regions of the world. The previously predominant image of 'timeless peasants' has given way to the image of fast-paced business people, mass consumerism and high-rise urban conglomerations. Yet much discourse remains entrenched in the polarities of 'East versus West', 'Tradition versus Change'. This series hopes to provide a forum for anthropological studies which break with such polarities. It will publish titles dealing with cosmopolitanism, cultural identity, representations, arts and performance. The complexities of urban Asia, its elites, its political rituals and its families will also be explored.

Hong Kong
The anthropology of a Chinese metropolis
Edited by Grant Evans and Maria Tam

Folk Art Potters of Japan
Brian Moeran

Anthropology and Colonialism in Asia and Oceania
Jan van Bremen and Akitoshi Shimizu

Japanese Bosses, Chinese Workers
Power and control in a Hong Kong megastore
Wong Heung Wah

The Legend of the Golden Boat
Regulation, trade and traders in the borderlands of Laos, Thailand, China and Burma
Andrew Walker

Cultural Crisis and Social Memory
Modernity and identity in Thailand and Laos
Edited by Shigeharu Tanabe and Charles F. Keyes

Asian Anthropology

**Edited by
Jan van Bremen,
Eyal Ben-Ari and
Syed Farid Alatas**

 Routledge
Taylor & Francis Group

LONDON AND NEW YORK

First published 2005
by Routledge
2 Park Square, Milton Park, Abingdon, Oxon OX14 4RN

Simultaneously published in the USA and Canada
by Routledge
270 Madison Ave, New York, NY 10016

Transferred to Digital Printing 2006

Routledge is an imprint of the Taylor & Francis Group

Typeset in Times New Roman by
Newgen Imaging Systems (P) Ltd, Chennai, India
Printed and bound in Great Britain by
Antony Rowe Ltd, Chippenham, Wiltshire

British Library Cataloguing in Publication Data
A catalogue record for this book is available from the British Library

Library of Congress Cataloging in Publication Data
   Asian anthropology / edited by Jan van Bremen, Eyal Ben-Ari, and
Syed Farid Alatas.
       p. cm. – (Anthropology of Asia series)
     Includes bibliographical references.
     1. Ethnology–Asia–Philosophy. 2. Ethnology–Asia–History.
3. Philosophy, Asian. 4. Anthropologists–Attitudes. 5. Indigenous
peoples–Education (Higher) 6. Racism in anthropology.
7. Asia–Social life and customs. I. Bremen, Jan van, 1946–
II. Ben-Ari, Eyal, 1953– III. Alatas, Farid, Syed. IV. Anthropology of
Asia series (Richmond, England).

GN625.A74 2004
306′.095–dc22   2004027729

ISBN 0–415–34983–4

Contents

Notes on contributors

Syed Farid Alatas is Associate Professor at the Department of Sociology, National University of Singapore, where he has been since 1992. A Malaysian national, he had his schooling in Singapore and obtained his PhD in Sociology from the Johns Hopkins University in 1991. He lectured at the University of Malaya in the Department of South-east Asian Studies prior to his appointment at Singapore. His book *Democracy and Authoritarianism: The Rise of the Post-Colonial State in Indonesia and Malaysia* is published by Macmillan (1997). His recent articles include 'The study of the social sciences in developing societies: towards an adequate conceptualization of relevance', *Current Sociology* (2001), 49(2): 1–19; (with Vineeta Sinha) 'Teaching classical sociological theory in Singapore: the context of Eurocentrism', *Teaching Sociology* (2001), 29(3): 316–31; 'Islam, Ilmu-Ilmu Sosial dan Masyarakat Sipil', *Antropologi Indonesia* (2001), 25(66): 13–22; 'Eurocentrism and the role of the human sciences in the dialogue among civilizations', *The European Legacy* (2002), 7(6): 759–70; and 'Academic dependency and the global division of labour in the social sciences', *Current Sociology* (2003), 51(6): 599–613. He is currently working on a second book in the area of the philosophy and sociology of social science and on another project on Muslim ideologies and utopias.

Eyal Ben-Ari is Professor of Anthropology at The Hebrew University of Jerusalem. He has carried out fieldwork in Japan, Singapore and Hong Kong on a variety of topics including Japanese white-collar communities, early childhood education in Japan, Japanese expatriates and the contemporary Japanese Self-defense Forces. In Israel, he has carried out research on Jewish saint worship and social and cultural aspects of the Israeli military.

Jan van Bremen obtained his PhD from the University of California at Berkeley in 1984, worked in the Department of Anthropology in the University of Amsterdam (1975–86) and joined the Centre for Japanese and Korean Studies at Leiden University in 1987. His specializations are Japanese anthropology and folklore studies, religion and society, and intellectual history. He edited *Ceremony and Ritual in Japan: Religious Practices in an Industrialized Society* (with D.P. Martinez, 1995); *Anthropology and Colonialism in Asia and Oceania* (with Akitoshi Shimizu, 1999); and *Wartime Japanese Anthropology in Asia and the Pacific* (with Akitoshi Shimizu, 2003).

Roma Chatterji is Reader in the Department of Sociology, Delhi School of Economics. Her research centres around folklore and the public sphere, illness experience and the anthropology of collective violence.

Jerry S. Eades is Professor of Asia Pacific Studies and Director of the Media Resource Center, Ritsumeikan Asia Pacific University, Beppu, Japan and Senior Honorary Research Fellow in Anthropology, University of Kent. His current research interests include migration, urbanization, tourism, higher education and the development of anthropology in East Asia. He is the author, editor or translator of over a dozen books, the most recent of which include *Globalization and Social Change in Contemporary Japan* (edited with Tom Gill and Harumi Befu, Trans Pacific Press, 2000), *Globalization in Southeast Asia* (edited with Shinji Yamashita, Berghahn, 2003), and *The Making of Anthropology in East and Southeast Asia* (edited with Shinji Yamashita and Joseph Bosco, Berghahn, 2004).

Grant Evans is Reader in Anthropology and Director of the Centre for Anthropological Research at the University of Hong Kong. His latest book is *A Short History of Laos: The Land In-between* (2002).

Takami Kuwayama is Professor in the Department of History and Anthropology at the Graduate School of Letters, Hokkaido University, Sapporo. He received his degrees from the Tokyo University of Foreign Studies and the University of California, Los Angeles. His recent publications include *Native Anthropology: The Japanese Challenge to Western Academic Hegemony* (Trans Pacific Press, Melbourne, 2004) and the Japanese translation of Joy Hendry's *An Introduction to Social Anthropology: Other People's Worlds* (Hosei University Press, Japan, 2002).

Okpyo Moon is Professor of Anthropology at the Academy of Korean Studies, Korea. She has written *From Paddy Field to Ski Slope: The Revitalization of Tradition in Japanese Village Life* (1989), *Countryside Reinvented for Urban Tourists* (2002), *Voluntary Associations in Japan* (2001) and edited many books in Korean including *New Women: Images of Modern Women in Japan and Korea* (2003) and *Yangban: The Life-world of Korean Scholar-gentry* (2004). Her current research interests are youth culture and generational relationships in Japan and Korea.

Frank N. Pieke is University Lecturer in the Modern Politics and Society of China and a Fellow of St Cross College, University of Oxford. His recent publications include *Transnational Chinese: Fujianese Migrants in Europe* (Stanford University Press, Stanford, CA, 2004, with Pal Nyiri, Mette Thuno and Antonella Ceccagno) and 'The genealogical mentality in modern China', *The Journal of Asian Studies* (2003), 62(1): 101–28. At Oxford, he is Director of the Institute for Chinese Studies and coordinator of the research programme on 'Sending Contexts' of the Centre on Migration, Policy and Society (COMPAS, 2003–8) funded by the British Economic and Social Research

Council. His research interests include local-level politics and administrative reform in rural China, rural development, political protest and migration, transnationalism and the overseas Chinese.

Michael Prager is Lecturer at the Department of Anthropology of the University of Muenster. Among his recent publications are articles on the history of anthropology, French social theory and the ethnography of South-east Asia. He is currently writing a book on the history of the Sultanate of Bima (Sumbawa, Indonesia).

Martin Ramstedt is currently Research Fellow at the International Institute for Asian Studies in Leiden. He is the author of 'Hindu dharma Indonesia – Das Verhältnis zwischen Religion und Staat bei der Entwicklung des Hinduismus im modernen Indonesien', in Martin Klein and Jens Krause (eds), *Umbruch in Südostasien: Fachbeiträge der Tagung des Arbeitskreises Südostasien/Ozeanien Berlin 1995*, Hamburg: Abera-Verlag, 1996, pp. 135–41; and 'Interkulturelle Kommunikation – wozu?', in Andreas Disselnkötter, Siegfried Jäger, Helmut Kellershohn and Susanne Slobodzian (eds), *Evidenzen im Fluß: Demokratieverluste in Deutschland*, Duisburg: Duisburger Institut für Sprachund Sozialforschung (DISS), 1997, pp. 205–31.

Vineeta Sinha is Assistant Professor at the Department of Sociology, National University of Singapore. Her research interests include the history and critique of concepts and categories in the social sciences, sociology and anthropology of religion, the practice of Hinduism in the Diaspora and the political economy of health care in medically plural societies. Her teaching includes courses in the area of classical sociological theory, sociology of religion, everyday life and food. She has a forthcoming book on Singapore Hindu Diaspora (NIAS and SUP). Some recent publications include 'Merging different sacred spaces: enabling religious encounters through pragmatic utilization of space?', *Contributions to Indian Sociology* (2003); 'Decentring social sciences in practice through individual actions and choices', *Current Sociology* (2002) and 'Teaching classical theory in Singapore: the context of Eurocentrism', with Syed Farid Alatas, *Teaching Sociology* (2001).

Acknowledgements

This volume owes its origins to presentations and debates in the workshop *Indigenous and Indigenised Anthropology in Asia*, which was held in 1997 at the Centre of Japanese and Korean Studies in Leiden University. The majority of the papers, rewritten and updated, appear in this volume. A number of chapters were added to give a more complete view of anthropology in Asia. The workshop and volume were made possible with the financial assistance of the Isaac Alfred Ailion Foundation, the Research School of Asian, African, and Amerindian Studies and the International Institute for Asian Studies in Leiden. Our thanks go to an anonymous reader; series editor, Shaun Malarney; and Stephanie Rogers and Laura Sacha of Routledge for their careful reading of the text, advice and support. We are also grateful to Hanneke Kossen for her unfailing editorial assistance.

Part I

Introduction

1 Asian anthropologies and anthropologies in Asia

An introductory essay

Eyal Ben-Ari and Jan van Bremen

The University of Notre Dame Department of Anthropology invites applications for a tenure-track position in the socio-cultural anthropology of South or Southeast Asia at the assistant professor level. A PhD qualification is required. We strongly encourage applications by scholars from this region and from other traditionally under-represented groups. Topical and thematic interests should include development, ecological, economic, environmental, or legal anthropology. The ideal candidate will have an active research program and be an excellent undergraduate teacher for our all-undergraduate program. Publications and teaching experience are highly desirable. The ideal candidate will share the department's commitment to a four-field approach in both teaching and collegial interactions. We will be especially interested in candidates who can involve undergraduates in research programs. The Department faculty are energetic and congenial and take research and teaching equally seriously. The University of Notre Dame is generous in its support for research. The position begins in August 2005; the teaching load is two courses per semester.

(http://www.aaanet.org/careers.htm)

Social/cultural anthropology of South Asia: The Department of Anthropology, Harvard University, is conducting a search to fill a faculty position in the social/cultural anthropology of South Asia at the level of Assistant or untenured Associate Professor. The topical and theoretical specializations are open, but the program seeks a faculty member whose research and teaching are complementary to the interests of the current faculty. The themes of interest include: gender and sexuality; the culture of the state; religion and nationalism; media, language, and the public sphere; science and technology; consumption and markets; the environment; the dynamics of diasporas; and sectarianism, violence, and politics. Candidates should have already conducted ethnographic fieldwork in one or more South Asian regions (broadly conceived, and including India, Sri Lanka, Pakistan, Bangladesh, or Nepal, and/or diasporic communities). Candidates should demonstrate a promise of excellence in both research and teaching and should expect to have completed the requirements for the PhD prior to their appointment. Their teaching duties will include offering courses at both undergraduate and graduate levels. The appointment will begin on 1 July 2005.

(http://www.aaanet.org/careers.htm)

Published in centers of academic life around the world, such employment notices regularly appear both in the professional anthropological newsletters and those of area studies. Such notices refer to university positions in which anthropological knowledge about Asia is created for consumption in our "professional community" and conveyed to students. But what kind of institutional arrangements and practices are entailed by such positions? What kind of ideals of professional conduct and career moves do such advertisements represent? What kind of knowledge do professional readers bring to bear on such announcements, so that they are made sense of?

In an essay devoted to the transformation of anthropology into an academic discipline, James Clifford, a central commentator on contemporary issues, candidly and carefully notes:

> My discussion here is largely limited to Euro-American trends. I join Gupta and Ferguson (chapter 1 of this book) in admitting my "sanctioned ignorance" (Spivak 1988; John 1989) of many non-Western anthropological contexts and practices. And even within the contested but powerful disciplinary "center," my discussion is primarily focused on North America and, to some extent, England.
>
> (1997: 219, n.1)

What kind of international order does Clifford assume in limiting his focus to the "center"? While his comments obviously reveal the structure of his personal and intellectual network, does his admission also convey the message that "real," "serious" anthropological work is done mostly in America and Britain? Can we learn anything from the fact that Clifford's confession of "ignorance" of anthropology elsewhere is placed in a marginal textual location, in a footnote?

This volume represents attempts at answering such questions. It examines the contexts within which anthropological knowledge in general, and such knowledge about Asia in particular, is produced and disseminated. In this introductory chapter we place our volume in the context of the ethnology of ethnologists (Scholte 1980) or the sociology of anthropological knowledge: an analysis of the social and cultural processes by which anthropological knowledge (of the social and cultural variety) about Asian societies is created. We follow Swidler and Arditi (1994: 317) to propose that academic knowledge be examined like other kinds of social knowledge around two analytical foci. First, we uncover how the production of knowledge about Asia is related to authoritative texts, career advancement, professional conduct and institutional locations. Here, we see knowledge as a set of skills and habits socially constructed and individually utilized to achieve strategic ends. Our second focus is on how anthropological practices and knowledge created by the anthropologists serve to produce and reproduce the larger system of social distinctions and social hierarchies within which anthropologists actively maneuver (Swidler and Arditi 1994: 317). In other words, we examine the question of how our professionalization replicates national, cultural, and international peculiarities.

Our model of anthropological work thus emphasizes how the moves of individual anthropologists serve, at one and the same time, to replicate and to reinforce and to shift such matters as relations between academic centers and peripheries, national academic boundaries, or notions of proper fieldwork.

Our contention along these lines is that it is impossible to focus only on the anthropology of Asia. We argue that an understanding of "things Asian" must take account of what has been variously termed the "international community" of anthropologists (Stocking 1982), a "World Anthropologies Network" (World Anthropologies Network 2003), or the "world system of anthropology" (Kuwayama 1997: 52). Our model underscores how the production of anthropological knowledge is situated in certain social, historical, and global contexts. Thus, a complementary aim of this introductory chapter is to show how an investigation of Asian anthropologies (anthropology by Asians, and the anthropology of Asian societies) may in itself proffer insights for understanding anthropology in our contemporary world.

After briefly justifying the focus on Asia, we set out the broad parameters of what may be termed the professional "folk model" which anthropologists hold. We then sketch out a number of key analytical metaphors or guiding images that best capture the diverse and changing nature of contemporary anthropology: centers and peripheries, the workings of the nation-state, an academic division of labor that produces "area studies," linguistic communities, the micro-politics of career moves, and a model of change and its limits.

Why Asia?

The reasons for examining anthropology in Asia have to do with historical and contemporary developments in Asian societies and with their varied anthropological traditions. First, this area includes a number of sites where anthropological traditions (formulated, for example, as folklore, ethnology, or "local" studies) have developed over a long period of time. Accordingly, Asia provides a number of cases which facilitate an inquiry into the distinctive traditions of "anthropological" scholarship (theories and methodological tools) created in societies outside the "West" (primarily, India, China, and Japan). Yet given our "global" focus, these diverse Asian cases also allow us to explore how local traditions of anthropology have interacted over the past two-hundred years or so with the discipline as it emerged in Western countries (Alatas, Chapter 11, in this volume).

Second, at the empirical level, Asia has rather dense concentrations of anthropologists that consistently produce and consume professional knowledge. Japan and China, to provide two examples, have the second and the third largest number of active anthropologists after the United States (Eades, Chapter 4, Pieke, Chapter 3, in this volume). In addition, the funds awarded for anthropological work by the Asian governments in the past decades have been complemented by the growing numbers of national and especially international conferences, symposia, and seminars held in (and about) the Asian societies. These emerging nuclei of anthropological work offer cases through which to explore what are perhaps the potential alternatives for producing anthropological knowledge.

Third, the sheer economic and political strength of countries in many parts of Asia is an issue which raises for anthropologists (as for other social scientists) problems related both to the place of resources in fostering the creation of anthropological knowledge and for understanding such postulated ideals as "East" and "West" or emergent thoughts about "Asian" identity. The economic success of many contemporary Asian societies forces Westerners (like the authors of this introduction) to face questions related to modernity (and post-modernity) in ways that African and (arguably) Latin American societies do not.

Fourth, the relative strength of the state in many Asian countries raises questions about the very nature of anthropology as a discipline that takes a critical or (conversely) a "contributory" attitude to authority. The actions and the activities of anthropologists in such societies aid us in clarifying the notions of professional autonomy, the political implications of anthropological work, and the manner by which anthropologists are committed to, and participate in, projects of social betterment or change.

A model profession

In attempting to understand how anthropological knowledge within and about Asia is produced, it is not enough to examine how the anthropological theories and the concepts have been developed in relation to the "Asian" issues ("caste society," "shame culture," or the "rice economies," for instance). No less important are questions about what may be termed a "professional folk model" of and the set of institutional and organizational practices through which this model is actualized. These questions center on how anthropological knowledge is produced within the professional communities to which anthropologists belong, and from which they derive their identity, receive rewards and sanctions for the use of certain tools and theories, and which govern what are defined as appropriate (and prestigious) sites and subjects of study.

Minimally, a profession is a body of persons engaged in a calling or an occupation which requires and produces a certain kind of knowledge. In anthropology, professionalism archetypically involves three central clusters of activities: doing research (fieldwork, field methods), writing texts (ethnographies, monographs), and "careering" in academic institutions (universities, associations, research centers, museums). To formulate the ideal of professionalism somewhat crudely, the image is one of a lone anthropologist (usually white-middle-class, frequently male) from a university in a "Western" (American, British, or French) center; he crosses national geo-political borders and the cultural boundaries to do an extended piece of fieldwork (usually a year or two) among another group; he returns to his university to "write-up" his research in a textual form called an ethnography; and it is this text (and accompanying articles published in journals) that is published and used as a means to advance a university career.

It is a "folk" model because it encompasses the assumptions and images that lie at the base of mundane or common sense knowledge we use in our anthropological world and has the unquestioned knowledge that "all" anthropologists know. It is a "professional" model because it provides the basic points of reference for "what we are" and "what we are trying to do" through which our specialist reality is constructed. To formulate this point by way of examples, anthropologists use this model to do such things as to describe and prescribe proper behavior in the field, to mark entrance via fieldwork into our community, and to give advice and support to new members trying to further their careers. While relatively simple, this model – and the clusters of activities it encompasses – is actually based on a complex array of practices, and arrangements.

By far the most discussed aspect of anthropological activity has been, and still is, fieldwork (Freilich 1977: 14). As a host of commentators have noted, although fieldwork is not only the "definer" of the peculiarity of our discipline, it is still considered the prime rite-of-passage into the profession (Agar 1980: 2; Langham 1981: xv; Gerholm and Hannerz 1982: 28; Wengle 1988; Srinivas 1996: 209). In a characteristic formulation, Messerschmidt (1989: 3) notes that

> In the past, it was considered a requisite and proper rite of passage for fledgling anthropologists...to leave the comfortable nest of our own social upbringing and brave the trials and tribulations of study in other lands, or at least among people other than our own. Research elsewhere, preferably abroad, was...an established tradition of the profession.

Based on the ideal of Malinowski's research in the Trobriands (Stocking 1983; Vincent 1991), fieldwork in our professional folk model entails the following components: a prolonged phase in a society other than one's own, hardships encountered upon entering the field, collecting information on the basis of participation and observation, and beginning to examine this data in the light of current theoretical formulations. This formulation also provides criteria for appraising such things as how much prestige should be awarded to a parti-cular stint of fieldwork (one mark being the amount of time spent in the field), or the "authenticity" of research (the distance between the culture studied and the anthropologist's "home" culture). It is on the basis of these criteria, for instance, that fieldwork projects are arrayed on a continuum, ranging from the more distant (and therefore more prestigious) to "anthropology at home" (Coleman and Simpson 2004: 28–30), which is sometimes labeled as fieldwork by default.

If fieldwork has been intensively discussed since Malinowski's time, the anthropological texts have been at the forefront of debates since the early 1980s. Our folk model dictates that on the basis of fieldwork, an ethnography – a book length monograph about a group and its life ways – should be published as a first major step on the way to a professional career. Despite current deliberations about experimental ethnographies (Marcus and Cushman 1982; Marcus and Fischer 1986), the basic criteria for appraising the "productivity" of anthropologists have not changed much in the past four or five decades. While it is true that anthropologists no longer look at whole cultures (Moore 1987: 735), they still build their careers on the basis of singular "whole" texts: such ethnographies are treated as "whole" social facts (Handelman 1994: 362). New ethnographies and experimental texts are still appraised and examined in the same way that older, "modernist" ethnographies have been scrutinized.

In other words, while many contemporary ethnographies may be written in experimental modes, they are still constitutive of modernist practices: they are written in the framework of universities, supervised and guided by mentors with resources, graded by internal and external readers, and funded by different research councils and fellowship bodies. Moreover, these texts often figure in professional evaluations that are central to academic practices such as employment promotion, conferring research funds, and assuring participation at the professional fora (Morris 1995).

For all of the stress on reflection among anthropologists during the past few decades, the least discussed aspect of careering has been the micro-politics of academic institutions (Nöbauer 2002). What Scholte (1980: 63) called the dearth of studies on the sociology of ethnological knowledge still persists. Pels and Salemink (1995) suggest that the central criterion for the allocation of prestige – and, we would add, power – in anthropology is place of work: within the academy (in central or marginal institutions)[1] doing practical or applied jobs (in NGOs, state frameworks or private companies); and at the periphery, the "no-longer" anthropologists. Despite critiques of this situation focussing on the strictures of academic budgets or the "industrial discipline" to be found in university departments (Fox 1991: 9; Gudeman 1998), this ideal ranking is still very much alive: for the vast majority of anthropologists an academic post is still preferable to employment as an applied researcher.

In positing this professional folk model and the practices by which it is put into effect, we are not arguing that there have been no alternative patterns that have emerged from it. For example, while Gupta and Ferguson (1997) review historical examples of alternative fieldwork styles, other scholars have suggested various possibilities for ethnographic writing (Van Maanen 1988; Behar and Gordon 1995). What we argue is that this model is the hegemonic one. The use of the term "hegemony" is not just a matter of using a fashionable expression. We maintain that this conceptualization goes beyond one predicated on notions of mainstream or normative representations or arrangements. The term hegemonic encompasses (at one and the same time) ideas about a socially legitimated and maintained hierarchy between alternative arrangements, and the centrality of the centers of anthropology in controlling not only material resources, but also dominating the very conceptual categories through which we anthropologists think about the professional reality within which we pursue our careers. As the system of domination and inequality becomes so lodged in cultural belief, it comes to appear natural and inviolate (Williams 1977). It is in this light that Gupta and Ferguson's (1997: 11) characterization of the "natural" choices which anthropologists face when choosing a field should be seen:

> [F]ield sites appear simply as a natural array of choices facing graduate students ... The question becomes one of choosing an appropriate site ... Just as the culturally sanctioned discourse of "hard work" and "enterprise" enables the structurally patterned outcomes of career choice in competitive

capitalism to disappear from view, so do the repeated narratives of discovering field sites "by chance" prevent any systematic inquiry into how those field sites come to be good places for doing fieldwork in the first instance. The very significant premises and assumptions built into the anthropological idea of the "field" are in this way protected from critical scrutiny, even as they are smuggled into the discipline's most central practices of induction, socialization, and professional reproduction.

We posit that "career" choices – where to study, under whom, what subjects, which methods to use – in contemporary anthropology should be seen in a similar manner. Anthropologists, we argue, usually adopt the professional model of careering as a "natural" taken for granted array of choices and options without attending to the "internal" professional and "external" political and economical structures that underlie it. At the same time, however, we find that Asian traditions of anthropology – in the sense of ongoing, actively created legacies – at once, replicate and question this model of professionalism.

Cores, peripheries, and colonialism

Probably the most common metaphor used to characterize macro aspects of contemporary anthropology has been that of "centers and peripheries." Building upon Uberoi's suggestions about metropolis–satellite relations, Gerholm and Hannerz (1982: 6) have developed this image as a central orienting notion for understanding "the world order of anthropology." In fact, perhaps because they published their work in a peripheral country (Sweden), it was not cited later in an American volume which took up many similar ideas (Gupta and Ferguson 1997: 27). The center–periphery metaphor centers on the relations between the hubs of our discipline and regional anthropologies within the structure of the world's political-economy. Gerholm and Hannerz (1982: 7) are worth quoting at length in this regard:

> We can look at this structure of center–periphery relations more or less in network terms, as a kind of sociometry of world anthropology. Which anthropologies, and anthropologists, do people in the discipline attend to across national boundaries, if any, and in what ways... [T]his is the pattern:
>
> (a) Metropolitan anthropologists largely confine their attention to what goes on at home, or possibly in one or more other metropolis.
> (b) The anthropologists of the periphery are concerned with what happens in the discipline in their own country and in one or more metropolitan anthropologies. To some, the former is of greater interest... to others it is the other way around...
> (c) The anthropologists of different countries of the periphery take little note of each other's work, at least unless it is brought to their attention through metropolitan anthropologies.

Within this structure, centers – primarily the United States, Britain, and France – influence the periphery through such channels as publication (journals or books), cultural and academic exchanges (Fulbright professorships or British Council fellowships), policies of scientific foundations, or training (Gerholm and Hannerz 1982: 10; Spencer 2000; Darnell 2001: 28–9; Eriksen and Nielsen 2001; Patterson 2001). The idea is that through their occupational socialization, anthropologists from the periphery tend to become tuned in to "the outside," to the world centers (Gerholm and Hannerz 1982: 8). As language is a central element in this order, it is not surprising that despite being published in Sweden, the journal that published Gerholm and Hannerz' book, *Ethnos*, is produced in English.

Whatever interest anthropologists may have in problems defined as important in their societies, in order to achieve recognition from the "centers," they must formulate their findings in terms of relevant theoretical models developed in the metropolis. For example, many Asian anthropologists find that they often have to "de-Asianize" their findings for external audiences from the centers. There may be two outcomes to this situation. Some local anthropologists may insist on defining their own professional agendas and the result is (from an "international" point of view) parochialism. This would be the case for certain brands of Japanese folklore that focus on questions of origin and authenticity (also Asquith 1998). Others may accept the agendas of the centers and the effect is not so much parochialism as marginalization in terms of the world system of anthropology.[2]

What is of importance in this model (and only hinted at by Gerholm and Hannerz), is that the authority of knowledge produced in the centers is grounded in patterns of social authority (Swidler and Arditi 1994: 311): it is primarily anthropologists at the metropolitan hubs that settle disputes and establish truth. For instance, the arrangement by which the departments in Singapore or Hong Kong consistently obtain the majority of their external academic examiners from the prestigious universities of Europe and North America is both an indicator, and a practice, that actualizes center–periphery relations. Along these lines, it is groups in the metropolis that create criteria for professional recognition, standards for field research, vocabularies for appraising career moves, and relevant audiences which are adopted by anthropologists at the cores and at the margins. Accordingly, it is primarily at the center that the professional folk model of professionalization and the undergirding of institutional arrangements have been developed.

The picture is, of course, more complex for as Gerholm and Hannerz (1982: 21) remind us, national anthropologies have their own centers and peripheries. Departments in mid- or lower-level universities in the centers may be no less marginal than such departments in various peripheries. Members of such departments often do not lead important sections in professional associations or assume editorships of major journals. Yet, centers at the periphery – Calcutta or Delhi in India, or Tokyo and Kyoto in Japan – may act as mediators for even more peripheral departments or groups at the margins by bringing in ideas from the international centers.

Gupta and Ferguson add an explicit awareness of the historical situatedness of centers and peripheries to the model developed by Gerholm and Hannerz. As they underscore, present-day formations are largely the outcome of developments in the world academic system over the past two hundred or so years. This growth has involved the reproduction of the objects, methods, and subjects of study defined by Western metropolitan centers in the peripheries, and in our case, Asian peripheries. Sinha (Chapter 7, in this volume), for instance, discusses the relatively "straightforward" importation of anthropology into India. Indian scholars studied "castes" and "tribes" and carried out fieldwork in order to produce ethnographies in the tradition of British social anthropology. At the same time, as she shows, the metropolitan centers themselves were conceptually and discursively constituted through the creation of the Indian "other": Europe itself was constituted through the creation of India (also Trouillot 1991).

On the more concrete level of professional conduct, it was the unequal relations between India and centers in the West that led to establishing the first department of anthropology in Calcutta, the creation of the first Indian journal of anthropology (*Man in India*), and the training of Indian anthropologists in Britain, the United States, and Germany. Sinha terms the continued peripheriality of Indian (and, for that matter, Chinese or Indonesian) anthropologies as part of "academic colonialism." Gupta and Ferguson formulate this situation as the "colonization of intellectual production" and show how it is reinforced by such "simple" realities as the fact that graduate students funded from US sources and doing fieldwork in India are paid twice as much as full professors in Indian universities. In addition, as they demonstrate, funding endows First World ethnographers with other advantages

> Journals in which First World ethnographers publish are not available in most libraries, and are much more expensive to subscribe to from foreign countries. In 1991, libraries in New Delhi cut back journal runs because the new fiscal regime imposed by the IMF raised the exchange rate, making journals prohibitively expensive.
>
> (1997: 45–6, n.42)

The new post-colonial and post-Cold War Asian anthropologies have been influenced primarily by Britain and America. While direct French influences were found in such places as Vietnam and Taiwan in the 1930s when a number of students pursued their doctoral studies in Paris (or outside Asia in such places as Quebec or Brazil), today such influences are often mediated through the English-speaking worlds. Malaysian, Korean, or Sri Lankan anthropologists, to put this picturesquely, read English translations of Bourdieu, Foucault, or Barthes.

An examination of other Asian cases reveals a more complex picture. A prime example is Japan which has been an independent core of anthropological research for many years. Partly an outcome of indigenous legacies of scholarship and partly a result of its economic and territorial expansion, Japan offers an instance of a non-Western form of links between anthropology and colonialism (van Bremen and Shimizu 1999; Kuwayama, Chapter 5, Moon, Chapter 6, in this volume). Before the Second World War Japan's colonies and protectorates in Taiwan, Korea,

Micronesia, and Manchuria provided Japanese anthropologists with subjects and objects of study. The establishment of study associations, university departments, and funding agencies within the country were complemented by the initiation of local outposts at its periphery: for example, the founding of a department of anthropology in Taipei in 1928 (Eades, Chapter 4, in this volume). As van Bremen (1996; also Chiu 1999) stresses in a comparative essay, the Japanese heritage of scholarship and the internal colonization of peoples within Asian states (China being the prime example – Evans Chapter 2, Pieke Chapter 3, in this volume), are indicators of the fact that "colonial anthropology is not entirely a thing of the past and not wholly a thing of the West" (van Bremen 1996: 40).

Japan continues to provide what is perhaps the most impressive example of an emergent world center. The economic development and increasing political clout of Japan are obvious factors that have led to the establishment and growing importance of the National Museum of Anthropology in Osaka (*Minpaku*) (van Bremen 1997b: 62), or to the fact that Japan now has the second largest number of practising anthropologists in the world, after the United States, with a national association of nearly 2,000 members (van Bremen 1996; Eades Chapter 4, in this volume). Indeed, it is not surprising to learn that in the past few decades, in addition to the large number of Chinese anthropologists sent to the United States for training, many have been dispatched to Japan as well (Pieke, Chapter 3, in this volume). Similarly, a number of Thai, Taiwanese, and Hong Kong anthropologists have also chosen to take their PhD degrees in Japan.

These developments should caution us: the world system of anthropology is itself changing. For instance, while many Indonesian (Ramstedt, Chapter 10, in this volume), and Malaysian anthropologists still take advanced degrees in America and Europe, an increasing number now go to Australia. Australia's emergence as a center of scholarship can be seen as a reproduction of the West's anthropological tradition. But given that many Australian scholars see themselves as being on the periphery of British intellectual traditions (Turner 1992) and the internal debates within Australia about its place in Asia, is this process a straightforward one of reproduction? What is the implication of Australian and Japanese money coming into the world system of anthropology? What kind of model of change captures these transformations?

Borders, boundaries, power, and the nation-state

Before addressing these questions, we return to the center and periphery model suggested by Gerholm and Hannerz. Despite their insistence on a network approach based on ties and exchanges, the constituent units of the world order of anthropology in their model are anthropological traditions developed in contemporary nation-states. Issues of state-control over "other" territories and populations have long been central elements in the relations between anthropology and authority (colonial or otherwise) (Ellen 1976). In many contexts, anthropological knowledge has often been linked (explicitly or implicitly) to the strategic interests of states. Thus, just as knowledge about India suited the concerns of Imperial

Britain so research about Southeast Asia went hand in hand with postwar American preoccupations (Gupta and Ferguson 1997: 9). In a related manner, as Eades (Chapter 4, in this volume) points out, the areas in which Japanese anthropologists have carried out fieldwork were closely connected to the interests of the pre-war Japan state: Japanese colonies including Sakhalin Island, the Kuril Islands, Korea, Taiwan and territories under Japanese rule in Micronesia, China, Mongolia, and Southeast Asia.

The links between anthropology and state-control are also involved in internal colonialism, in control of "domestic others" within nation-states (Gruber 1981). As Linke (1990: 126) notes, anthropology in such countries as Germany (and, we would add, Spain) involved not only knowing the populations of colonial countries through anthropology but knowing internal "peoples" through folklore: the "emergence of the population as a target of folklore research thus finds its early beginnings in the pragmatic concerns of the German states and not, as it is usually assumed, in the ideological concerns of the German romantic" (ibid.). Indeed, folklore research in Germany was launched during the period when new forms of state-control were instituted (hospitals, establishments of correction, education, and commerce) (ibid.: 131). From our perspective, what is of importance is not only the ways by which colonial patterns continue to animate present-day center–periphery relations, but also how they are entangled with states. Gupta and Ferguson observe:

> Decolonization has transformed field sites not merely by making it difficult, if not impossible, to move across national borders, but by affecting a whole host of mechanisms, from the location of archives to the granting of visas and research clearance. The institutions that organized knowledge along colonial lines have yielded to ones that organize it along national ones.
>
> (1997: 10)

China, for instance, when it closed its borders to foreign anthropologists unintentionally "encouraged" the study of Taiwan as a surrogate for scholarship on Han Chinese. Within China, while abolished as an independent branch of learning between the 1950s and 1970s (Zhou 1993), during the 1980s anthropology was reinstated as an appendage of the state, as a branch of knowledge contributing to the control of minorities (Evans, Chapter 2, Pieke Chapter 3, in this volume). In a more attenuated form, Provencher (1994: 56) observes that anthropologists doing research in Malaysia must sometimes take into account official views (as well as the tempers of some native Malay scholars) when studying "sensitive topics" such as ethnicity.

Yet formulating the issue in terms of state-"control" is too limiting. In many contemporary Asian societies, as Chatterji and Moon (Chapters 8 and 6, in this volume) argue, anthropology is linked not only to state-control and the effects of political boundaries, but also to active processes of state-making and nation-building. The most explicit case of mobilizing anthropology for nation-building tasks is probably Indonesia. Ramstedt (Chapter 10, in this volume) explains how applied anthropology in Indonesia was directed to foster "unity in diversity" (the government policy of national integration) and how courses given by anthropologists were to provide professionals such as lawyers, teachers, psychologists, public health officers, and priests with insight into the diversity and peculiarity of local cultures. As conceived of by representatives of the Indonesian state, anthropology was to work through government ministries, institutes of science and of national culture to mediate between tradition and modernity.

The link between anthropology and state power encompasses yet other complexities. Eades (Chapter 4, in this volume) explains that although carried out in colonial research institutes and funded by government, most research by Japanese anthropologists in China and Taiwan was so "academic" that it was useless for administrative or military use. A much stronger case is found in China where folklore was a source of opposition to state domination. "Atleast until the 1940s, Chinese folklore research furnished an ideology of popular resistance and not a mechanism of administrative control" (Linke 1990: 141). Chinese folklorists, who were intent on changing their society, promoted political programs concerned with literary and cultural reform in which the country's peasants were seen as the genuine source of a national heritage (ibid.: 141; Pieke Chapter 3, in this volume).

Indeed as contributors to this volume (Ramstedt Chapter 10, Evans Chapter 2, and Eades Chapter 4) and other scholars have shown (Kuper 1973; Sanjek 1993; Goody 1995; Lamphere 2003), anthropologists have often been openly critical of policy-makers. Pieke (Chapter 3, in this volume) points out that anthropology in contemporary China is heterodox and innovative and therefore, always potentially dangerous. Prager (1999) talks about the explicit opposition between anthropologists and state representatives in and around the effects of colonial domination or the granting of independence to local Indonesians. To generalize from Linke's (1990: 143) comparative investigation, such cases suggest that the political quest for social knowledge is not only an instrument of power, but that it can also serve as a basis for opposition.

Thus, the participation of anthropologists in state-mandated activities touches directly upon issues of professional autonomy. The self-image in the "folk model" of many anthropologists is that they have a deep-seated suspicion of state (and other kind of) powers. This belief, however, cannot go unopposed (for instance, see Evans Chapter 2 and Pieke Chapter 3, in this volume). In the past century in United States and Great Britain, and in other imperial and colonial nations in the world, anthropologists have by and large cooperated with their governments in administration, voluntarily or under duress, in the pursuit of empire, in battles against real or perceived social ills, and in the waging of wars (van Bremen 2003).

In reality, there is a great deal of ambiguity toward political commitment to, and mobilization by, state structures. Sinha and Chatterji (Chapters 7 and 8, in this volume; Jain 1997) show that Indian anthropology has long had a strong emphasis on applied aspects of the discipline, and Mahapatra (1997) encapsulates this point via a picture of "anthropologist as social activist." Where economic development and restructuring of societal domains are urgent priorities, the stress is often on social relevance (Alatas, Chapter 11, in this volume). Many anthropologists, thus, find themselves constantly justifying their existence to administrators and policy-makers on which they depend for most of their funding. Yet, as Sinha is quick to point out, relations with government are frequently characterized by a great deal of mistrust and skepticism. Indian anthropologists (like similar scholars around the area) are caught in a bind: they may be vilified through guilt-by-association with state powers[3] or commended for working for the betterment of society (Tambiah 1985: 347–8).

More generally, as studies of the state suggest, we must not presuppose a situation of strong state regulation but rather ask about its variable extent. We suggest that state regulation of anthropology runs between a strong control in communist countries as in China (Zhou 1993), an intermediate control as in Malaysia (Provencher 1994), through to an indirect control as in India. Asian cases direct us to ask about the relative autonomy of anthropology as an academic discipline and profession vis-à-vis the state. State autonomy is not a fixed structural feature of any governmental system because the potentials for state action change over time, as the organizations of coercion and administration undergo transformation (Skocpol 1985: 14; Evans *et al.* 1985: 351). In this respect, we must be wary of blaming all of anthropology's current woes on the colonial state. Colonial states are a type of state as are authoritarian, totalitarian, or democratic states. The effects of all of these kinds of states are analytically distinct from their colonial origins.[4]

Interestingly, the growing importance of Asian anthropologies with their explicit commitment to social betterment may bring about an engagement with questions of social responsibility in some "centers" now heavily influenced by de-politicized "post-modern" deconstructionist thought. In a curious way perhaps, the growing admission of Asian anthropologists into contemporary debates may rekindle older professional concerns with anthropology's emancipatory potential and commitment to social issues (Diamond 1981: 13). To speculate, this renewed call for social commitment will not be phrased in the same terms as those of the late 1960s and early 1970s, but will take into account such issues as the social positioning of anthropologists within various political projects. For example, it has become fashionable in the last few years to situate oneself in regard to (and often within) the ethnography one writes. Yet, apart from some attempts to tackle issues centering on what Americans call ethics in the field (as much a result of their legalist culture as of their Protestant heritage), there is very little sustained effort to discuss how we are situated with respect to what used to be called "action research" (i.e. research in which the investigator is part of the processes of social change). Some recent Asian ethnographies (Kinoshita and Keifer 1992; Chatterji, Chapter 8, in this volume) may serve as examples of prescriptive, value-laden alternatives to current politically sterile writings.

An international division of labor

But we would be wary of an over-optimistic view of such trends. Messerschmidt (1981) points out that while applied anthropology and ethnography at "home" in the United States have always had a commitment to the betterment of society, they have long been considered to be of a lesser stature. If this is still true, then it is not surprising that many Asians who have studied in such centers as America should have similar kind of attitudes. Furthermore, given that the majority of Asian anthropologists either study their "home" society or deal with applied research (or both) their very actions may further reproduce and reinforce their relative marginality.

If the first analytical metaphor we introduced was of centers and peripheries, and the second was the workings of the nation-state, the third is an international division of academic labor whose primary effect is to produce "area studies." Within academia, most of us belong in formal or informal senses to "area studies." To the question of "where are you located professionally?" we just as often answer "anthropology" as we do with such appellations as "Thai Studies," "Japanese Studies," "Chinese Studies," "Southeast Asian Studies," or "Hmong Studies." We belong to cross-cutting and overlapping scholarly communities. Such membership bears wider significance.

Historically speaking, the division of academic labor at the centers was, crudely speaking, sociology at "home" and anthropology in far away, "other" places. In the past few decades, this situation has grown more complex. On the one hand, there is a very gradual erosion of the lower prestige accorded "anthropology at home" with anthropologists at the center studying both "exotic," internal others, and the mainstream and the middle-class. On the other hand, despite these changes, Asian anthropologists (and more generally anthropologists from developing societies) do not investigate the cultures of the Western centers in any major way. Apart from a small but steady trickle of works – recent examples include Appadurai's (1996) work on America and Mori's (1999) work on Austria – Asian scholars in general and especially, those taking advanced degrees in the universities of the centers are encouraged to study their own societies and not those of the countries where they are located (Chatterji, Chapter 8, Evans, Chapter 2, Kuwayama, Chapter 5, Moon, Chapter 6, in this volume).

This predicament derives from how "area studies" are constructed through the institutional dynamics of the centers: through such matters as the relative advantage of Asians studying their own societies (primarily in terms of linguistic and social competence), their commitment to return home, the fit of their research projects with their supervisors' interests, the manner by which area studies are a social fact confronting any prospective student, the interests and preoccupations of scholarly societies, and the structure of scholarships and funding (Gupta and Ferguson 1997). But we would suggest that explaining this situation only in terms of resources and interests is reductionist. Japan, Korea, and Taiwan are good cases in point. They all have funds, foundations, universities, associations, and journals, but very few Japanese, Korean, or Taiwanese choose to study America or Britain from an anthropological point of view. Rather, their choices are curiously similar to those of anthropologists in "Western" societies barring one detail. Japanese, Koreans, and Taiwanese (i.e. from relatively affluent Asian countries) study not only the peripheries of their own societies but also the customs and mores of their own middle-class and mainstream groups. Interestingly, however, when they study "others," they are not European or American groups but rather cultures and societies in Asia, Africa, and Latin America. By studying themselves and societies that have been historically defined as "others" by Western anthropologists, they are of a necessity accepting the agenda governing professional appraisal as defined by the historical centers.

On a discursive level, as Gupta and Ferguson brilliantly show, Asian anthropologists participate in the reproduction of area specialization:

> Anthropology, more than perhaps any other discipline, is a body of knowledge constructed on regional specialization, and it is within regionally circumscribed epistemic communities that many of the discipline's key concepts and debates have been developed ... [I]t is precisely the naturalization of cultural difference as inhering in different geographical locales that makes anthropology such a regional science.
>
> (1997: 8)

Their analysis shows how theoretical notions about "culture areas" coalesce with the institutional politics of "area studies" and the global order of nation-states. Along similar lines, our volume provides examples of how "Asian Studies" are created and recreated. Take for instance, the volume's internal textual arrangement. The various contributions examine Indian, Japanese, Chinese, Indonesian, or Philippine anthropologies along with British, Dutch, French, or American ones. Based on the idea of discrete national anthropologies, our volume thus serves to further reproduce the assumption of a correspondence between states' geopolitical territories and the existence of "whole" cultures within them (see also Kuwayama, Chapter 5, in this volume). Much of scholarly writing about contemporary anthropology is thus suffused with categories of national affiliation. More generally, the idea of "area studies" fits well the center and periphery model as well as the image of the nation-state as the locus of anthropological work.

Yet, the idea of "area studies" also predicates the transnational character of anthropology as understood through the prism of national traditions of anthropology. Against this background we may well ask whether there is any meaning to "national" elements in the multinational character of contributors to this volume (Australian, British, Dutch, German, Indian, Israeli, Korean, or Japanese)? Does national affiliation bear any meaning for the concepts, theories, and professional vocabulary we use? What is a "national anthropology" in the context of an international profession with its own standards, autonomy, and models of expert roles?

In late 1989, the question of national influence was examined for the field of Japanese Studies, including Japan anthropology, in ten different countries. Different approaches were found to exist in aspects of scholarship, such as the formulation of problems, the collection and use of data, and the forms of reporting. The explanation is that the way scholars ask questions and the way they deal with data are influenced by cultural differences. While data collection is essential to any scholar, what may be done with data varies. Scholars may compile voluminous data in encyclopedic compendia, as Japanese or German scholars are wont to do. Others may rush to theorizing and hypothesis testing even before adequate data has been gathered, as Americans are wont to do. A third may take a more humanistic, interpretive approach, and write a major work as a mature scholar, as is likely the case in Europe (Befu and Kreiner 1992: 33).

Differences of this nature have been pointed out between American cultural and British social anthropology (Kuper 1999a,b). They are not only found to exist between Europe and America. Eades (Chapter 4, in this volume) argues that the empirical and humanistic tradition, today nearly abandoned in America and under threat in Europe, retains a high esteem by anthropologists in East Asia, who act as its present guardians and invigorators. It may lead the endangered approach to regain some of the ground it lost.

Common terms: interpretive communities and inequalities

Transnational ties have characterized our profession from its very beginnings. Urry, for example, observes that colonial anthropology was not only utilized to understand and control people, but was also utilized as a measure of imperialistic competition:

> Competition for colonies was also expressed in the size of respective ethnographic collections.... In the USA the Bureau of American Ethnology made British anthropologists eager to establish a similar body, an Imperial Bureau with government backing, but the British government did not take up the idea.
>
> (1993: 26)

One reading of this passage would emphasize the nationalistic motivations at base of separate national anthropologies. The establishment, operation, and continued funding of the National Museum of Ethnology in Osaka – as well as other major Japanese research institutes such as the International Research Center for Japanese Studies, the Japan Center for Area Studies, and the National Museum of Japanese History – can thus be seen as a postwar means to enhance Japan's international standing and prestige. This picture fits both the center and periphery, and nation-state metaphors for it involves a world system of anthropology which is based on competition between national establishments for stature and recognition.

This competition can, however, be understood in a complementary manner. We would propose that no less important than rivalry was the diffusion and the acceptance by members of the different national anthropologies of a set of common terms, a collection of ground rules by which international rivalry was played out (Ben-Ari 1998). Here, we follow Roland Robertson (1992: 135) who suggests that globalizing processes involve the "development of something like a global culture – not as normatively binding, but in the sense of a general mode of discourse about the world as a whole *and* its variety". We are thus led to the fourth image we suggest for understanding the world order of contemporary anthropology: interpretive or linguistic communities. This image is of a group of people who speak the same language and argue on the basis of a set of standard assumptions.

Along these lines, we caution against overstressing the differences between national traditions of anthropology. Anthropology as a discipline is predicated on what Boon (1982) has termed "the exaggeration of culture": we tend to examine the difference because from our perspective this is what seems to need an explanation. The nature of our disciplinary project, prevailing research strategies, theoretical orientations, and the reward structures of our profession often conspire to push us to select the most exotic materials to characterize and essentialize the groups we study, and to leave undescribed what seems simply familiar (Keesing 1989: 459). So, it is regarding our understandings of ourselves: we are led toward, and often rewarded for, stressing the dissimilarity between national traditions of anthropology.

A number of commentators have submitted that anthropology is characterized by common assumptions and practices – our professional folk model – that cross national and cultural boundaries. In his overview of the Gerholm and Hannerz' volume on national anthropologies, Stocking (1982: 181) concludes that "while the accounts of intellectual influence, institutional development, and substantive concerns differ in specific detail, there is little that qualifies as reinvented or radically alternative anthropology, and not too much specifically national uniqueness." And Dumont (1986: 205) posits that we belong to an international community of specialists comprising a discipline subject to its own rules. In this volume, we argue that what we have today is not a simple worldwide consensus about anthropological projects, but rather that the basic terms and the criteria which are used in discussions and contentions about the profession have been accepted by the majority of anthropologists during our time. To be sure, these terms and criteria have developed in the centers of Western scholarship and follow to a great degree the mythological mold established by Malinowski. But the striking similarity across national boundaries holds for such matters as our status hierarchies, journal policies, or the organization of professional bodies, and has direct implications for how we pursue our careers.

The emergence of common expertise and professional rules and procedures does not signal the formation of some kind of homogeneous or harmonious community. Issues of power, disparity, and dominance are as central today as they were in the past. Diamond, for instance, posits that

> the discipline is about as universal as the Singer sewing machine. It is a diffused technic that can be fabricated abroad. International anthropology has... become a uniform profession, put to the same uses in Bombay as in London, Tokyo, New York or Moscow.... An Indian and African anthropologist, trained in this Western technic, does not behave as an Indian or African when he behaves as an anthropologist... he lives and thinks as an academic European.
>
> (1980: 12)

The import of Diamond's contentions (also Kuwayama, Chapter 5, in this volume) lies in questioning any over-optimistic view of the "inter-" or "trans-nationalness" of our profession and in drawing our attention to issues of inequality that pervade it. Take the use of English in the majority of anthropological meetings and the dominance of English language publications in the anthropological world. The use of English is the outcome of how British influences have been reinforced by the economic, political, and cultural hegemony of the United States after the Second World War. Indeed, this volume itself is written in English for an international audience. But as Asad observes,

> because the languages of Third World societies – including, of course, the societies that social anthropologists have traditionally studied – are "weaker" in relation to Western languages (and today especially to English), they are more likely to submit to forcible transformation in the translation process than the other way around... Western languages produce and deploy desired knowledge more readily than Third World languages do.
>
> (1986: 157–8)

Linguistically speaking, Third World scholars, as well as many scholars located in non-English speaking countries, are at a distinct disadvantage in the international arena. Indeed, this situation of relative disadvantage lies at the base of Malaysian debates about establishing universities in which English is the language of instruction. English is a language of instruction in the University of Hong Kong. In the European Union, Leiden University among others is taking this course.

While mastery of (academic) English is a prerequisite for participating in "international anthropology," its use may be limited if there is a very large internal academic market as in China or Japan (Eades, Chapter 4, Kuwayama, Chapter 5, in this volume). Such academic markets – unlike those characterizing "small" societies like Malaysia – often allow professional advancement without publication or participation in English-language fora. The Japanese academic market, for instance, often assures a tenure without "publish or perish" pressures, makes available and legitimizes in-house publications, provides more opportunities for anthropologists to publish earlier in their careers, and has large readerships in the Japanese language (Eades, Chapter 4, in this volume). In other words, such academic systems offer alternatives for careering, publication, and the creation of knowledge.

Yet even relatively independent interpretive communities (groups of people sharing common assumptions and ways of looking at the world) are part of the structure of image of centers and peripheries. Talking back to the centers in the world language – now almost exclusively in the English language – can be done by anthropologists of the periphery, but it is done in a manner that is less fluent than scholars in these centers (Gerholm and Hannerz 1982: 9). Even secondary centers like China, India, and Japan can communicate among themselves, but they find that they are then cut off from the metropoles. Van Bremen suggests that the importance of English be seen as part of a complex historical model of linguistic communities which are segregated to different degrees:

> Apart from countries with absolutist regimes, like the former Nazi Germany or Communist Russia, and countries at war, the boundaries between metropolitan countries were transparent in the colonial period. The extent of the international contacts between anthropologists attests to it, as does the fact that anthropologists used four or five languages in scholarly communication until the middle of the century. Today some of those languages are no longer as widely used and new language enclaves have come into existence. As a result much scholarly work is unknown or under-used.
>
> (1996: 39–40)

The importance of this situation is that while anthropological knowledge continues to be produced in various national languages (Chinese, Japanese, and Indonesian, for instance), if one wants international recognition, one needs to present one's work in English.

Today the English language has become – as in all of modern academia – a standardizing device, a storehouse of common culture, and a resource and constraint (to attain international renown one must publish in English). Through translations of works written in the centers (now almost exclusively composed in English and French) or by way of international conferences and seminars, external works are filtered into local professional communities (Zhou 1993). The effect of this situation is both a greater homogenization of international anthropology and the reinforcement of power relations. Transnational activities, like the work of publishers or of journal editors, serve to reinforce relations between centers and peripheries. Indeed, Japan's emergence as a world center has involved the systematic translation of Japanese works into English and the establishment of book series in that language. The *Senri Ethnological Studies* is a noteworthy example. The series has been published irregularly since 1978 by the National Museum of Ethnology in Osaka, reaching a total of sixty-five volumes today (2004). This series presents work in English not only by scholars from Japan but also from a wide range of other countries in Asia and other continents. In 1998, the Japanese Society of Cultural Anthropology, at the time still named the Japanese Society of Ethnology, began to publish an annual in English, entitled the *Japanese Review of Cultural Anthropology*, as a supplement to the society's regular Japanese language journal, at the time still named the *Japanese Journal of Ethnology*, which received the new name of the *Japanese Journal of Cultural Anthropology* in 2004.

If our analysis holds, then it may explain another aspect of how the order of centers and peripheries and professional hierarchies is reproduced. Gerholm and Hannerz (1982: 8) propose that "[a]nthropologists writing in the national language may be popularizing or practical rather than academic, something one does to meet one's obligations to society and so not cut oneself off altogether from one's bases." The point, however, is that this movement – of linking oneself to one's home society and writing in one's local language – tends to reinforce the lower academic and professional standing of what are disparagingly termed "popularizers" of anthropology (MacClancy 1996). To put this point by way of example, writing in their own language Thai or Korean anthropologists may unintentionally reproduce their position as popularizers and as marginals.

The reproduction and production of knowledge

The kinds of relations that we have been discussing are all effected through the micro-politics of our profession. Wider configurations like center and periphery relations or membership in interpretive communities (all historically variable and culturally constructed) are accomplished, actualized through the institutional arenas within which anthropologists act. What is of significance here is that the production and reproduction of knowledge is "naturalized" through practical politics and career moves. These relations bear upon where and how we receive our training, situate ourselves within intellectual traditions, pursue our careers, and receive various kinds of reinforcements and sanctions. Yet, as we stated before, the micro-relations of power within the profession have been consistently left unanalyzed. If ethnography "is a historically situated mode of understanding situated contexts" (Comaroff and Comaroff 1992: 9–10) then what we are seriously missing is an examination of the intra-academic power formations of our profession, of mentor relations, funding decisions, support for publication, struggles for turf and territory, or the coercion involved in creating anthropological knowledge. With very few exceptions (Rabinow 1986, 1991; Sanjek 1993) we know very little about what Silverman (1981: xi) terms "the living and sometimes combative quality of theoretical development."

These questions have been systematically averted in anthropology because they are directly related to our careers. Accordingly, we could hardly expect anthropologists (even tenured ones) to discuss matters which could jeopardize their professional lives (Ben-Ari 1998). To be sure, these issues are very often discussed in the informal meetings of our institutional lives or, periodically, at the interstices of professional meetings. When they are published, they often appear in relatively unintegrated textual passages such as appendices, prefaces, forewords, footnotes, or acknowledgments (Ben-Ari 1987), or alluded to in the ubiquitous but as of yet unanalyzed obituaries (Darnell 1974: 291).[5] Rabinow (1986: 253) suggests that the taboo against specifying these power relations "is much greater than the strictures against denouncing colonialism...the micro-practices of the academy might well do with some scrutiny." These micro-practices, of course, include a variety of forms of prejudice and discrimination (based on sexism, classism, racism, and ageism) found in the anthropology departments of various societies. In Asian contexts, these practices involve such issues as Japanese perceptions of, and prejudice toward, foreigners (Hall 1998), the stress on Han Chineseness in China, or the pro-Bumiputra policies in Malaysia which govern appointments, admissions, and supervision of students. In fact, in the examination of Asian cases we are doubly limited. First, because the political situation in many countries precludes discussions of many "sensitive" topics (not even in the form of statistical analyses of hiring trends). Second, barring a few exceptions (Chan and Ho 1991; van Bremen and Shimizu 1999; Shimizu and van Bremen 2003) relatively little in the way of historical research which deals with the internal politics and struggles of such anthropological communities has been published for international audiences.

The following analysis is thus based on hints found in the scholarly literature and on our impressions as professional anthropologists. We take off from Gupta and Ferguson's (1997: 11) evocative image. For a given member of our profession pursuing his or her career the question usually boils down to finding a place where theoretical concerns, personal leanings, and career outcomes can most happily intersect. But various career choices – Who to align oneself with? Where to do fieldwork? Where and how to publish? What kind employment opportunities to pursue? – often appear to individuals looking at the professional community simply as "natural" arrays of alternatives. That these alternatives are structured by larger relations between anthropological traditions and the world's political economy is a fact usually hidden, or masked underneath a veneer of "normalness" (Gupta and Ferguson 1997). Furthermore, by following these alternatives, anthropologists replicate the very relations which structure these alternatives. At base of this image is a notion of reproduction: through pursuing career moves, doing research and acting within institutions and associations, we reproduce the very conditions within which we act. In other words, international centers and peripheries, state policies, and interpretive communities are refracted through the micro-politics of our profession to reproduce professional ideals and wider distinctions. Yet, contemporary anthropology is far too dynamic and changing to be understood through a simple focus on reproduction. We would posit a more complex model in which processes of reproduction are linked to production and transformation. A number of examples from Asia underscore this point.

Sinha (Chapter 7, also Alatas, Chapter 11, in this volume) raises a problem that many anthropological traditions that have developed outside the Western centers are grappling with. As she explains, Indian anthropologists often deal with a question touching at the very heart of their work: while claiming a uniqueness for "Indian anthropology" they also acknowledge commonalties with Western anthropology in terms of the methods, objects, and subjects of their study. Zhou (1993: 100) reports a similar discussion in contemporary China about the possibility of "a unique Chinese anthropology." In a different manner, in discussing the dominant rhetoric in contemporary Indonesia, Ramstedt (Chapter 10, in this volume) suggests that it is characterized by internal contradictions between colonial *Indologie*, the indigenous state philosophy, and American anthropological discourse. Thus, what we find in present-day Asia is not a total rejection of Western anthropological models. Many professionals in Asia continue to retain the sense of anthropology as a scientific discipline, the methods of fieldwork, the distinction between pure and applied research, and the definition of Asian societies as subjects of research. What is rejected is the totalizing imagery that has characterized previous work.

If totalizing images of Asian societies and cultures are rejected, then so are such images of national anthropologies. We need to understand and explain the multiplicity of voices and dissonance, and competing viewpoints that exist in them. Against the background of contemporary theoretical concerns we must be careful, for too strong a stress on reproduction may contribute to denigrating the critical facilities of professional "others" (Kuwayama 1997: 66), and thereby inadvertently reproduce colonialist assumptions. Just as we are wary of portraying our subjects of study as relatively homogeneous groups, so we must resist portraying anthropologists as members of unified cultural entities (national or otherwise), and clarify the ways in which they continually call into question one another's beliefs and opinions. For example, Zhou (1993) and Pieke (Chapter 3, in this volume) draw out the different ideas, opinions, and perspectives about anthropology that exist in contemporary China.

An image of anthropology that both reproduces professional assumptions and wider relations but is full of tensions and contentions, and incongruities and contradictions leads us to the question of change.

Change: entrepreneurship, nonlinearity, and networks

Many critiques of the world order of anthropology may be politically radical, but they are also theoretically conservative. They are politically radical because one of their central concerns has been to uncover the ways in which the anthropological profession is related to the existing power relations and to the reproduction of social and cultural distinctions of hierarchy and exclusion. They are theoretically conservative because they tend to stress reproduction – that is, the duplication – of unequal relations and discourses at the expense of delineating mechanisms of change. For example, while Gerholm and Hannerz suggest the continued importance of relations implicated by centers and peripheries, and Diamond stresses the export and adoption abroad of a "uniform profession," Gupta and Ferguson explicitly argue about the professional reproduction of distinctions and hierarchies. All these authors provide little in the way of a theorization of change, of the sources and trajectories of transformation in contemporary anthropology.

Where would one find these sources? Brian Moeran (1990) has written a provocative allegory of scholarly activity in the anthropological world. His story of the arrangements made for an exhibition for the ceramic pots he had fired in Japan, intimates that a prime analytic metaphor for understanding anthropological activity is that of entrepreneurship. In this imagery, anthropologists are accumulating, determined individuals who form networks and gather allies to push "their" products within an academic market place where ideas and resources are exchanged and bartered. The activities of Umesao Tadao, who established the National Museum of Ethnology in Osaka, and Matsubara Masatake, who recently founded the Japan Center for Area Studies, are examples of how entrepreneurial activity undertaken by an individual leads to the establishment of institutions where anthropological knowledge is produced.

Theoretically speaking, in this model macro-level change results from the activities of individuals pursuing their goals and visions of anthropological work. What is of importance here is how entrepreneurial activity is related to the internal dynamics of the academic marketplace. Evans (Chapter 2, in this volume) suggests that Asian anthropologists studying in metropolitan centers are taught that among the standards used to appraise their work are elements of reflection, critique, and creativity. To extend his argument, these elements themselves are later used as resources throughout people's careers. The point is that the critical facility, the ability for self-reflection, and the talent for offering alternative viewpoints which are part and parcel of academic work are linked to careering in the academic market place.

Similarly, generational dynamics within the academia are part of the manner by which younger scholars suggest new ideas, in order to make their mark. This kind of pattern may explain, for instance, how the critique of Clifford Geertz' work by his students is linked to their institutional activities and careering. As part of "making their academic" mark, his students undertook a systematic critique of his approach. Some contend that there is convergence between Japanese and Euro-American universities. But may this convergence, say in the use of Western theory and methods and the growing utilization of academic English, be related to the generational dynamics of Japanese anthropology? Is the mobilization of theoretical models, field methods, and textual formats borrowed from Western centers by younger Japanese scholars now coming into positions of power in Japan part of the way they are making "their mark"?

We do not, however, suggest that all anthropological activity can be simply reduced to the work of academic "businessmen" or "merchants" who consciously and intentionally follow rational strategies to achieve their aims. As Martin (1997: 135) muses, we may surely wonder whether all anthropologists, as scholars in general, can be characterized by a monadic, an agonistic, and a competitive approach to the world. Her suggestions center on another type of imagery, one that links the knowledge produced in the centers of knowledge (her academic citadels) with processes and events outside of them, with processes that may be distant or spatially discontinuous from them (Martin 1997: 136). The metaphor she introduces following Gilles Deleuze (Deleuze and Guattari 1986) is that of the rhizome. Rhizomes are very different in their internal order and pattern of development from "regular" plants. They differ in

> their function of shelter, supply, movement, evasion and breakout. The rhizome itself assumes very diverse forms, from ramified surface extension in all directions to concretions in bulbs and tubers.... Any point in a rhizome can be connected to anything other, and must be. This is very different from the tree or the root, which plots a point, fixes an order.
>
> (Deleuze in Martin 1997: 137)

Three characteristics of rhizomes are of importance for capturing the discontinuous, fractured, and nonlinear relationships between different anthropologies and between these anthropologies and their cultural and social contexts (Martin 1997: 137). First, because their development is commonly horizontal they can circumvent hierarchical relations (rhizomes make easy connections in many directions). Second, because their growth does not proceed linearly as in trees or roots, it cannot be predicted before the process begins. And, third, they are not perturbed by having their connections severed.

What does this metaphor allow us to understand? In the first place, it sheds light on what Gupta and Ferguson (1997: 39) (following Donna Haraway) term modes of building "web-like interconnections" between the different social and cultural locations of anthropologists. Common to both metaphors – rhizomes and webs – is the idea that many of our connections – personal, associational, and the-oretical – are nonlinear, are not predictable. In Martin's (1997: 138) imagery of academia as citadel, we begin to appreciate how some "people can peer over the castle walls; some can look through the holes in the walls. And others can trace the convoluted, discontinuous linkages between what grows inside the castle walls and what grows outside." From the perspective of the center and periphery model or the metaphor of nation-states, this implies looking at the myriad ways in which relative marginalization may be offset by networking, that is, the use of contacts around the world.

Given the dearth of empirical research on the actual ties that bind and separate anthropologists we can only offer a number of suggestions. Take the relations between rhizome-like ties and anthropological organizations as the American Anthropological Association (AAA) and the European Association of Social Anthropology (EASA). The AAA is made up primarily of American anthropolo-gists and is hierarchical in nature. To effect any major change, one must work through a national center and a set of hierarchical committees and legal processes. The EASA by contrast is composed of representatives and contingents from a vari-ety of countries including many small ones and appears to be much more open to loose coalitions and diverse initiatives. Thus, we suggest that the EASA may be more conducive to networking across national lines (also Amit 2004: xviii).

Of no less significance are, perhaps, means of electronic communication like the internet. In an evocative essay, Ribeiro (1997: 80) posits that we must think through the implications of new communication and data processing technologies on the creation of new forms of interaction, subjectivities, and collectivities. While Ribeiro's essay focusses on larger systems of interaction, we take his ideas to suggest that new technologies are central to the extension of the web-like inter-connections of our profession. These technologies made it easier for anthropolo-gists to cross national and regional borders, and to circumvent some of the boundaries between centers and peripheries. Two of the early examples of elec-tronic discussion groups within which Asian anthropologists and anthropologists of Asia began to participate are the Easianth and the ConsumAsian networks. During 1997 and 1998, the Easianth group has included discussions about rural Japan; information about the "Anthropology of Asia Series" edited by Shaun Malarney and published by Routledge and the University of Hawaii Press; a call for papers for the UCLA Graduate Students Symposium; a petition protesting the building of a replica of a Parisian bridge in Kyoto; obituaries; requests and refer-ences to various Websites related to Japanese, Chinese, Korean, Taiwanese anthro-pologies; and a notice on a conference on "Food and Ethnography" in Hong Kong.

During a similar period, and with participants from around the globe, the ConsumAsian net had discussions about globalization and popular culture; modernization, Westernization, and multinational companies; and the nation-state in the Asian context. In addition, it is in this virtual context that the Kuwayama–van Bremen exchange (Kuwayama 1997; van Bremen 1997b; Asquith 1998) was initiated, turning on the short- and long-term duration and importance of centers and peripheries in anthropology.

The groups participating in such networks provide examples of transnational virtual communities. They are not "imagined" communities in the sense of being politically constructed abstractions, but rather virtual in the sense of an "intermediate, parallel state between reality and abstraction.... The virtual reality is 'there' – it can be experienced, manipulated and lived as if it were real" (Ribeiro 1997: 78). They are "transnational" because of the ease with which such networks facilitate linkages and simultaneous discussions across national, institutional, and other boundaries. Such connections have other implications. For many years, some anthropologists in peripheral countries derived their power from being cultural brokers between the Western centers and their own countries (Gerholm and Hannerz 1982: 11). Today, the ease of relative access to the internet has led to many possibilities for circumventing such mediators. In addition, in many countries such as Japan the internet means that many problems of local library systems can be overcome without the vast expense of acquiring and maintaining the vast stocks of publications in Asian and other languages (Eades, Chapter 4, in this volume).

"Native anthropologists" and "professional others"

It has become rather trendy in the contemporary social science to discuss various aspects of "globalization" or "global trends." In anthropology, issues related to this trend focus on such fashionable terms as hybridity, creolization, border zones, and transnational scapes. From our perspective, what are of importance in these debates are not only attempts by anthropologists to deal with the reality of the global economy or of global cultural trends. We suggest that they direct us to engage with what has variously been termed "insider research" (Aguilar 1981), "native ethnographers" (Stephenson and Greer 1981), "native scholars" (Provencher 1994), "indigenous anthropologists" (Ramstedt, Chapter 10, in this volume), "native anthropologists" (Srinivas 1996: 212; Sinha, Chapter 7, in this volume), or "professional others" (Kuwayama, Chapter 5, in this volume).

All these terms designate the place of native anthropologists in specific social fields. Whether they are international anthropological celebrities like Arjun Appadurai, Veena Das, Aiwa Ong, or Partha Chatterjee or less acclaimed persons working in New Delhi, Hong Kong, or Manila, Asians are forcefully suggesting different ways of doing anthropology. To be sure, already by the 1930s anthropologists of Asian ancestry like Fei Hsiao-tung were making professional contributions to the discipline (Sanjek 1993: 16). What has changed is the political and economic situation within which Asian anthropologists now work and the degree to which they participate – directly or "virtually" – in centers of scholarly activity. There are two analytically distinct dimensions to the work of such "native ethnologists": the "structural" aspect of insider research and the specific histori- cal positioning of certain insiders. Aguilar (1981: 25), as a host of other com- mentators (Ablon 1971; Stephenson and Greer 1981; Jenkins 1984; Srinivas 1996: 211), examines the first dimension and observes that arguments for and against insider research

> rest on an implicit model that characterizes all researchers as either absolutely inside or outside a homogeneous sociocultural system... [A] more realistic model of the situation would view the local ethnographer as relatively inside (or outside) with respect to a multiplicity of social and cultural char- acteristics of a heterogeneous population.... They can strategically select among demographic locations and research topics... in order to regulate the degree of their social involvement and cultural immersion.

The problems for the Asian anthropologists who work within their own societies are usually phrased in terms of finding the right distance from the field and of the advantages and disadvantages their position holds. Thus, for example, Srinivas (1996: 203–4) suggests that his unique position as insider–outsider allowed him to appreciate how internally diverse India is. Van Bremen (1997b: 63) proposes that Asians often have the advantage of mastering multiple languages and therefore multiple perspectives. Eades (Chapter 4, in this volume) suggests that "native anthropologists" add much more complexity, detail, "liveliness," and thus angles that cannot be fully explained in contemporary theorizing.

But, there are vast differences between the historical situatedness of different native ethnographers. As feminist and critical theorists have shown us, differences in ideas are not only consequences of the different "interests" of social groups, or of their structural positions but of the differential effects of power in the genera- tion of gendered, or racialized knowledge (Swidler and Arditi 1994: 320). Thus, a Brahamin (Srinivas) who is studying his own caste, an ex-villager from China analyzing another village, or a Philippine intellectual investigating state power predicate different historical positions. In this sense, Asian anthropology repre- sents (arguably more than certain African or Latin American ones) an anthropo- logy that is actively and powerfully questioning. The very success of many Asian societies is in itself something through which the knowledge produced by Asian scholars is constituted.

On a discursive level, the specific configurations of power in and around Asia have led Asian anthropologists both to criticize the "center" and to deconstruct the "Third World." In the first instance, we can think of much current work as a continuation of Hsu's (1973) critique of the assumptions of a "White" American anthropology. Although not phrased in this manner, another example is Appadurai's (1996) deconstruction of America through his essay on "patriotism and its futures." In the second, and much more common, instance, scholars from Asia are continuously reconceptualizing the "Third World." This "world" is no longer assumed to be a fixed, essential object, but rather a series of historical positions, including those that enunciate essentialisms (Prakash 1990). Sinha (Chapter 7, in this volume) for example suggests that the Orientalist image of India has been vigorously contested by the Indian anthropologists who have pointed out the neglect of "non-Hindu," "non-tribal," and "non-caste" dimensions of Indian life. She echoes other calls for a questioning of the essentialist, the homogeneous, the reductionist, and the totalizing renderings of "other" peoples. Her chapter provides an example of an intellectual coalition between "native anthropologists" studying in their "home" societies and feminist, post-colonialist, and deconstructionist theorists.

A neglected aspect of the "deconstruction" of Asia, however, is related to a peculiarly Asian stress on looking at similarities (as opposed to differences) between societies and cultures. For example, while Japanese scholars have studied China for parallels and cultural links (Eades, Chapter 4, in this volume), Vishwanathan (1992) notes how much of Indian scholarship of Japan began from questions of similarity. These perspectives offer an enrichment of contemporary perspectives in suggesting that we may benefit from commencing our analyses from questions about similarity, continuity, and commonality and not essential sets of differences. In a related vein, fascinating questions raised by work on Asian cultures center not so much on Westernization as (to put this point by way of example) the Japanization of Korea, the Sinicization of China's minorities, or the cultural homogenization of the Indonesian archipelago.

In addition, the presence of Asian diasporas around the globe – speaking different languages and linked in diverse ways to their "homes" – may probe us to go beyond the borders of nation-states to analyze the distribution of cultural phenomena regardless of where they stand in relation to geo-political boundaries. A point hinted at by Pertierra (1995) is that Asian immigrants to, or diasporas within, various parts of the world question the confluence of nation, geo-political boundaries, language, and culture. The idea of Asian anthropologies privileges area and state and assumes a correspondence between geo-political boundaries and culture. But in questioning this assumption, diasporas may also change our notion of fieldwork as contained within a single location. For example, just like Jewish studies, so studies of Greater China would include not only (and obviously) China, Taiwan, Hong Kong, Singapore, and "traditional" abodes of "overseas Chinese" (like Indonesia or Malaysia) but also communities in places such as Canada, or the United States.[6]

New professional models

Asian anthropologists are offering more than reconceptualizations of centers and peripheries or of the links between geo-political and cultural entities. They have begun to offer extensions, enrichments, and alternatives to the hegemonic professional model.

The complex set of processes we term fieldwork is being augmented by Asian anthropologists in and around such practices as team research or carrying out multiple visits of short duration. For example, while research groups are something the Japanese and the Europeans have long been extremely good at organizing and funding (Tomiya *et al.* 1988; Eades, Chapter 4, in this volume), American scholars such as Messerschmidt (1981: 7), have suggested that research in uni- or multi-disciplinary groups may be especially suited to handle research in complex societies. At base of this idea, however, is not only pooling the resources of a number of professionals. The specific historical situatedness of different anthropologists prods us to consider, along with Campbell (1988) and Kuwayama (1997: 53), not only team research but also collaborative investigations which would include members of different national and other cultures.

Many Asian anthropologies are similar to the ethnological and folklore studies of Europe in another respect. In such places the "field" is

> always nearby and easy to visit; researchers spend a few weeks in rural areas collecting data and then come back to analyze them. Institutions are neither set up to grant research leaves of one year or more, nor are there funding agencies to support such "fieldwork." Furthermore, there is no assumption that after researchers return from "the field," their contacts with subjects will cease.
>
> (Gupta and Ferguson 1997: 28)

The normal use of such practices in Asia and its adoption by anthropologists in America or Britain may help to further confound the classic distinction between home and field, and disrupt the hierarchy of fields based on notions of distance from an archetypal anthropological "home" (Gupta and Ferguson 1997: 13).

The turn to the "textual" status of ethnographies has already brought about interesting discussions among anthropologists in centers of scholarship. For example, while Brian Moeran (1985) has integrated Japanese literary genres in an experimental ethnography, Kirin Narayan (1989) deals with similar issues in regard to genres of storytelling from India. To judge by these examples, perhaps we are beginning to see Asian influences on notions of what are considered proper, suitable anthropological texts. Asian influences not only inspire new ethnography, about which more is said later, but may also have a retroactive effect. It supports and may help to revise an anthropology that is geared mostly to elaborate empirical studies. That style has receded into the background in America followed by Europe, where the engagement with internal debates and theories, mostly the latest in fashion or with policy evaluations, is deemed more important than plain, long-term ethnography.

Some Asian traditions of anthropology offer a number of criteria for appraising professional advancement, which are different from those found in Western metropolitan centers. For example, Sinha (Chapter 7, in this volume) suggests that there is a demand on Indian anthropologists to grant greater prestige to applied anthropology than is usually accorded it. In other cases such as the Japanese (Asquith 1996; van Bremen 1997: 60; Eades, Chapter 4, in this volume) there is a great deal of prestige attached to the collection of data rather than to spinning out theories. Such instances signal an alternative to the strong stress on theory found in the centers. But perhaps, as Evans, Pieke (Chapters 2 and 3, in this volume), and Provencher (1994: 58) propose, the ultimate test for the influence of Asia on the centers will be when Chinese and Malaysian anthropologists (to take their examples) will study these very centers. This shift will entail changes in political economy and in professional definitions of what is interesting. For example, for a long time, American anthropologists studied the Japanese middle-class and themes that in their home countries would be studied by "sociologists." Yet, only lately have we found works that explicitly juxtapose the two societies (Mathews 1996).

A favorite metaphor used by (mainly) American academics is that of being at the "cutting edge" of theory or of a disciplinary field. This metaphor seems to concurrently capture the linear, aggressive, and intrusive tenor of many social scientific practices in this society. It is, perhaps, ironical that committed as they have been to holistic methods and perspectives, anthropologists nevertheless use this imagery as well. Perhaps, such metaphors are rooted in the prerequisites of "publish or perish" realities or in a general Western stress on linearity. Yet, anthropologists from and working about Asia have suggested somewhat softer approaches that are less "surgical" and more holistic. For example, Evans (Chapter 2, in this volume) – echoing older proposals (Krader 1980) – suggests that new views and new assumptions based on Buddhism or Chinese concepts of human nature may force us to reconceptualize many of our core theoretical notions.

Power, structure, and the limits of change

For all the stress on transformation and innovation, we are not arguing that issues of power, centrality, and structure are now gone. In this section, we examine the continued importance of conventional criteria for professional membership and advancement, and the persistence of centers and nation-states in the construction of anthropological knowledge. We commence from what is often seen as a major means for effecting change, the new electronic and communication technologies. Despite potentials for effecting new coalitions and ties, the web clearly does not lead to some kind of egalitarian set up. Virtual communities, no less than other groups, entail loci and effects of control and power. For instance, links via computer networks tend to be denser and stronger in the metropolitan centers. This situation means that virtuality may reinforce centerdness at the same time that it opens up new fora for discussions. In this sense, the image that Gerholm and Hannerz intimate but do not fully develop, the network as a mesh or tangle of interlinkages, captures both the relative centrality (or peripheriality) of different anthropologies, and the potentials for countervailing it.

On a more practical level, the implementation of open and equal discussion among anthropologists is limited by such things as the cost of computers, equipment, and services; access to network codes; and education and proficiency in English or computer languages (Ribeiro 1997: 78). Moreover, the stress on the potential of the net should not, at least at this stage, be taken too far. To a great degree, anthropological knowledge (like much of contemporary science) still has to be rendered into printed texts. Even while popular knowledge is increasingly visual, multi-channeled, and interactive, formal knowledge remains bound by print and reading (Swidler and Arditi 1994: 308). Our conjecture is that we will witness a bifurcation in the coming years: while formal anthropological knowledge will continue to appear in print, a great deal of informal professional knowledge will be disseminated by electronic media.

Kuwayama (1997: 53), suggests the metaphor of a computer conference or discussion group as a means to ameliorate the distance between Asian and Western anthropologists. His image is that of a (Roman or Greek) forum where issues will be dealt with, in an open and relatively egalitarian manner (the forum being a place of confrontation, experimentation, and debate). Asquith (1998), for her part, calls for an international dialogue and open discussions and cooperative steps toward resolving the inequality between Japanese and dominant Western scholarship. Ramstedt (Chapter 10, in this volume) begins his chapter by seeking grounds of similarity and difference in order to create an intercultural dialogue between anthropologists of different national or ethnic backgrounds. And Sinha (Chapter 7, in this volume) ends her chapter with a call to level the playing field between Western and non-Western anthropologists, so that good social science theorizing can take place. But notice that it is a Japanese, a Canadian, a German, and an Indian working in Singapore who suggest these arrangements. All see themselves and the societies in which they work as "equal" to, or part of, Euro-America in terms of international power relationships. But as Friedman (1987: 164–5) in somewhat abstract terms cautions us, we must realize that the "nature of the anthropological object [is] a construct dependent on a larger hierarchical relation between parts of the world. This relation is a material reality as well as an intellectual construction." The potentials for dialogue, open discussions, and cooperation then continue to depend on the larger political and economic relations between various centers and Asian peripheries.[7]

Conclusion

In this introduction, we have offered a number of analytical metaphors, or guiding images, that together help illuminate the dynamics of reproduction and change in anthropology. We have chosen these metaphors or images because of their value in illuminating – describing, explaining, interpreting – anthropological traditions in Asia and not because any particular one is the one and the best metaphor. Each has its advantages and disadvantages in terms of what it can and cannot illuminate. These images are of centers and peripheries, the nation-state, interpretive communities, and images of change like entrepreneurship and the rhizome through which the professional model of anthropology is both reproduced and produced. We explicitly argue for the superimposition of multiple metaphors in order to understand the complex reality of world anthropology. Our suggestion is that the profession is best conceptualized as a rather mixed (if not muddled) set of centers and peripheries, of small and larger coalitions, and of constant contentions and struggles over both resources and ways of looking at our joint project.

Friedman (1987: 164–5) suggests that one of the first principles of any social theory is understanding its own production. In this introductory chapter, we have located our volume within the processes by which the world order of anthropology is both produced, reproduced, and changed. The questions that we have addressed have to do with the ways in which the social locations and interests of individuals or groups of anthropologists make orderings of knowledge possible, and how their institutions and organizations are related to the production of both formal and informal types of professional knowledge. To take off from Swidler and Arditi (1994: 317), the analytical issue is not only knowledge of the world as produced by anthropologists, but also the knowledge we use to operate within our professional world. Thus, we end our introduction by alluding to Alatas's (Chapter 11, in this volume) epilogue. The volume as a whole, and the specific contributions contained within it, should be seen as opening up questions about the possibility of what he terms a "universal anthropology": on the potential for creating not some kind of simplistic anthropological knowledge somehow common to all anthropologists where and whenever they work, but rather negotiating a common set of criteria for assessing anthropological work based on a complex awareness of our various social and cultural locations.

> Showing that anthropological paradigms are existentially, socially, historically, and philosophically mediated is not identical to debunking one's colleagues or adversaries for selfish motives, vested interests, historical falsification, and ideological misrepresentation. To assert that anthropological knowledge is contextually situated and comparatively relative is not synonymous with reducing anthropological *praxis* to egomania, contamination, myth, or falsity.
>
> (Scholte 1980: 78–9)

Notes

1 Van Maanen (1995) suggests that anthropologists occupy themselves with three kinds of activities that in tandem are their craft and profession: fieldwork which consists of gathering data first-hand in particular places in the world; text-work consisting of the writing involved in noting down observations and conversations; and head-work in linking the ethnographies of others to one's work. Our additions to his list may be called career-work which consists of the moves and strategies anthropologists invest in, in order to pursue their vocation.

2 We thank Erik Cohen for this insight.

3 Compare this situation to African universities where anthropology departments are non-existent (due to the discipline's "colonialist" reputation), and research must be done in sociology, history, or economics departments, or in terms of studying oral literature (Gupta and Ferguson 1997: 29).

4 We thank Grant Evans for this point.

5 Such issues have sometimes been considered within historical cases, where distance and detachment buffer writers from any direct career implications (Stocking, Langham, or Urry, for example). It is much easier to bare how Boas or Mead controlled access to grants, publication, and academic posts than to explore how it is done in contemporary

anthropology. Current trends have been examined sometimes through macro statistical analyses of hiring trends or autobiographies by people – Hortense Powdermaker (1966) or Margaret Mead (1972), for instance – whose power enables them to disregard their dependence on others. Other investigations have been ethnographies written under pseudonyms (Cesara Manda 1982) or allegories (Flannery 1982; Moeran 1990). In the same vein, it is scholars outside the community – sociologists, philosophers, historians, biographers (Steward 1973; Lipset 1980; Vincent 1991) – who are most likely to pay attention to the struggles of the anthropological community. The title Leach (1984) gave his autobiographical essay captures the silences surrounding such issues and their exploration at a distance: "Glimpses of the Unmentionable in the History of British Social Anthropology." But even he is wary of extending his comments to the unmentionable in present-day British anthropology.

6 Thanks are due to Khun Eng Kuah for this point.
7 Similarly, Asquith (1998) cautions against adopting too facile a picture of change. She talks about "token internationals" or (to use our terminology) "token Asians" who speak English well, spend time abroad, publish English texts, and appear in English language fora in ways that reinforce the de-Asianization of local problems.

References

Ablon, Joan (1971) "Field method in working with middle class Americans: new issues of values, personality and reciprocity," *Human Organization*, 36(1): 69–72.

Agar, Michael H. (1980) *The Professional Stranger: An Informal Introduction to Ethnography*, New York: Academic Press.

Aguilar, John L. (1981) "Insider research: ethnography of a debate," in Donald A. Messerschmidt (ed.), *Anthropologists at Home in North America: Methods and Issues in the Study of One's Own Society*, Cambridge, UK: Cambridge University Press, pp. 15–26.

Amit, Vered (2004) "Introduction and guidelines," in Vered Amit (ed.), *Biographical Dictionary of Social and Cultural Anthropology*, London: Routledge, pp. xvii–xxii.

Appadurai, Arjun (1996) *Modernity at Large*, Minneapolis, MN: University of Minnesota Press.

Asad, Talal (1986) "The concept of cultural translation in British social anthropology," in James Clifford and George E. Marcus (eds), *Writing Culture: The Poetics and Politics of Ethnography*, Berkeley, CA: University of California Press, pp. 141–64.

Asquith, Pamela (1996) "Japanese science and Western hegemonies: primatology and the limits set to questions," in Laura Nader (ed.), *Naked Science: Anthropological Inquiry into Boundaries, Power and Knowledge*, New York: Routledge, pp. 239–56.

—— (1998) "The 'world system' of anthropology from a primatological perspective: comments on the Kuwayama – van Bremen debate," *Japan Anthropology Workshop Newsletter*, 28: 16–27.

Befu, Harumi and Josef Kreiner (eds) (1992) *Othernesses of Japan: Historical and Cultural Influences on Japanese Studies in Ten Countries*, H. Befu and J. Kreiner (eds), Monographien aus dem Deutschen Institut für Japanstudien der Philipp-Franz-von-Siebold-Stiftung, Band 1, München: Iudicium Verlag.

Behar, Ruth and Deborah A. Gordon (eds) (1995) *Women Writing Culture*, Berkeley, CA: University of California Press.

Ben-Ari, Eyal (1987) "On acknowledgements in ethnographies," *Journal of Anthropological Research*, 43(1): 63–4.

—— (1998) "Colonialism, anthropology and the politics of professionalization: an argumentative afterword", in Jan van Bremen and Akitoshi Shimizu (eds), *Anthropology and Colonialism: The Japanese and Dutch Experience in East and South-East Asia*, Honolulu, HI: University of Hawaii Press and London: Curzon Press, pp. 384–411.

Boon, James A. (1982) *Other Tribes, Other Scribes: Symbolic Anthropology in the Comparative Study of Cultures, Histories, Religions and Texts*, New York: Cambridge University Press.

Cambell, Donald (1988) *Methodology and Epistemology for Social Sciences: Selected Papers*, Chicago, IL: Chicago University Press.

Chan, Kwok Bun and Kong Chong Ho (1991) (eds) *Explorations in Asian Sociology*, Singapore: Chopmen Publishers.

Chiu, Fred Y.L. (1999) "Nationalist anthropology in Taiwan 1945–1995: a reflexive survey," in Jan van Bremen and Akitoshi Shimizu (eds), *Anthropology and Colonialism in Asia and Oceania*, London: Curzon Press.

Clifford, James (1997) "Spatial practices: fieldwork, travel, and the Disciplining of Anthropology," in Akhil Gupta and James Ferguson (eds), *Anthropological Locations: Boundaries and Grounds of a Field Science*, Berkeley, CA: University of California Press, pp. 185–222.

Coleman, Simon and Bob Simpson (2004) "Knowing, doing and being: pedagogies and paradigms in the teaching of social anthropology," in Dorle Drackle and Iain Edgar (eds), *Current Policies and Practices in European Social Anthropology Education*, Oxford: Berghahn, pp. 18–33.

Comaroff, John and Jean Comaroff (1992) *Ethnography and the Historical Imagination*, Boulder, CO: Westview Press.

Darnell, Regna (1974) "Part four: history from within the discipline," in Regna Darnell (ed.), *Readings in the History of Anthropology*, New York: Harper, pp. 289–96.

——(2001) *Invisible Geneologies: A History of Americanist Anthropology*, Lincoln, NE: University of Nebraska Press.

Diamond, Stanley (1981) "Introduction: anthropological traditions: the participants observed," in Stanley Diamond (ed.), *Anthropology: Ancestors and Heirs*, The Hague: Mouton, pp. 1–16.

Dumont, Louis (1986) *Essays on Individualism: Modern Ideology in Anthropological Perspective*, Chicago, IL: Chicago University Press.

Ellen, Roy F. (1976) "The development of anthropology and colonial policy in the Netherlands: 1800–1960," *Journal of the History of the Behavioral Sciences*, 12: 3–24.

Eriksen, Thomas Hylland and Finn Sivert Nielsen (2001) *A History of Anthropology*, London: Pluto Press.

Evans, Peter, Dietrich Rueschemeyer and Theda Skocpol (1985) "On the road to a more adequate understanding of the state," in Peter Evans, Dietrich Rueschemeyer, and Theda Skocpol (eds), *Bringing the State Back*, Cambridge, UK: Cambridge University Press, pp. 347–66.

Flannery, Kent V. (1982) "The Golden Marshalltown: a parable for the archeology of the 1980s," *American Anthropologist*, 84: 265–78.

Fox, Richard (1991) "Introduction: working in the present," in Richard G. Fox (ed.), *Recapturing Anthropology: Working the Present*, Santa Fe, KM: School of American Research Press, pp. 1–16.

Freilich, Morris (1977) "Field work: an introduction," in Morris Freilich (ed.), *Marginal Natives at Work: Anthropologists in the Field*, Cambridge, MA: Schenkman, pp. 1–37.

Friedman, Jonathan (1987) "Beyond otherness: the spectacularization of anthropology," *Telos*, 71: 161–70.

Gerholm, Tomas and Ulf Hannerz (1982) "Introduction: the shaping of national anthropologies," *Ethnos*, 1–2: 5–35.

Goody, Jack (1995) *The Expansive Moment: Anthropology in Britain and Africa*, Cambridge: Cambridge University Press.

Gruber, Jacob W. (1981) "The United States: racism and progress in the nineteenth century," in Stanley Diamond (ed.), *Anthropology: Ancestors and Heirs*, The Hague: Mouton, pp. 109–22.

Gudeman, Stephan (1998) "The new captains of information," *Anthropology Today*, 14(1): 1–3.

Gupta, Akhil and James Ferguson (1997) "Discipline and practice: 'The field' as site, method, and location in anthropology," in Akhil Gupta and James Ferguson (eds), *Anthropological Locations: Boundaries and Grounds of a Field Science*, Berkeley, CA: University of California Press, pp. 1–46.

Hall, Ivan (1998) *Cartels of the Mind: Japan's Intellectual Closed Shop*, New York: W.W. Norton.

Handelman, Don (1994) "Critiques of anthropology: literary turns, slippery bends," *Poetics Today*, 15(3): 341–81.

Hsu, Francis L.K. (1973) "Prejudice and its intellectual effect in American anthropology: an ethnographic report," *American Anthropologist*, 75(3): 1–19.

Jain, Ravindra (1997) "Obituary – Shyama Charan Dube," *Anthropology Today*, 13(1): 22.

Jenkins, Richard (1984) "Bringing it all back home: an anthropologist in Belfast," in Colin Bell and Helen Roberts (eds), *Social Researching: Politics, Problems, Practice*, London: Routledge, p. 64.

John, Mary (1989) "Postcolonial feminists in the Western intellectual field: anthropologists and native informants," in James Clifford and Vivek Dhareshwar (eds), *Travelling Theorists, Travelling Theories: Inscriptions*, Santa Cruz: UCSC Center for Cultural Studies, pp. 49–74.

Keesing, Roger M. (1989) "Exotic readings of cultural texts," *Current Anthropology*, 30(4): 459–89.

Kinoshita, Yasuhito and Christie W. Kiefer (1992) *Refuge of the Honored: Social Organization in a Japanese Retirement Community*, Berkeley, CA: University of California Press.

Krader, Lawrence (1980) "Anthropological traditions: their relationship as dialectic," in Stanley Diamond (ed.), *Anthropology: Ancestors and Heirs*, The Hague: Mouton, pp. 19–34.

Kuper, Adam (1973) *Anthropologists and Anthropology: The British School 1922–1972*, London: Allen Lane.

—— (1999a) *Culture: The Anthropologists' Account*, Cambridge, MA: Harvard University Press.

—— (1999b) *Among the Anthropologists: History and Context in Anthropology*, London and New Brunswick, NJ: The Athlone Press.

Kuwayama, Takami (1997) "Native anthropologists: with special reference to Japanese studies inside and outside of Japan," *Japan Anthropology Workshop Newsletter*, 26–27: 52–6, and 66–8.

Lamphere, Louise (2003) "The perils and prospects for an engaged anthropology: a view from the United States," *Social Anthropology*, 11(2): 153–67.

Langham, Ian (1981) *The Building of British Social Anthropology*, Dordrecht: Reidel Publishing Company.

Leach, Edmund R. (1984) "Glimpses of the unmentionable in the history of British social anthropology," *Annual Review of Anthropology*, 13: 1–23.

Linke, Uli (1990) "Folklore, anthropology, and the government of social life," *Comparative Studies in Society and History*, 32(1): 117–48.

Lipset, David (1980) *Gregory Bateson: The Legacy of a Scientist*, Englewood Cliffs, NJ: Prentice-Hall.

MacClancy, Jeremy (1996) "Introduction," in Jeremy MacClancy and Chris McDonough (eds), *Popularizing Anthropology*, London: Routledge, pp. 1–57.

Mahapatra, L.K. (1997) "Anthropology in policy and practice in India," *Studies in Third World Societies*, 58: 155–78.

Manda, Cesara (1982) *Reflections of a Women Anthropologist: No Hiding Place*, London: Academic Press.

Marcus, George E. and Dick Cushman (1982) "Ethnographies as texts," *Annual Review of Anthropology*, 11: 25–69.

Marcus, George E. and Michael M.J. Fischer (1986) *Anthropology as Cultural Critique: An Experimental Moment in the Human Sciences*, Chicago, IL: Chicago University Press.

Martin, Emily (1997) "Anthropology and the cultural study of science: from citadels to string figures," in Akhil Gupta and James Ferguson (eds), *Anthropological Locations: Boundaries and Grounds of a Field Science*, Berkeley, CA: University of California Press, pp. 131–47.

Mathews, Gordon (1996) *What Makes Life Worth Living? How Japanese and Americans Make Sense of Their Worlds*, Berkeley, CA: University of California Press.

Mead, Margaret (1972) *Blackberry Winter: My Earlier Years*, New York: William Morrow.

Messerschmidt, Donald A. (1989) "On anthropology 'at Home'," in A. Donald Messerschmidt (ed.), *Anthropologists at Home in North America: Methods and Issues in the Study of One's Own Society*, Cambridge: Cambridge University Press, pp. 3–14.

Moeran, Brian (1985) *Okubo Diary: Portrait of a Japanese Valley*, Stanford, CA: Stanford University Press.

—— (1990) "Making an exhibition of oneself: the anthropologist as potter in Japan," in Eyal Ben-Ari, Brian Moeran, and James Valentine (eds), *Unwrapping Japan: Society and Culture in Anthropological Perspective*, Manchester: Manchester University Press, pp. 117–39.

Moore, Sally F. (1987) "Explaining the present: theoretical dilemmas in processual ethnography," *American Ethnologist*, 14(4): 727–37.

Mori, Akiko (1999) *Tochi wo yomikaeru kazoku*, Tokyo: Shinyôsha.

Morris, Brian (1995) "How to publish a book and gain recognition as an academic," *Anthropology Today*, 11(1): 15–7.

Narayan, Kirin (1989) *Storytellers, Saints and Scoundrels: Folk Narratives in Hindu Religious Teachings*, Philadelphia, PA: University of Pennsylvania Press.

Nöbauer, Herta (2002) "Between 'Gifts' and 'Commodities': an anthropological approach to the Austrian academic field," in Caroline Gerschlager and Monika Moore (eds), *Women in the Exchange Society: (Self-)Deception and other Imponderables*, Amsterdam: Kluwer Academic, pp. 1–18.

Patterson, Thomas C. (2001) *A Social History of Anthropology in the United States*, Oxford: Berg.

Pels, Peter and Oscar Salemink (1995) "Introduction: five theses on colonial practice," *History and Anthropology*, 8(1–4): 1–35.

Pertierra, Raul (1995) "Counterfactual conditions of culture and their implications for integration: a Philippine example," *Philipinas*, 25: 49–64.

Powdermaker, Hortense (1966) *Stranger and Friend: The Way of an Anthropologist*, New York: Norton.

Prager, Michael (1999) "Crossing borders, healing wounds: the Leiden school of structural anthropology and the colonial encounter, 1917–1949," in Jan van Bremen and Akitoshi Shimizu (eds), *Anthropology and Colonialism in Asia and Oceania*, London: Curzon Press.

Prakash, Gyan (1990) "Writing post-Orientalist histories of the Third World: perspectives from Indian historiography," *Comparative Studies in Society and History*, 32(2): 383–408.

Provencher, Ronald (1994) "Anthropology in the Malayan Peninsula and Northern Borneo: orientalist, nationalist and theoretical perspectives," *Studies in Third World Culture*, 54: 47–71.

Rabinow, Paul (1986) "Representations are social facts: modernity and post-modernity in anthropology," in James Clifford and George E. Marcus (eds), *Writing Culture: The Poetics and Politics of Ethnography*, Berkeley, CA: University of California Press, pp. 235–61.

—— (1991) "For hire: resolutely late modern," in Richard G. Fox (ed.), *Recapturing Anthropology: Working the Present*, Santa Fe, NM: School of American Research Press, pp. 59–71.

Ribeiro, Gustavo Lins (1997) "In search of the virtual imagined transnational community," *Anthropology Newsletter*, 38(5): 78–80.

Robertson, Roland (1992) *Globalization: Social Theory and Global Culture*, London: Sage.

Sanjek, Roger (1993) "Anthropology's hidden colonialism: assistants and their ethnographers," *Anthropology Today*, 9(2): 13–18.

Scholte, Bob (1980) "Anthropological traditions: their definition," in Stanley Diamond (ed.), *Anthropology: Ancestors and Heirs*, The Hague: Mouton, pp. 53–87.

Shimizu, Akitoshi and Jan van Bremen (eds) (2003) "Wartime Japanese anthropology in Asia and the Pacific," *Senri Ethnological Studies*, No. 65, Osaka: National Museum of Ethnology.

Silverman, Sydel (ed.) (1981) *Totems and Teachers: Perspectives on the History of Anthropology*, New York: Columbia University Press.

Skocpol, Theda (1985) "Bringing the state back in: strategies of analysis in current research," in Peter Evans, Dietrich Rueschemeyer, and Theda Skocpol (eds), *Bringing the State Back In*, Cambridge: Cambridge University Press, pp. 3–37.

Spencer, Jonathan (2000) "British social anthropology: a retrospective," *Annual Review of Anthropology*, 29: 1–24.

Spivak, Gayatri Chakravorty (1988) "Can the subaltern speak?" in Cary Nelsona and Lawrence Grossberg (eds), *Marxism and the Interpretation of Culture*, Urbana, IL: University of Illinois Press, pp. 271–313.

Srinivas, M.N. (1996) *Village, Caste, Gender and Method: Essays in Indian Social Anthropology*, Delhi: Oxford University Press.

Stephenson, John B. and L. Sue Greer (1981) "Ethnographers in their own cultures: two Appalachian cases," *Human Organization*, 40(2): 123–30.

Steward, Julian H. (1973) *Alfred Kroeber*, New York: Columbia University Press.

Stocking, George W. (1982) "Afterword: a view from the center," *Ethnos*, 47(1–2): 172–86.

—— (1983) "The ethnographer's magic: fieldwork in British anthropology from Tylor to Malinowski," in George W. Stocking (ed.), *Observers Observed: Essays on Ethnographic Fieldwork*, Madison, WI: University of Wisconsin Press, pp. 70–120.

Swidler, Ann and Jorge Arditi (1994) "The new sociology of knowledge," *Annual Review of Sociology*, 20: 305–29.

Tambiah, Stanley J. (1985) *Culture, Thought and Social Action: An Anthropological Perspective*, Cambridge, MA: Harvard University Press.

Tomiya, Akimichi *et al.* (1988) "Small-type coastal whaling in Japan: report of and international workshop," *Occasional Publications*, No. 27, Edmonton, Alberta: Boreal Institute for Northern Studies.

Turner, Graeme (1992) " 'It works for me': British cultural studies, Australian cultural studies, Australian film," in Lawrence Grossberg, Cary Nelson, and Paula Treichler (eds), *Cultural Studies*, New York: Routledge, pp. 440–53.

Urry, James (1993) *Before Social Anthropology: Essays on the History of British Anthropology*, Switzerland: Harwood Academic Publishers.

Van Bremen, Jan (1996) "Anthropology and the colonial world: east-west parallels," *Kyoto Conference on Japanese Studies – 1994*, Kyoto: International Research Center for Japanese Studies, II: 33–42.

—— (1997) "Prompters who do not appear on the stage: Japanese anthropology and Japanese studies in American and European anthropology," *Japan Anthropology Workshop Newsletter*, 26–27: 57–65.

—— (2003) "Wartime anthropology: a global perspective," in Akitoshi Shimizu and Jan van Bremen (eds), *Wartime Japanese Anthropology in Asia and the Pacific: Senri Ethnological Studies*, Osaka: National Museum of Ethnology, 65: 13–48.

Van Bremen, Jan and Akitoshi Shimizu (eds) (1999) *Anthropology and Colonialism in Asia and Oceania*, London: Curzon Press.

Van Maanen, John (1988) *Tales of the Field: On Writing Ethnography*, Chicago, IL: Chicago University Press.

—— (1995) "The age of innocence: the ethnography of ethnography," in John van Maanen (ed.), *Representations in Ethnography*, Thousand Oaks, CA: Sage, pp. 1–35.

Vincent, Joan (1991) "Engaging historicism," in Richard G. Fox (ed.), *Recapturing Anthropology: Working in the Present*, Santa Fe, NM: School of American Research Press, pp. 45–58.

Vishwanathan, Savitri (1992) "Indian approaches to Japanese studies," in Harumi Befu and Josef Kreiner (eds), *Othernesses of Japan: Historical and Cultural Influences on Japanese Studies in Ten Countries*, Monographien aus dem Deutschen Institut für Japanstudien der Philipp-Franz-von-Siebold-Stiftung Band 1, Münich: Iudicum Verlag, pp. 281–93.

Wengle, John L. (1988) *Ethnographers in the Field: The Psychology of Research*, Tuscaloosa, AL: University of Alabama Press.

Williams, Raymond (1977) *Marxism and Literature*, Oxford: Oxford University Press.

World Anthropologies Network (2003) "A conversation about a World Anthropologies Network," *Social Anthropology*, 11(2): 265–9.

Zhou Daming (1993) "Review of a decade of the re-establishment of anthropology in China," *Social Sciences in China*, 2: 95–105.

Part II
Asia

2 Indigenous and indigenized anthropology in Asia

Grant Evans

I sometimes say to my Chinese students in Hong Kong, partly as gentle provocation, that we will know the age of colonialism is over when they choose to do their fieldwork in Britain, or Australia, or the United States, or some other "Western" country. That they rarely consider this to be an option is, perhaps, an interesting comment on the state of mind of young anthropologists in Asia. I have encountered a similar reluctance to analyze "the West" among Thai going to study anthropology overseas. I recall one friend writing a letter full of queries and wonderment about the local culture soon after her arrival in the United States in the 1980s. I replied, suggesting that she write her thesis on some aspect of American society. My suggestion was not taken up, and she completed her thesis on rural Thai society. Why was this? There are several reasons: certainly those with more radical leanings hope that their studies will "help the people" at home; some feel that not enough analysis has been done on their own societies; furthermore, often they are encouraged by their foreign supervisors who have usually done fieldwork in Thailand (but this applies equally to China or Indonesia, etc.) to pursue a home-centered line of research, and one suspects that this is partly because it keeps them vicariously in touch with "the field." In some cases, these foreign students are also obliged to study their own societies as a condition of their scholarships. Sometimes, however, foreign students beg-off doing fieldwork elsewhere because they claim that their language skills are not good enough. But usually, their English (or French, or whatever) is much better than most "Western" anthropologist's local language skills. So, is it simply that they cannot afford "field assistants" who will clarify pieces of slang, or render thick local accents into the standard form of speech? Or does their reluctance reflect some persistent "cultural cringe?"

Here, of course, we brush up against what has been until recently an enduring pattern in the practice of anthropology, that is, the advantages of affluent anthropologists from industrialized countries in the field. Their research has often taken place against a background of colonial rule and entrenched power differentials, in spite of the individual anthropologist's beliefs. As Kuper's (1973) study of the British social anthropologists shows, many of them were anti-colonial. This, however, did not change the objective asymmetry of their social relations in the field.

For a long time, the Japanese have studied other cultures in Asia, and this too needs to be set against a background of colonial practice (Van Bremen and Shimizu 1999). Japanese practice also appears to be partly influenced by ideas of cultural homogeneity. That is, if you want to study the "other" you go elsewhere.

Ethnocentrism has influenced Chinese anthropologists differently. It has been rare to find Chinese anthropologists elsewhere in Asia. They have tended to study the "other," that is the minorities, within China. More recently, however, Chinese anthropologists who have trained in foreign institutions have begun to focus on the Han. Chinese anthropologists from Taiwan or Singapore can, on the other hand, be found researching in other parts of Asia.

So, when we survey the big picture of Asian anthropology and anthropologists, its contours are blurred, and indeed our understanding of the evolution of the respective national traditions is, so far, inadequate.

American, European, or Australian scholars have until recently played a major part in the evolution of anthropological writing on Asia: historically this has been connected to colonialism, though this should not lead anyone to draw hasty conclusions about the "colonial nature" of their studies. There were, as we know, some instances in which the political developments of the time – the Cold War in Asia – influenced some anthropological projects, or at least ensured funding for them. During the Vietnam War, there was a controversy in Thailand about anthropological research there (Wakin 1992), and anthropologists such as Gerald Hickey worked closely with the US government in Vietnam – and, it should be said, he produced invaluable studies of the highland peoples there.

More importantly, the influence of "Westerners" in the anthropology of Asia has been a result of the affluence of these countries after 1945 and the expansion of higher education in them. Their liberal political systems meant that not only did students of anthropology have money for research, but they also had the freedom to choose where they would go. The main restrictions on them came from the governments of the countries where they wished to study, often as a result of post-colonial nationalist xenophobia. As Asian countries have become more affluent, and as higher education in them has expanded, we have seen similar developments in them. As I indicated earlier, Japanese, Taiwanese, Singaporeans, and south Koreans can now be found working all over Asia. Moreover, in conferences these days, one can see an important and refreshing shift in the cultural composition of the participants.

A fall in funding in the hitherto affluent countries has also led to a growing interest in their own "indigenous" anthropology, or "anthropology at home" (which I think was the title of one British book). This is also the background to the founding of the European Association of Social Anthropologists (EASA) some years back, and the apparent growth in anthropological interest in Europe. But in some respects this is a return to the founding folklorist traditions of ethnography in Europe. Of course, there are important theoretical issues involved in this shift too, but we should not lose sight of the effects of the mundane but fundamental issue of funding.

So, maybe we could say that in Europe, the United States, and Australia anthropology is indigenizing (at least, to a certain extent), while in Asia anthropology is simultaneously indigenizing and de-indigenizing.

But it is time to ask: What can *Indigenous and Indigenized Anthropology in Asia* possibly mean?

Well, it can simply mean that more people from Asia are conducting anthropology in Asia – either in their own countries or in other parts of Asia. This fact is obviously true. But the key issues that arise from this are: has this fact led to new questions being raised, a different type of practice for anthropology, and a new theory even? The latter, I suppose, is what is meant by the idea of indigenized anthropology.

But before we deal with these issues, I would like to make a rather long detour through a relatively little known field. A form of indigenous and indigenized anthropology has been practised in Asia for close to forty years – in the communist states of Asia.

Communism and indigeneity

One thing that communism in Asia did was to indigenize anthropology. Work by foreign researchers from anywhere was for a long time impossible in these states, then it became possible but under extremely restrictive conditions; in more recent times it is possible but still controlled. These restrictions even applied to "fraternal" comrades, so the few Soviet or Hungarian researchers in Vietnam, for example, were closely monitored. The main exception to this rule that I know of has been the fairly unimpeded access of Vietnamese ethnographers to Laos.

Indigenous anthropologists in these countries found their institutional base in Committees for Social Sciences, in Institutes of Ethnography or in sections of government departments, such as a Committee for Nationalities in a National Front for Reconstruction – or some such similarly named organization. As I have written elsewhere about Vietnamese Communist Anthropology (Evans 1985, 1995, 1999), these anthropologists identified with the developmental aims of the state and saw the minority peoples within their borders as "backward" and as requiring development as defined by the center. This mood remains strong among people in these institutions. Note also that their attention was focussed almost exclusively on what are called national minorities. Anthropologists – or ethnographers, as they are commonly known – did not study the Han Chinese or the Vietnamese. China's best known anthropologist Fei Tsiao Tung's studies of Han Chinese took place in the 1930s when he was a student at the London School of Economics. After 1949 his attention was directed toward the so-called "national minorities."[1]

The theoretical apparatus these anthropologists worked with was a Stalinist – Maoist version of Marxism, and the theory of nationalities that came out of Stalinist Russia. Anthropological theory in the "West" was dismissed as bourgeois and colonial or imperialist. Of course, if one wants to push a strong "nativist" line one could argue that these indigenous anthropologists were in thrall to a foreign theory, that is, Marxism. But such a claim is problematic as one ends up in a bizarre regression. So, extreme Russian nationalists today denounce Marxism as a Jewish theory, or a Jewish plot; and presumably Germans could do the same; while perhaps Jewish fundamentalists in the Middle East could denounce Marxism as "Western" and German. These are real possibilities within a "nativist" discourse.

Such claims, of course, raise the tricky problem of what constitutes a "foreign" theory. That is, how can one apply the idea of "foreignness" to a theory? But let me leave this question hanging for the moment.

The Chinese, for a complex set of reasons, took up Marxism and applied it to Chinese conditions, as did the Vietnamese and Lao and North Koreans, and so on. And a great deal of ink has been spilt on how they "indigenized" Marxism. I do not think anyone today would dispute the fact that the Chinese, the Vietnamese, and the North Koreans forced Marxism through their own cultural sieve, and rationalized this in all sorts of ways.

In other words, Marxism did not come into these societies in some pure form, nor did it operate in some pure theoretical space, but like all knowledge it was subject to local social, cultural, and political forces. (In this sense it parallels the fates of world religions – such as "foreign" Buddhism in China or in Thailand.) The Chinese, Vietnamese, and Lao anthropologists that I have met considered themselves to be Marxists, whatever their understanding of what that meant, and saw themselves applying that theory to "local conditions," and in many respects they thought they were "indigenizing" the theory. Most of them did this in good faith, and often of their own volition.

One of the consequences of the revolutions and the cutting off of intellectual life in these countries from "the imperialist West" was that for the next thirty years or so these anthropologists were impervious to theoretical developments in anthropology elsewhere. The main people they met with and went to conferences with and discussed theoretical and empirical issues with were themselves. Occasionally, they would discuss such issues with communist intellectuals from other countries. But, practically, they lived in an indigenous universe.

Another consequence of the revolution and the condemnation of the "Western" theory as bourgeois was that the foundation text for these ethnographers was Engels' *The Family Private Property and the State*, and perhaps some may have read excerpts from Morgan. Their work, therefore, was wedded to a very rigid view of the stages through which societies must pass – primitive communism, feudalism, capitalism, and so on. So in some respects, until very recently anthropology in these countries lived in a nineteenth-century evolutionist intellectual universe.

It was for this reason that people like myself felt they had stepped into a time machine and traveled backwards upon a first encounter with communist ethnographers in these countries. When reading their monographs or articles, or seeing them at work, it was as if one was observing an early twentieth-century British social anthropologist in, say, colonial Africa. Take photography as an example: if one looks back at photographs taken during the European colonial period in Asia (and here I have in mind the French in Indo-China in particular) there is a certain way of seeing that is at work. The "eye" of the camera is very much in the style of the observer and the observed: the colonial photographer looking at the native subject.[2] Only rarely do we find the conventions of "naturalism" that most modern anthropologists prefer – that is trying to be invisible, and trying to record non-staged events. When traveling and working with Lao or Vietnamese ethnographers, I have been struck by our different approaches to photography. They adopt what I identify as "colonial style," and will record staged events, and instruct people to put on their traditional clothing so that they can be photographed. And sometimes they will remark "you can see these people are giving up their traditions because they don't wear their traditional clothes anymore." Their positioning of the camera is symptomatic of an approach and an attitude.[3]

The feeling that one is experiencing the practice of high colonial anthropology in these communist countries is not an illusion either. I would argue that this indigenous practising of anthropology in Asia has, to date, been a form of colonial anthropology. Indeed, sometimes more blatant than anything we can find among European anthropologists who practised in Asia in the past.

Why do I say colonial? These anthropologists have self-consciously aligned themselves with the state in order to extend state control over ethnic minorities lying within the borders of the modern state. In this sense, it is internal colonialism – and we may wish to debate this concept. The first major task of anthropologists in China and in Vietnam and in Laos was to go and make an inventory of all the ethnic groups in the country, and to draw up criteria – social and cultural – for deciding on "nationality."[4] This so-called "cultural categorization" had real political effects concerning the granting of, for example, autonomous zones, or any other privileges that may go with minority status. It also meant excluding some groups who made claims to separate minority status, as well as the amalgamation of other groups who claimed to be separate. Once this was carried out this state assigned status became part of one's status as a citizen, and one's "nationality" was recorded on one's identity card. This power of creation or dissolution of groups is similar to the power of the European colonial state and its advisors to reinforce the power of particular chiefs and rajahs or not, to recognize the existence of certain groups or not, and to recognize certain types of land use or not.

Anthropologists are also required to identify so-called "reactionary" and "superstitious" practices – whether in religion, marriage practices, residential practices, and so on. In this sense they are true to the spirit of Morgan who wrote:

> It is one of the harsher, and at times even painful, office of ethnography to expose the remains of crude old cultures which have passed into harmful superstition, and to mark these out for destruction. Yet this work, if less genial, is not less urgently needful for the good of mankind. Thus, active at once in aiding progress and in removing hindrance, the science of culture is essentially a reformer's science.
>
> (cited in Tambiah 1990: 44)

I have recorded elsewhere, for example, how the Vietnamese in the southern highlands broke up the matrilineal longhouses there, claiming that they were a backward and primitive form. And as I note there, one can sense the incomprehension of these matrilineal cultures by the patrilineally oriented Vietnamese (Evans 1995).

I have met no mainland Chinese, Vietnamese, nor Lao ethnographer who has learnt a minority language. They expect the exchange to take place in the dominant "national" language. The only ethnographers who work in minority languages are minorities themselves who have been drawn into the Institutes of Ethnography or the Committees for Nationalities in order to carry out studies on their own peoples. Often, these people will operate as either interpreters and/or informants for ethnographers from the dominant ethnic group. In fact, these Institutes require a separate study. But from my observations in all three countries, they have been crucial vehicles for the upward social mobility of individual members of minorities, whereby they become trained and fluent in the dominant language and modes of thought, and apply these uncritically to their own peoples who they begin to see as backward, and indeed as a status they have left behind. In fact, they and their families migrate to the main cities, and they, or at least their children, begin to marry into the dominant group. Of course, I have no objection to cross-cultural marriage, but if one looks at the sociological role of these institutes it is not as some kind of representative institution for minority "voices," although one will find a greater tolerance in them of minority cultures than one will find in the society at large. They are institutions for the carrying out of state policy among minorities, and indeed most of their members agree that the state's policies with regard to the minorities are enlightened and correct.

It is true that among the mountains of material gathered by these ethnographers – and in terms of paper it is a lot – there is some interesting and important empirical material. It is, however, always placed in a theoretically inadequate framework and there is certainly no tradition of recording minority "voices," except perhaps their oral legends. Their studies will typically begin by trying to place the society in some traditional past, and within the pre-arranged categories of the Marxist evolutionary framework. The ethnography will be set out in standard categories of kinship, economy, religion, political organization, and finally a section on the good life under socialism. Indeed, I would argue that we learn relatively little about the working of these societies from this mountain of work, and in fact learn more about attempts by the state to codify the cultural boundaries of these groups.

In reflecting on the nature of so-called "indigenous" and "indigenized anthropology," what are we to do with a young Lao who has studied ethnography in Vietnam in Vietnamese, and who takes texts produced in Vietnam by the resident Black Tai in the Institute of Ethnography in Hanoi, back to Laos in order to use it as a basis of comparison with Black Tai communities in Laos? I had this experience when I first went up to Houaphan province in Laos in 1988 with a Lao ethnographer to start a study of Black Tai there.

When we reached the village site where we would be based, our research strategies were quite different. I began with the standard survey of the village, something that he found boring. What he had brought with him was a book in Vietnamese on the Black Tai from Vietnam and he set about using this book as a checklist to see whether the Black Tai where we were staying were "really" Black Tai. Soon, he confided to me that these Black Tai were forgetting their traditions as they could not recite to him histories of the Black Tai as found in his book, and as few of them knew how to read the traditional script, he decided there was little of interest to study. Meanwhile, my interest was focussed on cultural change, and any practices that may reflect this, and one quickly realized that studies of cultural change and what they meant to people were not on his agenda.

I have worked on and off with this person for almost ten years now. One of the first things I did was begin to pay for him to learn English for, as I argued, it was necessary for him to gain access to wider anthropological debates. I should also say that in our initial research in the north I was dependent on him to translate the local dialect into standard Lao for me, and he was often much quicker to see things happening in the village than me, but the irony was that he was not interested in them as an anthropologist. They were simply, for him, normal events that occurred in villages and did not require any special thought, such as a death ritual that happened while we were there.

Let me follow this person further in order to try to tease out what we could possibly mean by indigenous. His father was Black Tai, his mother Lao, he studied from junior secondary school to university in Vietnam and in Vietnamese, he is now married to a Vietnamese woman who lives with him in Laos, and they have three young boys. His ethnographic training is in Vietnamese, and most of his texts, until recently, have been in Vietnamese. More recently, he has had access to Thai and English texts. There is no doubt in my mind that his intellectual formation is special, but I find it hard to think how the term indigenous helps me to understand what he does or is.

Indeed, one can see in him, and among ethnographers in Vietnam and in China, a desire to "de-indigenize" their ethnographic practice and to learn more about anthropological developments in the "West," feeling now that what they have been doing and what they know theoretically to have been almost a waste of time and obsolete. What they can publish, however, remains strictly controlled by the state. What has distinguished the development of anthropology in these communist countries has been the recognition of ethnography by the state and its formal separation from sociology (unlike the evolution of the discipline in non-communist Asia). This has partly been a consequence of the object of research being defined as a study of minorities and not the majority population. Furthermore, a relatively large number of "indigenous" (i.e. minority) ethnographers were trained and employed by the state. I suspect, however, that with market-driven criteria increasingly entering the academic and state fields in these countries this situation is rapidly changing.

The communist states are an important example of large-scale indigenous practice of anthropology in Asia. Yet, they have produced no significant anthropological studies and no significant theoretical breakthroughs. Of course, one can object that these indigenous scholars were operating in totalitarian systems and not free to explore a "real" indigenous anthropology. But as I have suggested, this is not the way these indigenous scholars saw the problem, and moreover one has to deal with the fact that it was "indigenous" totalitarianism as well.

I say this because I want to problematize the idea of indigeneity and because I also think that hiding behind this idea is a notion that, for example, only Chinese can really understand Chinese culture and society, or Thai the Thai, and so on. This notion is inimical to anthropology.

Indigenized anthropology?

As Adam Kuper (1994) reminded us some years ago, ideas similar to those currently advanced by advocates of indigeneity have been associated with the extreme racist nationalism of Nazism in the past. One of the things we discover in such discourses, he says, is that some "natives" are more "native" than others are, that is, allegedly less polluted by foreign concepts or genes. (In Asia, one finds an invidious discourse in which both ideas are combined in the "naturalised" slur *Banana*, "yellow on the outside, white on the inside," applied especially to those "genetically pure" Chinese, Thai, etc., who have been brought up overseas.)[5] In the current debate what is one to do with an anthropologist whose parents come from different "racial"/cultural backgrounds? In such a discourse, they would seem to be permanently compromised – or one finds oneself assenting to an absurd case which argues that they can only study others like themselves. A key issue is, however, who has the power to define and manipulate the notion of "native," "indigenous," or whatever? Of course, some states have asserted this right – but should anthropologists?

Amphay Doré, who is of Lao and French parentage, in his autobiographical account of becoming a monk, proposes a more interesting and more complex line of thought:

> Ethnology, which I studied after psychology, gave me the elements for a more satisfactory definition [of myself]: through its ambition to understand a culture not only objectively but also from the inside, it gave a sort of justification to my state as a Eurasian: like a medium, I had the ability to translate from one language into another. Ethnology had, moreover, a global approach to reality, and this accorded well with my nature. It was through it, this western science, that I rediscovered the Asia of my childhood.
>
> (1974: 35)

Lack of "purity" may in fact be an advantage for an anthropologist! As I have argued elsewhere (Evans 1993), neither insiders nor outsiders to a culture have unambiguous advantages. I cite the problems, and I can now cite further cases, that so-called "indigenous" scholars have had in studying their own cultures, or in their own countries. And I suggest that probably one of the best solutions for anthropologists is collaborative research between insiders and outsiders.

Anthropology has always been committed to trying to understand other cultures and societies because, I would argue, of the importance of cross-cultural insights to anthropological theorizing. The practice of comparison (which of course has its own methodological problems) often raises questions and problems which do not occur if one focusses on a single culture. One can see this in the practice of anthropology in China in which anthropologists often become Sinologists and remain largely ignorant or uninterested in the rest of Asia. They become entrapped in a very powerful Sinocentric field (or is Sinocentrism indigeneity?). Their studies rarely proceed by way of comparison – except perhaps with "the West" (read the United States), when in fact more appropriate comparisons may be found in Asia. An obvious example of inappropriate comparison has been in discussions of the Chinese notion of "face." Anthropologists and psychologists have labored to show that Chinese are obsessed by "face," whereas Americans are not. The discussion has been oblivious to research on "face" (i.e. notions of pride, shame, etc.) in other Asian cultures, such as Thailand or Bali, for example. This is despite the fact that an essay by one of the world's most famous anthropologists, Clifford Geertz (1973), has dealt precisely with the question of the presentation of self among Balinese. I have no doubt that an anthropologist from Thailand or Bali working in China (or vice versa) would not miss the opportunity for comparison. And I have no doubt that comparisons of this kind would produce a more subtle understanding of "face" in everyday life in all of these cultures.

Earlier in this chapter I left a question mark hanging over the issue of so-called "foreign" theories. It is often asserted that anthropology is hopelessly compromised by the "Western" origins of its theories. And alongside such charges we may hear calls for a "Chinese Anthropology," or an "Asian Anthropology." To my knowledge, however, the claim that anthropology is irretrievably compromised has never been argued substantially or at length, and has more often than not rested on a nationalistic assertions of difference which are assumed to be common-sensically apparent. (Often these claims are little more than demagogy.) These assertions rarely demonstrate an understanding of "Western" intellectual history, of its radical shifts in perspective in recent centuries, or the diversity of "Western" thought, which is strongly marked by both romantic, idealistic discourses and rationalistic, scientific ones. Which is the "real West?" Therefore, I must agree with Maurice Godelier's reply to the question: "Is social anthropology indissolubly linked to the West, its birthplace?":

> anthropology is a mode of knowledge which has been able to take shape only by distancing itself from the West, by shifting its focus away from it and often by taking issue with its ethnocentric representations of the rest of humanity.
>
> (1995: 141)

This is not to argue that anthropological writings have not been, at times, shot through with ethnocentric assumptions that have compromised their findings. But, interestingly, it has been mainly "Western" scholars who have been most active in uncovering the hidden cultural assumptions in the works of their theoretical ancestors through the well-established practice of critique, which is fundamental to the anthropological tradition. In the current phase, the proven fallibility of the ancestors has led some people to become disillusioned with the larger aims of anthropology and we have seen a "post-modern" backlash and out-pourings of theoretical and personal *angst* about the practice of anthropology. The rejection of the "tradition" by post-modernism, not surprisingly, has provided ammunition for those arguing for indigeneity and the theoretical irrelevance of "the West." It is interesting to note, however, that this backlash has been strongest in the United States where the individualistic and subjectivist turn of post-modernism is culturally most appealing. (It is not insignificant that the French theoretical demigods of this turn have not spawned a similar movement among French anthropologists.) The sociology of knowledge that has always tried to locate theoretical shifts in social and cultural, rather than purely theoretical space is, unfortunately, not a well-developed field among anthropologists.

It has been the well-established theoretical practice of critique in anthropology which enables Godelier to draw the conclusion that:

> anthropology has already proved, through its best, and often highly unex-
> pected, results, that it is genuinely possible to construct a *metacultural vision*
> of humankind without abandoning cultural diversity.... The premise of the
> construction of a meta-cultural view of humankind (which will never be the
> spontaneous product of one perception or one culture), is that no specific
> culture, whatever its nature, can serve as a sole point of departure or centre
> of reference for the construction of a science of humanity.
>
> (1995: 155)

The widening of the cultural pool of practising anthropologists in Asia will sharpen our understanding of the cultural biases that may pervade our attempts to understand complex societies. Anthropology is now a cross-culturally shared tra-dition, and as we excavate the history of anthropology in each country, we are more able to fully understand the complex interaction between local traditions and this larger tradition – whether it be the impact of European folklore studies on Malinowski's formation, or Japanese imperialism on the evolution of Japanese anthropology.

Of course, there is another important issue raised by the debate around indigenous anthropology, and that is the degree to which intellectual systems of thought which do not have their origins in the European tradition can feed back into anthropology and contribute to its theoretical development. For example, can the extensive reflections of the nature of the mind by Buddhists lead to new forms of anthropological knowledge?[6] There have been many attempts by Asian psychologists and others to show that Buddhism can provide new perspectives on personality and the mind. But, unfortunately, most of them have been theo-retically disappointing (see, for example Sarachchandra 1958; Kawai 1996).

The Embodied Mind by three cognitive theorists (Varela *et al.* 1991) is perhaps the most theoretically powerful attempt to integrate Buddhist insights into our understanding of cognition, though I must leave it to others more knowledgeable in this area to decide on its long-term viability. In this regard, it is interesting to note that among psychologists there has been a more vigorous debate around the issue of indigenous knowledge and psychologies than there has been in anthropology. But the imprint of a positivistic and scientistic methodology in psychology finds its way into these debates, and indeed is the basis on which the results produced by cultural anthropology are rejected, because the "reliability, validity, and interpretation of the data are not strictly verifiable" (Kim and Berry 1993: 19). Nevertheless, the debate among them has also shown the problematical nature of an indigenous psychological theory (see Pandey *et al.* 1996).

The main changes to anthropological theory and practice will not come from some so-called "indigenous" transformation. It will come from the entry into anthropological discourse of people from increasingly diverse cultural and social backgrounds who will provide slightly new angles on old questions, arising perhaps from their exposure to different religious philosophies about the nature of humans, and they will bring with them new empirical data produced by an ever evolving world. In the long term, it will be this that will slowly re-shape anthropology's current contours.

We do not need an indigenous and indigenized anthropology in Asia, or anywhere else, but an anthropology that is more self-consciously and sensitively internationalized. In this respect, the time has come to problematize global categories like "the West" and perhaps "Asia" in anthropological discourse, and to carefully articulate their uses – especially the category "the West."[7] Its use is a theoretical habit that has been the source of a myriad of uninformed and false contrasts. A further serious issue is that many European and American anthropologists, when they are writing their articles and books in English (or other European languages), assume that they are writing for Europeans or Americans and forget that there is now a very large Asian (let alone African or Latin American) audience of anthropologists and other social scientists who are reading their literature. In fact, I would suggest, it is this feature of anthropological writing, far more than the concepts deployed, which betrays an ongoing ethnocentrism among American, Australian, or European anthropologists. On the other hand, many Asian anthropologists use the category "the West" in a way which shows no particular understanding of the content of that category, and its use largely derives from a long past political, nationalist context.

In this chapter I have tried to show: first, that we need to know more about the political, economic, social, and cultural coordinates which influence the practice of anthropologists in Asia; second, to illustrate through the examples of the communist states of Asia that the practice of so-called "indigenous anthropology" is fraught with problems; and finally to assert, along with Godelier, a metacultural vision of anthropology. Few anthropologists would deny the difficulties and complexities involved in anthropological research, but the challenge and excitement of it is admirably conveyed by Obeyesekere's reflections on his own anthropological practice:

> When I study a peasant village in Sri Lanka, I might do several things. I might make a personal self-discovery into my past; I might also make a critique of my own culture; I might see Sri Lanka not in isolation but in relation to the larger Indic or Hindu culture; I might see its parallels with Buddhist Burma and Thailand, and I might ask myself why is it different from Kenya or Highlands New Guinea or lowland New Jersey. What I do as an anthropologist is to understand culture, or a culture; and such understanding must surely be through the prism of my own cultural subjectivity. Yet the dialogue I carry on is not with the culture: it is an understanding about culture that I carry out in dialogical form with my colleagues from where it spills over into modern life and thought, influencing that life in a variety of ways.... While it cannot provide the energy, the blindness, and the passion that religious and political fundamentalism give to their adherents, it has at least the potential to influence a vision of a more humane world order.
>
> (1990: 274)

Notes

1 There are several studies of Fei's intellectual odyssey, but see Arkush (1981).
2 For a discussion of some of the issues relating to photography see the essays in Edwards (1992).
3 Of course, anthropology now questions the illusions of naturalist photography – but that is another issue.
4 For a brief account by one of the participants in this program see Huang (1994).
5 For a discussion of racialist ideas in Asia see the essays in Sautman (1994).
6 For an important discussion of how "Eastern" theories and Buddhism have influenced the development of European thought see Clarke (1997), especially chapter 9 for its influence on psychology.
7 Throughout this chapter I have been forced to use the self-conscious strategy of distancing myself from common-sense understandings of "the West" by always placing it in inverted commas. It is one of the virtues of Godelier's discussion that he provides a definition of what he means by the West (Godelier 1995: 144). One of the purposes of Jack Goody's (1996) thought provoking study is to overcome such simplistic polarities and to point to commonalties in heritage between "the East" and "West."

References

Arkush, David R. (1981) *Fei Xiaotong and Sociology in Revolutionary China*, Cambridge, MA: Harvard University Press.

Clarke, J.J. (1997) *Oriental Enlightenment: The Encounter Between Asian and Western Thought*, London: Routledge.

Doré, Amphay (1974) *Un Après-Gout de Bonheur: Une Ethnologie de la Spiritualité Lao*, Vientiane: Editions Vithagna.

Edwards, Elizabeth (ed.) (1992) *Anthropology and Photography 1860–1920*, New Haven, CT: Yale University Press.

Evans, Grant (1985) "Vietnamese communist anthropology," *Canberra Anthropology*, 8(1–2).
—— (1993) "Introduction: Asia and the anthropological imagination," in Grant Evans (ed.), *Asia's Cultural Mosaic: An Anthropological Introduction*, Singapore: Prentice Hall.
—— (1995) "The southern highlanders of Vietnam," in R.H. Barnes, Andrew Gray and Benedict Kingsbury (eds), *Indigenous Peoples of Asia*, Ann Arbor, MI: University of Michigan, Association for Asian Studies.
—— (1999) "Apprentice ethnographers: Vietnam and the study of Lao minorities," in Grant Evans (ed.), *Laos: Culture and Society*, Chiang Mai: Silkworm Books.
Geertz, Clifford (1973) "Person, time and conduct in Bali," in C. Geertz (ed.), *The Interpretation of Cultures*, New York: Basic Books.
Godelier, Maurice (1995) "Is social anthropology indissolubly linked to the West, its birthplace?", *International Social Science Journal*, XLVII: 143–58.
Goody, Jack (1996) *The East in the West*, Cambridge, UK: Cambridge University Press.
Huang, Shuping (1994) "The criteria of ethnic identification in China," in Barry Sautman (ed.), *Racial Identities in East Asia*, Hong Kong: Division of Social Sciences, Hong Kong University of Science and Technology.
Kawai, Hayao (1996) *Buddhism and the Art of Psychotherapy*, foreword by David H. Rosen, College Station, TX: Texas A&M University Press.
Kim, Uichol and John W. Berry (eds) (1993) *Indigenous Psychologies: Research and Experience in Cultural Context*, Beverley Hills, CA: Sage Publications.
Kuper, Adam (1973) *Anthropologists and Anthropology: The British School 1922–72*, London: Penguin.
—— (1994) "Culture, identity and the project of a cosmopolitan anthropology," *Man*, 29: 537–54.
Obeyesekere, Gananath (1990) *The Work of Culture: Symbolic Transformation in Psychoanalysis and Anthropology*, Chicago, IL: University of Chicago Press.
Pandey, Janak, Durganand Sinha and Dharm P.S. Bhawuk (eds) (1996) *Asian Contributions to Cross-Cultural Psychology*, New Delhi: Sage Publications.
Sarachchandra, Ediriweera R. (1958) *Buddhist Psychology of Perception*, Colombo: Ceylon University Press.
Sautman, Barry (ed.) (1994) *Racial Identities in East Asia*, Hong Kong: Division of Social Sciences, Hong Kong University of Science and Technology.
Tambiah, S.J. (1990) *Magic, Science, Religion, and The Scope of Rationality*, Cambridge, UK: Cambridge University Press.
Van Bremen, Jan and Akitoshi Shimizu (1999) *Anthropology and Colonialism in Asia and Oceania*, London: Curzon Press.
Varela, Francisco J., Evan Thompson, and Eleanor Rosch (1991) *The Embodied Mind: Cognitive Science and Human Experience*, Cambridge, MA: MIT Press.
Wakin, Eric (1992) *Anthropology Goes to War: Professional Ethics and Counter-insurgency in Thailand*, Madison, WI: University of Wisconsin, Center for Southeast Asian Studies.

Part III
East Asia

3 Beyond orthodoxy

Social and cultural anthropology in the People's Republic of China

Frank N. Pieke

Introduction

The conflicts, false starts and at times even almost complete annihilation that have characterized the development of anthropology in China make the title of this chapter much more than facile rhetoric. In Western academia, the legitimacy of a separate field variously called cultural anthropology, social anthropology or ethnology is usually taken for granted; in fact, much too much is taken for granted perhaps given the considerable overlap with adjacent fields such as sociology, geography, folklore studies, cultural studies, political science, economics, law, history or linguistics. China – and with it many other Asian, African and Latin American countries – on the other hand has always had a rather ambiguous attitude towards the division of labour within the Western social sciences and the humanities.[1]

In this chapter I will give neither a chronological outline of the development of anthropology in China nor a systematic overview of the current state of the anthropological field in the People's Republic of China (PRC). Other people are much better qualified to do this, and several easily accessible works in English or Chinese do already exist (McGough 1979; Wong 1979; Arkush 1981; Pasternak 1988; Guldin 1990, 1994; Guldin and Southall 1993; Wang 1997). What I will present in this chapter might best be called an anthropological view of Chinese anthropology. As an anthropologist working in China, I have had many conversations and more formal discussions over the years with Chinese colleagues and friends working in the disciplines of sociology, anthropology and ethnology. It was only after reading Gregory Guldin's book on Chinese anthropology (Guldin 1994; see also Pieke 1996), which is an excellent work on the period up until the 1960s, but rather disappointing in its discussion of more recent developments, that I realized that my impressions accumulated over the years began to amount to an informal ethnography of Chinese anthropology.

This chapter is an attempt to bring these impressions together. Its chief objective is to understand what anthropology means to Chinese social scientists and how this is often very different from the interpretations given to anthropology in Europe or North America. The chapter is also somewhat of an experiment in method. Presenting an abbreviated version of this chapter at the Distinguished

Lecture Series in Anthropology at Peking University in June 1998, I was struck by the differences between my own interpretations and those of the Chinese anthropologists and sociologists in the audience. I agree with many of the criticisms I received, in particular that this chapter falls short of providing a full ethnography of anthropology and the anthropological community in China as a whole. It is clear that my interpretations as an outsider cannot do full justice to the many disparate 'natives' point of view', and each native may therefore very justifiably feel that I have an insufficient grasp of the particulars of the situation that they find themselves in and their own localized ways to make sense of that situation.

Yet that is exactly the point of this chapter. The phenomenon of 'anthropology in China' (like all other social phenomena studied by anthropologists) cannot be encapsulated in one unequivocal truth, no matter how systematic or thorough the anthropologist has been. What this chapter (and anthropology more broadly) however can and should do is to juxtapose these different viewpoints and point out the underlying causes of their emergence, conflict and development. Anthropology does not present 'the natives' point of view' and cultures cannot be rendered as texts. Cultures are fields of discursive contention between many different native viewpoints. Although a particular anthropologist's interpretations of the nature and patterns of contention do not present the final word, they can contribute to the debates by presenting a view of the broader picture that often eludes the participants themselves. In this spirit, I sincerely hope that this chapter will be of some help to those scholars who are concerned with social and cultural anthropology in China. As this chapter will show, this is by no means an easy task, but I believe it will ultimately prove to be well worth the effort.

What are the social sciences supposed to do for China?

It is a truism that the introduction and growth of the social sciences in China cannot be separated from the challenge posed by the West. This was as true for eminent progressive scholars and revolutionaries in the past, such as Liang Qichao, Cai Yuanpei and Mao Zedong, as it is for leading intellectuals of today. In the May Fourth Movement of 1919 and the New Culture Movement in the 1910s and 1920s, 'science' was considered one of the root causes of the West's military and economic superiority over China.

The social sciences were part of the 'science' that was to be borrowed from the West as one half of the solution for China's ills.[2] Because of this specific genealogy, both 'science' and 'social science' have profoundly ambiguous connotations in China. Science will help break through the barriers of its traditional culture that is widely viewed as the cause of China's backwardness, and is thus an essential element in the long drawn out project of China's Enlightenment (Tu 1991). Yet science's dynamism can also be deeply subversive: if left unchecked, it will not only attack the harmful aspects of China's traditional culture, but may also obliterate much that is Chinese in China. According to some, there is no loss in that, but to most Chinese intellectuals and politicians this remains a disturbing notion.

Science in China is thus a metonym of the West as seen through Chinese eyes: on the one hand, the promise of progress, national strength, increased control over society and modernity, and on the other hand, the path to personal freedom, heterodox thought, political subversion and cultural obliteration. As Thomas Metzger in his discussion of the work of Ambrose King (Jin Yaoji) points out, this also implies that the West remains the benchmark for Chinese evaluations of China's development, implicitly denying China its own modernity (Metzger 1993). This is a point of some importance for anthropology, and I will return to it later.

With science and social science we have thus entered an extremely complex and multifarious discursive field. It could be argued – possibly at the risk of exhuming the body of the Frankfurter Schule – that the conditions of high modernity have largely subverted the Enlightenment project in the West. Science in the West is no longer the search for the control of reason, and reason is no longer the key to freedom, equality and brotherhood. Science in the West has been reduced to a profession in search of technical solutions to narrowly defined problems. The larger ideological and moral debates triggered by the quest for knowledge are carefully confined to the Academe, and have little impact on (and are largely incomprehensible to) society at large.

Cynical and seasoned as we are in the West, we are more often puzzled than anything else at the continued belief of Chinese intellectuals in both the curing powers and destructive potential of Western culture in general, and science in particular. Yet, to understand Chinese readings of that rarefied and peripheral academic discipline called anthropology, we have to take this larger discursive field into account. *Almost all* Chinese intellectuals consider their work to be more than a quest for knowledge that is important in its own right. Their scientific work ultimately aims at the discovery of the root causes of China's continued sorry state and at finding solutions for them.[3]

Chinese views on the future of China tend to focus on culture to an extent rarely found elsewhere. Since the simplistic *ti-yong* (substance-application) dichotomy of the late nineteenth century that insisted on the implicit superiority of China's essence, the argument usually runs as follows: China's problems ultimately lie with its culture, which is backward looking, oppressive and conservative. Smashing this old culture is thus a prerequisite for modernization and progress. Yet progress and modernization are merely instruments to restore the glory of China as a state, a nation and, ultimately, a civilization. Chinese culture can therefore not be all bad. Consequently, the good and progressive aspects of Chinese culture need to be preserved, moulded or even created and incorporated in China's new, modern civilization.

This argument, or parts of it, have informed and continue to inform thinking on modernization in China from Kang Youwei's constitutionalism around the turn of the century to the ravages of Mao's Cultural Revolution between 1966 and 1969, and from the aggressive iconoclasm of the celebrated TV series *River Elegy* in 1988 to the semi-ritual insistence on a socialist *spiritual* civilization as a complement to material civilization in post-reform China.

Chinese debates about civilization, Westernization, modernization, and progress are thus informed by specific meanings grafted onto concepts like science and social science. In view of this, it should come as no surprise that some Chinese intellectuals have turned to the 'science of culture', cultural anthropology, in order to understand and solve China's problems with its culture. Yet curiously enough, China has never become a hotbed of anthropological thought; if anything, anthropology as an academic discipline remains pitifully undeveloped. It is this paradox that I shall further explore in this chapter.

The inhibited growth of cultural anthropology in China

In the 1920s and 1930s, Chinese scholars of the Folklore Movement turned to the alive and real culture of the countryside as a source of the New Culture they hoped to create as an alternative to both the ossified literati culture and wholesale Westernization (Schneider 1971; Eminov 1978). Turning to the folk as a source of the nation is by no means unique to China: the Grimm brothers in Germany during the early nineteenth century had already done something very similar. Yet this type of work was by no stretch of the imagination anthropological in the way we understand it. The field of folklore studies (*minsuxue*) that is connected with the names of Gu Jiegang, Wolfram Eberhard, Lou Zikuang and Zhong Jingwen entails the documentation and collection of myths, stories, songs, customs, art and other aspects of non-literate and material culture in virtual complete isolation from the social and cultural fabric in which they are embedded.

In Chinese folklore studies, from the very beginning a tension exists between the goal of learning from the people and teaching and elevating the people. At first, the contradiction was not yet acute. The objective was to create a new culture based on, but not identical to, folk culture. In the 1930s, however, these two objectives became increasingly separated. The work of people like Gu Jiegang was primarily scholarly in nature. Other folklorists, however, were preoccupied with reforming the peasants for political and humanitarian reasons. Folklore studies became an instrument for the production and commodification of discrete items of culture for the hegemonic control or use by the state (Eminov 1978: 172).

The development of folklore studies under the Chinese Communist Party (CCP) was shaped by the same contradiction, with the senior folklorist Zhong Jingwen being the chief advocate of a scientific approach.[4] In 1957, Zhong paid the price for this when he was purged during the Anti-rightists Campaign. In the PRC, the goal of folklore studies is the collection of China's traditional non-literate culture and crafts before they die out. In line with Mao's directives during the 1942 Yan'an Forum on Literature and Art, folklore thus collected serves as the basis for the construction of a new, better culture for the masses. More bluntly put, folklore provides the raw material for the writers and artists who are the creators of China's socialist culture. In principle, a distinction is thus maintained between 'collecting' (*souji*) and 'editing' (*zhengli*) on the one hand, and 'creating' (*chuangzuo*) on the other. After the Anti-rightists Campaign in 1957 this distinction was increasingly lost on China's folklorists, who were made to see it as their main task to create a new folk culture in line with the Party orthodoxy. Only after 1981, with the attack on the 'Change the old into the new' (*Gai jiu bian xin*) movement, has a more academic view of folklore studies prevailed again, once more headed by grand old man Zhong Jingwen (Jia 1981; Ting 1987).

In the 1930s and 1940s, and largely independent from folklore studies, China perhaps came closest to developing a social and cultural anthropology of its own, with Wu Wenzao, who is almost unknown in the West, in a pioneering role. Yet, Fei Xiaotong more than anybody else showed the power that anthropological field studies can have. His books on rural development (*Peasant Life in China* 1939, *Earthbound China* 1945) and rural social structure (*From the Soil* 1992, *China's Gentry* 1953) are not just seminal academic works but continue to be important sources of inspiration for policy makers and their academic advisors. The continued importance of Fei's work derives directly from its grounding in British functionalist anthropology. His books are based on direct field work observation in real villages and towns, where institutions and practices are not studied in isolation but as functional parts of a total social structure. His two main discoveries are that Chinese farmers do a lot more than grow crops to survive, and that the relational way the Chinese define themselves is fundamentally different from Western individualism. These two findings may strike us as rather self-evident, but (sadly enough) urban Chinese sophisticates continue to find that they run counter to the ideas they have grown up with.

Yet as is well known, the post-1949 fate of Fei's anthropology has not been a happy one. Between the abolition of sociology and anthropology as bourgeois sciences in 1952 and he himself being branded a Rightist in 1957, Fei (as many of his colleagues) was put to work in the field of ethnology (*minzuxue*):[5] the study and classification of non-Han Chinese 'minority nationalities' (*shaoshu minzu*), a field of study whose intellectual mould is provided by Stalin's reinterpretation of Morgan's and Engels' evolutionism in 1942, and whose methods (documenting and gathering of isolated items of culture) derive more from folklore studies than from cultural or social anthropology.[6]

Yet Fei's scholarship encompasses much more than British functionalism transplanted on Chinese soil. Despite his lasting intellectual debt to Malinowski, he considered himself first and foremost a student of the Russian anthropologist Shirokogoroff who taught for many years at Beijing's Qinghua University, where Fei took an MA in sociology and anthropology before his sojourn to England (Pasternak 1988: 639–40). Shirokogoroff's anthropology was a comprehensive one, including the study of psycho-cultural worldviews and human biology. Both before and after 1949, Fei also thought himself as much a sociologist and ethnologist as an anthropologist, and indeed considers the issue of the disciplinary borders between them a moot point:[7]

As far as I am concerned, I have never made a clear distinction between anthropology, sociology and ethnology, and this unclear status has never influenced my work. This is an important point. I really have never changed the methodological objectives and theory of my research because its disciplinary name had changed. My research work has had a clear consistency. Perhaps this concrete example can make clear that a disciplinary name is of secondary importance. The key to scholarly success lies in a clear understanding of objectives, the improvement of methods and the development of theory. What kind of scholar other people call me is really not that important.

(1994: 3)

This pragmatic attitude is indicative of a broader trend in Chinese academia that has only become more pronounced after 1978. Only a small number of people in China call themselves cultural or social anthropologists. Both before and after 1949, most anthropology courses are taught in departments or institutes of sociology, ethnology or history. Specialized anthropology departments only exist in southern China. At Guangzhou's Zhongshan University, the anthropology department perhaps comes closest to an American-style four-fields anthropology. Until 1994, Xiamen University had a department of anthropology whose roots in the Museum of Mankind (*Renlei Bowuguan*) and the Department of History have led it to gravitate towards archaeology and material culture. In 1994, the anthropology department was abolished because its graduates could not find employment. Currently, Xiamen University only has a (research) Institute of Anthropology and the old Museum of Mankind (Li Minghuan, personal communication). Most recently, Yunnan University established a new department of Anthropology and Social Work (*Renleixue yu Shehui Gongzuo Xi*). Its anthropology section was earlier part of the Department of History and is strongly anchored in ethnology and American cultural anthropology.

Cultural or social anthropology in southern China is strongly linked to history, archaeology and ethnology. This seems the result of a curious blend of American four fields anthropology, which still is attractive to some of the older anthropologists trained before 1949, coupled with the Soviet division of labour imposed in the 1950s and a long-term sinicization process which both call for a stress on historical roots and a focus on non-Han people. Yet, the appointment in the 1990s of anthropology professors with an American PhD both at Xiamen and Yunnan were the first signs of a growing interest in Western (particularly American) anthropology, although this will not necessarily have to lead to the erosion of the distinctive nature of southern Chinese anthropologies.

In northern China, and more in particular Beijing, a very different situation pertains,[8] but oddly enough this has not led to the building up of an independent disciplinary base. Within the world of minority nationalities studies in the capital, a strong interest in anthropology exists. Ethnologists in Beijing are based at the Chinese Institute of Nationalities (now the University of Nationalities) and the Institute of Nationalities Studies of the Chinese Academy of Social Sciences (CASS). The latter is located at the same site as the University of Nationalities and is rather detached from the rest of CASS. Both institutions are confined to the study of non-Han minority nationalities; to them, promoting anthropology is a strategy to gain approval to work on Han Chinese as well (Ruan 1993). The issue of anthropology however has broader implications for the whole discipline of ethnology within and beyond Beijing, and I shall return to this later.

The second group of scholars with an anthropological interest are the folk-lorists around the successors of Zhong Jingwen at Beijing Normal University. Although I am personally the least acquainted with this group, I understand from conversations with former students there that many students are frustrated with the old-fashioned folklore studies taught by their teachers. Social and cultural anthropology and other more theoretically grounded disciplines are attractive to them as a way to work on issues beyond the rather sterile exercise of collecting, ordering and creating folklore.

Sociology is the third hegemonic academic discipline that, much like in pre-1949 Beijing, nurtures anthropology, primarily at the Institute of Sociology at CASS, the Institute of Sociology and Anthropology at Peking University, and more recently at the Department of Sociology at Qinghua University. The reasons for the sociologists' turn to cultural and social anthropology are somewhat more complex than those of the ethnologists and folklorists. First, Fei Xiaotong, the unrivalled dean of post-1978 sociology in China, was the founding head of first the Institute of Sociology at CASS and then the Institute of Sociology at Beijing University.[9] Although reportedly not in favour of an institutionally independent anthropology (more about the possible reasons for this in the next section), Fei does appreciate the specific contribution that the anthropological approach can make to a sociological study of China. During and after his tenure at these two institutes, Fei has made room for the appointment of young anthro-pologists at these institutes; at Beijing University he has even supervised several anthropology PhD students.

To Fei and many younger Beijing sociologists, anthropology stands for a combination of functionalism and holism, first-hand field work and qualitative methods. Since its re-establishment in 1979, Chinese sociology had been much influenced by American sociology with its heavy stress on quantitative methods. This was very attractive at the time. 'Hard' methods purport to construct objec-tive and unequivocal truth, an important argument for a fledgling discipline that wants to be taken seriously. In addition, such truth can be presented as uncon-nected to the political or ethical preferences of the scientist. A quantitative methodology thus protects the sociologist from the potential political fallout of his findings; it can even be a conscious strategy to make heterodox or even sub-versive messages more acceptable. By the late 1980s, however, and inspired by the relative political openness of the time, many younger sociologists became tired of cumbersome quantitative methods and the pallid conclusions to which they often led. To them, anthropology offered something new and exciting and, above all, different.

Recently, a related and further reason for sociology's interest in anthropology has come to the fore. After 1989, China's nationalistic turn has had a profound impact on the social sciences, with both sociologists and anthropologists calling for the 'sinicization' (*Zhongguohua*) or 'nativization' (*bentuhua*) as an integral aspect of 'disciplinary strengthening' (*xueke jianshe*) and weaning from the Orientalism that is thought to continue to inform the study of Chinese society by Westerners and Chinese alike (see also Chang 2004; Guldin 1994, chapter 12). Interestingly, sociologists look to anthropology's fieldwork methods and cross-cultural perspective to make sociology more relevant and suited to the complexities of Chinese society. Conversely, sociology could help anthropology break through the barriers of its traditional subject matter. As Ma Rong succinctly expressed at a discussion meeting:

> Today's close integration of sociology and anthropology carries on the experience of tradition and achievement of the older generation of sociologists, [who] adapted [literally 'integrated'*jiehe*, FP] anthropological methods to the analysis and research of the subject area of sociology; [this] both broke through the confines of anthropology's research area and objects, and made it possible for sociology's understanding of the complex social and cultural phenomena in human societies to transcend simple questionnaires and data, thus achieving the profundity that comes with a cross-cultural understanding. The mutual integration of sociology and anthropology is therefore in my opinion the key to the future 'nativization' of Chinese sociology and the new chance of research work.
>
> (Feng and Li 1997: 101)

A second factor in the capital's anthropological turn was the influence of returned foreign PhDs. Currently, several cultural and social anthropologists at the Institute of Sociology at CASS, the Institute of Sociology and Anthropology at Beijing University and the Department of Sociology at Qinghua University hold American, British, French or Japanese PhDs; several more former students or staff at these institutes are studying abroad or have already found employment at British or American universities. Through these diasporic links, Beijing's sociologists and anthropologists have become familiar with European, American and Japanese ideas about the place of cultural anthropology in the academic division of labour.

At first sight, my insistence on the inhibited growth of anthropology seems to be contradicted by the re-establishment of anthropology as a discipline with the onset of the reforms. In 1978, CCP propaganda chief and then head of the newly established Chinese Academy of Social Sciences Hu Qiaomu called a meeting for the re-establishment of sociology and anthropology (Rong 1996). Currently, Chinese anthropology boasts at least 2 professional journals and 3 professional organizations with thousands of members (Chen 1996).[10] Most of these members, however, seem to be volunteer or amateur folklorists and ethnologists.[11] Their work remains a largely untapped source of data on China's many local cultures and societies waiting for the professional anthropological researcher. As I have explained earlier, anthropology continues to be severely underfunded,[12] fragmented and with a very small institutional base either at the margins (in the South) or in the interstices of academia (in Beijing). In the words of Wang Mingming:

> until now, the discipline of anthropology in China has still not yet become a specialized and autonomous profession of teaching and research. Exploring anthropology under these circumstances, we must make clear to society with what kinds of work anthropologists should be occupied with and what kinds of contributions to society they can make. In a situation of increasing scholarly specialization, a vital task at present is to explain the disciplinary content of anthropology, to arrive through discussions at scholarly understanding and standards that are shared by all, and to go to the field to learn through personal experience what our own distinctive social position is. In addition to this, when being on our guard against a tendency to pragmatism, we can make clear to society the important duty that anthropology has to the life of humankind.
>
> (1997: 250)

Many reasons obtain for this state of affairs. Strong regional traditions dating back to the 1930s and 1940s, discussed earlier in this chapter, make the formation of any consensus on what anthropology is an almost impossible task. This has been much compounded by the imposition of a Soviet-style division of labour. Before 1949, anthropology at many universities was integrated with sociology. When the latter discipline was branded a bourgeois science and abolished in 1952, anthropology almost automatically suffered the same fate. At the same time, the anthropological turf of the study of minority nationalities was assigned to Stalinist ethnology, precluding the disciplinary blossoming that sociology witnessed after the political thaw of 1978 (Fei 1994: 3).

Yet anthropology's marginal status is currently also one of its chief attractions. Anthropology as an intellectual orientation promises access to other disciplines or alternative approaches that are at least partially out of reach of the hegemonic control of the party and the state. At the same time, this works against the establishment of anthropology as an institutionalized academic discipline.

A further cause of the fragmentation and inhibited institutionalization of anthropology are the endemic personal conflicts that reinforce the existing regional and disciplinary boundaries. The long-standing feud between Fei Xiaotong and Lin Yaohua, the grand old man of ethnology (Guldin 1994: 154), goes a long way in explaining the absence of formal cooperation between the ethnologists and the sociologists in the capital; similarly, Zhong Jingwen appears to have established his own independent kingdom of folklorists. More recently, the problems that exist in the relationships between the Institute of Sociology at CASS, the Department of Sociology at Peking University and the Institute of Sociology and Anthropology, also at Peking University, has made it impossible to join forces and push for a stronger institutional identity of cultural anthropology.[13]

The other major foster discipline of anthropology, ethnology, similarly seems to be riven by conflict, although in this case more substantial issues seem to be involved. At the most recent meeting of the Chinese Ethnological Association held in November 1997 in Nanning the debate on the 'nativization' of ethnology featured very prominently. Unlike the superficial similarity to the nativization debate in sociology, the issue here really seems to be the struggle between younger ethnologists who are well versed in foreign scholarship, and an old guard of ethnologists who feel threatened by this development. For the latter group, nativization simply amounts to a call to keep things as they are and foreign influences at bay. Younger scholars, on the other hand, acknowledge that ethnology ultimately is an offshoot of the importation of foreign anthropology into China in the 1930s and 1940s and find it indispensable for the further development of Chinese ethnology to infuse a large dose of the mother discipline: (foreign) anthropology. Naturally, they reject the notion that ethnology is a native Chinese discipline that ought to be nativized even further (Wang Qinghua, personal communication 1998; Weng 1998: 5–6).

'Anthropology' among Chinese ethnologists thus stands for much more than the possibility to study non-minority Chinese discussed earlier. It is ultimately tied into a debate on the nature of the discipline as a whole and a succession struggle among its incumbents. Yet, more substantive issues also feature in the larger debate on the future of ethnology and the role of anthropology therein. As Weng Naiqun points out, conventional ethnologists are increasingly hard put to find minority communities that have preserved their traditional culture and society intact, putting the blame for the bias in favour of the primitive and undeveloped onto the pre-1949 legacy of Western anthropology (Weng 1998: 1–2). Although I have trouble accepting the latter claim, I am a lot more sympathetic to the doubt that he expresses of the continued relevance of a search for pure and untouched cultures. What is much more relevant to the contemporary world, according to Weng, is for instance the increased cultural awareness of minority nationalities, leading to the reconstruction of their traditional culture for political purposes. Ethnology and anthropology can make unique contributions to the understanding of the uniquely Chinese pattern of the many changes brought about by the impact of modernization and globalization (Weng 1998: 6).

Regionally, the fundamental differences between the southern ethnological, biological, archaeological and historical and the northern sociological interpretations of anthropology came to a boil in January 1998 in the run-up to the *Second Session of the Advanced Seminar of Social and Cultural Anthropology of China*. At the last minute, mutual suspicions between the Beijing and Kunming organizers split the conference, which subsequently was held simultaneously both in Beijing and in Kunming.[14]

Fortunately, in Beijing at least individual researchers of all these groups and factions manage to communicate and cooperate, while their institutes continue to be at loggerheads. Informal discussion groups and more formal research projects thus provide important channels of communication and at least a degree of anthropological community building; in addition, the various institutes on occasion hire each other's students as staff.[15]

A more fundamental problem of anthropology in China than the enmities and debates alluded to earlier, is in my opinion that the social sciences have always been suspect in the eyes of the CCP, which is why both sociology and anthropology were outlawed only three years after the party's victory in 1949. The party proclaimed Marxism, after all just a social scientific theory, to be the absolute and eternal truth. This made the independent exercise of social scientific analyses not only a dangerous undertaking, as I have said earlier, but also a very threatening enterprise. Independent social scientific analysis may discover unpleasant facts about Chinese society that jar with the Communist Party's orthodoxy. The social scientific character of the ruling ideology potentially allows independent sociologists to turn these facts into a heterodox truth that undermines the ideological basis of the party's rule. Much of the growth of the social sciences in China is thus about a continual testing of the boundaries of acceptable social research, in which social scientists and the authorities negotiate the balance between innovativeness, orthodoxy, policy relevance and professional standards of social research.

Yet, this does not explain why in post-1978 China, sociology and other social sciences have been much encouraged and consequently grown into major academic disciplines, while anthropology has largely been left to fend for itself. We will therefore have to look further than the CCP's general suspicions of the social sciences to account for anthropology's continued inhibited growth. As said earlier, part of the explanation for this is that the post-1949 academic division of labour made anthropology largely redundant. This explains why anthropology graduates find it almost impossible to find jobs, the main reason for the abolition of the Anthropology Department at Xiamen University in 1994 (see p. 64). Yet, I believe more is at hand than just unfortunate circumstance. The core problem of Chinese anthropology is what I would like to call the ethnological basis of Chinese nationalism and socialism.

As Frank Dikötter has shown, the intellectuals around the turn of the century imagined that the Chinese nation were profoundly influenced by Western social Darwinism, evolutionism and racialist thinking. Shocked by Western racist condescension of the Chinese they turned to, among other things, anthropology for a scientific methodology to prove the equality of the yellow race (and especially the Chinese among them) and the white race in their superiority over all other races. Part and parcel of Chinese nationalism is therefore a scientific racialization of China's long-felt civilizational superiority (Dikötter 1992).

The CCP is very much heir to this definition of the Chinese nation, which is further strengthened by the incorporation of Morgan's and Engels' evolutionism into the socialist canon (Morgan 1877; Engels 1940; Shanin 1989). The CCP defines the PRC as a multi-national nation-state, an obviously ambiguous term,[16] and has used ethnology to construct the nationalities that make up the nation. The objective of the mammoth task of the classification of minority nationalities that continues until this day is to produce an objective, scientific account of this multi-national nation. All citizens are unambiguously assigned to one or the other specific group, either the majority Han Chinese, or else one among the fifty-five minority nationalities. All these groups are furthermore hierarchically ranked on the evolutionary ladder with the Han at the highest evolutionary stage (Fei 1981; Gladney 1991, chapter 2; Guldin 1991, 1994, chapter 6).[17]

The many ramifications of the CCP's classification do not concern us; just one important consequence should be mentioned here that has earlier been pointed out by Dru Gladney (1991: 306–12). The formalization of cultural differences *between* (artificially defined) groups renders insignificant (because not meriting separate group status) the cultural differences that exist *within* these officially sanctioned groups. Most significantly, this creates and upholds the fiction of a huge (91 per cent of the total population) homogenous Han Chinese majority that is the real backbone of the ostensible multi-national nation. Already in the early twentieth century were the 'invention of the Han' and the concomitant 'invention of the minority nationalities', essential aspects of the creation of a unifying nationalism by Sun Yat-sen, the founder of the Chinese nation; the CCP has simply systematized his ideas and carried them out on an unprecedented scale.

I would like to argue that the political sensitivity of anthropology-turned-ethnology-turned-minorities-classification can largely be traced to this ethnological basis of the Chinese nation. For decades, ethnology's job has been the official classification of minority nationalities. This implied and upheld the CCP's definition of the Chinese nation that is based on the fiction of the homogeneity of the Han and their essential difference from the minorities. When applied to ethnic divisions among the Han themselves, however, the very same classification methodology developed for non-Han minority nationalities would explode the myth of Han homogeneity. Similarly, studying interethnic relations between 'minority nationalities' and Han, or among groups within the same nationality (either Han or a minority) would very quickly lead to the conclusion that the boundaries drawn so carefully around the officially recognized nationalities are not so natural after all: cultural traits will come to be seen as interactive products and not objective facts.[18] Even more dangerously, any study of interethnic relations will rapidly have to confront the rough and tumble of exploitation, subjugation and exclusion that are at odds with the sanitized picture of harmonious relationships between China's nationalities.

Sociologists and ethnologists who are interested in the relations between nationalities in China are acutely aware of this problem. Many ethnologists tend to use a traditional, predominantly historical approach, studying for instance migratory patterns and the interaction between the Chinese imperial and republican governments and indigenous groups, yet others explicitly turn to Western anthropology as a source of ideas.[19] One problem they all seem to be grappling with is that China has inherited the strongly primordialist concepts of 'society', 'people' or 'nationality' from European and Marxist discourses on social and cultural difference (Shanin 1989).

A comparison with Soviet ethnology may be useful here. In the 1960s and 1970s, Soviet ethnologists struggled with a very similar problem when they tried to emancipate themselves from the stranglehold of Stalinist orthodoxy, sparking off a lively debate revolving around the term 'ethnos'. Yulian Bromley, in particular, developed this term into a very sophisticated analytical concept. In his work ethnos describes self-conscious social groups that persist over long historical periods. Ethnoses change under the impact of historical processes and social evolution, yet maintain their distinct nature (Bromley 1980; Dragadze 1980; Bromley and Kozlov 1989; Shanin 1989). The concept thus occupies a middle ground between the official Marxist dogmatic concepts of 'nationality' and 'society' and the Western circumstantialist concept of ethnic group. A conceptual debate such as this has not taken place, although recently the word *zuqun* has gained currency among sociologists and anthropologists as the equivalent to the modern Western term of 'ethnic group', while ethnologists increasingly use the word 'branch' (*zhixi*) when they wish to discuss differences between groups of the same nationality, including the Han. However, the latter concept merely provides a language to talk about difference, and not about the dynamics of the relationships between such groups.[20]

The present and future of anthropology in China

My brief overview of the inhibited growth of anthropology leads me to conclude that anthropology in contemporary China should not be called an academic discipline, but rather is a key word that is flexibly applied in several disconnected discursive communities. To some, particularly in southern China, anthropology is the broad integrated science of man subsuming the more specialized subfields of cultural anthropology, archaeology, biological anthropology, linguistics, folklore studies, ethnology, sociology and the like. Under the continuing influence of a Soviet-style division of labour this can be a dangerous strategy. More often, therefore, a narrower meaning is preferred that allows for the separate identity of ethnology alongside anthropology: anthropology thus becomes the ethnology of the Han-Chinese or a resumption of the dialogue with the mother discipline of Western anthropology (Yang 1996). To others who work in a sociological tradition, anthropology means social anthropology. This variously entails a stress on qualitative field work, cross-cultural comparison and community studies, or, more contentiously, the study of interethnic relations and historical connections between the Han and the minority nationalities, and the ethnic subdivisions among the Han themselves.

In such a fluid discursive field it is obviously very dangerous to draw firm conclusions about the indigenization of anthropology. Yet, this may be exactly what we should be looking for. China has assimilated and continues to assimilate Western anthropology not as an institution, but as a set of ideas, approaches and concepts. Unbundling anthropology proves to be a continual process. It draws from many disparate sources in world anthropology and leads in many different directions in China itself. The localized meanings that are grafted onto the concept of anthropology vary with the discursive uses to which it is put. These cannot be predicted in advance and shift and change over time. Anthropology in China is one example of what David Parkin has called 'latticed knowledge' (Parkin 1995). Globalization processes do not submerge and homogenize local cultures, but are continuously appropriated by local discourses. As such, anthropology and Coca Cola are very comparable aspects of global culture. Just as Coke is served piping hot in Shanxi province to fight the cold winters, so does anthropology acquire significances in Yunnan that are very different from those in Beijing.

Yet from anthropology's variable meanings, one constant element emerges. Anthropology in contemporary China is always heterodox, innovative and thus slightly dangerous. Chinese academics invoke anthropology because they want to say what the established categories of academic discourse are uncomfortable with (cf. Leach 1964) or do what the established academic division of labour hegemonically inhibits. Scholars in China who invoke anthropology therefore consciously play with fire, using the concept of anthropology as a discursive tool to limit the potential danger to themselves and especially the wider academic community of which they are a member.

Anthropology in China does not exist but does seem to have a bright future as a source of inspiration for other disciplines that are bogged down by the weight of official dogma or received wisdom. Yet China is only at the beginning of unravelling, translating and assimilating Western anthropology. China's unique way of indigenizing our discipline will come of its own only when anthropologically inspired researchers will shed their myopic gaze on China itself.

To return to the topic that I began this chapter with, Chinese intellectuals want to understand and cure China; in their search for solutions to China's (perceived) ills, some turn to anthropology. Few would quarrel with this, and I for one would like to argue that anthropology in any country ultimately strives towards a better understanding of the native culture(s). Yet, Chinese anthropologically inspired researchers do not realize that a fundamentally different understanding only comes about when one exposes one's own culture to comparisons with other cultures. Ultimately, analytical concepts and insights that emerge from the study of China will have to be put to the test of cross-cultural comparison. Anthropology thus really comes down to a hermeneutic cycle. Ideas derived from one's own culture are adapted for the analysis of other cultures. Thus modified, they are fed back into the ongoing debates in one's own anthropological community and wider society to be in turn applied to the study of other cultures, and so on.

I suspect that many researchers in China will agree with this, yet the actual research that follows from this realization is often seriously flawed, and a closer look at Western social and cultural anthropology may prove useful here. When social scientists talk about comparison, they almost invariably refer to the West ('Europe' or 'America'), ignoring the fact that the world is quite a bit larger than just China and its favourite other. However, there is one further point that needs some elaboration. Just as Western anthropologists can be accused of constructing an Orientalist image of China, a criticism with which I at least partially agree, so do Chinese anthropologists and other social scientists often work with an overtly stereotypical image and homogenous image of the West. Even more seriously, this image is often clearly Occidentalist in nature: a picture of the West is created as a neat mirror image of an equally neat and stereotypical image of China. Ultimately, the West's Orientalism is thus countered with a Chinese Occidentalism and its counterpart reverse Orientalism.

A stock comparison is, for instance, the Chinese's stress on human relationships, which is contrasted with the West's individualism. From this flow, a whole series of comparisons and contrasts that have very little to do with the lived-in reality of both China and Western countries (or at least the ones I am familiar with). Unfortunately, this Occidentalism and its counterpart reverse Orientalism tend to reinforce each other, forming a closed hermeneutic cycle that only few have managed to escape.

In my view these are serious problems that can however be solved. If one genuinely wants to understand oneself, one has to look at not one single but many cultures for contrasts and similarities and understanding of which should be grounded in solid ethnography of one's own and these other cultures, and should contrast one's own ethnography with those of anthropologists rooted in other traditions. In short, Chinese anthropology should build up its own, broad disciplinary tradition that can engage foreign anthropologies on an equal basis.

This is perhaps the true, and as yet not realized, potential of anthropology in China. An indigenous anthropology (whether formally institutionalized or not) only matures when it has built up a body of knowledge that is explicitly comparative and cross-cultural. Until that stage is reached, Chinese anthropology will merely remain an off-shoot of Western anthropologies that does little more than either systematize and make explicit indigenous stereotypes of Chinese culture, or else analyze China in terms of alien, Western anthropological ideas. By contrast, an indigenized anthropology autochthonously generates its own ideas, concepts and debates that are informed by an ongoing hermeneutics between one's own and other cultures and their anthropologies. Without this, old ideas are merely recycled and new ones can only be imported from an external (usually Western) source.

Ultimately, such an indigenized anthropology could also solve the long-standing problem, discussed in the beginning of this chapter, that Chinese intellectuals continue to refer to Western modernity as the only path of China's modernization. Producing accounts of Western and other societies from a Chinese point of view, a truly indigenized anthropology will be able to break through this closed hermeneutic cycle and thus contribute much to the development of a uniquely Chinese modernity. Such a reinvented anthropology would also make Chinese intellectuals more sensitive and appreciative of developments that already take place before their own eyes in China's villages, towns and cities, developments that are now often dismissed as aberrations or corruptions.

Seen from this perspective, training in non-Chinese field languages, funding of often expensive field work abroad (including, but not confined to the West!), and comparative studies are what China's anthropologically inspired disciplines need. The study of Western theories and methodologies are much less important from a long-term perspective and can even have profoundly deleterious effects. When pursued as an end in itself, the importation of Western ideas will only produce a faithful but sterile copy of Western anthropology that constantly tries to keep abreast of exciting developments and fashions that invariably take place elsewhere. To create a truly Chinese anthropology, Chinese anthropologists must turn away from their almost exclusive focus on Chinese societies and start the long and arduous march into the world beyond China.

74   *Frank N. Pieke*

Acknowledgements

I would like to thank Stephan Feuchtwang, Elisabeth Hsu, the participants in the International Workshop on Indigenous and Indigenized Anthropology in Asia, Leiden, May 1997 and the participants and audience of the Distinguished Lecture Series in Anthropology in honour of the centenary celebration of Peking University, Beijing, June 1998 for their comments on earlier drafts of this chapter. Obviously, much has happened since this chapter was written more than six years ago. Rather than try to account for the latest developments in Chinese anthropology, which would require substantial new research, I have decided to leave the chapter more or less as it is, with only a few changes and additions where appropriate. For a more recent discussion of my views on the anthropology of China and the 'indigenization' (*bentuhua*) of anthropology in China, see Pieke 2004.

Notes

1 Even this latter distinction between the social sciences and the humanities is not commonly used at all with the term *shehui kexue* (literally: the social sciences) usually denoting both the humanities and social sciences. One consequence of the absence of the distinction between the social sciences and the humanities has been that many people who were assigned positions in the new departments of anthropology and sociology in the 1980s were recruited from a broad variety of fields, including history, folklore and minorities studies.

2 The other half was democracy, shorthand for political reform and the establishment of a more accountable government. On the May Fourth and New Culture Movements, see Lin (1979) and Schneider (1971).

3 The thinking of Chinese intellectuals remains firmly embedded in what Tu Wei-ming has called the Enlightenment dilemma. This entails a fundamental belief in the force of reason and the malleability of individual and society that are Confucian in origin, coupled with a unilinear and forward looking concept of social development that is profoundly Western. This reading of the West's Enlightenment is fundamentally distorted by Chinese assumptions regarding the relationship between the individual and society. It ignores the most fundamental tenet of the West's Enlightenment, namely the inviolability of individuals and their rights even against the perceived reasonability of the collective interest. The Enlightenment is thus narrowed down to an instrument for the quest for renewed Chinese wealth and power, instead of a set of fundamental values and beliefs that are desirable ends in themselves (Tu 1991: 113–17).

4 Chen Kaige's film *Yellow Earth* (*Huang tudi*) gives a fascinating, if romanticized, view of the conflict between Mao's folklore collectors and the peasants whose culture they have come to harvest.

5 The Chinese word for ethnology, *minzuxue*, should not be confused with *minsuxue* (folklore studies) discussed earlier. It should also be borne in mind, however, that the distinction between *minzuxue* and *minsuxue* emerged only gradually in China. Especially before 1949, whether *minzuxue* should be translated as folklore or ethnology can often only be determined contextually.

6 A clear statement of the theoretical and methodological underpinnings of Chinese ethnology is given in Fei 1981. For a discussion of the intellectual roots of this tradition in the Central European concept of 'nationality' or 'people' (German *Volk*, Russian *natsional nost*) and Marxist evolutionism, see Shanin (1989).

7 Fei was a sociology undergraduate at Beijing's Yanjing University before he went on to Qinghua University. Quite possibly, he was emulating his teacher Wu Wenzao there, who also merged anthropological and sociological methods. See Pasternak (1988: 639) and Wang (1997: 238).

8 I will not discuss possible anthropologies in other areas since I have no knowledge of them. Here I would just like to note that Shanghais Fudan University does have some biological anthropology (Guldin 1994: 100), while the influence of British-trained Tian Rukang [Tian Ju-kang] may have lead to a continued interest in social and cultural anthropology.

9 The Institute of Sociology at Beijing University changed its name to the Institute of Sociology and Anthropology in 1992. The common parentage of the two institutes at Beijing University and at CASS does emphatically not mean that the two institutes, or at least their heads, are on good terms with each other. The capital's sociology is dominated by the alliances and animosities between its three main institutional bases (the Department of Sociology at Beijing University, the Institute of Sociology and Anthropology at Beijing University, and the Institute of Sociology at CASS); a detailed study of the nebulous politics that this involves would easily be enough for a full-length paper in itself.

10 National professional organizations are the Chinese Anthropological Association (Zhongguo Renleixue Xuehui), the Chinese Association of Urban Anthropology (Zhongguo Dushi Renleixue Hui) and the Chinese Association of Visual Anthropology (Yingshi Renleixue Hui). Two of these associations publish their own newsletter: the *Newsletter of the Chinese Anthropological Association* (Zhongguo Renleixue Xuehui Tongxun) and the *Newsletter of the Chinese Association of Urban Anthropology* (Zhongguo Dushi Renleixue Hui Tongxun). In addition, several conference volumes and books have been published under the aegis of these organizations. For details see Chen (1996: 1–3).

11 It is quite likely that many of these researchers were also active in the 1960s and the 1970s, when folklore and ethnology carried out field work despite the hostile political climate of these days. This work remains largely unpublished until this day, but should be very interesting if it were ever be made publicly available. I would like to thank Dr Kuah Khun Eng, Kuala of Hong Kong University for bringing this to my attention.

12 The most telling illustration is that fact that the 1987 and 1992 meetings of the Chinese Anthropological Association could not be convened, but were held as 'written meetings' (*bah*), that is, through the submission of written papers only.

13 Since this chapter was written, the situation seems to have become even more complicated with the reestablishment of the Department of Sociology at Qinghua University in May 2000. Several prominent sociologists and anthropologists from the United States, CASS, Peking University and People's University were attracted by the opportunities and salaries that a new, well-funded department offered them. Simultaneously, Peking University's ambitions to merge its Institute and Department of Sociology and start a full Department of Anthropology have become mired in personal issues, only one of which was the unfortunate dismissal of rising star Wang Mingming after a very unfortunate case of plagiarism (see *People's Daily* English edition 16 January 2002 http://fpeng.peopledaily.com.cn/200201/16/eng20020116_88767.shtml; *Christian Science Monitor* 22 January 2002 http://www.csmonitor.com/2002/0122/p16s02-legn.htm; both were last accessed on 11 May 2004). Finally, even more recently the CASS Institute of Sociology at last established a centre of anthropology, but again its fate seems to have been hamstrung by personal rivalries from the start.

14 Personal rivalries no doubt played a role as well in this split, but the organizers of both seminars were reluctant to discuss these. One indication though is that he attended the Kunming seminar, thus cold-shouldering the seminar organized by Peking University's Institute of Sociology and Anthropology which is still very much dominated by his rival Fei Xiaotong.

15 Somewhat facetiously, we could conclude that Fei Xiaotong's distinction between the organizational mode of association (*tuanti geju*) of Western society and the differential mode of association (*chaxu geju*) of Chinese society applies equally well to the differences between the anthropologies of China and the West (Fei 1992, chapter 4).

16 I am acutely aware of the many pitfalls of translating both *minzu* (people, nationality) and *guojia* (nation, state, country), but believe that my translation is an adequate rendition of what Chinese mean with *duominzude guojia* or phrases similar to that. I have chosen to translate *guojia* as nation-state rather than nation, because this is exactly the ambiguity that the term is meant to express. China is not a federation, but a unified state. Minorities are nationalities in name only: they are no nations with the right of secession. These individual nationalities therefore are incorporated into one nation dominated by the most advanced nationality, the Han. Ultimately, all nationalities will evolve and thus assimilate into the Han: the objective laws of social evolution will solve the contradictions of the multi-national nation-state.

17 Minorities are not always the gullible informants or passive victims they may seem to be. As Cai Hua points out in his study of the Na in Yunnan province, the Na strongly resist the work of Chinese ethnologists that reinforce Chinese Orientalist stereotypes regarding the promiscuity and primitivism of the Mosuo (the minority to which the Na have been assigned). On the other hand, the local Na cadres actively lobby for recognition as a separate minority that will bring special bureaucratic privileges for the Na population and prized sinecures for the cadres (Cai 1997).

18 One example of this is the study of the Hakkas, who are officially Han, and their relationship to the She, who are an official minority but culturally and linguistically very similar to the Hakkas. It is all the more intriguing that this is a field of study which is currently being developed by anthropologists at Xiamen University (Jiang 1995; Chen 1996: 10).

19 One example is a group of scholars in Xinjiang Normal University who recently set up an Institute of Cultural Anthropology (Wenhua Renleixue Yanjiusuo) to give themselves more room to tap into Western anthropology and study the relations between minority groups in Xinjiang (Dilmurat Omar, personal communication 1998).

20 I am aware that the concept of ethnos is no longer universally accepted among Russian ethnographers since the breakup of the Soviet Union, because it does reify the cultural distinctiveness of social groups in a way not dissimilar to the concepts of 'culture' or '(unrepresented) nation' in the currently politically correct climate in the West and particularly the United States. Ethnos is now a concept espoused by more conservative ethnographers, while others argue for the use of the Western term ethnic group (Tishkov 1998 and commentaries). I would argue, however, that Russian ethnologists can meaningfully debate these issues, because the concept of 'ethnos' does have a circumstantionalist side to it that prepared the way for an appreciation of the specific analytical value of the concept of 'ethnic group'. The Chinese concept of *minzu* (nationality) lacks this dimension. In the present political and intellectual climate in China, it is perhaps better to remould this concept by adding a circumstantionalist dimension to it, instead of discarding it altogether in favour of a transplanted Western concept.

References

Arkush, R. David (1981) *Fei Xiaotong and Sociology in Revolutionary China*, Cambridge, MA: Harvard University Press.

Bromley, Julian and Viktor Kozlov (1989) 'The theory of ethnos and ethnic processes in Soviet social sciences', *Comparative Studies in Society and History*, 31(3): 425–38.

Bromley, Yu (1980) 'The object and subject matter of ethnography', in Ernest Gellner (ed.), *Soviet and Western Anthropology*, London: Gerald Duckworth & Co., pp. 151–60.

Cai Hua (1997) *Les Na, une Société sans Père ni Mari* [The Na, a society without father or husband], Paris: Presses Universitaires de France.

Chang, Maukuei (2004) 'The movement to indigenize the social sciences in Taiwan: origin and predicaments', Unpublished paper.

Chen Guoqiang (1996) 'Zhonghua Renmin Gongheguo Shi'er Nian (1981.5–1993.4) Lai de Renleixue ji Fazhan (1981.5–1993.4)' [Anthropology and development in the People's Republic of China in the past twelve years (May 1981–April 1993)], in Chen Guoqiang and Lin Jiahuang (eds), *Zhongguo Renleixue de Fazhan* [The development of Chinese anthropology], Shanghai: Shanghai Sanlian Shudian, pp. 1–11.

Dikötter, Frank (1992) *The Discourse of Race in Modern China*, London: Hurst & Company.

Dragadze, Tamara (1980) 'The place of "ethnos" theory in soviet anthropology', in Ernest Gellner (ed.), *Soviet and Western Anthropology*, London: Gerald Duckworth & Co., pp. 161–70.

Eminov, Sandra (1978) 'Folklore and nationalism in modern China', in Felix J. Oinas (ed.), *Folklore, Nationalism, and Politics*, Columbus, OH: Slavica Publishers, pp. 163–83.

Engels, Friedrich (1940) *The Origin of the Family, Private Property and the State*, London: Lawrence and Wishart.

Fei, Hsiao-tung [Fei Xiaotong] (1939) *Peasant Life in China*, London: Routledge & Kegan Paul.

—— [Fei Xiaotong] (1945) *Earthbound China*, Chicago, IL: University of Chicago Press.

—— [Fei Xiaotong] (1953) *China's Gentry: Essays on Rural–Urban Relations*, Chicago, IL: University of Chicago Press.

—— [Fei Xiaotong] (1981) *Toward a People's Anthropology*, Beijing: New World Press.

Fei Xiaotong (1992) *From the Soil: The Foundations of Chinese Society*, A Translation of Fei Xiaotong's Xiangtu Zhongguo with an introduction and epilogue by Gary G. Hamilton and Wang Zheng, Berkeley, CA: University of California Press, Chinese original first published in 1948.

—— (1994) 'Guanyu Renleixue zai Zhongguo' [About anthropology in China], *Shehuixue Yanjiu*, 50(2): 1–4.

Feng Xiaoshuang and Li Haifu (1997) 'Jiaqiang Xueke Jianshe Huiying Weida Shidai: "Zhongguo Shehuixue de Xueke Jianshe" Xueshu Taolunhui Zongshu' [Strengthen disciplinary construction – meet the requirements of a great era: A summary of the scholarly discussion meeting on 'Disciplinary Construction of Chinese Sociology'], *Zhongguo Shehuikexue*, 5: 96–105.

Gladney, Dru C. (1991) *Muslim Chinese: Ethnic Nationalism in the People's Republic*, Cambridge, MA: Council on East Asian Studies, Harvard University.

Guldin, Gregory Eliyu (ed.) (1990) *Anthropology in China: Defining the Discipline*, Armonk, NY: M.E. Sharpe.

—— (1991) 'The organization of minority studies in China', *China Exchange News*, 19(2): 7–12.

—— (1994) *The Saga of Anthropology in China: From Malinowski to Moscow to Mao*, Armonk, NY: M.E. Sharpe.

Guldin, Gregory and Southall, Aidan (eds) (1993) *Urban Anthropology in China*, Leiden: E.J. Brill.

Jia Zhi (1981) 'Guanyu Shehuizhuyi Shiqi Minjian Wenxue Gongzuo de Fangzhen Wenti' [Concerning the problems of guiding principles in folk literature work in the socialist period], *Minjian wenxue* [Folk Literature], 7: 116–28.

Jiang Binzhao (1995) 'Shilun Kejiade Xingcheng ji Qi yu Shezu de Guanxi' [An exploration of the emergence of the Hakkas and their relationship with the She nationality], in

Ma Qicheng and Bai Zhensheng (eds), *Minzuxue yu Minzu Wenhua Fazhan Yanjiu: Qingzhu Lin Yaohua Jiaoshou Congjiao Liushi'er Zhounian Jinian Wenji* [Research on ethnology and the development of nationalities' cultures: Festschrift on the occasion of Professor Lin Yaohua's sixty-two years of teaching], Beijing: Zhongguo Shehui Kexue Chubanshe, pp. 183–99.

Leach, Edmund (1964) 'Anthropological aspects of language: animal categories and verbal abuse', in E.H. Lenneberg (ed.), *New Directions in the Study of Language*, Cambridge, MA: The MIT Press, pp. 23–63.

Lin Yü-Sheng (1979) *The Crisis of Chinese Consciousness: Radical Anti-Traditionalism in the May Fourth Era*, Madison, WI: University of Wisconsin Press.

McGough, J.P. (ed.) (1979) *Fei Hsiao-tung: The Dilemma of a Chinese Intellectual*, Armonk, NY: M.E. Sharpe.

Metzger, Thomas A. (1993) 'The sociological imagination in China: comments on the thought of Chin Yao-chi (Ambrose Y.C. King)', *Journal of Asian Studies*, 52(4): 937–48.

Morgan, Lewis H. (1877) *Ancient Society, or Researches in the Lines of Human Progress from Savagery through Barbarism to Civilization*, Chicago, IL: Charles H. Kerr & Company.

Parkin, David (1995) 'Latticed knowledge: eradication and dispersal of the unpalatable in Islam, medicine and anthropological theory', in Richard Fardon (ed.), *Counterworks: Managing the Diversity of Knowledge*, London: Routledge, pp. 143–63.

Pasternak, Burton (1988) 'A conversation with Fei Xiaotong', *Current Anthropology*, 29(4): 637–62.

Pieke, Frank N. (1996) 'Review of Gregory Eliyu Guldin, the saga of anthropology in China: from Malinowski to Moscow to Mao', Armonk, NY: M.E. Sharpe, 1994, *The China Quarterly*, 148: 1388–9.

——(2004) 'China and anthropology', in Xin Liu (ed.), *New Reflections on the Anthropological Studies of (greater) China*, Berkeley, CA: Institute of East Asian Studies, University of California, pp. 153–77.

Rong Guanqiong (1996) 'Tantan Fazhanzhong de Woguo Wenhua Renleixue' [A discussion of our country's developing cultural anthropology], in Chen Guoqiang and Lin Jiahuang (eds), *Zhongguo Renleixue de Fazhan* [The development of Chinese anthropology], Shanghai: Shanghai Sanlian Shudian, pp. 21–42.

Ruan Xihu (1993) 'Present tasks of urban anthropology in China', in Greg Guldin and Aidan Southall (eds), *Urban Anthropology in China*, Leiden: Brill, pp. 8–13. Originally published as 'Dangdai Zhongguo Dushi Renleixue de Ji Xiang Renwu', pp. 3–10 of the Chinese edition of the same volume, Ruan Xihu (ed.) *Dushi renleixue*, Beijing: Huaxia Chubanshe, 1990, pp. 3–10.

Schneider, Laurence A. (1971) *Ku Chieh-kang and China's New History: Nationalism and the Quest for Alternative Traditions*, Berkeley, CA: University of California Press.

Shanin, Teodor (1989) 'Ethnicity in the Soviet Union: analytical perceptions and political strategies', *Comparative Studies in Society and History*, 31(3): 409–24.

Ting, Nai-tung (1987) ' "Folk literature run by the folk": a new development in the People's Republic of China', *Asian Folklore Studies*, 46: 257–71.

Tishkov, Valery A. (1998) 'US and Russian anthropology: unequal dialogue in a time of transition', *Current Anthropology*, 39(1): 1–17.

Tu Wei-ming (1991) 'The enlightenment mentality and the Chinese intellectual dilemma', in Kenneth Lieberthal, Joyce Kallgren, Roderick MacFarquhar and Frederic Wakeman, Jr (eds), *Perspectives on Modern China: Four Anniversaries*, Armonk, NY: M.E. Sharpe, pp. 103–18.

Wang Mingming (1997) *Shehuixue Renleixue yu Zhongguo Yanjiu* [Social anthropology and China research], Beijing: Sanlian Shudian.

Weng Naiqun (1998) 'Shijie zhi Jiao Fansi Zhongguo Minzuxue' [Reflections of Chinese ethnology at the turn of the century], Unpublished paper.

Wong Siu-lun (1979) *Sociology and Socialism in Contemporary China*, London: Routledge & Kegan Paul.

Yang Kun (1996) 'Tan Renleixue yu Minzuxue de Guanxi' [On the relationship between anthropology and ethnology], in Chen Guoqiang and Lin Jiahuang (eds), *Zhongguo Renleixue de Fazhan* [The development of Chinese anthropology], Shanghai: Shanghai Sanlian Shudian, pp. 17–20.

4 Anthropologists of Asia, anthropologists in Asia

The academic mode of production in the semi-periphery

Jerry S. Eades

As the introduction to this volume stresses, ethnography does not arise spontaneously in a vacuum: the conditions of production and the careers and affiliations of the producers are of the greatest importance, not only in understanding individual ethnographies, but also in locating them and the national traditions to which they belong within the "world system" of anthropology, as described by Kuwayama (2004). In this chapter, I examine the conditions of production of anthropology in Asia, concentrating mainly on Japan and China, and compare them with developments in other parts of the world. This may sound an overly broad enterprise, but it also reflects the course which my own academic career has taken over the years, starting in West Africa, then gravitating to the United Kingdom, and finally ending up for more than a decade in Japan, where I have become increasingly concerned with the Asia Pacific. I have also found myself increasingly involved in making anthropology by Asian scholars available to "the discipline," that is, international dissemination through editing and translation.

In this chapter, therefore, I discuss first the dynamics of the development of anthropology at the center as an ideal type. Second, I discuss the development of anthropology in Asia, concentrating on China and Japan, to see how and why it differs from the central ideal type. Third, I look at the differences between the research traditions in the West and Japan in relation to China. Finally, I consider how likely it is that these various traditions will coalesce into a global anthropology during the twenty-first century, and the forces which might shape this development.

Anthropology as ideal type: the development of a discipline

A decade ago, I attempted a systematic comparison of the development of anthropology in West Africa – one of the main stamping grounds of British anthropology until the 1960s – and China (Eades 1995). I argued that the development of the discipline in "normal" circumstances during the postwar period took place through three main phases. The first phase, building on prewar work, was one in which the main task was to map and classify the main cultural areas (as in the International African Institute's massive Ethnographic Survey of Africa), and to carry out sampling in the form of detailed research on individual villages within these major cultural areas. This was followed by a second phase in which the political economy and historical processes became the main focus of attention, partly because of the greater availability of historical data, and partly because the region itself was changing rapidly under the impact of decolonization, economic change and political instability. Much of this work was influenced by neo-Marxist concepts such as dependency, underdevelopment and the world-system, and the data and methods used increasingly overlapped with those of history and the other social sciences. Finally, a third phase ensued in which the study of cultural forms came to the fore, though still grounded in an understanding of the political economy and the development of social and gender relations within it.

I argued that similar phases could also be seen in the development of the discipline in China, despite the discontinuities which followed the 1949 revolution. Research on "China" of course continued, either indirectly, through interviews with informants who had been in China, or by using Hong Kong and Taiwan as surrogate fields for investigating the dynamics of Chinese society. In China itself, of course, there was the huge volume of work carried out in connection with the development of minorities policies before and after the Cultural Revolution (Wong 1979: 78–92; Guldin 1994: 105–8), an enterprise similar to the kinds of regional classification exercises taking place elsewhere, despite the obvious idiosyncrasies of Marxist–Leninist–Mao Zedong theory. The work in Hong Kong and Taiwan in the late 1960s and early 1970s also reflected the kinds of changes taking place worldwide: an increased interest in history, an increased awareness of the importance of the global political economy, and the integration of micro-level fieldwork with more extensive quantitative techniques. The developmental sequence is most clearly seen in the fine series of monographs on the New Territories of Hong Kong, inspired originally by Freedman, but actually written by Baker (1968), Potter (1968), James Watson (1975), and Rubie Watson (1985). Baker was a student of Freedman's and worked in a village where Freedman himself had intended to work, concentrating on the classic themes of kinship and ritual. James Watson helped Potter with his work on the Hong Kong economy, before writing his own study of a village that had gone global through the establishment of the Chinese catering trade in the United Kingdom. Rubie Watson's study is of economic differentiation within the village, showing how and why access to wealth and power can vary between individuals, even within the same village and the same lineage, the key variable being access to land. The cumulative body of work on the New Territories was also important as showing how quite small differences in ecology and economy within a surprisingly small area can produce large variations in patterns of development. The sequence of books represented a gradual shift away from classic themes of the lineage and ritual toward studies of social and economic change, culminating in James Watson's work in global migration. A similar trend is visible in the work on Taiwan. One feature of this and other Taiwanese work was that the researchers were able to draw on Japanese records and census data which were of a higher quality than anything available on the Mainland.

By this time, Mainland China itself had started to open up for research, and some of the old Hong Kong and Taiwan hands began to move there as well, as did their students. During the early years of the Chinese revolution, the only detailed accounts came from radicals such as William Hinton (1966, 1983) and David and Isabel Crook (1959, 1966) who managed to stay on in China while most other foreigners left. But during the late 1970s and early 1980s, their work was complemented both by work based on interviews of mainlanders in exile in Hong Kong, and, later, by a new generation of accounts based on fieldwork. Initially, these generally focused on individual villages (e.g. Endicott 1988; Siu 1989; Potter and Potter 1990), but they gradually came to encompass the cities (e.g. Jankoviak 1993; Davis 2000) and ethnic minorities (e.g. Gladney 1991; Harrell 2000; Schein 2000). Even though some kinds of research became more difficult in the wake of the Tiananmen Square upheavals in 1989 (see e.g. Rudelson 1997), the work in China by the mid-1990s was starting to catch up with themes which had been important in other parts of the world since the late 1980s: urban life, consumption, the media, cultural production, and the social construction of ethnicity. Interestingly, an increasing number of the studies were by Chinese scholars who had been trained in the West and in Japan. These scholars provided some interesting insights into the differences between Japanese and Western research and writing. But before comparing these bodies of work, I will first trace the development of anthropology since the early twentieth century in Japan.

Japanese anthropology: nationalism, colonialism, and centrifugal researchers

The rapid speed of development of the Japanese economy and polity in the wake of the Meiji "restoration" of 1868 has often been commented on. What is not often realized by Western scholars is just how rapidly academic disciplines from the West were transplanted and institutionalized in Japan. In the case of anthropology, many of these developments predated those in the West. In the case of the establishment of academic associations, the publication of learned journals, and the employment of anthropologists by the government to help gather information on the nascent colonial empire, Japan was sometimes ahead of both Europe and America (for detailed accounts, see Askew 2004; Yamashita 2004).

In the late nineteenth century, the anthropology that developed was of course evolutionary, and was preoccupied with questions similar to those being asked in the West, such as the origins of the Japanese race, their relationship with regional minorities such as the Ainu in Hokkaido and the peoples of Okinawa, the origins of the Imperial Family, and the development of (a distinctive) Japanese culture. As Askew notes (2004), early answers to these questions in the case of Japan tended to be rather eclectic and often fanciful, but no more so than the answers to similar questions being proposed in Europe and America. In Japan, the work of early European observers and Japanese scholars tended to influence each other. Indeed, the founding myth of Japanese anthropology relates it to the discovery and excavation of a shell-mound near Tokyo by the American biologist, E.S. Morse, and the reactions of Japanese scholars to it. Morse claimed to have found evidence of cannibalism, and the debate over this and related issues provided a rallying point for Meiji intellectuals, as well as suggestions that the best people to interpret the past of Japan were the Japanese themselves.

They key figure in all this was Tsuboi Shôgorô, who established the first anthropological association, *Jinruigaku no Tomodachi* (Friends of Anthropology), together with the first journal. As Askew notes (ibid.), there is a direct line of descent between these and the present-day Japanese physical anthropologists, and their association and journal. However, Tsuboi was also indirectly responsible for many of the developments in Japanese cultural anthropology as well, as he befriended and taught Torii Ryûzô, a most influential figure and leading field-worker in Japanese anthropology during the colonial period (Askew 2003). In an astonishingly full career, Torii traveled extensively through Northeast and Southeast Asia, recording the societies he observed, both in his published written accounts and in the hundreds of photographs which he took all over the region. As more and more territories came under Japanese control, Taiwan in 1895, Korea in 1910, Melanesia in 1918, and parts of China during the 1920s and 1930s, Torii quickly included them in his travels (Askew 2004: 60; Yamashita 2004: 91–2).

As in the cases of Britain, France, and the United States, anthropology became part of the colonial effort, even though it is not clear what impact, if any, it had on colonial policy. The Japanese colonial governments carried out large-scale ethnographic surveys of the colonies, gathering a mass of information which is still basic to the study of Taiwan, Korea, and parts of China. In Taiwan, much of the effort went into documenting the aboriginal areas of the island, in which the government had invested huge resources to bring them under administrative control. Japanese became not only the language of education, but also a *lingua franca* in these areas which is still spoken by some of the older people (Eades 2003). In Korea, there was also considerable ethnographic research. After the departure of the Japanese in 1945, this was dismissed by many Korean scholars as a "distortion" of Korean society, though more recently this position has been re-evaluated (Kim 2004: 262–3). The Japanese colonial government set up imperial universities in Seoul and Taipei, in addition to those in Japan, and much of the research was based there. Toward the end of the colonial period, they also set up a number of research institutes around their empire and sphere of influence: an Institute of Oriental Culture in Tokyo (which still survives as part of the University of Tokyo), an ethnic relations institute, and a northwestern research institute in Mongolia. Apart from the Institute of Oriental Culture, these were closed at the end of the War, but the researchers who began their careers there went on to become the leaders of the revival of anthropological research in the postwar period. The academic anthropologists were not the only ones working within the Japanese empire during this period: as Yamashita has shown, there were also amateurs whose work is nevertheless still of interest to Micronesian specialists (Yamashita 2004: 99–102).

In the pre-war period, therefore, Japanese anthropological research was concentrated in six main areas: the main islands of Japan itself, along with Northern

China, Taiwan, Korea, the Ainu in Hokkaido, and Okinawa. Since then, the regions of interest to Japanese researchers have changed considerably, as shown by Sekimoto's analysis (2003) of the subject matter of articles in the *Japanese Journal of Ethnology* over the years. Generally, he argues, there has been a centrifugal tendency in Japanese anthropology, and during each period researchers have tended to move as far away from Japan for their field material as they can. After 1945, research of any kind was considerably curtailed as the Japanese economy recovered, but as soon as the funds became available once more, Japanese researchers began to move rapidly across the globe. Rather like the British and Americans, but unlike anthropologists in other Asian countries, Japanese anthropologists have tended to value overseas over domestic research. The recent series of survey articles in the English-language *Japanese Review of Cultural Anthropology* shows just how widely they now range. In addition to a considerable volume of research being carried out in Southeast Asia, which is perhaps the most popular region at the moment, there are also significant numbers of researchers in Latin America and Africa. In contrast, there are surprisingly few working in North America or Europe, and even there the main object of study is often Japanese migrants. As a percentage of the total research, the work being carried out in the six areas which predominated before 1945 is now comparatively small. In the case of China, this work is being carried out not only by Japanese scholars, but also by Chinese scholars living and working in Japan. The total volume of anthropological research being carried out by scholars based in Japan is immense: the Japanese Society of Cultural Anthropology currently has around 2,000 members, and its annual meetings draw together several hundred participants, with several panels running concurrently. It is probably the largest anthropological society in the world, with the exception of the American Anthropological Association (AAA) itself. And yet this work is surprisingly little known in the outside world, for reasons that are worth considering in more detail.

The academic mode of production in Japan

Elsewhere, I have argued that both the differences and lack of communication between Japanese anthropology and anthropology in other places in the world can be explained not so much in terms of theoretical differences as more mundane considerations, such as conditions of employment and the structure of the publishing industry (Eades 2000). Even though a handful of Japanese scholars over the years have enjoyed reputations outside Japan (the obvious examples are Mabuchi Tôichi before the Second World War and Nakane Chie in the postwar period), the number of anthropologists based in Japan and writing in Japanese who contribute to mainstream Western journals and monographs series is very small indeed. Very few books written in Japanese are translated, and the result is that these scholars are seldom mentioned in the standard citation indices.

Outside scholars seldom quote their work, unless they have sufficient interest in Japan and the neighboring countries to want to refer to the Japanese-language literature. This has clearly nothing to do with the quality of the research and data, as we will see in the case of the work on China. The Japanese research tradition in anthropology is well known for its meticulous accumulation of data over the course of repeated field-trips in areas such as the cataloging of plant or animal species and their diffusion, and the micro-level observation of interaction, gesture, and conversation. Japanese scholars are also well informed about the latest theoretical ideas emanating from the West, as the work of leading theoretical gurus is regularly translated into Japanese. In my earlier paper (ibid.), I have argued that the reasons for this "intellectual balance of payments" problem are rather as follows: first Japanese academic traditions are different not so much because they have developed separately, but because things have changed so rapidly in the West in the postwar period. In the early postwar period the academic mode of production in Japan was very similar to that in other countries, and it remains so. If anything, it is the United States and, to a lesser extent, the United Kingdom that are out of line with the rest of the world, even if the hegemony of English means that they are seen by many scholars as role models to which the rest of the world should aspire. Second, the changes which have taken place in the United States and United Kingdom have led to drastic changes in publishing patterns over the years, with increasing emphasis on a small number of prestigious peer-reviewed journals and academic presses as the outlets most highly rated in the Anglo-American academic labor market. Third, the competition to publish through these prestigious outlets has meant increasing delays in the time it takes to publish in the West, which in the case of some journals and presses can be measured in years rather than months. The review process can take months, as can the process of copy-editing, much of which is concerned solely with the elimination of repetition or the imposition of uniformity in house style, making very little difference to the actual quality of the work. Fourth, many academic publishers publish small print runs of books in hardback only, making their profits through high prices rather than volume of sales. The end result is that many distinguished monographs end up selling a few hundred copies worldwide: by the time they are reviewed (which can also take several years), most of the copies have already been sold, so that positive reviews, in effect, have very little effect on sales. A final point is that the competitive environment has led to an emphasis on theory and writing style as hallmarks of excellence rather than richness of data. Graduate students at the leading American universities learn to write in what might be described as "house discourse" early on in their postgraduate training, as can be seen from their fluent presentations at AAA conferences, replete with the latest jargon and buzzwords. This provides yet another barrier for the non-native English speaker in competing for space in the recognized outlets.

The Japanese publishing industry, by contrast, is incredibly efficient by Western standards. Most Japanese universities have in-house journals, in which a large percentage of academics publish most of their work. These can be produced in a matter of weeks rather than years. Having got their research findings out of the way, the authors then move on rapidly to the next research project.

Publishers are also much more efficient than in the West, most books taking a maximum of six months in press, including editing, proofreading, and (in some cases) even translation. Print runs tend to be longer than in the West, the books are cheaper, salaries are higher, and Japanese academics are avid readers. So work published in Japanese tends to reach a larger audience than work published in English, especially in Japan.

It might be added that there is considerable variation between disciplines in the extent to which Japanese authors make the effort to publish in English. In science, technology, and engineering, there is a much longer tradition of publishing in English, perhaps because much of this research is carried out in collaboration with foreign scholars. Even within anthropology, Japanese physical anthropologists have had an English-language journal rather longer than the socio-cultural anthropologists. Socio-cultural anthropology follows a pattern more typical of the humanities in Japan, where the bulk of publishing is in in-house journals, and where the emphasis is on the local rather than the international audience. Even though the Japanese higher education system and labor market is becoming more competitive as will be discussed later, jobs are still based largely on personal networks, a situation which can be likened to the United Kingdom before 1970, when the number of anthropology departments was very small, and where much of the recruitment was handled informally by a small network of powerful professors with close personal relationships. In Japanese anthropology, patron–client links with senior professors is still the best way to get a permanent job, as well as research funding and part-time jobs until a permanent job materializes. I have no hard data, but my impression is that Japanese scholars tend to be older than their Western counterparts when they complete their PhDs (an optional extra for many Japanese university teachers until the 1990s), and when they get their first permanent jobs. As with the United Kingdom in the early postwar period, recruitment based on old-boy networks also means that the profession has been dominated by graduates from a few small prestigious universities, notably Tokyo, Kyoto, and Tokyo Metropolitan. But once a permanent job has been obtained, there is no further need to compete for tenure, and university teachers are relatively free to pursue their own teaching and research pursuits, with less pressure to continue publishing and obtaining research funding that scholars typically experience in the West. Salaries are still based on age rather than performance, and by international standards they are generous, especially as they often include substantial research, transport, and housing allowances. Promotion to full professorships between the ages of 45 and 50 is generally assured, and the Japanese employment system differs from the Euro-American system in that it is an *inverted* pyramid. Most of the incumbents are full professors, with a smaller number of associate professors, and an even smaller number of lecturers (tenured assistant professors). Even though the Japanese economy has experienced a long recession since 1991, it has been nothing like as traumatic as the collapse of the British economy in the late 1970s and early 1980s, and the demographics of the Japanese profession mean that there is a steady stream of retirements and reappointments.

Japanese anthropology and theory

The Japanese attitude to theory is well reflected in the survey articles in the first four editions of the *Japanese Review of Cultural Anthropology*. In volume 2, for instance, Itô Abito, a senior professor at Tokyo University, discussed Japanese anthropological research on Korea, though much of what he says also applies to China. (Perhaps significantly, he was also the supervisor of Nie Lili whose work is discussed later.) Itô observes that even though anthropology was imported from the West, and continues to be influenced by it, it also has to be appreciated within its own intellectual context (Itô 2001: 39). "The Japanese mode of adaptation to the world system of anthropology" he argues, "is complex because of the wide variety of commitment among scholars to different social settings or audiences" (ibid.: 40). "However," he continues, "most Japanese anthropologists specializing in Korea have been more attracted by the descriptive style of folklore studies, in response to a particular audience in Japan which is more interested in the substantive reality and less interested in the scientific theories and analytical categories used elsewhere in the world" (ibid.). Later on he adds, "The Japanese style of research is often characterized as narrowly focused ethnography with an emphasis on description. It is also regarded as being weak in terms of its theoretical framework by western or Korean social scientists trained in the West" (Itô 2001: 45). However, from the Japanese perspective, "This [i.e. the Western] approach which puts the emphasis on the logical system, may appear to be more 'scientific' than the Japanese approach, but may also be seen as being less satisfactory in terms of the observation and description of concrete examples than the more substantive Japanese approach" (ibid.).

Itô therefore argues that the Japanese way of anthropology really is different: the emphasis is on imparting the facts gathered together with the personal experiences of gathering them directly, rather then analyzing them according to the current theoretical fashions and preoccupations of the international scholarly community. This clearly fits well with Japanese publication practices that make the results of research available to other scholars quickly and efficiently, through publication in in-house journals or in the form of short research notes and communications. It also goes along with the pattern of research funding in Japan through the Japanese Ministry of Education, in which funds are made available for a specific academic year, and cannot be transferred to other years. These grants often require a research report to be completed and printed by the end of the year as well, which reinforces the need to publish quickly. Given the current differences in the Japanese and Western academic modes of production, it is not, therefore, surprising that the product is different as well, as will be seen from a comparison of the work of Chinese scholars of similar age and background working in Japan and the United States, respectively.

Expatriate Chinese anthropologists in America and Japan

Some of the most interesting work on China since the early 1990s has been carried out by a new generation of Chinese scholars, born in the People's

Republic of China (PRC) but educated in the West and now based in the United States, such as Yan Yunxiang, Jing Jun, and Liu Xin. What is often not realized, however, is that a group of scholars of very similar backgrounds ended up in Japan rather than in China during the 1980s, and now work and publish there, mainly in Japanese. The best known of them are probably Nie Lili, Han Min, and Qin Zhaoxiong. All three are bilingual in Japanese and Chinese, and all three have also written in English from time to time (including Han's PhD thesis, later revised as Han 2001). All three have full-time teaching or research positions at major institutions in Japan. As such, they tend to follow the Japanese literature as a guide to issues and styles of writing, and their work therefore makes a very interesting comparison with that of the scholars based in the United States.

There are, of course, many Japanese anthropologists in Japan carrying out work on China. In the late 1980s and early 1990s, initial reports of much of this research was presented at the regular meetings of a research group called *Sen'innokai*, and a list of their activities gives a good idea of the major themes with which these scholars were engaged (Suenari *et al.* 1995: 327–32). The same volume brought together some of the work of the members of the group with other papers which had been presented at a panel at the AAA Annual Meeting in San Francisco in November 1992, with papers on classic themes such as affinal relations, ancestor worship, *feng shui* geomancy, and ethnicity. Three of the papers dealt with Taiwan, two of them concerning the Sinicization of aboriginal groups. Segawa later contributed a review article of recent research on China to the *Japanese Review of Cultural Anthropology* (Segawa 1998), and a recent bilingual publication edited by Yokoyama (2004) provides a survey of work carried out on Chinese minorities by scholars from both Japan and the West from the same period. Little, if any, work was carried out in Mainland China for twenty years after the Second World War, though some Japanese-based scholars, like the Americans, used Hong Kong and Taiwan as surrogates for Mainland China.

But it is perhaps the major monographs by the Chinese scholars which are of main interest here, and here I examine three of them dating from the early 1990s. Coincidentally, all three of them dealt with areas of China little explored by Western scholars, namely Liaoning, Anhui, and Hubei provinces. Thus, the work is not only interesting in its own right, but also from the comparative perspective of China as a whole. First, it helps fill in some of the major gaps in the ethnographic map of China and its rural sociology in the aftermath of the post-economic reforms. Second, it is possible to compare it directly with the work of the members of the same generation of Chinese scholars based in the United States during the same period, as I describe later.

Given that Nie Lili's two main teachers, Fei Xiaotong in China and Itô Abito in Japan, were both village specialists themselves, it is not surprising that she chose a village in her father's area of origin as her field site. (She herself had been brought up in the city, where she worked in an electronics factory when the rest of the family was sent to the countryside during the Cultural Revolution.) However, the starting point for her analysis is similar to that of Freedman and the earlier Hong Kong school, that is, the structure of the lineage (Nie 1992, chapter 2).

Here, Nie faced considerable difficulties because the genealogy of her village had been almost entirely destroyed during the Cultural Revolution.

The bulk of the book provides a political history of the village, from the republican period and the Manchukuo period under Japanese control through Liberation and the subsequent upheavals to the post-Mao period of economic reform. During the post-Liberation land reform, the richer members of the village were stripped of their assets and allocated poor quality land. They remained stigmatized by their "bad class background" for a generation, until the economic reforms of the late 1970s (Nie 1992, chapters 6–7). The character who emerged as de facto village boss during this period was one Wang Longchen, thanks to his ability to build and maintain a powerful social network. Wang's colleagues managed to gain access to all kinds of resources, from food coupons at the time of the Great Leap Forward, to control of jobs and the registration system, which made it possible for the children of some villagers to look for better jobs in the towns.

By the end of the Cultural Revolution, most households in the village were nuclear households, and parents and children generally lived apart, even when the parents were elderly and widowed. Many of the villagers were abandoning agriculture, handing over their fields to others (often their children) and concentrating on the production of poultry and clothing (Nie 1992, chapter 8). Most households now had some form of income outside agriculture. Some men became building laborers in the towns and cities of the region, while others established small enterprises in the village. The most successful entrants to the poultry industry were the younger more literate villagers, able to read about scientific farming and to muster the energy to market their product. In the building trade, it was the bosses of the gangs who made the money: for the laborers themselves earnings were much more limited, not least because of the seasonality of the work in the harsh Manchurian climate. The roles of the village head and party secretary were also changing: they now needed to be economic managers rather than political wheelers and dealers, and some of them were not up to the job. Some of them were resented because of their behavior during the earlier political campaigns, and they lacked the trust and networks to cope with the changed conditions. Because they had better education, the members of the former landlord and rich peasant classes now began to prosper once more. All this had a dramatic impact on relations within the family. By the late 1980s, the divorce rate had increased as women with their new sources of income were no longer prepared to tolerate incompetent and lazy husbands. Children were no longer prepared to support their parents, and brothers found themselves in competition for their parents' favors towards themselves and their children – and for their assets when they died.

All in all, even though Nie's starting point was the structure of the lineage and the traditional Confucian morality underpinning it, by the end of her account not much of these were left. They have been undermined by the growth of the state in the twentieth century, the ideological shift from lineage to party brought about after the communist revolution, and the shift from the lineage to commune and then to the market as the basis of social organization in the post-Mao period.

Han Min's (2001) monograph on a village in Northern Anhui also focuses on the lineage, though in this case the genealogy survived the Cultural Revolution to provide the framework for the whole study (she presents much of it in pull-out form in Han 2001: 33). The structure of the book is broadly similar to that of Nie. Han's book also contains a historical account of the fortunes of the lineage members from the early twentieth century to the present day, via the republican period and the Sino-Japanese war (chapter 3), Liberation, the Great Leap Forward, and the Cultural Revolution (chapter 4), and the economic reforms of the Deng era (chapter 5). But there are also differences. The responsibility system in Anhui led to agricultural boom rather than decline, thanks to cotton production controlled by women. This gave them considerably greater power in marriage transactions, now that their labor and the social networks to which they give access had become more valuable (Han 2001, chapter 6). The waning power of the party, at the grass roots level, at the time of the research is also interesting. As in Nie's village, the economic reforms meant a substantial loss of influence for the village administration. Han reports one instance of a father refusing to allow his son to take over the position of local party secretary. His explanation: "the situation under the responsibility system has become more complicated. The work of a secretary involves displeasing people. I told my son, if you take the post, I will disown you" (Han 2001: 135).

The third major work from this period, that of Qin (1994), as yet remains unpublished in English, though it also covers similar ground. It is divided into three parts, dealing in turn with history and politics (part I), social structure and ritual (part II), and economics and politics (part III; for an English account see also Qin 2002). Individual chapters deal with themes similar to those discussed by Nie and Han: traditional religion, the structure of the household, marriage, life cycle rituals, and the various stages of economic revolution and reform after 1949. Nie's work was completed first, and all three scholars knew each other well, so it is perhaps not surprising their village studies also took on a similar form. However, because they all covered such similar ground in such detail, it makes it possible to see the similarities and differences between the studies, as for instance in the changing economic status of women, the reasons for boom or bust in local agriculture, and the revival or otherwise of traditional beliefs and rituals, depending on how much of their infrastructure survived the revolution. All three are fully rounded monographs in the tradition of both Fei's work from an earlier period (as mentioned earlier, Nie studied under Fei in Beijing before moving to Japan), and have much in common with north American accounts of villages during the same period, for example, those by Siu, Endicott or the Potters.

The American school

Compared with the Japanese studies, the monographs by the Chinese scholars based in the West are much more precisely focused theoretically and in terms of subject matter. The most overtly historical of them is Jun Jing's *The Temple of Memories* (1996), which deals with the revival of lineage ideology in a village in

Gansu from the period of economic reforms onwards. The two main themes of the book are suffering, and the attempts of the local community to recover from it (1996: 20). The villagers traced their descent back to Confucius, and migration from his home town of Qufu in Shandong. From the time of Liberation, the village and its temple suffered a series of disasters: attack by the People's Liberation Army (PLA) during the communist takeover, a flood and relocation in the face of hydraulic engineering in the 1960s, and disruption of ancestor worship during the Cultural Revolution. As in Han's village in Anhui (2001, chapter 8), the end of the Mao era allowed a revival of the ancestral cult and the genealogy, and the construction of new temples. Jing's conclusion is that "Broadly speaking, this religious domain of village life is becoming a strong, alternative base of power and authority precisely because it is tied to the increasingly noticeable assertion of local identity, voluntary associations, and community" in contemporary China (1996: 176).

The framework of Yan's *The Flow of Gifts* is provided by lists of wedding presents, which are recorded at the time of the wedding and later carefully reciprocated. His fieldwork was carried out in a village in Northern China, which he previously lived in after being "sent to the countryside" during the Cultural Revolution (1996: 2). Theoretically, the starting point for the study is classic exchange theory deriving from Marx and Mauss, via Annette Weiner and Marilyn Strathern (ibid.: 4–13). He examines the ways in which continuous exchanges among members of a close-knit community create and express networks of social relations. He distinguishes no less than twenty-one different types of gift exchange (ibid., chapter 3), and their role in network building within the village. He also looks at the ethics of gift exchange, and its role in power relations (chapter 4), before launching into the analysis of the marriage transactions themselves (chapter 5). His conclusions are that with the desocialization of Chinese society, establishing networks through gift exchange has become increasingly necessary for individual villagers to survive in the rapidly changing Chinese society. Earlier in the book, he argues that the importance of affinal ties has increased, along with the decline of the patrilineal institutions on which social organization used to be based. This ground is also covered in detail in Han Min's study (2001, chapter 6), but she begins with the lineage, and is thus able to show the articulation of exchange, affinal relationships, and lineage in much more detail.

If Yan's focus is gift exchange, that of Liu's *In One's Own Shadow* is Bourdieu's theory of practice and *habitus*. "Practice is not a result of conscious determination. The effects of action always exceed or are richer than its intention.... The crucial point here is that something exists only *in* practice – only in the ways of talking, the ways of doing, the ways of behaving, and so on" (2000: 23). Individual actions in Liu's village were a mixture of the traditional, the revolutionary and the modern, but "social life in northern rural Shaanxi was essentially characterized by a lack of any mode of moral economy.... In other words, there was no consistent 'moral' order to guide and determine social action or cultural meaning" (ibid.: 182). How individuals manage and navigate this kind of society in transition provides one of the main themes of the book, in a series of vignettes drawn from weddings, funerals, and mass meetings. Though theoretically very different, his account is reminiscent of that of Nie, who records her sense of surprise at the level of family conflict in the village when she began her own research (1992: 9).

Comparing the six works is a fascinating exercise. In fact, the ground that they cover is in many ways very similar, and most of the major themes are dealt with in at least two or three of the monographs. By the time the American-based scholars turned their dissertations into published books, the "cultural turn" in anthropology was well underway. The Japanese work, in contrast, was written slightly earlier, and is closer to the American models of the 1980s. Certainly, the three American books are beautifully written and theoretically highly sophisticated, especially the one by Liu. And yet, together they raise a practical question: which of them is more likely to be of interest as records of the liberation, collectivization, and reform periods of Chinese history in a generation or so? Because the Japanese works cover in so much detail similar processes in different parts of China, it is arguable that they will provide the more useful baseline, especially when read together with the earlier studies by American scholars of the post-reform period. The three village studies by the Chinese scholars based in the United States are rather shorter, more limited in scope, and less rich in empirical detail. Liu's book provides some interesting case studies of ritual and the use of space, but it is difficult to piece together an overall picture of the community from the vignettes he provides, interspersed as they are with theoretical meditation. As accounts of lineage structure, none of the other studies approaches the level of detail of Han's who provides a genealogy of the entire local lineage as a grid on which all the *dramatis personae* of her account can be placed, something of a *tour de force* in itself. As I found when we worked together on a paper on marriage and the plight of the single men, she had almost total recall of the village residents and their life histories (Han and Eades 1995; reworked in Han 2001, chapter 6). This was the result of a remarkable piece of participant observation in which she was able to play various roles in relation to different groups of villages (Han 2001: 219–22): as an adopted daughter of a village notable, as a member of the party with a military background and credentials, as a confidante of the younger married women with their various domestic problems, and as a scholar who could help decipher the genealogy and ancient ancestral monuments.

Japanese and Western anthropology: a convergence?

In the previous section, I dealt with some of the differences between the work of Chinese scholars based in America and Japan, as a telling case of the differences in anthropological approach between the two countries. In this final section, I consider the possibilities for a convergence between the two schools. Is Japanese anthropology changing, and what are the forces propelling the change?

Japanese academe as a whole is undergoing something of an upheaval at the moment, along with many other core Japanese institutions, after more than a decade of economic recession. The Koizumi government is committed to deregulation and privatization as a general policy, and the recent granting of a new independent status (*dokuritsuhôjinka*) to the national universities is just one example of this (Goodman 2001). At the same time, as the universities are facing the consequences of a declining birthrate, they are also having to face the increasing spread of the "audit culture" which has pervaded British universities increasingly since the Thatcher era of the 1980s. It is clear that the British model is one which the Japanese Ministry of Education has at the back of its mind, as is clear from some of the more recent policies (cf. Eades 2001). The last two years have seen major initiatives to improve the quality of teaching and research in Japanese universities as a whole: the Center of Excellence (COE) Program, which has awarded large sums of money to around 200 departments and research groups around the country to raise the standard of their research to "international level," and the Center of Learning (COL) Program which attempts to reward significant innovations in teaching. The knock-on effect of the COE is likely to put more pressure on individual academics and departments to obtain research funding and publish their results internationally, rather than in the usual in-house journals.

Meanwhile, the academic associations seem to be moving in a similar direction. The Japanese Society of Ethnology (*Nihon Minzoku Gakkai*) finally concluded the long debate over its name and future, by voting overwhelmingly to change it to the Japanese Society of Cultural Anthropology (*Nihon Bunkajinruigakkai*) (Cheung 2004). What this means in practice is that the older ethnological wing of the association is in decline, and the mainstream now consists of scholars who are more committed to communicating with colleagues internationally. Some initiatives are already underway: the *Japanese Review of Cultural Anthropology* is just one of a number of Asian-based English or bilingual journals to appear on the market recently, and Japanese anthropologists now regularly organize panels at the larger international conferences. The Japanese Society of Cultural Anthropology itself is very concerned with its own internationalization. However, this is not the end of national anthropologies, as Shinji Yamashita, Joseph Bosco, and myself have recently argued elsewhere (2004). Styles of publication are clearly linked to the intended audience. No doubt, Japanese anthropologists will continue to publish in Japanese for their large domestic audiences, but they will also publish increasingly in English.

There are still bottlenecks, of course, one of the most important of which is language. On the one hand, the number of native speakers of English with editing skills living and working in Asia is steadily increasing, as is the economic clout of the region. On the other hand, editing and translation are extremely time-consuming. They are also very expensive services if they have to be purchased on the open market. There is, therefore, an argument for both the governments and academic associations of countries like Japan to fund systematic translation of some of the best work into English as soon as it appears in Japanese. Foundations that fund major literary prizes might also be persuaded to invest some resources in making these works more widely available internationally, more quickly.

There are other good reasons for attempting to integrate the anthropologies of the Asian semi-periphery into the mainstream of global anthropology. Each generation adds its questions to the anthropological agenda, and when these questions are initially posed, they tend to stimulate lively theoretical debate.

Ultimately, the issues they represent disappear from view, or are taken on board as received wisdom, after which it is back to business as usual. From the mid-1960s to the 1980s, French structuralism, French Marxism, American development theory, and feminism succeeded each other rapidly as issues which had to be addressed. However, the "cultural turn" in Anglophone anthropology has produced a subculture and a style of writing within the discipline in which many of the virtues of earlier generations seem to have been forgotten: clear thinking, the presentation of rich data, lively description, quantitative and historical evidence, chronological narratives, and detailed accounts of real people doing real things in real locations. In some of the best of the Asian work, many of these virtues still survive, and international collaboration could serve as a useful reminder of this to the rest of us. In world-systems theory it is often the semi-periphery which produces the surprises and the innovations. As we head into a twenty-first century in which the majority of scholars writing in English will no longer necessarily live either in the United States or United Kingdom, it could well be the countries of the semi-periphery which will increasingly take the lead in the ongoing saga of anthropology and its vicissitudes within the academic mode of production.

References

Askew, D. (2003) "Empire and the anthropologist: Torii Ryûzô and early Japanese anthropology," *Japanese Review of Cultural Anthropology*, 4: 133–54.

——(2004) "Debating the 'Japanese race' in Meiji Japan: towards a history of early Japanese anthropology," in S. Yamashita, J. Bosco, and J.S. Eades (eds), *The Making of Anthropology in East and Southeast Asia*, Oxford and New York: Berghahn, pp. 57–89.

Baker, H.R. (1968) *A Chinese Lineage Village*, Stanford, CA: Stanford University Press.

Cheung, Sidney C.H. (2004) "Japanese anthropology and depictions of the Ainu," in S. Yamashita, J. Bosco, and J.S. Eades (eds), *The Making of Anthropology in East and Southeast Asia*, Oxford and New York: Berghahn, pp. 136–51.

Crook, I. and D. Crook (1959) *Revolution in a Chinese Village*, London: Routledge.

——(1966) *The First Years of Yangyi Commune*, London: Routledge.

Davis, Deborah (ed.) (2000) *The Consumer Revolution in Urban China*, Berkeley, CA: University of California Press.

Eades, J.S. (1995) "The new Chinese anthropology: a view from outside," in M. Suenari, J.S. Eades, and C. Daniels (eds), *Perspectives on Chinese Society*, Canterbury: University of Kent, Centre for Social Anthropology and Computing, pp. 274–91.

——(2000) "Why don't they write in English? Academic modes of production and academic discourses in Japan and the West," *Ritsumeikan Journal of Asia Pacific Studies*, 6: 58–77.

——(2001) "Reforming Japanese higher education: bureaucrats, the birthrate, and visions of the 21st century," *Ritsumeikan Journal of Asia Pacific Studies*, 8: 86–101.

——(2003) "Ethnographies of the vanishing? Global images and local realities among the aborigines of Taiwan," in S. Yamashita and J.S. Eades (eds), *Globalization in Southeast Asia*, Oxford and New York: Berghahn, pp. 226–52.

Endicott, S. (1988) *Red Earth*, London: I.B. Tauris.

Gladney, Dru (1991) *Muslim Chinese*, Cambridge, MA: Harvard University Press.

Goodman, R. (2001) "The state of higher education in East Asia: higher education in East Asia and the State," *Ritsumeikan Journal of Asia Pacific Studies*, 8: 1–29.

Guldin, G. (1994) *The Saga of Anthropology in China*, Armonk, NY: M.E. Sharpe.

Han Min (2001) *Social Change and Continuity in a Village in Northern Anhui, China*, Osaka: National Museum of Ethnology (Senri Ethnological Studies 58).

Han Min and J.S. Eades (1995) "Brides, bachelors and brokers: the marriage market in rural Anhui in an era of economic reform," *Modern Asian Studies*, 29(4): 841–69.

Harrell, S. (2000) *Ways of Being Ethnic in Southwest China*, Seattle, WA: Washington University Press.

Hinton, W. (1966) *Fanshen*, New York: Monthly Review Press.

——(1983) *Shenfan*, New York: Random House.

Itô, Abito (2001) "Japanese research on Korea," *Japanese Review of Cultural Anthropology*, 2: 39–64.

Jankoviak, W.R. (1993) *Sex, Death, and Hierachy in a Chinese City*, New York: Columbia University Press.

Jing, Jun (1996) *The Temple of Memories*, Stanford, CA: Stanford University Press.

Kim, K. (2004) "The making and indigenization of anthropology in Korea," in S. Yamashita, J. Bosco, and J.S. Eades (eds), *The Making of Anthropology in East and Southeast Asia*, Oxford and New York: Berghahn, pp. 253–85.

Kuwayama, Takami (2004) "Native anthropology: the Japanese challenge to Western academic hegemony," Melbourne: Trans Pacific Press.

Liu, Xin (2000) *In One's Own Shadow*, Berkeley, CA: University of California Press.

Nie, Lili (1992) *Ryu Ho* [Liu Village], Tokyo: Tokyo University Press.

Potter, Jack M. (1968) *Capitalism and the Chinese Peasant*, Berkeley, CA: University of California Press.

Potter, S.H. and J. Potter (1990) *China's Peasants*, Cambridge, UK: Cambridge University Press.

Qin, Zhaoxiong (1994) "Chûgoku Kohokushô no nôson no shakai henka, 1949–1993" [Social change in a village in Hubei Province, China, 1949–93], PhD dissertation, Department of Cultural Anthropology, University of Tokyo.

——(2002) "Changes in Chinese lineage and politics: a case study from rural Hubei," *Japanese Review of Cultural Anthropology*, 3: 3–30.

Rudelson, J.J. (1997) *Oasis Identities*, New York: Columbia University Press.

Schein, L. (2000) *Minority Rules*, Durham, NC: Duke University Press.

Segawa, M. (1998) "Anthropological studies in Japan of Chinese society: 1900–1997," *Japanese Review of Cultural Anthropology*, 1: 7–32.

Sekimoto, T. (2003) "Selves and others in Japanese anthropology," in A. Shimizu and J. van Bremen (eds), *Wartime Japanese Anthropology in Asia and the Pacific*, Osaka: National Museum of Ethnology (Senri Ethnological Studies 65), pp. 131–43.

Siu, H. (1989) *Agents and Victims in South China*, New Haven, CT: Yale University Press.

Suenari, M., J.S. Eades, and C. Daniels (eds) (1995) *Perspectives on Chinese Society*, Canterbury: University of Kent, Centre for Social Anthropology and Computing.

Watson, James (1975) *Emigration and the Chinese Lineage*, Berkeley, CA: University of California Press.

Watson, Rubie (1985) *Inequality among Brothers*, Cambridge, UK: Cambridge University Press.

Wong, Siu-lun (1979) *Sociology and Socialism in Contemporary China*, London: Routledge.

Yamashita, S. (2004) "Constructing selves and others in Japanese anthropology: the case of Micronesia and Southeast Asian Studies," in S. Yamashita, J. Bosco, and J.S. Eades (eds), *The Making of Anthropology in East and Southeast Asia*, Oxford and New York: Berghahn, pp. 90–113.

Yamashita, S., J. Bosco, and J.S. Eades (2004) "Asian anthropologies: foreign, native, and indigenous," in S. Yamashita, J. Bosco, and J.S. Eades (eds), *The Making of Anthropology in East and Southeast Asia*, Oxford and New York: Berghahn, pp. 1–34.

——(eds) (2004) *The Making of Anthropology in East and Southeast Asia*, Oxford and New York: Berghahn.

Yan, Yunxiang (1996) *The Flow of Gifts*, Stanford, CA: Stanford University Press.

Yokoyama, Hiroko (ed.) (2004) *The Dynamics of Cultures and Society among Ethnic Minorities in East Asia*, Osaka: National Museum of Ethnology (Senri Ethnological Reports, 50).

5   Native discourse in the "academic world system"

Kunio Yanagita's project of global folkloristics reconsidered

Takami Kuwayama

Introduction

Kunio Yanagita (1875–1962) is widely regarded as the founder of Japanese folklore studies or folkloristics.[1] Not only are his writings numerous, there is also a voluminous secondary literature on his works and career. Unfortunately, most of them have not been translated into other languages, and Yanagita's contributions are little known outside Japan.[2] In this chapter, I will discuss an important aspect of his thought, which, for one reason or another, has been neglected by earlier scholars – the idea of "global folkloristics." Presented in his 1934 book, *Minkan Denshôron (The Science of Popular Tradition)*, this could have developed into a major international project, but has remained to date an unfinished task, the potential significance of which has yet to be explored.

Different interpretations are possible, but I contend that global folkloristics was conceptualized as an attempt to study folk cultures throughout the world by examining them first in their native country or nation and then comparing and generalizing the research results on a global scale. This idea was innovative, for it regarded all people studied by folklorists, including so-called "natives," as active agents of research into their culture. Whether "primitive" or "civilized," Western or non-Western, literate members of the world's community were regarded, at least potentially, as knowledge producers. As such, Yanagita's vision is useful in examining anthropological practice in today's postcolonial age, when the traditional boundary between the colonizer/describer and the colonized/described has increasingly become blurred.

In my recent book, *Native Anthropology* (2004), I maintained that decolonization after the Second World War has changed "natives" (henceforth used without quotation marks) in the non-Western world from passive objects of representation to active agents of ethnography. This change has occurred, in part, as a result of the spread of education in former colonies: many of the natives are now able to read and critically examine what has been said about them. Moreover, professionally trained members of the native community have learned to write about their history and culture in their own language from their own perspective. Their views often conflict with those of scholars from the former colonizing powers.

Despite such change, natives' voice has seldom reached the metropolitan West, where much of the esteemed knowledge about them is produced and disseminated to the rest of the world. I submit that this situation has been brought about by what may be called the "academic world system," in which the "center" is occupied by a few major Western countries – in the case of anthropology, the United States, Great Britain, and to a lesser extent France – which together have relegated other countries, including small European countries, to the "periphery." The imbalance of power between the center and the periphery is such that it is difficult for the two parties to negotiate on an equal basis. Yanagita's global folkloristics has a potential to change this system into a structure that gives equal representation to both central and peripheral scholars because, in my interpretation, it was designed to create "dialogic space" open to all academics from around the world. As I will demonstrate later, this space was envisioned as a forum in which different kinds of knowledge produced in different parts of the world were compared and examined without privileging one or a few dominant countries.

Yanagita's vision, however, reveals some of the limitations characteristic of modern intellectuals in developing countries. Particularly problematic is his cultural nationalism, which lurks in the assertion that only natives can understand their culture and are therefore qualified to study it. Academically speaking, this assertion derived from the priority Yanagita placed on the natives' "embodied understanding" over the outsiders' "analytical understanding" – a point I will discuss in detail in the following section. Politically speaking, it stemmed from his desire to defend Japanese culture from Western encroachment by eliminating Western researchers from the study of Japan. This desire, in turn, sprang from Yanagita's attempt to "know" and "possess" Japan's culture, which reflected the strong nationalism of modern Japan.

Here I first outline Yanagita's global folkloristics under eight headings, then show its significance for today's anthropology, and finally discuss its limitations. My interpretation is based on the newly edited *Yanagita Kunio Zenshū (Complete Works of Kunio Yanagita*, 38 volumes*)*, which started to be published in 1997.

Re-viewing global folkloristics

An explanation of terminology is required at the outset. The expression Yanagita used for global folkloristics is *sekai minzokugaku*, "world folklore studies," which first appeared in *Minkan Denshôron*.[3] The first chapter of this book also introduced another important concept, *ikkoku minzokugaku*, which literally means "one-country folklore studies." Whether these concepts form a contrasted pair or a complementary relationship is a point of contestation, one I will discuss shortly. For now, suffice it to say that *sekai minzokugaku* and *ikkoku minzokugaku* will be translated throughout as "global folkloristics" and "national folkloristics," respectively.

The scope of global folkloristics

It is widely argued that Yanagita was solely interested in the study of Japan, and refused to compare it with other countries. His concept of national folkloristics has often been cited in support of this argument. Global folkloristics, on the other hand, has been considered to involve cultural comparison. For this reason, national and global folkloristics have long been regarded as having opposite orientations.

A careful reading of Yanagita's writings reveals this to be a misunderstanding. Contrary to the common supposition, he conceived of national and global folkloristics as two sides or stages of the same project, regarding the former as the constituent unit of the latter. In other words, he expected each country to establish an academic tradition of its own, through which it would employ local theories and methods to investigate its own folk customs. Once a sufficient number of countries had embarked on this process, he thought a global community of folklorists would naturally emerge. Global folkloristics was therefore conceptualized as a sort of "town meeting" in which folklorists gathered from different parts of the world to exchange their ideas and research findings. As Yanagita (1998b: 25) remarked, "We should first establish national folkloristics in order to prepare the ground for creating global folkloristics in the future."

Global folkloristics and comparative folkloristics

On one of the rare occasions when Yanagita discussed cultural comparison, he defined *hikaku minzokugaku* (comparative folkloristics) as a field that studies the folk customs of different countries by comparative methods (Yanagita 1964). Drawing on this definition, later generations of Japanese folklorists have argued that comparative folkloristics "aims to capture Japaneseness by comparing Japan's folk culture with that of other people" (Sano 1998: 116). They have, however, paid little attention to how comparative folkloristics is different from global folkloristics. In many cases, the two fields have been considered almost identical.

In my view, there is a fundamental difference between the two. This difference concerns the meaning of "comparison" involved in each field. In comparative folkloristics, the objects of comparison are the different folk cultures in different parts of the world. For example, Japan is compared to Korea or China or both, and by examining the similarities and differences between these countries, scholars draw conclusions about what makes Japan distinctive. Collaboration with local researchers is encouraged throughout the process. By contrast, global folkloristics compares different *kinds of knowledge* produced by folklorists in different parts of the world. In the study of Japan, for example, research is first carried out exclusively by Japanese scholars. It is only after they have analyzed their findings according to their own academic traditions that foreigners are invited to examine the relative merits and demerits of the overall research results. Thus, until native or local scholars have completed their analysis, foreigners are excluded because, according to Yanagita, they do not know the local culture well enough. This exclusion was derived from Yanagita's deep conviction that no outsider could fully appreciate another people's culture – a reflection of his nationalism.

The objective of global folkloristics

Nowhere in *Minkan Denshôron* is the objective of global folkloristics clearly stated, although the following passage, taken from the opening paragraph of the second chapter, sheds some light on the issue:

> The mission of the science of popular tradition is not complete merely because the discipline of folkloristics has been established in a country, such as Japan, where data are plentiful. Our aspirations should be aimed higher. If our methods of investigation are systematic enough to deserve the name of science, and if they prove truly useful in exploring that part of human history not accessible to conventional historiography, which relied on archival documents for verification, then our experiments should be applied to the study of our neighboring countries, and even to those unfortunate races that exist without a country. Furthermore, it is not the exclusive right of other disciplines to attempt to discover the forces and laws underlying this exceedingly complex universe that we now conceive of as constituting a single entity. We must discard our old habit of taking pleasure in making small discoveries, and instead we must be determined to contribute to the great task of discovering human unity.
>
> (Yanagita 1998b: 34)

Since Yanagita regarded folkloristics as a branch of historiography, his emphasis on discovering "laws" and "unity" appears, at least initially, to contradict such a notion. He was, however, interested in studying the general *pattern* of history, the ways in which the daily lives of ordinary people are changed, rather than unique, momentous events. Yanagita was, in fact, strongly influenced by British empiricism, as his definition of folkloristics as an "inductive science" shows (ibid.: 191).

Community studies, national folkloristics, and global folkloristics

Yanagita strongly advocated community studies called "*kyôdo kenkyû*" (literally, the study of one's hometown). His major work in this field, *Kyôdo Seikatsu no Kenkyûhô (Methods in the Study of Community Life)*, was published in 1935. In this book, and elsewhere, Yanagita emphasized that community studies should begin at home, namely, with the study of one's own village or town – a view compatible with his assertion that natives should be active agents of research into their culture. In the 1930s, Yanagita founded a nationwide network of amateur researchers. These researchers reported their local findings to Yanagita and his associates stationed in central Tokyo, who then subjected them to detailed analysis, and from this they drew more generalized, nationwide conclusions. Yanagita was convinced that the entire nation of Japan constituted a single community. Thus, a particular local community was not studied as an end in itself, but was treated as the basic unit for comparison on a national scale.

His notion that global folkloristics comprises a community of folklorists from around the world may be considered an extension of this approach. He conceived of global folkloristics as involving two stages of development: (1) establishing in each country a distinctive tradition of folkloristics on the basis of community studies carried out in different parts of the country; and (2) establishing a global science of folklore by integrating the different types of national folkloristics practiced in different parts of the world. In Yanagita's mind, then, community studies, national folkloristics, and global folkloristics constituted a continuum. The following passages clearly attest to this point:

> If a powerful institution is located at the center [of Japan], we can collate all the locally conducted research and make the overall results available to the wider, national community . . . I sometimes dream of making an international network of knowledge exchange.
>
> (Yanagita 1998b: 75–6)

> Data collected and analyzed in each country should actively be translated. Taking language or ethnic groups as the basic unit, we should first create a domestic community of scholars and then engage in international collaboration.
>
> (Ibid.: 81)

Relationships with ethnology/anthropology

In 1925, when Yanagita was browsing in a used bookshop in Berlin, he met by chance Franz Boas, a German-born Jew who, having emigrated to the United States, was teaching anthropology there. According to Yanagita, Boas told him that in German the terms "folkloristics" and "ethnology" roughly corresponded to *Volkskunde* and *Völkerkunde*, respectively. Yanagita's distinction between folkloristics and ethnology (what is more commonly known today as cultural anthropology) seems to have been influenced by this German classification. For example, he defined folkloristics as "research from the inside, conducted in a small number of advanced countries in order for them to know about themselves," and, ethnology, as "research from the outside, conducted to teach the people of advanced and civilized countries about the various ethnic groups in the world" (ibid.: 40).

Because of his conviction that only natives can fully appreciate their culture, Yanagita regarded folkloristics as superior to ethnology, remarking, "Foreigners' observations, however carefully made, are no equal to the compatriots' insights into their culture. Folklorists have demonstrated this to ethnologists" (ibid.: 38). At the same time, he welcomed the advance of ethnological research, which showed that some "primitive" customs had survived in the civilized societies of Western Europe well into the twentieth century. Contending that this finding had greatly stimulated the study of one's own culture, Yanagita stated, "The advance of ethnology will further stimulate the growth of folkloristics in each country. Eventually, it will help establish global folkloristics. This is the mission of ethnology" (ibid.: 48).

The establishment of national folkloristics by natives

Yanagita declined to compare Japan with other countries, not because he found cultural comparison worthless, but because he believed the time was not yet ripe for such study. Because of his conviction that only natives could understand their culture, Yanagita asserted that until tribal peoples possessed the ability to study themselves, a truly meaningful comparison of the world's cultures would be impossible.

Yanagita repeatedly argued that the deeper layers of a culture are inaccessible to outsiders. In *Seinen to Gakumon* (*Youth and Scholarship*), published in 1928, he wrote, "As foreigners' descriptions of Japan show, outsiders' observations and conjectures are prone to gross mistakes, no matter how elaborate their research methods are. The language barrier is mainly responsible for this. Thus, we can hardly put our complete confidence in their research" (Yanagita 1998a: 27). In *Minkan Denshôron*, Yanagita developed a famous model of folklore research consisting of three parts. The first is concerned with visible phenomena, which just scratch the surface of a folk culture. This is the level of research done by "travelers." The second part is concerned with audible phenomena, which are more complex than the first because understanding them requires language competence, but are still not particularly deep. Research on this level is undertaken by "temporary residents." The third part is the most complex, being concerned with what Yanagita called "*shin'i genshô*" (literally, psycho-semantic phenomena) or mentalities. There are some arguments about whether or not Yanagita had consulted, in formulating his ideas, Malinowski's *Argonauts of the Western Pacific* (1922), in which a similar model of ethnographic research was proposed.[4] But that is not important in our context. The point is that whereas Malinowski had no doubt about the outsiders' ability to understand the native mind, Yanagita considered it practically impossible. As he remarked, "After all, foreigners cannot probe into *shin'i genshô*. We have to wait until natives have learned to look at themselves objectively" (Yanagita 1998c: 347).

Global folkloristics and Japan's mission

Yanagita vehemently maintained that it was Japan's mission to establish a strong, national tradition of folkloristics before any other non-Western country did so. This contention was based on his observation that although "primitive" societies had many materials useful for folklore research, their people lacked the ability to investigate them for themselves. By contrast, "civilized" societies in Western Europe had the intellectual resources, but were hampered in their efforts by modernization, which had buried the old cultural layers, making them difficult to find. Yanagita regarded Japan as an ideal place for folklore research because, although a modern nation, it had industrialized relatively late and had thereby retained access to the old world, while gaining the resources needed to study it provided by the new. As he remarked, "Among the Japanese, the facts of everyday life speak for an age that is becoming a past.... In many cases, thinking about them is at the same time collecting data, as well as making classifications and generalizations. Nowhere in the world is it possible to collect materials necessary for historical reconstruction as easily and as perfectly as in Japan" (Yanagita 1998b: 31). Japan was therefore a "treasure island" of folklore research (Yanagita 1998c: 215). This in-between status of Japan stemmed from its liminal position in modern, international politics: Japan was dominated by the Western powers in the wider world, but in Asia it was a great regional power with its own colonies.

Yanagita was moved by nationalistic sentiments when he commented that whereas "primitive" people had to be represented by Westerners, the Japanese possessed the intellectual resources to represent themselves. Criticizing outsider research as "touching the skin, but failing to reach the heart," he wrote, "Herein lies the great misfortune of uncivilized people who do not possess historians of their own. Since they are incapable of studying their past, they must have it represented by foreigners with motivations. By contrast, the Japanese are fortunate enough to be able to trace the history of our culture, if only we have the will to do so" (Yanagita 1998c: 234). Yanagita further commented, "Even if foreigners flock together to make scientific observations, the results will be no more than those of the 'five blind men and the elephant.' It is truly significant that our fellow countrymen, who are familiar with the world's scholarship, are setting out to study our own culture" (Yanagita 1998a: 160). The following statement summarizes Yanagita's intellectual nationalism: "We must study ourselves. Not only should we attempt to know ourselves better, we must also lead Western folklorists who have gone astray. This is Japan's noble mission" (1998a: 171).

Yanagita's counter-hegemonic discourse

Yanagita was counter-hegemonic in two respects. First, he challenged mainstream Japanese scholarship, especially orthodox historiography, which relied almost exclusively on written records for describing the lives of great individuals. This orientation contrasted with Yanagita's emphasis on the importance of collecting data through fieldwork, which enabled the writing of the history of what he called "*jômin*" (literally, ordinary people or the plebeians).

Second, Yanagita challenged Western academic hegemony. In the opening chapter of *Seinen to Gakumon*, he praised the advance of Western ethnology on the one hand, and criticized its colonial roots on the other. He contended that "white men's activities" had posed a serious challenge to young, ambitious Japanese people. He was angered when he found that no Japanese had been invited to attend an international conference on Pacific studies to be held in Brussels. He objected, saying that Japanese scholars should participate because Japan is a "major nation in the Pacific region" (Yanagita 1998a: 29). Similarly, in *Minkan Denshôron*, Yanagita denounced a world almanac of folklore, edited by a Swiss scholar, for being too Western-centered. As he remarked, "How can they call it 'international' when there is no reference to Japanese research, which has played an important role in the development of this field? No future almanac would be complete without Japanese participation. They *must* invite us" (Yanagita 1998b: 81).

Today, Yanagita is often criticized for having been indifferent to the politics of folklore, especially to the connection of Japanese folkloristics with Japan's own colonial rule. These criticisms are legitimate, but they point to one important aspect of modern Japan and overlook another. From the late nineteenth century onwards, the Japanese colonized and ruled much of the Asia Pacific region, but they were dominated by the Western powers in the wider world. This duality regarding Japan cannot be overemphasized because now that Japan has achieved a status comparable to that of any major Western country, it is a fact too frequently overlooked. Referring to the future of folkloristics, Yanagita wrote, "Considering the possibility that this discipline would flourish in countries like Japan, where data are plentiful, we should be prepared to re-write Western theories by reconsidering them in the light of the Japanese data" (Yanagita 1998b: 155). Such counter-hegemonic discourse may only be understood by considering the Western domination of Japan in almost every field, including scholarship.

The contemporary significance of global folkloristics

Proposed in the 1930s, Yanagita's vision contains some outdated ideas. At the time, however, when natives were merely treated as objects of research, being "inscribed" in the academically authorized ethnography by colonizers, his view of natives as active agents of research into their own culture was innovative. In today's postcolonial age, this position deserves serious attention because, as noted at the beginning, the boundary between the seer/describer and the seen/described has become increasingly blurred. People who used to be considered docile subjects unable to speak for themselves have, on various occasions, spoken up, as the native rights movements in many parts of the world show. The anthropologist's gaze has been returned. Later, I will examine the international context in which this change has occurred, and discuss the contemporary significance of global folkloristics.

Decolonization

The situation in which anthropologists find themselves today is completely different from what it was after the end of the Second World War, when many of the colonies attained political independence. The "primitive world," where a good deal of anthropological fieldwork was conducted, has almost disappeared as it has been integrated into the so-called "Third World." It is no longer an isolated, self-contained community without power. Rather, its collective representation is often more conspicuous than each of the former colonizers. Under these circumstances, and owing to the spread of education among the formerly subjected people, anthropologists have encountered a new kind of aliens to whom they have seldom paid attention – natives as readers of ethnography who have written about their culture. Significantly, these natives have often objected to the anthropologists' accounts, thereby contesting their authority. A case in point are the Samoans' criticisms of Margaret Mead, which, even before the publication of Derek Freeman's controversial book (Freeman 1983), were said to be quite widespread, but which are now heard forcibly as the result of the two figures' debate (Yamamoto 1997). Gone are the days when anthropologists could freely gather data in the field and interpret it in books and articles without considering the reactions of the people they were describing.

The describer, too, has changed. Historically speaking, anthropology developed as a science that aimed to explain the "exotic" people, whom the Westerners had encountered as they sought to expand their influence throughout the world – hence the "colonial roots" of anthropology. Today, this discipline is no longer a monopoly of the West. In Japan and India, for example, soon after anthropology was established in the West as a professional discipline, local intellectuals interested in the study of culture established their own schools of research, drawing on their country's academic traditions. Yanagita's folkloristics was one such school. Afterwards, some leading members of the native community went to Europe or America to receive advanced training in anthropology. Like Japan's Eiichiro Ishida and India's M.N. Srinivas, they were instrumental in strengthening the anthropological foundation of their country after returning home. The so-called "indigenization" of anthropology began, and local traditions have been reproduced through higher education. In this process has emerged a professional group of natives who study and write about their own culture in their own language from their own perspective – native anthropologists. Although often overlooked, anthropological education in the West has helped spread the discipline to the rest of the world, including the former colonies. Native anthropologists, who, given their professional expertise and the distance between them and their Western counterparts, may be called "professional Others," are increasing both in number and power. In some countries, Westerners have already found it difficult to pursue their research without consulting them in one way or another. Far from docile research objects, they are now "dialogic partners," possessed of the skills to communicate with, and in some instances, talk back to, the former colonizers.

The "world system" of anthropology

Despite such change, the natives' voice is barely heard in the academic center of the dominant Western countries. When they strongly protest against what they think are complete misunderstandings on the part of Western academics, a most notable case of which is the dispute between Haunani-Kay Trask and Jocelyn Linnekin over the "invention" of Hawaiian values (Trask 1999), their arguments tend to be labeled "subjective" (and, therefore, unworthy of serious attention) or be simply dismissed as "political propaganda" (and, therefore, unworthy of the name of scholarship). Many factors are at work here, but I contend that this unfavorable treatment results from the imbalance of power in the "academic world system," rather than from the alleged deficiencies of native scholarship.

Every field of knowledge constitutes a "world system." As mentioned at the outset, in anthropology, three major Western powers – the United States, Great Britain, and France – occupy the "center" (core) of this system, which together has relegated other countries to the "periphery" (margin). (For the semi-periphery, see Kuwayama 2004: 48–63.) As Tomas Gerholm (1995) pointed out, the relationship between the center and the periphery may be likened to that between the main-land and remote islands. The former can go through their life regardless of what happens to the latter, whereas the latter is dependent on the former for basic needs. Similarly, central scholars can ignore peripheral research without putting their career at risk, while the opposite is hardly true. Furthermore, peripheral scholars, in their desire to keep up with the latest research at the center, have so eagerly forged ties with the center that they have neglected relationships among themselves. Thus, there is frequent "ferry traffic" between the mainland and the islands, but the traffic is sporadic between the islands, which have remained iso-lated from each other. This explains why peripheral scholars are surprisingly ignorant of each other's writings, regardless of their geographical proximity. Furthermore, communication between one part of the periphery and another is ordinarily conducted in the central language(s), English in particular, and ideas tend to be framed using prestigious theories produced at the center. Indeed, peripheral anthropologists find it difficult to understand each other unless they relate their own tradition to that of the central countries (e.g. calling Japan's Masao Yamaguchi, a national celebrity, a "Japanese Victor Turner") – a practice that is realistic, given the anonymity of native scholarship outside the country, but which causes resentment among the people thus acknowledged. All in all, native anthropologists, however brilliant, find it practically impossible to negotiate with central ones on an equal basis.

Put succinctly, the "world system" of anthropology defines the politics regard-ing the production, dissemination, and consumption of knowledge about other peoples and cultures. Influential people at the center have the power to decide what kinds of knowledge should be evaluated highly and, thereby, given author-ity. They maintain and strengthen their status by publishing, for example, peer-reviewed journals, which, for non-conformist scholars working on the margin, function as a means of censorship. Another often-used strategy is to give presti-gious awards to their own colleagues they admire. By contrast, knowledge pro-duced by peripheral scholars, however valuable, tends to be treated as an inferior product or as something that is significant only in the local context, and indeed it is often dismissed outright, unless it meets the standards set by the center. Thus, "local knowledge," to use the celebrated phrase of Clifford Geertz, is appreciated only when it is rendered intelligible to the powerful elites at the center.

The need to create dialogic space

To overcome this situation, a forum for dialogue, a "dialogic space," is necessary in which central and peripheral scholars can exchange opinions freely as equal part-ners. Yanagita's idea of global folkloristics as a constellation of the different national folkloristics practiced in different parts of the world is useful in this regard.

Certainly, questions may be raised about whether or not the nation can be treated as the unit for scholarship. We must remember that there are always different, often competing, traditions within a nation. Also, the world is rapidly globalizing, and there is a constant flow of people, goods, and information across national boundaries. Despite the internal diversity, however, and in the face of globalization, the nation continues to function as the basic unit of international order. In fact, the ideal of nation-state is far from defunct today, when the human population is threatened with many crises that can hardly be solved by the traditional order based on national sovereignty. If anything, globalization has triggered nationalistic reactions in many parts of the world, and it is widely recognized that globalization goes on simultaneously with localization, hence the neologism "glocalization."

The same is true with scholarship. Different nations have produced different academic traditions, which have been reproduced and reinforced by teaching. These traditions are clearly revealed in the ways conferences are organized, journals are edited, and books are published, to say nothing of the styles of argument. Through external influences, whether political or philosophical, changes do occur in scholarship, but foreign ideas are almost always incorporated to suit the local conditions. To appreciate the continued importance of the nation for scholarship, consider this fact: throughout the world, academic organizations have been, and continue to be, named after the nation (e.g. the *American* Anthropological Association (AAA), founded in 1902; the *Japanese* Society for Cultural Anthropology, which, until March 2004, was known as the Japanese Society of Ethnology, founded in 1934). To my knowledge, no serious suggestions have ever been made to change such names.

Given this reality, Yanagita's vision, outdated as it is in some respects, is worth reconsideration. At least, it offers some insights into the question of how the academic world system may be changed to give equal representation to the hitherto neglected peripheral/native scholarship. Junzo Kawada, one of the leading anthropologists in Japan, remarked that Yanagita's view of "primitives" as active agents of research, which, in Kawada's opinion, had been presented as a hope to be realized someday, rather than as a reality, is coming true. He gave two major reasons for this: the appearance of native anthropologists in former colonies and the globalization of information.

> In Europe, in the case of African studies, students come from Africa to study at major universities in large numbers. They carry out research on their own country and write doctoral dissertations, which are then submitted to French universities, for example. Furthermore, they can read and critically comment on the works of French scholars who have conducted research in Africa. The interaction between the researcher and the researched is far more frequent today than in the past. Not only has it become possible to check each other's research, they now have closer ties ethically. Politically and economically, too, the world's societies are closely bound up with each other. Under these circumstances, outside researchers can no longer feign indifference toward the people they study, for their research may entail adverse consequences. The scientific prerogative of "detachment," which Western ethnologists and

anthropologists used to postulate between themselves and their research objects, is no longer tenable.

(Kawada 1997: 65)

Yanagita argued that when foreign travelers return from their journey to a distant land, "people accept them as the sole experts on that place and do not question what they have said" (Yanagita 1998b: 35). He also wrote, "The scarcity of research into one region by different scholars has made it difficult to compare their descriptions" (ibid.: 36). Regarding this as a major deficiency of ethnology, he further commented that he had made it a rule to read Western descriptions of Japan before evaluating the overall credibility of their ethnography. "The literate Japanese are in a position to work as inspectors," said Yanagita. Today, these "inspectors" are native anthropologists or "natives who talk back." Despite the persistent inequality in the academic world system, they have finally entered the theater as actors or actresses creating their own performances. In this new situation, Yanagita's global folkloristics provides a model, though far from complete, for creating a worldwide forum for dialogue open to all academics as equal partners.

The use of the Internet

The Internet provides a powerful means of creating the dialogic space discussed earlier. Unlike conventional methods of communication, such as the print media, in which information flows in one direction from the sender to the receiver, the Internet has made it possible to connect diverse people bilaterally, and instantaneously, on a global scale. In particular, it has proved to be a boon for researchers living in marginal, isolated areas of the world. The so-called "digital divide" that exists today between rich and poor countries will, hopefully, disappear or diminish considerably, as the technology advances further. The complex question of translation remains unsolved at this stage, but, theoretically, it has become possible to engage in dialogue in ways inconceivable only a decade ago. For example, if ethnographic data are made public on the Internet, simple factual mistakes or misunderstandings, derived from the researcher's unfamiliarity with the details of local life, may immediately be corrected by, among others, the people described. It will also allow different interpretations to be written in from all the people concerned with the culture under discussion. Eventually, such undertakings will change people's perception of natives from passive objects of representation to dialogic partners, and of peripheral scholars in the academic world system from lesser members of the profession to equal research partners. Furthermore, an innovative use of the Internet has the possibility of producing new styles of ethnographic writing. Among them is "plural authorship," in which more than one writer creates texts collectively in the manner of *renga* (linked verse), a classic style of Japanese poems. Until recently, such ideas have existed only in the realm of imagination, but they are within our reach today.

There are, of course, many practical problems to be solved before all this becomes a reality. In particular, the question of how to assign and protect academic credit needs a thorough examination.[5] It would also be premature to expect too much of the Internet, for not only does it help to promote communication across national borders, it can also spread misunderstandings instantaneously throughout the world. It remains, however, that we have entered a new technological age that makes dialogic space possible in ways unimaginable in Yanagita's age.

Can only natives "understand" their culture?

In this section, I will examine a major problem in Yanagita's global folkloristics – his assertion that only natives can fully understand *(wakaru)* their culture and are therefore qualified to study it. In *Minkan Denshôron, Kyôdo Seikatsu no Kenkyûhô*, and *Gakumon to Seinen*, Yanagita repeatedly expressed deep misgivings about a foreigner's ability to explore the native mind. This skepticism stemmed partially from his methodology, in which the analysis of folk terminology was considered to be the basis of folklore research. As he remarked, "The spiritual life of a people is expressed in their art of language.... It is inaccessible to foreign travelers who speak different languages. Some people take delight in translating into English the American Indians' verbal art, but can they truly *ajiwau* (literally 'taste,' meaning 'appreciate') it? I think not. The distinctive *aji* (taste) of one's language may only be appreciated by one's compatriots" (Yanagita 1998b: 134).

No one would seriously disagree that language is an expression of the folk spirit *(Volksgeist)* and that no cultural understanding would be complete without a mastery of the local language. To argue, however, that only natives can appreciate their culture is tantamount to saying that non-natives, including folklorists, have little or nothing to contribute. Since Yanagita devoted his life to establishing folkloristics in Japan, it is unlikely that he had intentionally made statements that contradicted his mission. I would therefore submit that Yanagita's view was derived from his distinct conception of *wakaru* or "understanding." Ironically, he made remarks that seemingly contradicted his mission because he was unaware of how his own conception was deeply embedded in the Japanese way of thinking.

In my interpretation, when Yanagita made statements, such as, "After all, it is impossible for outsiders to know how local people feel," and "People brought up under different circumstances will never understand" (Yanagita 1998c: 367), he referred to the difficulties of appreciating local life with the *body*, rather than questioning the outsiders' ability to grasp it cognitively. In other words, he was questioning whether non-natives could experience the culture they studied as the natives experienced it. This type of understanding is similar to "empathy," which entails the sharing of emotions with other people. Emotions are mediated by the body, which, as will be discussed later, has been contrasted with the mind in Cartesian dualism.

Yanagita's use of the word *ajiwau* (taste) clearly attests to this point. Although it was used figuratively, tasting something involves the functioning of a bodily apparatus – the tongue. Indeed, the Japanese concept of *wakaru* suggests something more than cognitive understanding based on the rational mind: it implies a full-bodied experience that transcends abstract thinking. For the Japanese, and, certainly for Yanagita, it is not sufficient to understand by *atama* (head). More important is the ability to learn something using the entire *karada* (body). The favorite Japanese expression "*minitsuku*" (attaching to the body, which, in this particular case is pronounced "*mi*," meaning the body or *karada*), as in *Chishiki ga minitsuku* (literally, knowledge has been attached to the body), clarifies this point. In this context, Takie Lebra's observation that the Japanese *karada* may best be understood as the "minded body" is illuminating (Lebra 1993). We may even go one step further and say that *wakaru* is analogous to the Zen ideal of "no dependence on words," which holds that truth lies in bodily experience, not in words (Suzuki 1940: 7).

H.D. Harootunian put it well when he observed that, for Yanagita, understanding meant "getting inside, beneath the surface" (1998: 148).

> For this reason, he and his followers dismissed ethnography: because it consisted of reporting from the perspective of an outsider, it could never hope to reach the interior of folk experience.... The discipline of native ethnology [i.e., Japanese folkloristics] put the investigator inside the scene of investigation to become one with it.... Despite his celebration of scientific rigor and its implied openness, Yanagita came close to promoting a methodology restricted to those who, like himself, were inside the scene.... Understanding the folk required not interpretation but empathy. The study of native ethnology meant probing beneath the surface to locate those deeply embedded unconscious habits of mind that ceaselessly regulated the repetitive rhythms of everyday life. The investigator had to be in a position to recognize what constituted the fund of spiritual beliefs that the folk took as second nature, which would remain forever beyond the powers of the outsider to grasp.
>
> (Ibid.: 148–54)

By contrast, modern Western thinking generally draws a sharp dividing line between the mind and the body – a reflection of the pervading influence of Cartesian dualism. Representing the domain of reason, the mind is regarded as superior to the body, which is believed to be affected by emotion. For Westerners, understanding something means grasping it by the power of reason, and this conception is central to their notion of rationality. Empathy plays only a minor role because it is mediated by the body, which is considered to be emotional and irrational. This is, of course, not to say that the body has been neglected in Western philosophy. Some scholars, including Immanuel Kant, have noted the importance of bodily experience in their attempt to overcome the limitations of the mind/body dualism. By and large, however, Cartesian dualism has exerted a lasting influence on Western thought, so that understanding is identified with a logical analysis clearly articulated by words.

The Enlightenment grew out of this intellectual tradition. Advocating the supremacy of the mind, it successfully developed science by the power of reason to a degree unknown in human history. Significantly, it was against this current of ideas that romanticism emerged. Represented in the writings of the German philosopher Johann Gottfried Herder, romanticism rejected the Enlightenment ideals of rationality and universality, celebrating instead non-rational aspects of human thought (Mautner 1999: 488). Herder's "cultural pluralism," which came from his admiration of local and national traditions, was an important source of inspiration for the rise of nationalism in developing countries within Europe (ibid.: 247). As Mikako Iwatake (1996) pointed out, romanticism contributed to the formation of folkloristics as a "national discipline" in the less developed parts of the modern world, including Japan.

Yanagita was strongly influenced by the British empiricism, as his definition of folkloristics as an "inductive science" shows. On a deeper level, however, he was fascinated by German romanticism. Masao Oka, Yanagita's contemporary who, after returning to Japan from his study at Vienna University in the 1930s, helped found Japanese anthropology, made this observation:

> Yanagita's scholarship developed when Japan was full of nationalism. The Japanese people's view of their country as "backward" relative to the West had fostered a strong national consciousness among them. Thus, they resisted the influx of Western ideas and commodities. It was a period when the search for Japan's distinct culture began, and the need to maintain and strengthen the Japanese spirit was emphasized. Japanese folkloristics, therefore, has had fundamental similarities with its German counterpart.
>
> (1979: 82)

Kazuhiko Komatsu, a leading figure in Japanese folkloristics today, maintained that to "know" something is to "possess" it, contending that a strong desire to possess one's culture is hidden in the study of folklore (Komatsu 1998: 202). Edward Said essentially made the same point when he argued in *Orientalism* (1978) that the study of a foreign culture is a form of domination over that culture. Since Yanagita called his discipline "*jiko shôsatsu no gaku*" (a science of introspection), he was mainly interested in "knowing" his country. As I see it, the ensuing desire to "possess" Japan caused Yanagita to develop a strong cultural nationalism, which eventually resulted in the attempt to exclude foreign (especially Western) researchers from studying Japan. He justified this attempt in terms of their alleged inability to *wakaru* the Japanese mind. On the level of cognition, however, understanding is possible for any person intelligent enough to analyze what he or she has seen. Yanagita, therefore, discounted the foreigners' ability on the grounds that they could not possibly have a full-bodied experience of Japanese culture. I propose to call Yanagita's conception "embodied understanding," as contrasted with the Western approach that emphasizes rational thinking, which is called here "analytical understanding."

Lest my arguments become too complex, I will refrain from discussing Yanagita's relationship with his fellow Japanese researchers, notably amateur researchers called "*kyôdoshika*" (people studying their hometown's history), whom Yanagita incorporated into Japan's nationwide network of folklorists. Two comments are in order, however. First, in terms of *kyôdo kenkyû* (the study of one's hometown), Yanagita was at a disadvantage because, living in central Tokyo and not being a native of the research community, he was subject to the same criticisms he had made of non-Japanese scholars. Second, Yanagita tried to solve this dilemma, whether consciously or unconsciously, by arguing that natives paid so much attention to the details of everyday life that they frequently overlooked its essence. In other words, contrary to his statement about the alleged inability of non-Japanese people to have a full-bodied experience of the culture, Yanagita here gave priority to the outsiders' "analytical understanding" over the natives' "embodied understanding." In this way, he privileged his own inside/outside position vis-à-vis other researchers of Japan, both foreign and local.

Yanagita's "arrogance" is not the issue here. Rather, the problem is with his desire to exclude foreigners, which, in my interpretation, endangers the very foundation on which the idea of global folkloristics rests. As explained earlier, in comparative folkloristics, collaboration with foreign researchers is encouraged, whereas in global folkloristics they are excluded until natives have produced tangible research results. However, the study of culture almost inevitably involves comparison, and a folkloristics that lacks the outsiders' perspective is incomplete because, as Yanagita himself argued, natives take for granted and overlook what outsiders can easily see. He in fact warned against the "danger of attempting to accomplish community studies exclusively by natives' knowledge" (Yanagita 1998b: 77). Thus, even if a distinctive tradition of folkloristics is successfully established in each nation, its deficiencies will soon be revealed when examined against other traditions. Furthermore, the natives' strong desire to "know" and "possess" their culture will necessarily clash with the equally strong desire of interested outsiders to study and know it. When this happens, it becomes practically impossible to engage in dialogue without a head-on confrontation. Yanagita's assertion, then, that only natives can understand their culture is inimical to the realization of global folkloristics.

Influenced by romanticism, Yanagita's writings were literary and required empathy on the part of a reader. After Japan's defeat in the Second World War, he remarked, "We used to carry out research without having foreign readers in mind. I thought it was demeaning to have them read our works" (Yanagita *et al.* 1965: 59). Another thing Yanagita failed to anticipate was the spread of Japanese studies throughout the world, after the war. Today, the study of Japan is a thriving field, and there are all sorts of discourse about the country and its people. Under these circumstances, we should be wary of a cultural nationalism that allows only natives to "know" and "possess" their country. It is also important to note that there are different types of understanding, such as "embodied" and "analytical," and that they are complementary, rather than mutually exclusive. The study of one's own culture may only be opened to the global community when we remember this.

Conclusion

I conclude by elaborating on the last point. In both folkloristics and cultural anthropology, the concept of culture occupies a central place. As Ernest Gellner (1983) and Nagao Nishikawa (1992), among others, have shown, this concept developed concurrently with that of the modern nation-state. Thus, culture and politics are indistinguishably related, and it is impossible to separate one from the other. Since the 1980s, when culture began to be examined in relation to nationalism, anthropologists have been forced to reconsider their intellectual foundation, for many of them have been rather indifferent to the politics of culture.

In this reflective moment, a basic question we must ask is "Who owns culture?" Obviously, what is being addressed here is not the universal pattern of culture that is supposedly shared by all human beings, but rather a particular culture that has been developed by a particular group of people, usually called an "ethnic group" or simply a "nation," over a long course of time. This problem of "cultural ownership," if you will, is inevitably related to that of "cultural subjects/agents" and the "right" to represent them.

Culture as understood earlier is associated with the history and the folklore of a given people. We must remember, however, that it also allows different peoples with different collective memories to *live* it if they have chosen to do so, or, for one reason or another, have been forced to do the same. Culture, then, is both a product of the people who have developed it *and* the property of the people who currently live it, whether or not they are genealogically related to each other. Seen in this way, we may argue that culture is common property of all human beings – something that may be appreciated across the ethnic or the national boundaries, which consequently defies a claim to an exclusive ownership by the people who have made it. As such, the right to represent it belongs to everyone, whether native or non-native.

This is, of course, not to deny the natives' contributions to the growth of their culture. Nor is it intended to allow uncommitted outsiders to speak of other peoples in ways that would offend their dignity. All that is being claimed here is that culture is an open, not a closed, entity. Thus, Japanese culture is not an exclusive property of the Japanese people. It belongs, rather, to the people who have chosen (or have been destined) to live it as their own. Unlike theatrical masks, culture cannot be worn or removed easily, but human beings have the freedom to live a new culture, and, conversely, discard the culture in which we were born, even though the latter is an emotionally disturbing process.[6] This dual freedom of choice is, I submit, based on the ideal of common humanity.

In the 1930s, Kunio Yanagita proposed the ambitious project of global folkloristics. His mission was noble, but it was abandoned mid-stream by Yanagita himself, who, in his later days, described it as a "failure." This miscarriage resulted from his refusal to broaden his perspective beyond Japan, rather than from any specific theoretical weaknesses. Born in modern Japan, characterized as it was by a strong nationalism, Yanagita was unable to resist the powerful desire to "know" and "possess" his culture. Our task, then, is to develop the positive aspects of his intellectual legacy and create the much-needed dialogic space in which people with different national backgrounds can participate on an equal basis for a better understanding of culture.

Acknowledgments

Earlier versions of this chapter appeared both in Japanese (Kuwayama 2000) and in English (Kuwayama 2004: 64–86). It should be noted that there are overlaps between the latter and the present work because of the delay in publishing this volume.

Notes

1 In terms of the scope of research, Japanese folkloristics is much broader than its counterparts in English-speaking countries. It is not much different from today's cultural anthropology, except that it mainly studies the researcher's own culture, its traditional aspects in particular, under the rubric of *minzoku* (the folk).
2 Some of Yanagita's major works have been translated into English (Yanagita 1957, 1970, 1972, 1975). Among the useful critiques of Yanagita, written in English, are Kawada (1993), Koschmann *et al.* (1985), Morse (1990), and Tsurumi (1975).
3 Only the introduction and the first chapter of this book were written by Yanagita himself. The remaining chapters were written by one of his students, who had hand-recorded his lectures delivered in his house. This fact is partially responsible for the scant attention paid to the global folkloristics.
4 Malinowski (1922) classified the objects of ethnographic research into three categories in ascending order of complexity: (1) the organization of the tribe and the anatomy of its culture; (2) the "imponderabilia" of actual life; and (3) the native mind.
5 A major obstacle to "Internet ethnography" is the current system of academic evaluation. When reviewed for tenure or promotion, scholars are ordinarily required to show their list of publications. In this system, by far the most important consideration is the number, as well as the quality, of books and articles printed *on paper*. This fact inevitably makes scholars protective of their writings, thus unwilling to share ethnographic data with other people, until they are actually *printed*. If, however, the system is changed in such a way as to consider the frequencies of access to one's web site, for example, along with the quality of other people's comments it has drawn, the situation will probably change dramatically. New technology requires new methods of evaluation.
6 Soon after the First World War, Edward Sapir maintained that in order for an individual to attain spiritual growth, he should have the courage to discard the culture into which he was born. As he remarked, "Once the individual self has grown strong enough to travel in the path most clearly illuminated by its own light, it not only can but should discard much of the scaffolding by which it has made its ascent. Nothing is more pathetic than the persistence with which well-meaning applicants to culture attempt to keep up or revive cultural stimuli which have long outlived their significance for the growth of personality" (Sapir 1949: 324). He called such an attempt a "spiritual crime."

References

Freeman, Derek (1983) *Margaret Mead and Samoa: The Making and Unmaking of an Anthropological Myth*, Cambridge, MA: Harvard University Press.
Gellner, Ernest (1983) *Nations and Nationalism*, Oxford: Blackwell.

Gerholm, Tomas (1995) "Sweden: central ethnology, peripheral anthropology," in Han F. Vermeulen and Arturo Alvarez Roldán (eds), *Fieldwork and Footnotes: Studies in the History of European Anthropology*, London: Routledge.

Harootunian, H.D. (1998) "Figuring the folk: history, poetics, and representation," in Stephen Vlastos (ed.), *Mirror of Modernity: Invented Traditions of Modern Japan*, Berkeley, CA: University of California Press, pp. 144–59.

Iwatake, Mikako (1996) *Minzokugaku no Seijisei* (The Politics of Folklore), Tokyo: Miraisha.

Kawada, Junzo (1997) "Nichiô Kindaishi no naka no Yanagita Kunio" (Kunio Yanagita in the Modern History of Japan and Europe), *Seijo Daigaku Minzokugaku Kenkjûjo Kiyô* (The Bulletin of the Center for the Study of Folklore, Seijo University), 21: 37–66.

Kawada, Minoru (1993) *The Origin of Ethnography in Japan: Yanagita Kunio and His Times* (translated by Toshiko Kishida-Ellis), London: Kegan Paul International.

Komatsu, Kazuhiko (1998) "*Minzoku Chôsa no Niruikei*" (Two Types of Folklore Research), in Ajio Fukuta (ed.), *Minzokugaku no Hôhô (Methods in Folkloristics)*, Tokyo: Yûzankaku.

Koschmann, J. Victor, Keibo Oiwa, and Shinji Yamashita (eds) (1985) *International Perspectives on Yanagita Kunio and Japanese Folklore Studies* (Cornell East Asia Series 37), Ithaca, NY: Cornell University East Asia Program.

Kuwayama, Takami (2000) "Yanagita Kunio no Sekai Minzokugaku Saikô" (A Reconsideration of Kunio Yanagita's Global Folkloristics), *Nihon Minzokugaku* (The Bulletin of the Folklore Society of Japan), 222: 1–32.

—— (2004) *Native Anthropology: The Japanese Challenge to Western Academic Hegemony*, Melbourne: Trans Pacific Press.

Lebra, Takie Sugiyama (1993) "Culture, self, and communication in Japan and the United States," in William B. Gudykunst (ed.), *Communication in Japan and the United States*, New York: State University of New York Press.

Malinowski, Bronislaw (1984) *Argonauts of the Western Pacific: An Account of Native Enterprise and Adventure in the Archipelagoes of Melanesian New Guinea*, Prospect Heights, IL: Waveland Press (Orig. 1922).

Mautner, Thomas (ed.) (1999) *The Penguin Dictionary of Philosophy*, Harmondsworth: Penguin Books.

Morse, Ronald A. (1990) *Yanagita Kunio and the Folklore Movement: The Search for Japan's National Character and Distinctiveness*, New York: Garland Publishers.

Nishikawa, Nagao (1992) *Kokkyô no Koekata* (Beyond National Boundaries), Tokyo: Chikuma Shobô.

Oka, Masao (1979) *Ijin Sonota* (Strangers and Others), Tokyo: Gensôsha.

Sano, Kenji (1998) "Hikaku Kenkyû" (Comparative Study), in Ajio Fukuta (ed.), *Minzokugaku no Hôhô* (Methods in Folkloristics), Tokyo: Yûzankaku.

Sapir, Edward (1949) *Selected Writings of Edward Sapir in Language, Culture, and Personality*, Berkeley, CA: University of California Press.

Suzuki, Daisetz T. (1940) *Zen to Nihon Bunka* (Zen and Japanese Culture), Tokyo: Iwanami Shoten.

Trask, Haunani-Kay (1999) *From a Native Daughter: Colonialism and Sovereignty in Hawai'i* (revised ed.), Honolulu, HI: University of Hawai'i Press.

Tsurumi, Kazuko (1975) "Yanagita Kunio's work as a model of endogenous development," *Japan Quarterly*, 22(3).

Yamamoto, Matori (1997) "Samoa-jin no Sekushuariti Ronsô to Bunka-teki Jigazô" (The Debate on Samoan Sexuality and Cultural Self-Portraits), in Shinji Yamashita and Matori Yamamoto (eds), *Shokuminchi-shugi to Bunka* (Colonialism and Culture), Tokyo: Shinyôsha.

Yanagita, Kunio (1957) *Japanese Manners and Customs in the Meiji Era* (translated and adapted by Charles S. Terry), Tokyo: Ôbunsha.

—— (1964) "Hikaku Minzokugaku no Mondai" (Problems in Comparative Folkloristics), in *Teihon Yanagita Kunio-shû* (The Works of Kunio Yanagita, Standard Edition), Volume 30, Tokyo: Chikuma Shobô.

—— (1970) *About Our Ancestors* (translated by Fanny H. Mayer and Yasuyo Ishikawa), Tokyo: Japan Society for the Promotion of Science.

—— (1972) *Japanese Folk Tales* (translated by Fanny H. Mayer), Taipei: Orient Cultural Service.

—— (1975) *The Legends of Tôno* (translated with an introduction by Ronald A. Morse), Tokyo: Japan Foundation.

—— (1998a) *Seinen to Gakumon* (Youth and Scholarship), in Yanagita Kunio (ed.), *Yanagita Kunio Zenshû* (The Complete Works of Kunio Yanagita), Volume 4, Tokyo: Chikuma Shobô (Orig. 1928).

—— (1998b) *Minkan Denshôron* (The Science of Popular Tradition), in Yanagita Kunio (ed.), *Yanagita Kunio Zenshû* (The Complete Works of Kunio Yanagita), Volume 8, Tokyo: Chikuma Shobô (Orig. 1934).

—— (1998c) *Kyôdo Seikatsu no Kenkyûhô* (Methods in the Study of Community Life), in Yanagita Kunio (ed.), *Yanagita Kunio Zenshû* (The Complete Works of Kunio Yanagita), Volume 8, Tokyo: Chikuma Shobô (Orig. 1935).

Yanagita, Kunio, Shinobu Orikuchi, and Eiichiro Ishida (1965) "*Minzokugaku kara Minzokugaku e*" (From Folkloristics to Ethnology), in Yanagita Kunio (ed.), *Minzokugaku ni tsuite* (On Folkloristics), Tokyo: Chikuma Shobô.

6 Korean anthropology

A search for new paradigms

Okpyo Moon

Introduction

Anthropology as an imported discipline has a relatively short history in Korea. Its major academic body in the country, the *Korean Society for Cultural Anthropology*, celebrated its fortieth anniversary in 1998 and its first department was established in 1961 at Seoul National University. After some 40 years of history, however, there are still only nine university departments teaching the subject (five as independent degree courses and four as joint courses with archeology), and one graduate course offering master and doctoral degrees in cultural anthropology. Compared with related disciplines such as sociology whose first department was established in 1946 yet now has 39 departments with independent degree courses, or political science with 55 departments throughout the country,[1] we may note that the growth of anthropology has been extremely limited in Korea. While it is true that university politics often reflect power relations other than those of a more academic nature, we can hardly deny that the present institutional status of anthropology indicates the obvious fact that the subject has failed to gain its due recognition in the intellectual world in Korea.

The apparent failure of Korean anthropology to establish its identity and to have its voice heard may be partly understood as a consequence of the recent historical circumstances of the country. It is the study of culture that has long provided a basis for the identity of anthropology. Culture is conventionally conceived as a way of life that groups of people residing within a specific locality share. This varies in regions, tribes, or nations, and it has been expected that anthropologists point out these differences. Anthropology has, therefore, been known mainly for its study of other cultures. In Korea, however, the tradition of on-site fieldwork in other cultures had not been established for various political and economic reasons; the main body of anthropological work has been done on Korean society itself. It is only since the 1980s that we find sporadic attempts by Korean anthropologists to study other cultures (Moon Okpyo 1997a).

When dealing with their own society, anthropologists largely concentrated on illuminating the nature of traditional culture. The emphasis upon the study of traditional culture, it seems, provided Korean anthropology with a way of distinguishing itself from other areas of social science that dealt mostly with contemporary phenomena. "Traditional culture," conceptualized as something preserved in rural communities not yet exposed to the drastic alterations of urbanization and industrialization, was often approached as being isolated, without much consideration of the outside forces impinging upon it. The popularity of such topics as the kinship system or shamanism among the first-generation Korean anthropologists reflects the efforts to demonstrate the uniqueness of "Korean culture."

The preference of earlier Korean anthropologists to portray traditional culture as a closed system embedded in the lives of local communities, however, soon proved to be detrimental to dealing with more urgent issues in a rapidly changing society like Korea. In the political turmoil of the immediate post-liberation years (since 1945) and in the devastation of Korean War (1950–3), for instance, the most urgent concerns of social scientists seemed to be economic issues, such as the elimination of absolute poverty or political issues such as the ideological opposition that was causing constant instability within the country. With the industrialization and rapid economic development from the 1960s to the 1980s, worsening social inequality and political oppression became the issues that occupied most social scientists in the country. In such an atmosphere, the culture or nature of the human being, the subject that anthropology is known to profess, could barely draw anyone's attention. During that time, as demonstrated in their growth at academic institutions, the political sciences, economics, and sociology were regarded as the major areas that provided knowledge for the people trying to grasp the nature of and adjusting to their rapidly changing circumstances. Although various ethnographic attempts had been made to take into account the power relations and history within the context of their subjects' lives, dealing mostly with micro-situations, anthropology was in general unable to satisfy the people's need for grand theories or prescriptions.

Several changes in Korean society recently, however, seem to promise a new consideration for the relevance of anthropological knowledge. The first of these is related to what may be termed as an indigenization movement in Korean academia. The movement started in the 1970s, with the increasing influx of Western scholarship and was heightened in the general mood of anti-foreign power and nationalism of the 1980s. More recently, the move is being reassessed with rising skepticism concerning grand theories that claim universal validity across time and space. Many social scientists in Korea have begun to feel the need to develop indigenous theories rooted in the social, cultural, and historical realities of Korea itself and to avoid the uncritical reception of foreign theories. Anthropology, which has always emphasized the description of the actual world of daily life from a native point of view, may have something to offer with regard to these efforts. The fact that anthropological studies have largely concentrated upon detailed analyses of local reactions to macro processes may also be taken into account in this consideration.

Second, another area for anthropological contribution can be found in relation to the boom of "area studies" in Korea. With the relative growth and expansion of the Korean political and economic power, opportunities for inter-cultural contact have increased substantially. Unlike in other advanced countries where area studies began much earlier after the Second World War, in Korea an institutional basis for providing contemporary information about other societies and cultures was almost non-existent until quite later on. It was only after the 1988 Seoul Olympics that institutions for training area specialists began to be established at the university level. The 1990s saw a dramatic increase in these institutions and some began to employ anthropologists. It is true that, even in this area, the need for cultural understanding has always been felt much later than that for gathering immediate information on political and economic matters. In the long run, however, we may expect a significant contribution to this new development from anthropologists, who usually have long-term experience in the cultures they specialize in, as well as a considerable proficiency in the language concerned.

Finally, a new relevance of anthropology may be found in relation to the growing need for constructing identity in the multipolar, globalized, postcolonial situation in which all of us now live (Moore 1996). Increases in the movements of people, commodities, information, technology, etc., that characterize modern society make it increasingly difficult to assume culture as being something coherent and integrated that is bounded by specific locality. In the contemporary cultural situation, it is often possible that those sharing the same space (say, parents and children, males and females, etc.) may live in distant worlds to each other. Such a situation raises problems in the study of culture. With the growing perception that there can be multi-voices within what used to be considered a coherent and unified system, that is, culture, it becomes problematic to represent a culture with a single (dominant) voice. What becomes more important is to, instead, demonstrate the relationships between the sub-cultural communities that comprise one culture. Similarly, under the circumstances, culture or identity can better be described not as a shared, super-organic entity or amalgam of specific elements of a static nature but as a process of construction. It stands to reason then, that anthropologists are perhaps better equipped than others for studying these processes.

After a brief review of the backgrounds for major paradigm shifts in the history of Korean anthropology, I will discuss in more detail about the possibilities for a new relevance of anthropological knowledge. What will be ultimately attempted is a search for an identity for anthropology as an independent discipline in the academic milieu of contemporary Korea.

Anthropology as studies of traditional culture

The earliest attempt to approach traditional Korean culture was made mainly by the folklorists. In fact, if we include works in this category in the history of anthropology, it may reach back much further to the colonial period (1910–45) and even to the late Chosôn period (1392–1910). The search for Korean identity born among the scholars of the School of Practical Learning (*sirhak*) of the eighteenth century was inherited during the colonial period by nationalist scholars in the form of Korean Studies or the Koreanology Movement (*Chosônhak undong*) of the 1930s and 1940s.[2]

One of the adherents of the Korean Studies Movement was An Chaehong (1891–1965), who defined Korean Studies as the "systematized knowledge constructed from studies of things unique to Korea, characteristics of Korean culture, and distinctive traditions of Korea" (Chôn Kwan-u 1974: 52). Although the major concern of these earlier Koreanology scholars was the discovery of "Korean-ness" in rather metaphysical forms,[3] some of their works contain abundant materials in the presently important fields of folklore studies, for example, myths, shamanism, folk tales, customs, and so forth. In fact, history, classics, literature, and folklore were the major fields of Korean Studies of this period although these fields were not clearly differentiated.

In the late 1930s and early 1940s, we find more studies about Korean traditional culture by such folklorists as Song Sôkha and Son Chint'ae who participated in the new Society for Korean Studies called *Chindanhakhoe* founded in 1934 (Yu Kisôn 1990). The Society mostly consisted of scholars trained either at *Keijo* Imperial University or in Japan, who occupied a somewhat different position in the intellectual world of colonial Korea. In contrast to the rather uncompromising nationalism of the earlier period, some historians labeled them as neo-nationalists. Their studies of Korean history, literature, and folklore were more concerned with scientism and positivism than with national identity or cultural superiority (Yi Kibaek 1972; Kim Chôngbae 1979; Nam Kûn-u 2000, 2002). It is true that such terms as scientism and positivism were often used to avoid political and ideological commitment in the colonial situation.[4] In the midst of indiscriminate oppression and censorship toward the end of the colonial period, it became indeed much more difficult to deal with politically sensitive issues. It is perhaps due to this repressive political atmosphere that we find an increasing emphasis on history in the folklore studies of this period. For instance, if specific folklore items were studied as elements to explain a more holistic concept of culture, national character, or "mind" in the earlier studies, the main focus was now placed upon their origins, history, and typology without much consideration for the social and political contexts in which they were practiced. This unfortunate turn in the tradition of Korean folklore studies continued into the 1950s and, to a larger extent, until today.

Political implications aside, however, we may trace some connection between the preoccupations with traditional culture found among earlier generation Korean anthropologists and the folklore studies of the colonial period. In fact, it was mostly folklorists who first formed an anthropological association in Korea in 1946.[5] It was also this folkloristic tradition that dominated the Korean Society for Cultural Anthropology (*Han'guk Munhwa Illyuhakhoe*) when it was first established in 1958. Until the 1960s, therefore, anthropology and folklore studies were not clearly differentiated. The main body of the studies by members of Korean Society for Cultural Anthropology was carried out in relation to such topics as shamanism, the folk belief system, folk games, legends, myths, seasonal festivals, and rituals centered on the traditional agricultural cycle of village life, etc.

While dealing with the same subjects, these folklore-oriented scholars differed in their approaches to traditional culture from their later, more sociologically oriented colleagues, in that folklorists approached their subjects largely as residual customs. Reconstruction of models from often-obsolete customs, relying on the memory skills of the elderly, and meticulous recordings were heavily emphasized. From the viewpoint of later, more sociologically oriented critics, these studies "de-contextualized" their subjects by concentrating upon description and classification of folk customs *per se* without providing an analysis or interpretation of their meanings to the lives of the people. The culmination of this type of folklorist domination of the studies of traditional culture in Korean anthropology can be found in the Nationwide Survey of Folk Customs (*Chôn'guk minsok chonghap chosa*) carried out by the Korean Society for Cultural Anthropology.[6]

Anthropology as community studies: 1960s and 1970s

Conscious efforts to differentiate anthropology proper from this folklorist domination began to emerge in the early 1970s. The 1970s were a period in Korea of the expansion of universities and when disciplinary identities were reclaimed. Some anthropologists began to feel uneasy about the situation of anthropology being more or less identified with folklore studies. They claimed that anthropology should be classified as a field in the social sciences and asserted breaking away from the humanistic tradition of earlier folklore studies. Among the folklorists themselves, there were two different factions. One group emphasized the relatedness between anthropology and folklore studies and recommended that folklore studies remain as a sub-field of anthropology by trying to adopt anthropological perspectives and methodologies. Others, however, argued that folklore studies should claim its own independent disciplinary identity by divorcing itself from anthropology and from the Korean Society for Cultural Anthropology to which most of them belonged at the time.

Those who maintained the former position were, in fact, the older generation folklorists who were mostly trained during the colonial period and had some knowledge about how anthropology was practiced in the West. It was this group who voted for the designation of "Anthropological Society" instead of "Folklore Society" when they first gathered and formed an academic society after the War.[7] Despite these elements, however, institutional separation between the two subjects gradually began and folklorists' participation in the Korean Society for Cultural Anthropology notably decreased after the mid-1970s. In the long run, this unfortunate outcome was brought about mainly as a result of anthropologists' frustration about the so-called "butterfly-collecting" style folklore studies that often lacked any theoretical perspective. The conflict and antagonism between the two disciplines and the confusion surrounding their identities were finally concluded when the Department of Anthropology at Seoul National University, which started as a joint degree course with archeology in 1961, was separated from the latter and joined the College of Social Sciences as an independent department in 1975.

Along with these developments, there was a major shift in the study of traditional culture in the late 1960s and 1970s. The transformation was from the type centered on folklore studies to a more anthropological type of community studies. Village ethnography depicting the lives of people and the inter-connectedness of social institutions has indeed been a clear feature distinguishing anthropology from folklore studies since the 1960s. The concept of traditional culture as folk customs was replaced with a system of social institutions, and many detailed descriptions and analyses of traditional institutions were produced during this period. Unlike the case of precedent folklore studies, the studies of this latter type were characterized by relatively longer-term fieldwork within a particular community. They both shared, however, a common interest in clarifying unique aspects of Korean traditional culture.

Perhaps, the most popular topics in anthropological studies during this period were kinship and family structure. It seems that many scholars assumed that kinship systems were an area in which the distinctiveness of Korean traditional culture can be clearly understood. A detailed ethnography of a traditional upper-class lineage village published in 1964 by Kim Taekkyu can be considered a pioneering example in this area (Kim Taekkyu 1964). Subsequently, there have been numerous studies published with specific focus on such related areas as family, kinship, lineage, and marriage relations. Indeed, both in depth and scope, kinship studies are the area where Korean anthropology has made the most substantial contribution.[8] Yet, while these contributions clarifying characteristic features of Korean social structure should be fully acclaimed, many anthropological studies on kinship during this period failed to provide a wider analytical perspective. For instance, while family structure, inheritance patterns, lineage organizations, and practices of ancestor worship were described and analyzed in great detail with regard to specific localities, not many attempts were made to explain why these practices differed with region and class, and what these differences meant.

Similarly, few attempts have been made to interpret the role of kinship in contemporary social, political, and economic contexts. Beyond being a traditional institution that is losing importance, kinship may also be an active agency in mediating state power and private authority, as a ground for allegiance at local level politics, or as a basis for identity, in a modern urban context. Its importance seems to be particularly notable in Korea, where recently there has been a resurgent movement in lineage ideology and ancestor worship (Kim Kwang-ôk 1992, 1994a; Kim Ilch'ôl *et al.* 1998). These phenomena indicate the continuing importance of family and kinship ideologies in contemporary Korean society and thus need to be further investigated and theoretically accounted for by anthropologists.

In the 1970s and 1980s, we also find various attempts to theorize basic principles that govern Korean traditional culture. Kang Shinpyo (1974), for instance, put forward a dyadic model for conceptualizing Korean cognitive structure. Adopting Levi-Straussian structuralist ideas, Kang argued that reality is a manifestation of underlying cultural principles and, in case of Korean culture, those underlying principles can be understood as "dyadic cognitive structures" (*taedaejôk injugujo*). According to him, one may discern a singular system of cultural grammar underlying all Korean behavior whether it is in politics, economics, religion, art, or elsewhere. Kang's unique contribution in developing theories concerning Korean culture is not in his theoretical scheme itself, however, but in his continuous efforts to substantiate his argument by providing numerous examples at various levels of Korean behavior (Kang Shinpyo 1974, 1980, 1985, etc.).

Others argued that reciprocity is the basic principle by which Korean behavior can be best understood and explained (Yi Mun'ung 1977; Kim Chuhi 1981; Chôn Kyông-su 1984). Kim Chuhi, for instance, elaborated on the basic relational pattern underlying the institution of reciprocal labor exchange (*p'umasi*) widely reported in traditional agricultural communities and extended it as a general explanatory tool to all types of social relationships found in Korean society. She argued that the principle of reciprocity could be used to explain all kinds of relationships found in Korean society, living or dead. The relationships may include among the living those of parents and children, kin, friends and neighbors, and those between dead ancestors and their descendants in Confucian ancestor worship, between shamans and their clients in shamanic rituals, or between clergymen and their congregation in Christian churches (Kim Chuhi 1981, 1991). An interesting element of her conceptualization of reciprocity was that she included psychological dimensions in her scheme and maintained that people were impelled to reciprocate in order to regain emotional balance.

One may enumerate many other attempts made by anthropologists of this period to discover and theorize distinctive features of Korean traditional culture. The difference between them and earlier folklorists was the fact that their works were based on long-term anthropological fieldwork and their arguments were substantiated by detailed ethnographic descriptions. The validity of individual claims aside, what was characteristic of many of these studies was their implicit assumption of the monolithic nature of Korean culture. It was often assumed that culture is something shared and agreed upon, and not much attention was given to the possibility for sub-cultural differences between regions, classes, and gender, or to the possibility of conflicts and clashes among them. This may be partly the result of the village study attitude that purports "what one finds in such-and-such village is representative of Korean culture." The fact that many of these studies were conducted as preparations for a doctoral dissertation at a foreign university may have contributed toward this tendency in that their audiences were mostly foreigners who were not familiar with the diversity in Korean culture and history.

Even when heterogeneous elements were admitted, they were often presented in a simple juxtaposition without any systematic attempt to analyze how these contrasting elements interacted with each other. A clear example of such an attitude can be found in the oft-adopted dualistic model of Korean culture such as Confucianism/shamanism, hierarchical/egalitarian principles, and lineage/non-lineage villages, etc. Unlike the usual practices in anthropological studies of other cultures that mostly deal with the natives, the ruled, the folk, and the peasants as opposed to the ruling class, in Korea, anthropological studies of traditional culture were often biased toward the elite culture. The studies of the Confucian tradition of *yangban* (literati-official class) lineage villages provided an apt means toward this end.

The studies of non-lineage villages or shamanic traditions, on the other hand, were juxtaposed with the Confucian elite tradition as representing the commoners' tradition with the assumption that the commoners were less exposed to Confucian influence. The topic of shamanism, for instance, has always occupied an important position in Korean studies, in general. It has not been considered simply as a belief system adhered to by a few, but more often as something that embodies the essence of purely native, non-alien elements in Korean culture transmitted from the primitive past (Ch'oe Kilsông 1978; Cho Hûng'yun 1983; Chang Chugûn 1986, etc.). Under these dualistic perspectives, Korean villages were classified into two categories, the lineage villages of the *yangban* class and the non-lineage villages of the commoners. These two types of villages were then characterized by hierarchical, authoritarian, group-oriented patterns of human relationships on the one hand and democratic, egalitarian, individualistic ones on the other (Yi Mangap 1973; Ch'oe Shindôk 1982; Yi Kwanggyu 1986, etc.). Confucian and shamanic traditions were divided on the similar line as representing different sectors of the Korean population.

Such typological approaches, however, tend to blind us from seeing the internal differentiation within the same class whether it be *yangban* or commoners. They also prevent us from seeing the role of the individual actor in the social or cultural system by assuming individual behavior, which is determined by cultural tradition automatically dictated by class. The fact that those who belonged to the elite class in the traditional estate system do not necessarily occupy an elite position in the modern class system further weakens the basis of cultural typologies and determinism. In other words, one may say that anthropological treatment of sub-cultural diversities needs to proceed beyond simply recognizing and juxtaposing them to an analysis of how individual actors select and manipulate the diverse cultural resources available to them as social, economic, and political strategies in the modern context.[9]

Political economic anthropology in the 1980s

Since the late 1970s, a new trend emerged in Korean anthropology. The emphasis shifted from the description of cultural tradition as a static entity to an analysis of social and cultural changes in a modern context. The works of Han Sangbok in the area of economic and applied anthropology may be considered as the leading examples of this new trend. Han Sangbok was, in fact, the very figure who actively initiated in the early 1970s the previously mentioned separation of anthropology from folkloristic tradition. His works and those of his followers in the Department of Anthropology at Seoul National University greatly contributed toward establishing a distinctly sociological tradition that subsequently characterized Korean anthropology for about a decade or so (Kim Kwang-ôk 1987: 59).

One may say that the attempts to discover prototypes, underlying structures, key cultural principles, and the like that were previously discussed all share in common a presupposition of the a priori autonomy of culture and thereby present a very limited view concerning control of human actors over culture.

In other words, with a view of seeing all cultural phenomena as the mechanical manifestation of underlying principles, it is difficult to explain cultural change or the constructive power of human actors in producing culture. The approaches of Han Sangbok and his disciples drastically differed in type of view, in that they turned their eyes from culture and folklore to social institution and economic condition as being the major determinants of human behavior. A comparative study of three fishing villages by Han (1977), for instance, revealed how the functions of social and cultural institutions might differ with ecological conditions and the nature of economic activities.

His major concern was in understanding the nature of the changes occurring in the cultural traditions of Korea which, he sees, had mostly been established during the late Chosôn period (Han Sangbok 1980b, 1985). To him and to those who followed a similar line in the late 1970s and early 1980s, culture was not a given cognitive structure or psychological disposition but something that was determined by external conditions, material bases, economic opportunities, technological development, and availability of resources. They also took the view that significant changes had occurred in Korean society as a result of colonization and incorporation into the world economy and attempted to show how these factors had affected the Korean way of life. This shift in interest may in part reflect the search for relevance of anthropological knowledge in the explanation of fundamental changes that Korean society underwent in the 1970s and 1980s.

Unlike in the village ethnographies of the earlier period in which villages were approached mostly as self-sufficient microcosms that preserved traditional culture, the interests shifted to the complicated process by which village communities were connected to broader society, state, market, and the world. Moreover, rather than focusing on the elite class subculture, anthropologists were now more interested in the lives of groups such as rural farm families, the urban poor, and the newly emerging working class. The sites for fieldwork of Korean anthropologists were accordingly diversified. While village community studies predominated during the 1960s and 1970s, an increasing number of anthropologists now studied urban slum communities (Pak Kyeyông 1984; Kim Ûnshil 1984), construction sites (Hwang Ikju 1985), market places (Kim Uyông 1984), and so on.

Indeed, the major interests of those who did graduate work at Seoul National University during the 1980s were to understand the nature of social structural factors impinging upon the lives of those in agrarian or urban sectors of industrializing Korea.[10] Widely adopted were theoretical concepts of social formation, articulations of modes of production, and dependency theories that had been developed in the French Marxist School or in the School of Anglo-American political economic anthropology of the 1960s and 1970s. The 1980s were a period when capitalist penetration and social inequality were major concerns of the Korean social sciences in general; anthropology closely shared these concerns. In this regard, therefore, we may say that it was also the period when the interactions between anthropology and other fields of social sciences such as sociology, economics, and political science were most active.

The emphasis upon "material base" being a definitive factor of the human condition noted in the Korean anthropology of the 1980s may be understood as a frustrated reaction against the anthropological practices of the previous genera-tion. Both the folklore-oriented studies and the community studies of the 1970s pursued uniqueness of culture as being the major explanatory factor for diversity in the way of life. But, such studies largely neglected the material conditions in which the uniqueness was created. In the political economic anthropology of the 1980s, on the other hand, one finds a dangerous disregard of culture. This gener-ation of anthropologists preferred seemingly more concrete concepts such as socio-economic conditions, ideology, power relations, capitalists, and the assem-bly line as explanatory tools and tended to avoid the ambiguity and vagueness inherent in the concept of culture (Kim Kwang-ôk 1995: 83).

Perhaps as a reaction against the cultural determinism implicit in the studies of the previous generation, Korean anthropology of this period was heavily biased toward social structural determinism and again tended to lose sight of the human actors. This is dangerous, however, because it deprives anthropology of its very basis for identity. The fact is that not only rationality but also belief systems, or the general worldview, that underlie political, economic, and social behavior, were often overlooked. Consequently, it seemed that Korean anthropology, freed from the dominance of folklore studies, had become a branch of sociology.

Changing concept of culture: challenges in the 1990s

It is often said that we live in a world that is completely different from the one we inhabited only a few decades ago. The post-structuralist, post-modernist concep-tion of the world as "de-centered, fragmented, compressed, flexible, and refrac-tive" quickly affected Korean academia, and toward the end of 1980s and into the 1990s, culture suddenly emerged as the concern of everyone. Culture-related articles filled the pages of major newspapers and books with the word "culture" in the title superseding those with the terms "social" or "political-economic" as best sellers in social sciences. "Sociology of culture" emerged as a popular major among sociologists and academic societies for cultural policies (*Munhwa Chôngch'aek Hakhoe* 1995) and cultural economics (*Munhwa Kyôngje Hakhoe* 1997) were formed. The term, culture (Korean: *munhwa*), indeed, seems to have become the key word in almost all academic disciplines in Korea and anthropologists can no longer claim a monopoly of its study.

A considerable dissimilitude can be noted, however, between the conventional anthropological understanding of culture and what is conveyed by the term in this new popularization. In the latter, culture more often means concepts such as pref-erences, images, styles, consumer tastes, leisure, and art, but not a way of life or a way of thinking in its totality that is taken to distinguish a group of people residing in a specific locality from others. Nor is it something that can be grasped in long-term fieldwork in a small community as an integrated totality. Instead, it is often understood as fragmentary and thus approached as something that can be understood through subjective and impressionistic experiences in contemporary culture studies without much reference to the works accumulated in anthropology. Due to these differences in understanding and the resultant suspicion, there exists some tension between those in cultural studies and anthropologists. And, as elsewhere in the world, Korean anthropology is facing yet another challenge to deal with these changing circumstances: to reinvent the purpose of study and methodologies that may guarantee it an independent identity (Moon Okpyo 1995).

Into the 1990s, therefore, we note various efforts on the part of Korean anthropologists responding to these changing circumstances. First, there appeared a growing perception that culture no longer exists as something that functions within a bounded locality but as something that is being constructed, consciously manipulated, and politically transacted. Second, culture appears as something that is produced, performed, and consumed as a commodity in the context of tourism or otherwise. The subjects of MA theses submitted to Korean departments of anthropology clearly demonstrate these shifts in interests reflecting the redefinition of the concept of culture.[11]

Perhaps the most notable shift is in the conscious effort made on the part of anthropologists to recover the culture neglected in the studies of the 1980s that had emphasized a political economic aspect. Now, anthropologists showed increased sensitivity to the role of culture in defining and mediating class relations or hegemonic processes rather than to the material basis of the power structure itself. Ch'ae Suhong (1991), for example, examined the process by which counter ideologies were formed and emanated among shop floor workers through performance art. Ch'oe Horim (1993) and Chin P'ilsu (1994) explored the process by which power structures and authority systems were produced and reproduced through cultural means at the assembly line. Other studies dealt with how company culture is constructed and utilized as resources for creating belongingness and identity among workers (Chang Chông'a 1995; Chang Hojun 1995).

The emphasis upon process rather than system can be seen in the studies of traditional culture as well. In the studies of shamanism, for instance, the focus is now on its practice as cultural processes that occur in specific social, political, and economic contexts rather than on the reconstruction of its prototypes or on the detailed description of what was practiced in the past. Kim Sôngnye's study of Cheju Island shamanism, for instance, shows how shamanism is used as a ritual space to represent and transmit people's historical consciousness that is otherwise muted by official power (1989). Other studies of shamanism include that of Ch'oe Chôngmu (1987) in the contexts of cultural nationalism, and that of Kim Kwang-ôk (1994b) as resources for the politics of resistance. Kim Sôngnye (1992), in particular, has attempted to deconstruct discourses surrounding shamanism and its studies since the colonial period.

The second notable movement is partly related to the efforts of indigenization. These efforts were concentrated upon reformulating research topics as well as developing methodologies and theories appropriate to the features unique to Korea. It was increasingly felt, for instance, that those developed in the present-oriented anthropology of the West, and of the United States in particular, could not satisfactorily explain the historical depth of Korean reality. Unlike most societies studied by anthropologists in the West, Korea is a society with a long history in which state politics have played a central role in shaping people's lives and anthropologists began to realize that these aspects needed to be seriously taken into account as an indispensable element in any interpretation of Korean culture. There was also a growing awareness of the need to relate the phenomena observed in contemporary Korean society and culture to the unique historical experience of the Korean people of colonization, war, division of the country (and of families), North–South confrontation, military dictatorship, fierce student and civil movements for democratization, rapid industrialization and urbanization, not to mention the recent impact of globalization. These historical events have had strong repercussions on the lives of Korean people at both personal and collective levels, and anthropologists working on Korea very frequently come across invocations of those memories in their fieldwork situation.

How to incorporate and account for ordinary people's historical knowledge and consciousness in anthropological researches and writings has therefore become one of the major issues in Korean anthropology in the 1990s. Reflecting this new line of interest, a study group for historical anthropology was organized as a sub-group of the Korean Society for Cultural Anthropology in the early 1990s. Also, a group of young historians, anthropologists, and folklorists who are interested in folklore studies but dissatisfied with the butterfly collection style of the past generation established a separate Society for Historical Folklore. The members of the historical anthropology group have carried out research specifically focused on reconstructing popular memories and narratives that are often muted in the official historical discourse (Yun Taeklim 2003; Yu Ch'ôl-in *et al.* 2004). It was in the same context that the Korean Society for Cultural Anthropology organized a workshop on oral history in December 1999 at the Academy of Korean Studies with specific focus upon the possibility of methodological cooperation between anthropology and history. At the Academy of Korean Studies,[12] there appeared an interdisciplinary study that attempted to combine anthropological fieldwork and analyses of old documents in order to reconstruct the life-world of *yangban*, the ruling literati officials of the Chosôn period (Moon Okpyo 2004).

Another notable trend in Korean anthropology can be found in the growing interests in the study of subcultures. The growing urban middle class population (Moon Okpyo *et al.* 1992; Kim Ûnhi 1993, 1995), the urban poor (Cho Ûn and Cho Okla 1992), and youth culture (Yang Chaeyông 1994; Cho Hyejông 1996) were among the particularly focused areas during this time. More attention has been given to regional differences as well and various societies for the study of local culture have been formed (Ch'oe Hyôp 1994).

The interest in the issue of gender may also be considered as part of this development (Korean Society for Cultural Anthropology 1997; Yun Taeklim 2001; Moon Okpyo 2003). The 1990s have also witnessed a growth in the studies of the Koreans abroad and the phenomena of diaspora in general, also of other cultures. The studies of other cultures by Korean anthropologists, in particular, have notably increased since the late 1980s to include not only Japan and China but also many South and Southeast Asian, African, South American, and

European countries (Moon Okpyo 1997a). With the accumulation of the studies of other cultures, many attempts at cross-cultural comparisons have also appeared.

On the whole, the features that distinguish the Korean anthropology of the 1990s from that of the previous periods can be found in the diversification of research interests. Greater sensitivity toward class, gender, and regional differences within what is commonly designated as Korean culture, or toward a need for cross-cultural comparison with the growth of the studies of other cultures, has been mentioned already. Studies of ethnicity issues in relation to Koreans abroad, as well as to the foreign workers coming into Korea (Yi Chôngdôk 1993; Yi Ukjông 1994), or studies of consumption and lifestyles attempted by a few Korean anthropologists reflect efforts to deal with culture in globalized contexts (Moon Okpyo 1997b; Yi Jeong-duk 2002). Interests in post-colonial issues and cultural identity, in the relationship between the state and private lives, in the culture industry, in environmental discourses, in tourism, and culture change, to mention just a few, have been emerging as new areas of inquiry for Korean anthropologists.

Conclusion: the future of anthropological knowledge in Korea

In the globalized context of today's world, Korean culture exists as a hybrid of foreign and native elements, and it has often been questioned as to what all Koreans share. With the development of the culture industry supported by high technology and the free transfer of information, Korean teenagers have perhaps more to share with teenagers in other countries than with their parents or grandparents who live in the same geographical space with them. In their preferences, in behavior patterns, in values, and worldview, for instance, Korean youngsters may be more like the youth of Hong Kong, Japan, or the United States than elderly Koreans. A similar kind of cultural fragmentation seems to be occurring not only between generations or classes but also between urban and rural, male and female, and more than anything else, between North and South Koreans who have been separated from each other for more than half a century now.

The situation indicates that we can no longer assume a boundary between cultures as automatically given. Localities or nationalities no longer function as such and, it is becoming increasingly difficult to study culture by concepts and frameworks that have been familiar to us in conventional anthropology. In other words, it does not seem possible nowadays to designate any cultural elements as "Korean" or to list them as representatives of the lives of all those, or at least a dominant sector of those, who live in modern Korea. This does not mean, however, that the relevance of anthropological knowledge can no longer be claimed. The blurring of traditional cultural boundaries does not necessarily mean that they no longer exist, or that they have lost all unique characteristics. On the contrary, it means that new cultural boundaries are constantly being constructed and identities created. Moreover, we see in this process that cultural resources, both traditional and modern, are widely and openly selected, adopted, manipulated, or even consumed.

Acknowledgment

This chapter is reprinted with the permission of *The Review of Korean Studies*, Vol. 2. September 1999 (pp. 113–37).

Notes

1 This number includes departments of international politics and international relations.
2 It is said that the term *Chosônhak* was first adopted by Chŏng Inbo in 1931 in his *Chosôn Kosô Haeje* (Bibliographical Notes of Korean Classical Literature) and used widely until early 1940s, by scholars like Ch'oe Namsôn, Shin Ch'aeho, An Chaehong, and Mun Ilp'yông, etc.
3 Concepts like the "Korean spirit" (*Chosôn ûi ôl*) advocated by Chŏng Inbo or the "Korean mind" (*Chosônsim*) by Son Chint'ae are a few examples of this (Kim Kwang-ŏk 1998).
4 For more detailed analyses of the issue, see Kim Kwang-ôk (1998), Pak Hyônsu (1993, 1998), and Kim Kyông'il (1998).
5 The Society was known as Chosôn Anthropological Society (*Chosôn Illyuhakhoe*) at first but soon after renamed as the *Taehan* Anthropological Society and continued its activities until 1949 (Han Sangbok 1974, 1980a).
6 The Korean Ministry of Culture and Information subsidized the Survey that began in 1968 in South *Chôlla* Province and was completed in 1981, with the publication of the North and South *Hamkyông* Province edition.
7 There was in fact a short-lived Korean folklore society, *Chosôn Minsokhakhoe* (Korean Society for Folklore Studies) formed in 1933 (Han Sangbok 1974), but many folklorists later chose to adopt the title, "anthropological society," in the belief that folklore studies should ultimately develop into the wider discipline of anthropology. Among older generation folklorists who maintained this position were Kim Taekkyu 1985, Yi Tuhyôn, Chang Chugûn, Yim Sôkjae, and Ch'oe Kilsông. For more details, see Yi Tuhyôn, Chang Chugûn, and Yi Kwanggyu 1983.
8 See Ch'oe Chaesôk 1966, 1979, 1983; Yô Chungch'ôl 1980; Yu Myônggi 1977; Yi Kwanggyu 1977, 1980, 1991; Song Sônhee 1982; and Kim Yonghan 1989. The works listed here and later are not meant to be exhaustive, but include only those that I regard as typically representing the trends of the period discussed. Additionally, it should be noted that the studies of foreign anthropologists on Korean society are not covered here.
9 In the case of shamanism, for instance, recent studies show that it is often utilized by establishment and dissident movement leaders alike, to achieve their own political ends (Kim Kwang-ôk 1994b).
10 For a comprehensive list of MA and PhD dissertation topics submitted to the anthropology departments of Korean universities, see Kim Kwang-ôk (1987: 81–7).
11 There are three universities in Korea, Seoul National University, Yôngnam University, and Academy of Korean Studies that offer doctoral degrees in anthropology, but the number of dissertations completed is yet too small to be used as an indicator of the general trend of the direction of research.
12 The Academy of Korean Studies is a national organization, established in 1978 for the purpose of teaching and research in Korean Studies. Since the early 1980s, it has been engaged in collecting old documents dispersed throughout the country at individual lineages, Confucian Schools and Buddhist temples, and making them available for research in microfilm and on online spaces.

References

Ch'ae Suhong (1991) "Nodongja kyekûp inyôm hyôngsông kwajông e kwanhan yôn'gu" (A Study of Formation of Working Class Ideology), Unpublished MA Thesis, Seoul National University.

Chang Chông'a (1995) "Kiôp inyôm yupo wa suyong yangsang e kwanhan yôn'gu" (A Study of Dissemination and Accommodation of Corporate Ideology), Unpublished MA Thesis, Seoul National University.

Chang Chugûn (1986) *Han'guk minsok non'go* (Essays on Korean Folklore), Seoul: Kyemyôngsa.

Chang Hojun (1995) "Kongdongch'ejôk kiôp munhwa tamnon ûi hwalyong kwa kwagô ûi chaekusông" (Manipulation of Community-type Corporate Cultural Discourse and Reconstruction of the Past), Unpublished MA Thesis, Seoul National University.

Chin P'il-su (1994) "Pongje kiôp chag'ôpjang munhwa e kwanhan yôn'gu" (A Study of Shop Floor Culture of a Clothing Factory), Unpublished MA Thesis, Seoul National University.

Cho Hûng'yun (1983) *Han'guk ûi mu* (Korean Shamanism), Seoul: Chông'ûmsa.

Cho Hyejông (1994) *Tal-sikminji sidae chisig'in ûi kul ilki wa sam ilki* (Reading Books and Lives of the Intellectuals of the Post-colonial Age), Seoul: Tto hana ûi munhwa.

——(1996) *Hakkyo rûl kôbuhanûn ai, ai rûl kôbuhanûn hakkyo: Ipsi munje ûi chôngch'i kyôngjehak* (Children who Refuse Schools, Schools that Refuse Children: Political Economy of the Entrance Examination Issue), Seoul: Tto hana ûi munhwa.

Cho Ûn and Cho Okla (1992) *Toshi pinmin ûi sam kwa konggan: sadangdong chaekaebal chiyôk ûi hyônjang yôn'gu* (Life and Space of the Urban Poor: A Field Research of Sadangdong Redevelopment Area), South Korea, Seoul: Seoul National University Press.

Ch'oe Chaesôk (1966) *Han'guk kajok yôn'gu* (A Study of Korean Family), Seoul: Iljisa.

——(1979) *Chejudo ûi ch'injok chojik* (Kinship Organization of Cheju Island), Seoul: Iljisa.

——(1983) *Han'guk kajok chedosa yôn'gu* (A History of Korean Family System), Seoul: Iljisa.

Ch'oe Chôngmu (1987) "The competence of Korean Shamans as performers of folklore," Unpublished PhD Thesis, Indiana University.

Ch'oe Horim (1993) *Saengsanjik kwallija ûi chiwi wa yôkhal ûi pyônhwa e kwanhan yôn'gu* (A Study of the Change of the Status and Role of Production Management Workers), Unpublished MA Thesis, Seoul National University.

Ch'oe Hyôp (1994) "Honam munhwaron ûi mosaek" (On the Character of *Honam* Culture), *Han'guk munhwa illyuhak* (Korean Cultural Anthropology), 25: 29–45.

——(ed.) (1997) *Illyuhak kwa chiyôk yôn'gu* (Anthropology and Regional Studies), Seoul, Korea: Nanam Publishing House.

Ch'oe Kilsông (1978) *Han'guk musok ûi yôn'gu* (A Study of Korean Shamanism), Taegu: Hyôngsông Ch'ulpansa.

——(1986) *Han'guk ûi chosang sungbae* (Korean Ancestor Worship), Seoul: Yejônsa.

Ch'oe Shindôk (1982) *Han'guk nongch'on e kwanhan sahoe illyuhakjôk yôn'gu* (A Social Anthropological Study of Korean Villages), Seoul: Samildang.

Ch'ôn Kwan'u (1974) *Han'guksa ûi chaeinsik* (A Reconsideration of Korean History), Seoul: Iljogak.

Chôn Kyông-su (1984) *Reciprocity and Korean Society: An Ethnography of Hasami*, Seoul: Seoul National University Press.

Han Sangbok (1974) "Han'guk munhwa illyuhak ûi pansông kwa chihyang" (Reflection and Orientation of Korean Cultural Anthropology: The Field of Cultural Anthropology) *Han'guk munhwa illyuhak* (Korean Cultural Anthropology), 6: 213–17.

——(1977) *Korean Fishermen: Ecological Adaptation in Three Communities*, Seoul: Seoul National University Press.

——(1980a) "Illyuhak" (Anthropology) in *Mun'ye yôn'gam* (Yearbook of Literature and Art), Seoul: Munye chinhûng'wôn.

Han Sangbok (1980b) "Han'guk'in ûi kongdongch'e ûishik e kwanhan yôn'gu" (A Study of Community Consciousness of Koreans), in *Han'guk ûi sahoe wa munhwa* (Korean Society and Culture), Sôngnam: Academy of Korean Studies, 3: 141–84.

—— (1985) "Han'guk'in ûi saenghwal yangsik kwa sago bangsik" (Lifestyles and Modes of Thoughts of Koreans), in Han Sangbok (ed.), *Han'guk'in kwa han'guk munhwa: illyuhakjôk chôbkûn* (Koreans and Korean Culture: An Anthropological Approach), Seoul: Shimsôldang, pp. 292–300.

Hwang Ikju (1985) "Han'guk kônsôl'ôp ûi koyong kujo e kwanhan yôn'gu" (A Study of Employment Structure of Korean Construction Industry), Unpublished MA Thesis, Seoul National University.

Kang Shinpyo (1974) "Tong asea esô ûi han'guk munhwa" (Korean Culture in East Asia), *Han'guk munhwa illyuhak* (Korean Cultural Anthropology), 6: 191–4.

—— (1980) "Han'guk'in ûi chôntongjôk saenghwal yangsik ûi kujo e kwanhan shiron" (A Preliminary Study of Korean Traditional Way of Life), *Han'guk ûi sahoe wa munhwa* (Korean Society and Culture), Sôngnam: Academy of Korean Studies, 3: 231–316.

—— (ed.) (1985) *Han'guk munhwa yôn'gu* (Studies of Korean Culture), Seoul: Hyôn'amsa.

Kim Chông-bae (1979) "Shinminjokjuûi sagwan" (Neo-Nationalist History), *Munhak kwa chisông*, Spring(9–1): 37–50, Seoul: Munhak kwa Chisôngsa.

Kim Chuhi (1981) "*P'umasi*: patterns of interpersonal relationships in a Korean village," Unpublished PhD Thesis, Northwestern University.

—— (1991) *P'umasi wa chông ûi in'gan kwankye* (Interpersonal Relationships of Reciprocal Exchanges and Human Feelings), Seoul: Jipmundang.

Kim Ilch'ôl, Moon Okpyo, Kim Pildong, Song Jeong-ki, and Han Donyôn (1988) *Chongjok maûl ûi chônt'ong kwa pyônhwa* (Tradition and Change in a Lineage Village), Seoul: Paeksan.

Kim Keongil (Kim Kyông'il) (1998) "Intellectual context of Korean Studies in Colonial Korea," *The Review of Korean Studies*, 1(1): 53–75, Sôngnam: The Academy of Korean Studies.

Kim Kwang-ôk (1987) "Hankuk illyuhak ûi Pyôngka wa Chônmang" (Appraisal and Prospect of Korean Anthropology), *Hyônsang kwa insik*, 11(1): 53–89.

—— (1992) "Socio-political implications of the resurgence of ancestor worship in contemporary Korea," in Nakane Chie and Chien Chiao (eds), *Home Bound: Studies in East Asian Society*, Tokyo: Toyo Bunko, pp. 179–203.

—— (1994a) "Munhwa kongdongch'e wa chibang chôngch'i" (Cultural Community and Local Politics), *Han'guk munhwa illyuhak* (Korean Cultural Anthropology), 25: 116–82.

—— (1994b) "Ritual of resistance: the manipulation of shamanism in contemporary Korea," in C. Keyes, L. Kendall, and H. Hardacare (eds), *Asian Visions of Authority*, Honolulu, HI: University of Hawaii Press, pp. 195–219.

—— (1995) "Han'guk illyuhak ûi Pansông kwa Kwaje" (Reflections and Tasks of Korean Anthropology: Personal and Reflexive Appraisal), *Hyônsang kwa insik*, 19(2): 75–102.

—— (1998) "Iljesigi toch'ak chisig'in ûi minjok munhwa insik ûi tûl" (Concepts of National Culture among the Native Intellectuals under the Japanese Colonialism), *Pikyo Munhwa Yôn'gu* (Cross-cultural Studies), 4: 79–120.

Kim Sôngnye (1989) "Chronicles of violence, rituals of mourning: Cheju Shamanism in Korea," Unpublished PhD Thesis, University of Michigan.

—— (1992) "Musok chôngtong ûi tamnon punsôk" (Discourse Analysis of Shamanic Traditions), *Han'guk munhwa illyuhak* (Korean Cultural Anthropology), 22: 211–44.

Kim Taekkyu (1964) *Tongjok burak ûi saenghwal kujo yôn'gu* (A Study of Life Structure of a Lineage Village), Taegu: Ch'ônggu taehak ch'ulpanbu.

——(1985) *Han'guk nonggyông sesi ûi yôn'gu* (A Study of Yearly Agricultural Rites in Korea), Kyôngsan: Yôngnam University Press.

Kim Ûnhi (1993) "Il, kajok kûrigo sôngyôkhal ûi ûimi" (Meanings of Work, Family and Gender Roles) in Korean Society of Social History (eds), *Han'guk kûnhyôndai kajok ûi chaejomyông* (Reconsideration of Korean Modern Family), Seoul: Munhak kwa Chisôngsa.

——(1995) "Munhwajôk kwanyôm ch'egyerosô ûi kajok: Han'guk toshi chungsanch'ûng ûl chungshim ûro" (Family as Cultural Ideological System: With Reference to Korean Middle Class), *Han'kuk munhwa illyuhak* (Korean Cultural Anthropology), 27: 187–214.

Kim Ûn-shil (1984) "Han'guk toshi pin'gon ûi sônggyôk e kwanhan yôn'gu" (A Study of the Characteristics of Urban Poverty in Korea), Unpublished MA Thesis, Seoul National University.

Kim U-yông (1984) "Ch'ônggwamul tomae sijang chungmae in ûi kyôngje haengwi" (Economic Behavior of Middlemen in Fruit Wholesale Market), Unpublished MA Thesis, Seoul National University.

Kim Yonghan (1989) "A study of Korean lineage organization from a regional perspective: a comparison with Chinese system," Unpublished PhD Thesis, The State University of New Jersey Rutgers.

Korean Society for Cultural Anthropology (eds) (1997) *Sông, kajok kûrigo munhwa: Illyuhakjôk chôpgûn* (Gender, Family and Culture: Anthropological Approaches), Seoul: Chipmundang.

Moon Okpyo (1995) "Illyuhak, hyôndai munhwa punsôk, han'guk hak: ironjôk, pangbôpronjôk yôn'gye ûi kanûngsông" (Anthropology, Contemporary Culture Studies and Korean Studies: A possibility for theoretical and methodological communication), *Han'guk ûi sahoe wa munhwa* (Korean Society and Culture), Sôngnam: Academy of Korean Studies, 23: 49–84.

——(1997a) "Han'guk illyuhak ûi chiyôk yôn'gu tonghyang" (Trends of Area Studies in Korean Anthropology), in Ch'oe Hyôp (ed.), *Illyuhak kwa Chiyôk yôn'gu* (Anthropology and Regional Studies), Seoul: Nanam, pp. 89–128.

——(ed.) (1997b) *Han'guk'in ûi sobi wa yôga saenghwal* (Consumption and Leisure Life of Koreans), Sôngnam: Academy of Korean Studies Monograph Series: 97–9.

——(ed.) (2003) *Shinyôsông: Han'guk kwa ilbon ûi kûndae yôsôngsang* (New Women: Images of Modern Women in Korea and Japan), Seoul: Ch'ôngnyônsa.

——(ed.) (2004) *Chosôn yangban ûi saenghwal segye* (The Life-world of Korean Scholar Gentry), Seoul: Baeksan Press.

Moon Okpyo, Yim Pong-kil, Kim Kwang-ôk, Chôn Kyông-su, and Kim Pu-sông (1992) *Toshi chungsanch'ûng ûi saenghwal munhwa* (Lifeways of Urban Middle Class), Sôngnam: Academy of Korean Studies Monograph Series: 92(10).

Moore, Henrietta L. (ed.) (1996) *The Future of Anthropological Knowledge*, London: Routledge.

Nam Kûn-u (2000) "Shin minjokjuûi minsokhak chaego" (A Reconsideration of Methodologies of Neo-nationalist Folklore Studies), *Yôksa minsokhak* (Historical Folklore Study), 10: 147–72.

——(2002) "Chosôn minsokhak kwa sikminjuûi: Song Sôkha ûi munhwa minjokjuûi rûl chungsim ûro" (Korean Folklore Studies and Colonialism: With reference to the cultural nationalism of Song Sônkha), *Han'guk Munhwa Illyuhak* (Korean Cultural Anthropology), 35(2): 99–126.

Pak Hyônsu (1993) "Ilche ûi chosôn chosa e kwanhan yôn'gu" (The Survey Works on Korea by Imperial Japan), Unpublished PhD Thesis, Seoul National University.
——(1998) "Han'guk munhwa e taehan ilje ûi sigak" (Colonialism and the Japanese View of Korean Culture), *Pikyo Munhwa Yôn'gu* (Cross-cultural Studies), 4: 35–78.
Pak Kyeyông (1984) "Muhôga chôngch'akji chumin ûi kyôngje haengwi e kwanhan il koch'al" (A Study of Economic Activities of the Residents of an Unauthorized Urban Settlement), Unpublished MA Thesis, Seoul National University.
Song Sônhee (1982) "Kinship and lineage in Korean village society," Unpublished PhD Thesis, Indiana University.
Yang Chaeyông (1994) "Ch'ôngsonyôn chiptan ûi taejung munhwa suyong kwajông e kwanhan yôn'gu" (A Study of Popular Culture Receptions by Youth Groups), Unpublished MA Thesis, Seoul National University.
Yi Jeong-duk (Yi Chôngdôk) (1993) "Social order and contest in meanings and power: Black boycotts against Korean Shopkeepers in poor New York City neighborhoods," Unpublished PhD Thesis, City University of New York, USA.
——(2002) "Globalization and recent changes to daily life in the Republic of Korea," in James Lewis and Amadu Sasse (eds), *Korea and Globalization: Politics, Economy and Culture*, London: RoutledgeCurzon, pp. 10–35.
Yi Kibaek (1972) "Shin-minjokjuûi sagwan ron" (A Discussion on Neo-nationalist Historiography), *Munhak kwa chisông*, Seoul: Munhak kwa Chisôngsa, Autumn(3–3): 509–28.
Yi Kwanggyu (1977) *Han'guk kajok ûi sajôk bunsôk* (A Historical Study of Korean Family), Seoul: Iljisa.
——(1980) *Han'guk kajok ûi kujo bunsôk* (An Analysis of Korean Family Structure), Seoul: Iljisa.
——(1986) "Puraksaenghwal ûi taerip kwa chohwa rûl tonghan chilsô ûisik" (Order Consciousness through Opposition and Harmony in Village Life), *Han'guk ûi sahoe wa munhwa* (Korean Society and Culture), Academy of Korean Studies, 6: 181–212.
——(1991) *Han'guk ûi kajok kwa chongjok* (Korean Family and Lineage), Seoul: Minûmsa.
Yi Mangap (1973) *Han'guk nongch'on sahoe ûi kujo wa pyônhwa* (Structure and Change of Korean Rural Society), Seoul: Seoul National University Press.
Yi Mun'ung (1977) "Han'guk sahoe e issôsôui hohyesông ui myôtgaji ch'ukmyôn (Some aspects of Reciprocity in Korean Society)," *Chindanhakbo*, 43: 143–54.
Yi Tuhyôn, Chang Chugûn, and Yi Kwanggyu (1983) *Han'guk minsokhak kaesôl* (An Introduction to Korean Folklore Studies), Seoul: Hag'yônsa.
Yi Ukjông (1994) "Kungnae bangladesh nodongja tûl ûi saenghwal shiltae wa chôk'ûng chôllyak e kwanhan sarye yôn'gu" (A Case Study of Living Conditions and Adaptive Strategies of Bangladesh Workers in Korea), Unpublished MA Thesis, Seoul National University.
Yô Chungch'ôl (1980) "Ch'wirak kujo wa shinbun kujo" (Village Structure and Status Structure), *Han'guk ûi sahoe wa munhwa* (Korean Society and Culture), Sôngnam: The Academy of Korean Studies, 2: 97–154.
Yu Ch'ôl'in, Song Doyông, Kim Unhi, Oh Myông'sôk, Yun Taeklim, Yun Hyôngsuk, Han Kyông'ku, and Ham Hanhi (2004) *Illyuhak kwa chibang ûi yôksa: Sôsan saramdûl ûi sam kwa yôksa ûishik* (Anthropology and Local History: Life and Historical Consciousness in Sôsan), Seoul: Akanet.
Yu Kisôn (1990) "Namch'ang Son Chin-tae ûi 'tosokhak/minsohak' ûi sôngkyôk mit yôn'gu pangbôbnon e taehan koch'al" (A Study of the characteristics and methodology of Son Chin-tae's ethnography and folklore), Unpublished MA Thesis, Department of Anthropology, Seoul National University.

Yu Myôngki (1977) "Munjung ûi hyôngsông kwajông e kwanhan koch'al" (An Investigation on the Process of Lineage Formation), *Han'guk munhwa illyuhak* (Korean Cultural Anthropology), 9: 123–6.

Yun Taeklim (2001) *Han'guk ûi mosông* (Marternity in Korea), Seoul: Mirae illyôk yôn'guwôn.

——(2003) *Illyuhakja ûi Kwagô yôhaeng: han ppalgaeng'i maul ûi yôksa rûl ch'azasô* (An Anthropologist's Trip to the Past: In Search of the History of a Communist Village), Seoul: Yôksabipyôngsa.

Part IV
South Asia

7 'Indigenizing' anthropology in India

Problematics of negotiating an identity

Vineeta Sinha

Colonialism, anthropology and the 'native'

The seventeenth and eighteenth centuries saw increased contact between rapidly expanding 'West' and 'non-Western' societies, manifested especially in the form of colonial encounters. However, 'European'[1] interaction with the 'Orient' did not begin with colonialism, with sound evidence of much pre-colonial and non-hegemonic (J. Abu-Lughod 1989) interaction. This chapter explores a facet of this encounter through detailed analysis of a single empirical case. I demonstrate how pre-colonial interaction, colonialism and the discipline of anthropology crystallized both a geographical space (i.e. India as a legitimate culture area) and an intellectual space ('Indians' as exotic human others) for subsequent social scientific investigation. This recognition carries important consequences for contemporary efforts to indigenize anthropology in India.

For at least half a century, non-Western scholars have called for the liberation of the social sciences from colonial hegemonic influences. The need to divest both the conceptualization and practice of social science disciplines, of Eurocentric and orientalist biases has been the guiding rationale of this project. One recent variant of such desire is carried in the English word 'indigenization', which has over the last few decades found numerous proponents. The aspiration to build autonomous, indigenous social science traditions is not new, having been with us from the 1950s, culminating in efforts to localize, nativize, nationalize and indigenize received social science wisdom. The literature on 'indigenization' of the social sciences is complex and multi-dimensional. Without denying important internal differences, it would be fair to say that fundamentally the various voices have challenged the ideological, institutional, theoretical and methodological dominance in social science domains from the core academic and intellectual centres located largely in the West. Despite the prevalence of these ideas, it has been suggested that this challenge has not culminated in a coherent epistemological and theoretical agenda. There is indeed a multiplicity of voices and positions; I interpret this as empowering rather than as a failure as it means that the question of indigenization has not been deemed to have been settled once and for all by my predecessors, making it possible to add yet another voice. This remains a core reason for my continued engagement with issues within this domain.

A further impetus comes from approaching the subject as a 'liberating discourse' (S.F. Alatas 1993). Historically, the calls for 'academic independence' and overcoming the 'captive mind' (S.H. Alatas 1977) closely paralleled the push for political liberation from colonial rule carried in the Third World nationalist movements. The emergent scholarly work served to signal a conceptual, epistemological, methodological and above all a political critique of dominant concepts, categories and dichotomies of investigation used in mainstream social science traditions. The essentialist, homogeneous, reductionist, totalizing and monolithic renderings of the 'other' (largely marginal, colonial and subjugated peoples) typically produced in mainstream social science accounts was problematized and calls made to redress these. The beneficiaries of such a critique have been more than those interested in 'indigenizing' various social science disciplines. It is clear that the by now common-place critique of essentialist tendencies in 'European'/'Western' orientalist discourses about 'other' peoples and places, launched by feminist, post-colonialist, post-orientalist and deconstructionist theorists, was in a very serious way already anticipated and embedded in the discourse about 'decolonizing' the social sciences. Presumably, the various proponents of indigenization intended to generate a social science that avoids the essentialism, problematic reification and stereotypical tendencies inherent in 'mainstream' social science. I have chosen to explore these issues using the case of anthropology in India as it is not particularly problem-ridden or unique in its experience of attempting to 'indigenize' anthropology. Rather, I use the Indian material to accomplish these aims:

- To abstract and identify elements that typify indigenization efforts in Indian anthropology.
- To underscore the problematics inherent in indigenization agendas that are rooted in weak conceptual frameworks.

My argument about India and Indian anthropology is explicated in two steps. First, I demonstrate that the constitution of India's 'otherness' predates anthropological attempts to categorize India and Indians as relevant objects of anthropological inquiry. Ideas about India were in currency before both the colonial and the anthropological encounters between Europe and the subcontinent. Second, I draw connections between these pre-existing images and the development of anthropological studies in India, outlining the discourse surrounding efforts to create a specifically 'Indian' anthropology. These discussions reveal the complex and problematic ways in which 'native anthropologists' (Kuwayama 2003, 2004) have tried and continue to claim a separate agenda for Indian anthropology, premised upon a different, non-Western image of India. While the image of India as an exotic 'other' holds for Western constructions of anthropology, the dialectics of constituting India both as 'self' and 'other' characterize an attempt to craft an indigenous anthropology in India today.

Constitution of India's otherness

The terms 'India', 'Africa' and 'America'[2] and the images they conjured in the minds of Christian Europeans were as much constructions as was 'Europe' itself, arising out of lengthy colonial interactions between the representations of European imperial and local wielders of power in pluralistic, plurinational regions. Just as the meanings attached to the label 'Negro' changed dramatically after Atlantic slavery, and there were no 'Indians' in the Americas before Hispanic conquest, so also the 'Hindoostan' and 'Hindoos' that emerged after the British encounter were unlike the imaginations of other Europeans prior to this episode.

An analysis of the intellectual heritage of anthropology must be grounded in pre-existing European knowledge and debates about the Orient. Anthropology did not invent but has inherited the 'savage slot' with its various 'others' including natives and primitives (Trouillot 1991). In appropriating this slot as the epistemological and methodological foundation of their discipline, anthropologists have reconstituted and transformed it in critical ways. It was never a monolith in the first place. Over time anthropology has added new variants to this category.

The constitution of India's otherness was a complex historical process to which my brief treatment cannot do full justice. Clearly, images and evaluations of India, the land, its peoples and customs, changed greatly between the sixteenth and twentieth centuries. Neither is the process purely a concern with the past. The discovering and labelling of the other still goes on. My intentions are to demonstrate that (a) European[3] discussions of India have focused on its religion, language, law, state, political economy and social structure (Inden 1990); (b) such foci have led to the selection of specific traits that were, and continue to be, perceived as 'Indian' – Sanskrit, caste, Hinduism, rural and socially rigid; and (c) the association of these traits with India are perpetuated in scholarly accounts of India, including anthropological narratives.

The lead taken by Greek geographers, historians and philosophers is evident in the early contact between India and Greece. These contacts may have been facilitated by the development of land routes along India's north-eastern and, particularly, north-western borders (Kaul 1979). The Portuguese 'discovery' of the route around the Cape of Good Hope into the Indian Ocean (the Greeks' Erythraean Sea) and to India heralded a new phase in sea travel, maritime trade and sustained interaction between Europeans and Indians. Knowledge about Indian religions, languages (particularly Sanskrit), customs such as *sati*, caste, garb, eating habits (Thapar 1979: 19) and royal courts revealed India as a land of the fantastic and the fabulous. Ptolemy's geography and the *Periplus* of the Erythrean Sea provided significant geographical data on 'India' to primarily Christian audiences up to the 1500s (ibid.: 6). During the sixteenth century, increased Portuguese, Dutch, Italian and English presence redefined existing European images of India's territorial boundaries (Lach 1968: 340–1).

Clearly, the places described in these varied accounts as 'India'[4] are not the same as the geographical and socio-political entity known as India today. There does not seem to be a single territorial 'indigenous' label used to designate what is today called 'India'. Denotations such as *Aryavarta* (the country of the Aryans) and *Bharat*, the name of a mythic ancient King, have sometimes been applied by the inhabitants of India to this geographical entity. In medieval, renaissance and colonial accounts the words 'Hindoostan' and 'Indostan' are frequently used interchangeably with India. Thus, the very boundaries of territories within India today (not to mention the labelling of these as territories as India) were as much a construction by outsiders[5] as the social, cultural, religious and political descriptions of this land and its peoples.

Significantly, a Europe that imagined India was not itself a pre-existing entity. It was constructed simultaneously while 'inventing' India and other such groupings as an 'other'. Inden makes this point elegantly:

> I will argue that Euro-American Selves and Indian Others have not simply inter-acted as entities that remain fundamentally the same. They have dialectically constituted one another.
>
> (1990: 3)

The mould in which India was cast reflected European preoccupations in the seventeenth and eighteenth centuries more than it reflected an empirical reality. Europe's concern with emerging industrial capitalism and the growth of cities, the rise of bureaucracies, debates on reason and rationality, the romantic imagination, Christianity and religion, individualism, politics and statehood and equality profoundly influenced their debates about Asia and the East.

Notwithstanding the existence of published material on India in Europe through the sixteenth and seventeenth[6] centuries, Marshall (1970: 2–3) argues that 'wide-spread European discussion of India took place mostly in the second half of the 18th century', primarily from British perspectives. Much of this discussion centred on Indian religion and specifically on Hinduism and its relationship to caste and the Sanskrit language.[7]

The Indian debate in British circles engaged missionaries, travellers, traders and intellectual elites starting from about the eighteenth century. The administration of India as a Crown colony in 1858 created a need to make sense of India's location within the British Empire. Romantic renderings of India are captured in the imagination of a group of English civil servants who arrived around 1780, under the governorship of Warren Hastings. The most notable being Sir William Jones, whose interests in India included law, religion, language and literature amongst others. He served as a Supreme Court judge in 1783, learned Sanskrit and asserted that Greek, Latin and Sanskrit had common origins.[8] On Hinduism, he noted that 'the omnipresence, wisdom and goodness of God' was 'the basis of Indian philosophy' (Marshall 1970: 40). For him, the apparent eroticism of the *Bhagvat Purana* and *Gita Govinda*[9] was 'no proof of depravity in their morals' (ibid.: 41). Other English writers in the second half of the eighteenth century who portrayed Hinduism in a positive and favourable light include John Zephaniah Holwell, a surgeon who served in the East India Company in Bengal. He described Hinduism as belief in 'one God, eternal, omnific, omnipotent and omniscient'; the apparent polytheism was 'to be taken only in a figurative sense' (ibid.: 27). Charles Wilkins, who translated the *Bhagvad Gita*,[10] described Hindu commentators very positively. The later work of German Indologist Friedrich

Schlegel further exemplifies such romantic interpretations of India. According to Schlegel:

> this philosophy contains a multitude of the sublimest reflections on the separation from all earthly things, and on the union with the God-head; and there is no high conception in this department of metaphysics, unknown to the Hindoos.
>
> (1890: 160)

Mysticism and other-worldly concerns pervade descriptions of Indian philosophy, mentality and religion in these accounts. The work of missionaries and romantic Indologists[11] led to the definition of India as a society marked by extreme religiosity, structured hierarchically by caste and as a land of imagination. Other features attributed to India were its 'otherworldly' and non-rational orientation, an idea systematically emphasized by Max Muller,[12] who published his *The Sacred Books of the East* (1879) and *India: What it can Teach Us?* (1883). These endeavours to understand India reflect a process whereby the self also encounters and constructs itself through a discovery of an other. Interestingly, William Jones had planned to undertake the writing of *Britain Discovered*,[13] a project that would underscore the point that the discovery of India involved an effort '...to define both an Indian and a British identity' (Majeed 1990: 219). It however did not materialize.

Despite these positive evaluations, '...(British) opinion was beginning to harden against Hinduism' (Marshall 1970: 41) at the end of the eighteenth century. This attack against Hinduism was led in England by Evangelical Christians and social reformers. Charles Grant, writing from India about Hindus in 1785, says 'It is hardly possible to conceive any people more completely enchained than they are by their superstition.' William Wilberforce, the abolitionist hero, '...inferred that the natives of India, and more particularly the Brahmins, were sunk into the most abject ignorance and vice' (Marshall 1970: 42). By the early years of the nineteenth century, Hindus (and Indians) were presented as superstitious, primitive and idol-worshippers, and the British presence rationalized as one of civilizing the natives.

James Mill, a British philosopher and historian, in his *The History of British India* in 1858, analyses Indian society, about which William Thomas (in the Introduction to the 1975 edition) states:

> India became a field in which the philosopher's ethical theories and legal schemes could be put to the test.

Mill's concern in the *History* was less with constructing an image of India as such, and more with demonstrating what he considered to be universal philosophical truths.[14] He criticized Jones's romanticization of India and his celebration of the 'Indian imagination'. Mill associated the 'imagination' with conservatism and argued instead in favour of instrumental rationality as a rhetoric of reform in India (Majeed 1990).

From James Mill to Hegel, accounts of caste,[15] based on travellers' tales and missionaries' and administrators' reports, have made 'caste into the central pillar of their constructs' (Inden 1990: 82–4). In these treatises, all aspects of Indian social life were linked to castes. Caste was seen as an essential marker of social, religious, cultural, economic and racial aspects of Indian identity. It was further invoked by British and German scholars to explain India's intellectual degradation, vulnerability to conquest, the presence of a rigid social order, absence of individualism and her static, unchanging nature.

The social institution of caste was defined as peculiarly Indian, and tied inextricably to Hinduism,[16] such that attention to these two (defined negatively) was seen to be integral to understanding Indian civilization. The earlier reverential stance towards Indian customs, articulated by Warren Hastings in 1773, had undergone dramatic change by the middle of the nineteenth century, particularly after the Indian Sepoy Mutiny of 1857. By the turn of the twentieth century, India was perceived as predominantly Hindu – a distinct, backward, primitive cultural region, as opposed to the European civilization. The discourse on caste was further elaborated through German and British debates on the political economy of Europe and Asia. Scholars like Sir Henry Maine and Monier-Williams characterized India as a land of villages. Marx and Engels in their discussions of the Asiatic mode of production contributed indirectly to the discourse about Indian villages.

Marx depicted Indian villages as self-sufficient, static communities, lacking a free market, a state, private property and a competitive spirit (Ghosh 1984). The Indian village was declared to be a fundamental unit of analysis for India.

Collectively the indological, orientalist and colonial discourses have led to a particular essentialist construction of India, whose otherness was achieved through an equally essentialist definition of Europe or the West as the 'self'. A complex of uniquely defining features culminated into an exclusive definition: the existence of castes, varieties of Hinduism, an agrarian and primitive economy, patterns of kinship and social organization and the absence of distinctive national unity. India was what the West was not: rural, mystical and irrational, intensely religious, inegalitarian, oriented towards the collective rather than the individual, traditional, technologically backward and stateless.

Anthropology in India did not emerge in an intellectual vacuum. The boundaries of British discourse preceding institutionalization of the discipline in India have shaped anthropological studies about India in definite ways. Why, for instance, does talk about India even today inevitably bring to mind labels like 'Hindu', 'caste', 'villages' – which have assumed the status of 'foundational categories' (Mathur 2000) to mention just a few? Part of the answer lies in a specific construction of India up to the late nineteenth century and its accompanying discourse which forms the background against which non-Indian scholars initiated anthropology in India. Indian anthropologists are aware of this intellectual history in attempts to produce an Indian variant of this discipline. But this enterprise itself is fundamentally linked to the history of anthropology in India, to which we now turn.

Anthropology in India

Anthropological research in India, in the late nineteenth century, came on the heels of the imaginings and discourses just detailed. Studies of caste and social stratification, kinship, family and social organization, religious rituals, beliefs and institutions, customs and folklore, Indian music, dance and painting, village communities and tribes have preoccupied both non-Indian and Indian scholars well into the twentieth century.

A review of the Indian anthropological literature reveals a relatively 'straight-for-ward' and unproblematic account of the importation of the discipline to India and its subsequent development therein (Dube 1973; Mahapatra 1997). However, this history also recognizes and articulates colonial and imperialist links with anthropology, particularly in works produced over the last two decades (Prakash 1990; Mathur 2000). Surajit Sinha's (1971)[17] historical sketch of anthropology in India leads to a three-part periodization: the British colonial period (1774–1919), the pre-independence period (1920–49) and the post-independence era (1950–to date).

During the first phase, the colonial roots of Indian anthropology are evident in studies initiated by the British colonial administrators and missionaries. These documentaries of the native social and cultural life were undertaken to facilitate effective colonial administration. The exercise also generated detailed ethnographic monographs about aspects of caste, village life and religiosity. Indian social scientists are well aware that 'Anthropology . . . was entangled in an orientalist project' (Patel 2002: 272). The foundations of Indian anthropology were laid between 1891 and 1931, when with the launching of the Census of India, the empirical study of caste and tribes came into existence. At the same time, Indian scholars[18] conducted research on Indian tribes producing ethnographic monographs in the tradition of British social anthropology.

In the pre-independence period, the formalization of the discipline in India was secured with the establishment of the first Indian Department of Anthropology at the University of Calcutta in 1920 (Patel 2002). The following year saw the publication of 'the first full-fledged Indian Journal of Anthropology, *Man in India*' (S. Sinha 1971).[19] In this crucial period, Indian anthropologists were still trained in Britain, the United States and Germany, but the dominant influence of the British anthropological traditions is apparent in the works produced.

In the final phase, nationalistic ('Swarajist') and independence movements injected a political dimension to intellectual debates in Indian anthropology. There was an increasing patronage from the Indian government to teaching and research in anthropology (ibid.: 3). Although the model of British anthropology prevailed, the input of American scholars in Indian studies increased at this time.[20] This last influence further shifted the anthropological focus from 'tribe' to 'caste' and 'village', from 'tribals' to 'peasants', and spurred an interest in culture and personality studies and in the interactions of 'little communities' with 'great traditions' (Singer 1972). Most significantly, following the nationalist call for political independence, Indian anthropologists made a strong case for 'indigenizing' the social sciences in India (Dube 1973; Fahim 1982; Pathy 1988b).

A case for an 'Indian' anthropology

Anthropological research in India over the last five decades has undoubtedly been redefined in dramatic ways. Mathur (2000) itemizes these shifts eloquently and names five important developments. I discuss only one – the concern with producing indigenous forms of knowledge. Notwithstanding this rethinking, studies of India today by Indian and non-Indian scholars still reproduce the image of India as an exotic 'other', and through the particular project of indigenizing anthropology, the image of India as an exotic self. This orientalist and indological image of India has, however, been contested vigorously in recent years, particularly, by Indian scholars (Ahmad 1972; Thapan 1988; Bhattacharyya 2004). They also point to the blatant neglect of non-Hindu, non-tribal, non-caste dimensions of Indian life, and to the dearth of urban and political studies in the anthropological literature, emphasizing India's cultural, socio-economic, religious and political heterogeneity, thus questioning the British presentation of India as a monolith. However, it would be erroneous to suggest that there is anything resembling a unified homogeneous voice in Indian anthropological discourse. The contestations and controversies are many and the following pages show where these are located and how they are articulated.

Contemporary situation in Indian anthropology[21]

Evaluations of social sciences disciplines in India (including anthropology) point to an 'intellectual crisis', which Indian anthropologists express in various terms (Danda 1981; Pathy 1988a). These include a perceived 'lack of enthusiasm and creativity' (Misra 1972), the inability to generate new theories and methods, a stifled growth of the discipline because of limited resources, a lack of coherence and proper direction, irrelevance of anthropological researches to India, the mindless imitation of the Western anthropological models (Sharma 1990) and, contradictorily, the fact that Indian anthropology is 'lagging' in comparison to Western research.[22] This self-reflexivity leads to such questions as 'Is Indian anthropology dead/dying?' (Basu and Biswas 1980) and 'And why an Indian sociology?' (Ray 1989). There are, however, voices that claim greater achievements for Indian anthropology and argue that the discipline has 'come of age' (Atal 1976; Hasnain 1988). However, the predominant view since the late 1960s supports the urgency of re-evaluating and redefining the content and priorities of Indian anthropology.[23] But recent readings of the field have called for a more nuanced evaluation of crisis with more precision (Chatterjee 2002).

Local anthropologists consistently emphasize the need to carve out a suitable niche for the discipline both in an Indian and a global context. This new image for Indian anthropology is articulated largely as a call for a unique and distinct anthropology relevant to the particularities of India. However, the designing of an Indian anthropology has turned out to be more problematic than envisaged. 'Indian-ness' is not a pre-existing agreed upon entity, but instead has to be constructed. In wanting to present their profession as particularly 'Indian', Indian anthropologists struggle to chart a unique course for their discipline. Yet, the fact that they must craft their profession against the background of epistemological, methodological and *historical commonality* with Euro-American anthropology exacerbates their problems. In a sense, Indian anthropologists are trapped within their own history as anthropologists. How do Indian anthropologists claim 'uniqueness' while acknowledging a common history with Western anthropology?

One way out of this predicament, alluded to by some Indian anthropologists (Roy 1986; Khare 1990) is to invoke a new and different beginning for Indian anthropology which temporally precedes colonialism and the birth of anthropology in the West. This invention of indigenous roots attributes anthropological insight to ancient Indian texts such as the *Laws of Manu* as well as to teachings of Sri Aurobindo, Rabindranath Tagore, Mohandas Karamchand Gandhi and other Indian humanists. Inherent in these sojourns into an Indian past is an attempt to redefine not just the history of Indian anthropology but its very epistemology and methodology. For example, Vidyarthi has this to say about the 'Indian-ness' of anthropology:

> But it does not mean that social anthropology in India should overlook what may be termed 'Indianness' of its science. Perhaps to some extent it has not done so, as it has not progressed under the spell of unthinking imitation.... Then, we have had our own sets of social thinkers who have given thought to the social problems from time to time and who have also given direction to them.... Also, with the series of thinkers, ancient scriptures like the *Vedas*, *Upanishads*, *Smritis*, *Purarnas* and *epics* etc. are full of social facts and they need to be studied carefully to develop 'Indianness' in the social anthropology of India, which should be specially used in the study of cultural process and civilizational history of India.
>
> (1980: 20)

This search for 'Indian-ness' has led to a range of difficulties in practice. It is not a pre-existing agreed upon entity, but instead has to be constructed and negotiated through a maze of diverging perspectives.

'Indian-ness' of anthropology in India

The category 'Indian anthropology'[24] is widely used by Indian anthropologists, and some invoke the label 'native anthropologist'[25] to denote their identity. However there is no consensus on the content of either category, both of which are contested. The project of nativizing anthropology combines the following elements: study of India and privileging relevance of anthropological research to Indian problems, which is to be undertaken in a different way by Indians, but not closed to non-Indian scholars; and using Indian rationale, thus producing Indian theories.

This self-conscious call for a 'national' anthropology does not mean a total rejection of Western anthropological models. In their constructions of anthropology, Indian anthropologists retain selected elements from the anthropology of the West, such as the definition of anthropology as a scientific discipline, the methodology of fieldwork and participant observation, the distinction between pure and applied research, and the definition of India as the subject of anthropological discourse. The specific orientalist presentation of India and the perceived dominance of Western ideas in Indian social scientific research are rejected. The rejection of such 'academic colonialism' is expressed in the need for the relevance of anthropological research to the Indian context. Misra expresses a view that is shared by a majority of contemporary Indian scholars:

> that Indian social scientists have not been able to establish their own traditions but instead play a role which is subservient to the foreign 'masters'.
>
> (1972: 92)

Attention is drawn to 'academic colonialism' (K.S. Singh 1984) and the 'servitude of the mind of Indian academics' (Misra 1972; Saberwal 1983). The explicit invocation of the term 'swaraj' (from Hindi: literally 'self-rule'), in a discussion of Indian social sciences (Uberoi 1968) conflates the desire for self-rule and political liberation with the need for 'decolonizing' anthropology in India (S. Sinha 1971: 1).

Given the common historical, epistemological and methodological commonalities between anthropology in India and its Western counterparts, how 'native/ indigenous' can 'Indian' anthropology be? Can one attempt to craft an anthropology peculiar to an 'indigenous' Indian context? The rhetoric of indigenization has effectively opened a Pandora's box. The attempts to nativize anthropology lead to the contestation of such categories as 'India', 'Hindu', 'Indian-ness', 'indigenous' and 'Indian anthropology'.

Consensus on the content of these categories and the nature of Indian 'roots' (Jairath 1984) has turned out to be impossible. A number of inherent difficulties impede indigenization of Indian anthropology. How is the notion of 'Indian-ness' to be translated? What constitutes 'Indian-ness?' Who defines it? Given the tremendous ethnic, religious, political, ideological and socio-economic diversity that characterizes Indian society, how is the proposed 'indigenization of anthropology' from an 'Indian' perspective to be accomplished? (Bailey 1959; Ahmad 1972; Thapan 1988). Indian anthropologists are conscious of these problems, as Pathy exemplifies:

> But it must be acknowledged that there are *multiple versions* of indigenization, including those popularized by the multinational foundations as well as ruling classes. The tragedy of indigenization is its failure to take account of the country's socio-cultural diversity and multiple centres of culture and history.
>
> (1988a: 18, italics added)

Ironically, the debates reveal that the very heterogeneity of Indian social life that is used to contest and 'correct' orientalist renditions of India, now itself becomes an obstacle. This problem has to be overcome in order to even contemplate a consensus about conceptualizing the categories 'Indian' and 'indigenous'.

The indigenization of anthropology is further expressed as: the need to conduct research that is 'substantively Indian' and to generate methods and theory that are specifically 'Indian' (Thapan 1988). The need for an Indian viewpoint has been reiterated by many scholars (Roy 1986; Madan 1991; Uberoi 1968, 1974; Y. Singh 1970; S. Sinha 1971; Sahay 1976; Vidyarthi 1980). Attempts made by Indian anthropologists to articulate an Indian viewpoint culminate in such rhetorical questions as 'Is there an Indian way of thinking?' (Ramanujan 1989) and 'Is there an Indian tradition in social/cultural anthropology?' (S. Sinha 1971) which have no quick or easy answers.

Applied anthropology and development

One more manoeuvre with which Indian anthropology attempts to create its own space is the emphasis on India constructed in opposition to 'Western' nations. India is what the West is not to Indian anthropologists: Third World, non-Western, under-developed, with specificities such as extreme poverty, problems of nation-building and rural development, social and economic inequality, tribal groups unevenly integrated and overpopulated. In so defining their object of study, Indian anthropologists claim a fundamentally different agenda for their anthropology. They attest that from the earliest days of Indian independence, Indian anthropology was set up in direct opposition to Western anthropology, itself crystallized as a monolith. Binary oppositions such as 'applied' versus 'pure' research, 'practice' versus 'theory' and 'abstract theorizing' versus 'application of knowledge' have been, and continue to be, invoked to sustain the claimed incompatibilities (Mahapatra 1997; Mathur 2000; Patel 2002).

The emphasis in Indian anthropology[26] since the independence of India has indeed been on development (Mahapatra 1997; Patel 2002) and planned social change. This reflects the context of a newly independent Third World country where economic development and the restructuring of societal domains become urgent priorities. The explicit engagement of anthropologists in India with the British colonial government, particularly, in relation to the welfare of tribes, meant that anthropologists continued to perceive themselves as affiliated with administrators and policy-makers in independent India. In the 1950s and 1960s, there was a great deal of enthusiasm and hope for the contributions that anthropological knowledge could make towards a 'better India'. Anthropology then presented itself not only as able to diagnose social problems but also as qualified to provide solutions (Sachidananda 1980: 16; Roy Burman 1982; Mathur 1987; Halbar 1991). This enthusiasm has waned somewhat since the 1970s. The reality of the tensions between administrators and anthropologists has come forcefully to the fore (Mathur 1980; Dang 1982).

This desire to be seen as an 'applied science' strongly marks Indian anthropology today. This is not to suggest that Indian anthropologists see themselves as engaging exclusively with the applied components of their discipline. Many insist on a need to engage in anthropological research with the aim of consolidating the theoretical framework of the discipline (Y. Singh 1970; Saberwal 1983), renewing a call for theorizing that cuts through all periods of Indian anthropology. The crucial difference today is that the future of Indian anthropology is perceived by its practitioners to lie in its ability to demonstrate its social relevance to problems within the Indian context (Pathy 1987; Hasnain 1988; Guha 1989; K.S. Singh 1991; Srivastava 1991).[27]

Despite the noted crises in Indian anthropology, its practitioners do hold a vision of the future for their discipline. Sarana and D. Sinha (1976: 216) invoke the phrase 'anthropological self-study' to describe Indian anthropology in India. The juxtaposition of anthropology with analysis of the self might seem to be a contradiction in terms. But, these two anthropologists theorize self-study by Indians as follows:

> One of our greatest drawbacks is the lack of other-culture studies by Indian anthropologists. It is high time that we did develop expertise in this field because research among other cultures has been the forte of anthropology.... However, what has until now been our weakness will prove to be a source of strength in the very near future. We do not think there is any other country in the world where anthropological self-study has been conducted by native-born anthropologists for almost seven decades. Before long, anthropologists of all countries, particularly the developing countries, will have to start studying their own culture. We cannot anticipate the kinds of problems these native anthropologists will face. This new aspect of anthropology in almost every country will encounter growing pains. The only exception will be India, which has long passed that stage.
>
> (Ibid.: 217)

A significant number of anthropologists in India, in recent years, have stated their research agenda as one where the production of knowledge is aimed directly at the solution of social problems (Patel 2002; Chatterjee 2002). However, there are real differences in stating what anthropologists should do, what they can do, what they actually do and what is done with the knowledge produced. The inclination of Indian anthropologists to advocate applied aspects of the discipline have much to do with the structural frameworks within which anthropology has operated in the past, and continues to do so.

The patronage accorded to anthropological organizations in India by governments (as early as 1880s), have created a dependence upon the state. The bulk of anthropological research is funded by the Central for various State governments (Chatterjee 2002). Funding from private organizations or philanthropists is practically non-existent. Resources are scarce. What little is available provokes intense competition from other social sciences. In such a context, it makes sense that Indian anthropologists feel the need to demonstrate the relevance of their research to administrators and policy-makers. In order to legitimate their cause,

Indian anthropologists have to present themselves as committed to planning, development and nation-building (Hebbar 2003). They must demonstrate the usefulness of their craft in the real world to be seen as relevant and legitimate.

The one domain of Indian society where Indian anthropologists have always exercised their leadership role is in the administration of tribal affairs.[28] Although Indian anthropologists have, in recent years, tried to expand their repertoire by carrying their research to other areas such as education, housing, population studies, rural planning, structures in the workplace and urban contexts, tribal welfare and the concern with scheduled castes and tribes have remained their expertise. In a sense the administrator–anthropologist's preoccupation with 'primitives' and 'tribes' and the early engagement of Indian scholars with the same issues continue to haunt Indian anthropologists today. The perceived existence of the 'tribes' in India and efforts to properly locate them in Indian society then ironically continues to legitimate Indian anthropologists.

Apart from influencing policy decisions vis-à-vis scheduled tribes and castes, and some presence in 'government-sponsored statutory institutions and corporations' (Mahapatra 1997), it would be fair to say that their accomplishments in nation-building tasks have been minuscule. Yet, it is curious that the rhetoric of 'relevance of anthropology' to address urgent practical, social problems has been in currency amongst practitioners for about four decades. Another way of getting at the same point is to pose other questions: What are the structural constraints under which Indian anthropologists function? What can they do? What options do they have in terms of real bread and butter issues such as getting jobs? What avenues are open to them apart from research and teaching in academia? Tribal research institutes in various parts of India, the Anthropological Survey of India and the Indian Council of Social Science Research, in addition to the universities, absorb the bulk of graduating anthropologists. A large number of anthropologists have to look elsewhere. The various government departments can and do potentially utilize such individuals (Chatterjee 2002) and it would thus seem that Indian anthropologists can find avenues for making themselves heard and potentially apply their knowledge to solve practical problems. However, by the admission of Indian anthropologists themselves, a great deal of distrust, mistrust, scepticism and suspicion characterizes their relationship with 'the government' (Sachidananda 1980: 17–18). Many anthropologists argue that the tensions between themselves and 'the government' make it difficult to use anthropological knowledge for solving real problems.

Clearly, these directions in contemporary Indian anthropology cannot be explained by structural factors in isolation from others. However, the material and economic considerations, compounded by political factors, profoundly influence how the discipline in India is conceptualized and presented by its practitioners. This is not to argue that this situation is either unique or specific[29] to the Indian scene, but to underscore that the reality of limited institutional resources greatly affects the very survival of the profession. The last observation may provide a partial explanation for at least the explicitly stated anthropological agenda of Indian anthropologists couched in terms of applied research and not only abstract theorizing.

Problematic of negotiating an identity: re-thinking 'indigenization'

The English word 'indigenization' came into popular currency in social science discourses in the late 1970s and 1980s, adding to earlier vocabulary of decolonizing, disengaging and delinking from centres of social science power. Today, however the term has fallen into some disrepute and has been rejected even by earlier adherents, although sufficient numbers remain committed to the underlying political and intellectual project. This rejection is rooted at least in the awareness that to begin with the term and the agenda have been inadequately conceptualized. Proposals have been made to continue the project using instead a different language of generating 'counter-Eurocentric' and 'alternative' discourses. In these altered modes, the indigenization project continues to engage a number of different parties: laypersons, development planners, politicians, government authorities, funding agencies and academics, alerting us to varied and contested interpretations of the label, some of which border on nativism and chauvinism in the outright rejection of all 'Western' forms of social science knowledge. Through these usages, the term is loosely invoked and assigned a taken-for-granted set of meanings. This popular but unproblematized invocation has rendered the project of rethinking and remaking social science disciplines ambiguous and obscure, and the agenda poorly formulated.

As I have argued previously (V. Sinha 1997), despite strong criticism of the term and the agenda it carries, a discourse on 'indigenization' in the social sciences does exist. But this is marginal to mainstream social science as practised both in the core and in the periphery. Even if the terms 'indigenous', 'native' and 'indigenization' are admittedly problematic, it is clear that the inherent agenda of rethinking social science foundations and their relevance in specific socio-cultural contexts cannot be as easily dismissed. Whereas at the level of practice, participants in the field show tremendous energy and industry, the conceptual components receive far less attention. This has meant that the categories in use in this field remain inadequately conceptualized. The empirical translation of an indigenization agenda that is rooted in weak conceptual foundations is thwarted both by theoretical and political difficulties. Such a programme is open to charges of parochialism and chauvinism, and critiqued on these grounds even by proponents of indigenization. Most proponents of indigenization either spend little energy conceptualizing 'indigenization', or bypass the conceptual dimension altogether in favour of the mechanics of 'how to indigenize' a particular discipline. I have argued elsewhere (V. Sinha 1997, 2002) for the need to reconceptualize the notion of indigenization, and proposed for consideration a set of seven issues, attention to which might facilitate a more workable indigenization project in practice. But applying some of these to the Indian case reveals yet again how tricky and awkward the translation exercise really is.

One element in the indigenization of anthropology of India is an effort to identify the 'Indian-ness' of the discipline. I suggest that this equation of indigenization with 'Indianization' with a search for the essence of what it means to be 'Indian' is both conceptually and politically problematic, and runs the risk of being labelled parochial, chauvinistic and exclusionary. A meaningful conceptualization necessitates problematizing the epistemological and political status of the categories 'indigenous' and 'native' in anthropology as well as the relations between colonialism and anthropological knowledge production, something only more recent anthropological works in India attend to, and which is largely missing in the earlier long-standing indigenization discourse. Third World anthropologists have attempted to claim the category 'native' to mark refashioned identities and a discipline, without the marginalizing and subjugating tone it has carried. Although, many groups defined as 'native/other/indigenous' have embraced the label and attempt to redefine it, it is equally crucial to ask what are the consequences of being labelled 'indigenous' and/or 'native'. The example of Indian anthropologists is a case in point (Karlsson 2003).

A version of indigenization that does not adequately theorize a shared common history (through colonial and imperial encounters), with Western social science is also wanting. In claiming a distinct historical, epistemological, methodological and political space for their discipline, Indian anthropologists cannot start as if from a clean slate. The eighteenth and nineteenth-century images of the 'Indian Subcontinent' that informed early anthropological researches in India constitute their intellectual inheritance. In this sense the latter's claims for 'nativity' does not and cannot justify a complete break with the Western anthropological traditions. The challenge is to find meaningful ways of theorizing this link. Also, a sound conceptualization of indigenization is neither a categorical rejection of all Western input, nor does it seek to replace Eurocentrism with nativism or any other dogmatic position. Over the last decade, anthropological works in India do not reveal simplistic statements about the possibility of Indianizing anthropology, particularly as completely de-linked from its counterparts in the North. Through the combined influence of 'Subaltern Studies Collective in India' (Mathur 2000: 93) and feminist scholarship, Indian anthropologists have revisited in a critical mode the 'entanglement' of anthropology with both the colonial and nationalist projects. A more sophisticated attempt to make sense of links with Western academia avoid literal reading of 'indigenization', preventing a search for 'indigenous' roots and the 'essence' of Indian-ness, Chinese-ness or African-ness etc., as defining features of an indigenized discipline.

Although the 'core–periphery' dichotomy in the world of social science needs to be problematized, realistically speaking a divide does exist and, more importantly, structures unequal relations within the global academic and intellectual arenas. Associated with this partition is a specialization or division of labour vis-à-vis social scientific research (Pletsch 1981). It has been pointed out that while scholars from the West are generators of concepts and theory (of universal and comparative value), their non-Western counterparts are viewed largely as providers of empirical material and local knowledge (S.F. Alatas 2000). In a radical rethinking exercise, this traditional global division of labour, the intellectual specialization and academic dependency (S.F. Alatas 2003) would be questioned, challenged and transformed. In a larger context, the issue is an important one of what is to be the nature of relationship between the kind of social science research that is done by 'Western' scholars and their 'non-Western' counterparts.

Scholars who define indigenization through attention to an applied dimension are caught in something of a double bind, as is seen in the Indian case through the opposition between applied and pure research. Given the structural constraints under which many Third World social scientists operate, there are tensions between the demands of a 'pragmatic' nature (satisfying regional/localized interest) and the exigencies of engagement with a wider global community of scholars and intellectuals. How does one remain relevant to local/regional particularities and yet engage with larger theoretical issues of a universal and comparative nature?

Unfortunately, by defining their agenda as 'applied', Indian anthropologists are further marginalized from the concerns of Western anthropology. Furthermore, the explicit particularizing of Indian anthropology leads to a disengagement (perhaps unintentional) of Indian scholars from current issues deemed relevant in Euro-American anthropology. But such distancing is mutual. The lack of attention to native scholarly discourses in anthropology in the West is evident. At the same time, the need to pay attention to and conceptualize indigenous discourses and accord voices to native informants is fashionably reiterated in current anthropological writings. Are the agendas set by Indian and Western anthropologists so mutually incongruent to warrant this double silence? I submit that in these times of acknowledged crises in anthropology, it is crucial to *theorize* the silence of anthropologists both in the core and in the periphery.

Notes

1 This chapter is grounded in the awareness that none of these words – Western, European, non-Western can be used without the necessary problematization.

2 The choice of 'India', 'Africa' and 'America' is not arbitrary. Granting heterogeneity in colonial experiences some commonality can nonetheless be abstracted. Any discussion of India without reference to Africa, and vice-versa, is necessarily incomplete.

3 In using the term 'European' I am aware that Europe was itself not a pre-existing entity before the sixteenth century. I focus primarily on British and to some extent German contributions which culminated in constructions of India in highly specific terms.

4 Interestingly, the designation of the lands beyond the Indus river as 'India' is attributed to Alexander, whose contacts were confined to areas in the north-west of the subcontinent. The totality of India, stretching from northern Kashmir to southern Kanyakumari was not implied in European accounts of 'India'. Other territorial descriptions referred to India's coastal areas and ports. Knowledge of interior regions was fairly limited.

5 The word 'Hindu' can be traced to its origins in the Old Persian and Avestic languages. According to Steingass' *A Comprehensive Persian–English Dictionary*, the word 'Hindu' means 'an Indian', 'black', 'slave', 'servant' and 'infidel' (1947: 14–15). The Aryans first used the word *Sindhus* to refer to the modern Indus river. In Vedic literature *Sindhu* was used as an appellative noun for 'river' in general. Persians in the eighth century referred to the river as 'Hindu' (al Faruqi and Sopher 1974: 73) and by extension used the same word to describe those who lived beyond the Sind or the Indus Valley (Ling 1985: 142).

6 By the sixteenth century Indians were of course not the first or the only 'other' known to Europeans. The Spanish encounters with Indians in the Americas predate Spanish, Portuguese and British experiences of Indians in Asia.

7 By Indian religion European scholars meant primarily Hinduism and neglected Buddhism and Islam in such discussions (Marshall 1970; Inden 1990). British designation of 'Hinduism' as the religion of India and Sanskrit as the sacred language of India reveal the sources of European knowledge about India. English civil servants like Jones and Halhed relied on Brahmin priests to learn Sanskrit from and for selection and translations of Indian texts. Scholars (Mukherji 1985) have argued that 'too little attention has been paid to the Indian contribution' (Mukherji in Rocher 1989: 627) in the project of British Orientalism. In the eighteenth-century India, numerous pandits (Hindu Brahmin priests) and maulavis (Muslim religious experts) entered British service, particularly in British courts as interpreters of Hindu and Muslim law (Rocher 1989).

8 Jones, however was not the first European to read Sanskrit or translate Indian texts. The French scholar Anquetil-Duperron went to India in 1754 and made translations of the *Upanishads* (Schwab 1984).

9 Surmised to have been composed in South India in early tenth century AD. It is by far the most popular of all the Puranas. The latter literally mean 'ancient stories or lores'. As part of Hindu sacred literature, they contain popular encyclopedic collections of myth, legend and genealogy, varying greatly as to date and origin.

10 Literally 'The Lord's Song'. A part of the Indian epic poem Mahabharata, it is a dialogue between the warrior prince Arjuna and his friend and charioteer Lord Krishna. It has been dated to the first or second century AD.

11 Indology as a study of Indian civilization was not a monolithic set of ideas. Besides German, French and English varieties of Indology, individualistic interpretations lent further heterogeneity to Indological discourses.

12 According to Alvares:

> This myth of the absolutist nature of Indian philosophy was repeated so often everybody came to accept it as gospel truth: the average Hindu was turned into a dreamy visionary and his philosophy into a world-and-life denying dogma.
>
> (1991: 47)

13 In Majeed 1990, quoted from Lord Teignmouth's Memoirs of the Life, Writings and Correspondence of Sir William Jones, 1804.

14 A similar argument can be made about Marx's, Hegel's and Weber's writings on India. Their agendas were larger than a particular concern with India. In European philosophical, political, religious and economical debates, India was used both as data and as a testing ground for theories. Regardless of their explicit motivations for focusing on India, it is nonetheless crucial that their pronouncements have critically shaped imaginings and discourses of India, including the anthropological.

15 The word 'caste' is not one of Indian origin and is not traceable to any Indian language. The Indian application of the word *caste* comes from the Portuguese casta which means 'race, breed or lineage'.

Indological accounts of caste in India refer to the varna system, a classificatory scheme found in Vedic texts. The four-fold occupational division in the *Laws of Manu* has been described by Indologists as a scheme of elaborate and rigid social classification. This interpretation reveals European reliance upon Vedic textual sources and Brahmins as the religious authority in India.

However, Indian scholars have questioned such a presentation of caste. Srinivas (1951) has argued that the real unit of the 'caste system' is not *varna* but *jati*, which he defines as 'a very small endogamous group practising a traditional occupation and enjoying a certain amount of cultural, ritual and juridical autonomy' (ibid.: 24). He further questions the rigidity of the caste system in Indological accounts (ibid.: 30).

16 An identical relationship between caste and Hinduism has been assumed by scholars from Max Weber to Monier-Williams to Louis Dumont. Weber (1958: 29), relying on written sources concluded 'Before anything else, without caste there is no Hindu.'

Srinivas, however, sees caste as the 'structural basis of Hinduism... (which) occasionally even survives conversion to Christianity and Islam'.

17 In contrast to Surajit Sinha's (and also Dube 1971) dating of the origins of Indian anthropology to 1774 which coincides with the establishment of the Asiatic Society of Bengal, Sarana and Dharni Sinha (1976: 210) attribute the birth of Indian anthropology to the late nineteenth century.

18 In early twentieth century, Indian scholars like S.C. Roy and L.K. Ananthakrishna Iyer undertook studies of Indian castes and tribes in the tradition of administrator–anthropologists. This focus on tribal populations such as the Oraon, the Munda, the Birhor, among others, continued well into the 1940s. In these studies, the tribal populations were constructed as the 'other' by pioneering Indian anthropologists.

19 The first department of Sociology in India was set up in Bombay in 1919. The boundaries between sociology and anthropology in India, both historically and today, are not as rigid as in parts of Europe and North America. Practitioners of both disciplines acknowledge great areas of overlap (Betellie 1993; Patel 2002) but others assert a distinction between them (Guha 1989). It is quite common for anthropologists and sociologists in India to cross over disciplinary boundaries, both in their research and teaching. The best known example of this is the Indian scholar, M.N. Srinivas who is appropriated by both disciplines.

20 Efforts to create an anthropology or sociology peculiar to India or South Asia have not occupied only Indian scholars. In 1957 the combined efforts of Louis Dumont and David Pocock 'for a sociology of India' led to the establishment of the most prestigious social science Indian journal today, *Contributions to Indian Sociology*. They argued that Indian sociology should lie at 'the confluence of sociology and indology'. This has proved to be a highly controversial proposition, generating tremendous debates among both Indian and non-Indian scholars (Peirano 1991). In recent years Mckim Marriott's (1989, 1990) call for an 'Indian ethnosociology', in addition to being highly controversial has led to lively debates about both the need for an 'Indian' social science and its content. The fact that both these debates spanning the last thirty years have been made by 'non-Indians' has not gone unnoticed by Indian scholars, which gives the latter greater cause to insist on independence from Western intellectual influences.

21 My discussion of Indian anthropology is confined to what is labelled cultural anthropology in North America. Physical anthropology and archaeology are included in the teaching curriculum of Indian anthropology. Linguistics is only just beginning to make inroads in anthropology curriculum in India.

22 D. Sen phrases the problem thus:

> Cultural anthropology, like other branches of Anthropology, has been imported from the West. Therefore, it is expected there will be a lag in catching up with the latest trend in the field in the west.
>
> (1974: 57)

23 In 1963 the publication of *Anthropology on the March* aimed to 'arouse the interest of many, and in particular, of those who are interested in the welfare of tribes and backward communities'. In a different but related vein, in 1968, Indian social scientists organized a conference on the subject of 'Urgent Research in Social Anthropology'. In the introductory address N. Ray stated, 'We have assembled here for one brief week to consider and define in theoretical and practical terms the priorities of research problems in the field of social anthropology in India in the near future, and to suggest and plan, as precisely as possible, practicable ways and means by which scarce resources can be brought to bear on selected problem-areas and geographic regions.'

24 Some Indian theorists have queried the need for an Indian anthropology or sociology (Atal 1976; Ray 1989). While they legitimate theorizing in particular contexts, they argue that anthropology's status as a 'universal' science makes it difficult to propose its national variants. The reasons for this are not entirely clear to me. The invocation of

national varieties in anthropology is not a new idea. Anthropologists in Great Britain and the United States have claimed national differences in their profession. More recently anthropologists in parts of the Arab world (J. Abu-Lughod 1989), Italy (Saunders 1984) and Japan (Kelly 1991; Kuwayama 2003, 2004) have similarly claimed regional and nationalist specificities in their practice of anthropology.

25 Anthropologists from other Third World countries also use this label synonymously with the phrase 'Third World Anthropologist' (Bennoune 1985). Both these labels are used variously to signify a differential identity from First World anthropologists.

26 Anthropologists in newly independent India were joined by sociologists, political scientists and economists, similarly engaged in redefining their disciplines vis-à-vis the nationalist project of rebuilding India.

27 The point is made forcefully by Sahay:

> It is high time that the anthropologists also feel this urge and feel themselves concerned with the burning and practical problems, which not only face any particular cross section of society, but the country or its people as a whole. With their specialized knowledge of culture, they should come forward to suggest solutions of the problems like unemployment, population-explosion, crisis of conscience disintegration, lack of national character, and be of real help in successful implementation of some national programmes of our...Prime Minister (Indira Gandhi), and the like.
>
> (1976: 17)

28 Verrier Elwin, an English missionary turned anthropologist, served as an advisor on tribal affairs to Jawaharlal Nehru. Upon the advise of the former, Nehru devised a plan for the appropriate administration of tribes in India. Elwin's contributions have taken on the proportion of a 'myth'/'legend' in Indian anthropological circles, but were at the time vehemently opposed by some Indian anthropologists. Amongst them was G.S. Ghurye who argued that the best solution to the tribal 'problem' was to assimilate them into mainstream Hindu society. Keeping them in isolated 'national parks' he elaborated would lead to accusations that anthropologists were trying to keep the tribes 'primitive' to facilitate their discipline's interests.

29 The varied attempts to indigenize sociology in Taiwan (Chan 1993; Sun 1993; Yeh 1994), Japan (Kuwayama 2003, 2004) and China (Guldin 1995) provide interesting comparative material.

References

Abu-Lughod, Janet L. (1989) *Before European Hegemony: The World System AD 1250–1350*, New York: Oxford University Press.

Ahmad, Imtiaz (1972) 'For a sociology of India', *Contributions to Indian Sociology*, New Series, 6: 172–8.

al Faruqi, I. and D. Sopher (1974) *Historical Atlas of the Religions of the World*, London: Collier Macmillan Publishers.

Alatas, Syed Farid (1993) 'On the indigenization of academic discourse', *Alternatives*, 18(3): 307–38.

——(2000) 'Academic dependency in the social sciences: reflections on India and Malaysia', *American Studies International*, XXXVIII: 2.

——(2003) 'Academic dependency and the global division of labour in the social sciences', *Current Sociology*, 51(6): 599–613.

Alatas, Syed Hussein (1977) *The Myth of the Laze Native*, London: FrankCass.

Alvares, Claude (1991) *Decolonizing History*, New York: The Apex Press.

Atal, Yogesh (1976) *Social Sciences: The Indian Scene*, New Delhi: Abhinav Publications.

Bailey, F.G. (1959) 'For a sociology of India', *Contributions to Indian Sociology*, 3: 88–101.

Basu, Amitabha and Suhas K. Biswas (1980) 'Is Indian anthropology dead/dying?', *Journal of Indian Anthropological Society*, 15: 1–14.

Bennoune, Mahfoud (1985) 'What does it mean to be a Third World anthropologist?', *Dialectical Anthropology*, 9: 357–64.

Beteille, Andre (1993) 'Sociology and anthropology: their relationship in one person's career', *Contributions to Indian Sociology*, New Series, 27(2): 291–304.

Bhattacharyya, Gayatri (2004) 'Bhudev Mohkopadhyay and Reverse Anthropology', *Journal of Indian Anthropological Society*, 39(2): 139–51.

Chan, Hoiman (1993) 'Some metasociological notes on the sinicisation of sociology', *International Sociology*, 8(1): 113–19.

Chatterjee, Partha (2002) 'Institutional context of social science research in South Asia', *Economic and Political Weekly*, 31 August, 3604–12.

Danda, Ajit (1981) 'On the future for anthropology in India', *Journal of Indian Anthropological Society*, 16: 221–30.

Dang, B.S. (1982) 'Future of applied anthropology in India', *Indian Anthropologist*, 2: 31–7.

Dube, S.C. (1973) *Social Sciences in Changing Society*, Lucknow: Ethnographic and Folk Culture Society of UP.

Dumont, Louis and David Pocock (1957) 'For a sociology of India', *Contributions to Indian Sociology*, 1: 7–22.

Fahim, Hussein (ed.) (1982) *Indigenous Anthropology in Non-Western Countries*, Durham, NC: Carolina Academic Press.

Fox, Richard G. (ed.) (1991) *Recapturing Anthropology*, Santa Fe, NM: School of American Research Press.

Ghosh, Suniti Kumar (1984) 'Marx on India', *Monthly Review*, 35: 39–53.

Guha, Ramachandra (1989) 'Sociology in India: some elective affinities', *Contributions to Indian Sociology*, 23(2): 339–46.

Guldin, Gregory Eliyu (1995) *The Saga of Anthropology in China*, Armonk, NY: M.E. Sharpe.

Halbar, B.G. (1991) 'Anthropology and the modern world', in Halbar and Khan (eds), *Relevance of Anthropology*, Jaipur: Rawat Publications, pp. 289–301.

Halbar, B.G. and C.G. Hussain Khan (eds) (1991) *Relevance of Anthropology: The Indian Scenario*, Jaipur: Rawat Publications.

Hasnain, Nadeem (1988) *Readings in Indian Anthropology*, New Delhi: Harnam Publications.

Hebbar, Ritambhara (2003) 'Social science policy in the new millennium', *Economic and Political Weekly*, 31: 2118–20.

Inden, Ronald B. (1990) *Imagining India*, Oxford: Basil Blackwell.

Jairath, Vinod K. (1984) 'In search of roots – the Indian Scientific Community', *Contributions to Indian Sociology*, 18(1): 109–29.

Karlsson, Bengt G. (2003) 'Anthropology and the "Indigenous Slot": claims and debates about Indigenous Peoples' status in India', *Critique of Anthropology*, 23(4): 403–23.

Kaul, H.K. (ed.) (1979) *Travellers' India: An Anthropology*, Delhi: Oxford University Press.

Kelly, William W. (1991) 'Directions in the anthropology of contemporary Japan', *Annual Review of Anthropology*, 20: 395–431.

Khare, R.S. (1990) 'Indian sociology and the cultural other', *Contributions to Indian Sociology*, 24(2):177–99.

Kuwayama, Takami (2003) ' "Natives" as dialogic partners; some thoughts on native anthropology', *Anthropology Today*, XIX: 1.

—— (2004) *Native Anthropology*, Melbourne, vic: Trans Pacific Press.

Lach, Donald (1968) *Southeast Asia in the Eyes of Europe: The Sixteenth Century*, Chicago, IL: The University of Chicago Press.

Ling, Trevor (1985) *A History of Religion: East and West*, London: Macmillan.

Madan, T.N. (1991) 'Relevance in social anthropology: some observations', in Halbar and Khan (eds), *Relevance of Anthropology*, Jaipur: Rawat Publications, pp. 283–7.

Mahapatra, L.K. (1997) 'Anthropology in policy and practice in India', *Studies in Third World Societies*, 58: 155–78.

Majeed, Javed (1990) 'James Mill's "The history of British India" and utilitarianism as a rhetoric of reform', *Modern Asian Studies*, 24: 209–24.

Marriott, Mckim (1989) 'Constructing an Indian ethno-sociology', *Contributions to Indian Sociology*, 23(1): 1–38.

—— (ed.) (1990) *India Through Hindu Categories*, New Delhi: Newbury Park.

Marshall, P.J. (ed.) (1970) *The British Discovery of Hinduism in the Eighteenth Century*, Cambridge, UK: Cambridge University Press.

Mathur, H.M. (1980) 'Anthropology and public administration', in L.P. Vidyarthi and K.N. Sahay (eds), *Applied Anthropology and Development in India*, New Delhi: National Publishing House.

—— (1987) *Anthropology and Development in Traditional Societies*, New Delhi: Vikas Publishing House.

Mathur, Saloni (2000) 'History and anthropology in South Asia: rethinking the archive', *Annual Review of Anthropology*, 29: 89–106.

Mill, James (1858) *The History of British India* (3 vols), London: Baldwin.

Misra, P.K. (1972) 'Social science researches in India: their relevance', *Journal of Indian Anthropological Society*, 7: 89–96.

Mukherji, Abhijit (1985) 'European Jones and Asiatic Pandits', *Journal of the Asiatic Society*, XXVII: 43–58.

Muller, Friedrich Max (ed.) (1879) *The Sacred Books of the East*, London: Clarendon Press.

—— (1883) *India: What it can Teach Us?*, New York: Funk & Wagnalls Company.

Patel, Sujata (2002) 'The profession and its association: five decades of the Indian sociological society', *International Sociology*, 17(2): 269–84.

Pathy, Jaganath (1987) *Anthropology of Development: Demystifications and Relevance*, New Delhi: Gian Publishing House.

—— (1988a) 'Emerging frontiers of anthropology from Third World perspective', *Indian Anthropologist*, 18(1): 11–19.

—— (1988b) 'In pursuit of indigenization: trends and issues on building sociology for India', *The Journal of Sociological Studies*, 7: 70–84.

Peirano, Mariza G.S. (1991) 'For a sociology of India: some comments from Brazil', *Contributions to Indian Sociology*, 25(2): 321–7.

Pletsch, Carl E. (1981) 'The three worlds, or the division of social scientific labor, circa 1950–1975', *Society for Comparative Study of Society and History*, 23: 565–90.

Prakash, Gyan (1990) 'Writing post-orientalist histories of the Third World: perspectives from Indian historiography', *Comparative Studies in History and Society*, 32: 383–408.

Ramanujan, A.K. (1989) 'Is there an Indian way of thinking? An informal essay', *Contributions to Indian Sociology*, 23(1): 41–58.

Ray, Rabindra (1989) 'And why an Indian sociology?', *Contributions to Indian Sociology*, 24(2): 265–75.

Rocher, Rosane (1989) 'The career of Radhakanta Tarkavagise, an 18th century Pandit in British employ', *Journal of American Oriental Society*, 109: 627–33.

Roy, S.C. (1986) 'The study of anthropology from the Indian viewpoints', *Man in India*, 66(1): 81–93 (1st published in 1937).

Roy Burman, B.K. (1982) 'Applied anthropology today and tomorrow', *Indian Anthropologist*, 12: 23–9.

——(1987) 'Third World anthropology and the related sciences: the issues', *Eastern Anthropologist*, 40(4): 349–57.

Saberwal, Satish (1983) 'For a sociology of India: uncertain transplants, anthropology and sociology in India', *Contributions to Indian Sociology*, 17(2): 301–15.

Sachidananda (1980) 'Planning, development and applied anthropology in India', in L.P. Vidyarthi and K.N. Sahay (eds), *Applied Anthropology and Development in India*, New Delhi: National Publishing House.

Sahay, K.N. (1976) 'Teaching of anthropology in India', *Indian Anthropologist*, 6(1): 1–19.

Saloni, Mathur (2000) 'History and anthropology in South Asia: rethinking the archive', *Annual Review of Anthropology*, 29: 89–106.

Sarana, Gopal and Dharni Sinha (1976) 'Status of socio-cultural anthropology in India', *Annual Review of Anthropology*, 5: 209–25.

Saunders, George R. (1984) 'Contemporary Italian cultural anthropology', *Annual Review of Anthropology*, 13: 447–66.

Schlegel, Friedrich von (1890) *Philosophy of History*, translated by James Burton Robertson, London: George Bell.

Schwab, Raymond (1984) *The Oriental Renaissance: Europe's Rediscovery of India and the East, 1680–1880*, Gene Patterson-Black and Victor Reinking (trans.), New York: Columbia University Press.

Sen, Dharani (1974) *Indian Anthropology Today*, Calcutta: Department of Anthropology, Calcutta University.

Sharma, K.N. (1990) 'Western sociology with Indian icing', *Contributions to Indian Sociology*, 24(2): 251–8.

Singer, Milton (1972) *When a Great Tradition Modernizes: An Anthropological Approach to Indian Civilization*, New York: Praeger.

Singh, K.S. (1984) 'Colonialism, anthropology and primitive society: the Indian scenario (1928–47)', *Man in India*, 64(4): 400–11.

——(1991) 'Relevance of anthropology', in Halbar and Khan (eds), *Relevance of Anthropology*, Jaipur: Rawat Publications, pp. 181–6.

Singh, Yogendra (1970) 'For a sociology of India', *Contributions to Indian Sociology*, 4: 140–4.

Sinha, Surajit (1971) 'Is there an Indian tradition in social/cultural anthropology: retrospects and prospects', *Journal of Indian Anthropological Society*, 6: 1–14.

Sinha, Vineeta (1997) 'Reconceptualising the social sciences in non-Western settings: challenges and dilemmas', *Southeast Asian Journal of Social Science*, 25(1): 167–81.

——(2002) 'Decentring social sciences in practice through indiavidual acts and choices', *Current Sociology*, 51(1): 7–26.

Srinivas, M.N. (1951) *Religion and Society among the Coorgs of South India*, London: Oxford University Press.

Srivastava, V.K. (1991) 'Some issues in the anthropology of development', in Halbar and Khan (eds), *Relevance of Anthropology*, Jaipur: Rawat Publications, pp. 303–18.

Steingass, F. (1947) *A Comprehensive Persian–English Dictionary*, London: Kegan Paul, Trench, Trubner and Co.

Sun Chung-Hsing (1993) 'Aspects of "Sinicisation" and "Globalisation"', *International Sociology*, 8(1): 121–2.

Thapan, Meenakshi (1988) 'Contributions and the sociology of India', *Contributions to Indian Sociology*, 22: 259–72.

Thapar, Raj (ed.) (1979) *The Invincible Traveller*, New Delhi: Vikas Publishing House.

Trouillot, Michel-Rolph (1991) 'Anthropology and the savage slot: the poetics and politics of otherness', in Richard G. Fox (ed.), *Recapturing Anthropology: Working in the Present*, Santa Fe, NM: School of American Research Press.

Uberoi, J.S. (1968) 'Science and Swaraj', *Contributions to Indian Sociology*, 2: 119–24.

——(1974) 'New outlines of structural sociology, 1945–1970', *Contributions to Indian Sociology*, 8: 135–52.

Vidyarthi, L.P. (1980) *Aspects of Social Anthropology in India*, New Delhi: Classical Publications.

Weber, Max (1958) *The Religion of India: The Sociology of Hinduism and Buddhism*, Hans Gerth and Don Martindale (trans. and eds), New York: The Free Press, Macmillan Publishing Co.

Yeh Chi-jeng (1994) 'A sociological analysis of indigenization in social research', *Hong Kong Journal of Social Sciences*, 3: 52–78.

8   An Indian anthropology?

What kind of object is it?

Roma Chatterji

As one of the three anthropologists from Delhi University studying Dutch society, I was often asked whether there was anything "Indian" about my disciplinary perspective. While being personally irritated by the naive condescension implicit in this question, I still find it important to address precisely because of the assumptions that it reveals about anthropology itself.

Anthropology, as the study of alterity *par excellence*, has the difficult task of confronting the issues, both ethical and political, that alterity connotes. What does the fact of otherness do to the perspective that anthropology brings to bear on the societies that it studies? Recent criticism from within the discipline shows that questions of scale were directly related to the way a society could be thought of as other. For example, the Nuer could be identified as a small stateless society only by ignoring their place in the British colonial empire (see Last 1995). Thus, the characterization of some societies as small scale and simple is not so much a feature of these societies in their contemporary state but rather a result of the anthropologists' own orientation. That this methodological orientation, that is, the ethnographic method involving participant observation over a fairly long period of time in the society being studied, has a political agenda, is the focus of the recent historiography of the anthropological cannon. Talal Asad (1973) shows that British functionalist anthropology, while claiming to have contributed to world knowledge by providing detailed ethnographies of "primitive" societies, also contributed to the structure of power represented by the colonial system. Functionalist anthropology was used to implement and justify the system of indirect rule in Africa by which the colonial system exercised power through the so-called "traditional political" institutions.[1]

Not surprisingly then, anthropology became suspect in many of the former colonies given the assumption that those who were studied by anthropologists were primitive. Ramkrishna Mukherjee quotes a conversation with a North African student in Paris in 1948, "Today we are 'tribals' and the 'anthropologists' study us; but tomorrow we shall attain independence, and then we shall be 'people' and the 'sociologists' and 'political scientists' will come to study us!" (1986: 86). In pre-Independence India, the nationalists considered anthropology an instrument of colonial policy to keep sections of the population away from the national mainstream (Srinivas and Panini 1986). After Independence, it was sociology that was influenced by nationalist concerns, addressing issues around identity politics, agrarian relations, and development. Tribal and caste groups were studied not for the purpose of documenting the cultures of dying or fast changing societies, but rather to study the process of change itself. Interestingly, structure-functionalism, the fieldwork method associated with British social anthropology, was used by many Indian sociologists in opposition to earlier tendencies of explaining contemporary institutions by placing them in the context of sacred Hindu scriptures (ibid.). Thus, sociology and anthropology were distinguished not so much in terms of method but rather in terms of whether the societies they studied were thought to be contemporaneous with themselves or not.

In the process, of course, the scale of the community typically studied by the method of structure-functionalism was modified. Thus, Srinivas, one of India's most illustrious post-independence sociologists, made a significant contribution to the study of ritual by linking the hierarchies of ritual purity and pollution, in terms of which social groups were stratified, to the strategies these groups adopted to change their ritual behavior (Srinivas 1997). Communities came to be seen from within a civilizational perspective. Traditional institutions like caste came to be studied as dynamic processes transformed through the modern political structures of democracies. Srinivas, an anthropologist trained in Britain like many scholars of his generation, marked this change in focus by designating himself a sociologist and naming the department he set up in Delhi University, a sociology department. This department still teaches a combination of what in the West would be called sociology and social anthropology.

A stranger in one's own society

The generation of post-independence "sociologists," like M.N. Srinivas and T.N. Madan, used participant observation to relate to the empirical reality of India. For Srinivas (1997), village studies became a window to the study of Indian civilization. He saw a dissonance between the "book view" and the "field view" of Indian society especially when the texts taken to construct the picture of society were normative in character. He thought of Indian sociology as a study of "the self in the other and not that of the absolute other" (1997: 21).

Madan chose to study his own community, the Pandits of the Kashmir Valley, partly for the reason that a brief field trip in a "tribal" area in central India as an MA student made him feel that anthropological fieldwork was degrading to the subject of observation (1998: 150). By choosing to study his *own* community he was "transforming the familiar into the unfamiliar by the decision to relate to it as an anthropologist" (1994: 114).[2]

What happens to the "ethnographic gaze" when it is turned on one's own society? Veena Das (1998a) in an insightful discussion of Evans-Pritchard's work on witchcraft among the Azande, talks about the anthropologist's need to secure the reality of the other. She says that anthropologists use concepts to make other societies knowable in terms of laws, rules, and patterns of authority. But beneath the seeming objectivity of anthropological texts that render other societies as rationally ordered, perhaps there lurks another voice, the voice of "unreason," the acknowledgment that the reality portrayed by the anthropologist is experientially enigmatic. I quote:

> a glimmer of fear of the other's reality may be found in Evans-Pritchard's description of how he came to suspect that he was falling into unreason when he was tempted by the notion that the moving light he saw from his tent might after all be a witch as Azande theories suggested despite his firm belief that witches did not exist.
>
> (Das 1998a: 43)

In her own writing Veena Das increasingly uses the concept of voice to position herself critically vis-à-vis the classical anthropological cannon of writing, that is, "knowledge produced by the intimacy of fieldwork...the participant observation mode which paradoxically produces the exotic other" (1995: 6). Unlike the distant representations produced by the "ethnographic gaze," the use of "voice" points to the position of the one who makes the representation. It allows representations to become like utterances that position the speaker and in which the circumstance in which words are uttered become part of their meaning (cf. Gould 1998: 53). Voices must be heard to become significant. Anthropological representations are disaggregated to become a play of voices that appeal to the potential listener, asking to be heard. The anthropologist becomes both the voice as well as the listener.

What does it mean to say that the anthropologist becomes the voice for the field? Is there not a danger that the anthropologist will appropriate the voices of the field by claiming to speak on their behalf; and even more dangerous perhaps, by claiming an empathy with the society she studies, she reproduces the silences that it produces about itself? (cf. Cavell 1997).

In her recent work on violence and everyday life, Das (1997) says that it is only by transforming the anthropological experience into an act of witnessing that the anthropologist is able to avoid the dangers of both the distant ethnographic gaze as well as the silencing empathetic voice. The anthropologist as witness engages with the voices of those who sustain relationships in everyday life. Writing specifically about the violence that followed the Partition of the Indian subcontinent in 1947, she shows how public violence mutates into intimate violence in the domestic context. She uses the biographical method to reveal the patient work of care that individuals undertake to repair relationships that have been tainted by the collective violence. She calls this the "souling" of culture, a recognition of the fact that human beings must actively engage in "creating themselves and others as cultural beings" (2000: 2). As she says, the idea of the soul is usually associated with the interiority that lies behind the exteriority and facticity of the body. Therefore, to recognize another person as a soul is to recognize that beyond the external facticity of the body available to the public gaze, there is also a unique being that transcends it. Das uses the concept of voice to capture this uniqueness of being, a uniqueness that transcends anthropological representations of persons, as role playing actors or as embodiments of cultural meanings. Voice, as I have said, is oriented to the act of listening, it demands an acknowledgment from the other. When the anthropologist recognizes her "informants" as "voices," she acknowledges that they too are other to their own society in the sense that they share the anthropologist's sense of unease with larger questions of culture and society, and like her must struggle to achieve their unique understanding of social phenomena. In this sense, the phenomenologist position of the stranger is para-digmatic for the way persons and the anthropologist as one such person receive culture and learn to achieve a life in society (Schutz 1970).

Voice, event and sociality

For the social scientists who were writing at the time of Independence, the study of Indian society was tied to the nationalist project of conceptualizing India as a unity in both cultural and political terms. Thus, for sociologists like Srinivas, this meant the articulation of cultural diversity within a largely Hindu civilizational perspective and for the historians of modern India this meant a concentration on the Civil Disobedience Movement that gave the Indian public a consciousness of its unity. In the late 1970s, a group of young historians disillusioned with what they called the "post colonial nation state" and its failure to disrupt its links with colonial modes of governance, came together to produce a series of texts on sub-altern histories that were severely critical of modern Indian historiography. They accused the historians who wrote on Indian nationalism of elitism and said that what was missing from this representation of Indian history was the "politics of the people" (cf. Guha 1998).

> For parallel to the domain of elite politics there existed throughout the colonial period another domain of Indian politics in which the principal actors were not the dominant groups of the indigenous society or the colonial authorities but the subaltern classes and groups constituting the mass of the laboring population and intermediate strata in town and country – that is, the people. This was an *autonomous* domain, for it neither originated from elite politics nor did its existence depend on the latter.
>
> (Guha 1982: 1)

This failure on the part of the nationalist historians was partly due to the mode of conceptualizing the historical archive only in terms of the "big event." Instead, the subaltern historians concentrated on fragmentary sources, on the "debris of the past" (Guha 1987), in order to interpret the silences that surround the official documents that made up the historical archive.[3] Thus, in what is now considered a classic work of subaltern historiography, Ranajit Guha (1987) reconstructs nineteenth-century rural Bengali society and its structures of caste domination and patriarchy from an *ekrar* (a legal term for a confession of guilt) submitted to the district court by a woman who inadvertently helped cause her daughter's death by assisting in the abortion of her "illegitimate" child. By reading this document "against the grain," Guha is able to imaginatively reconstitute the context of this event. He reads the actions of the various persons described in the document so as to give them agency and thus bring them back to the historical arena.

Similarly, Shahid Amin takes an incident in Chauri Chaura in northern India during the Civil Disobedience Movement in 1922 when a group of "nationalists" burned down a police station and juxtaposes different representations of it, some culled from judicial records and nationalistic writings of that period while others are local recountings of the event from the relatives of the actors in the 1980s. What is significant for us is that he calls this an exercise in historical fieldwork. In fact, the subaltern historians have been instrumental in breaking down disciplinary boundaries between the social sciences in India today.

Given that most social science disciplines have now adopted anthropological fieldwork techniques to complement their particular modes of data collection, anthropologists and sociologists in India have increasingly begun to re-think their disciplinary boundaries, especially in terms of what is supposed to constitute fieldwork. For instance, a recent collection of fieldwork accounts edited by Meenakshi Thapan (1998) distances itself from previous Indian collections of this kind by taking on a decidedly prescriptive tone. While all the articles fall within the *genre* of writing that is called reflexive anthropology and problematize the self/other polarization that "classical" anthropological writing assumes, at least two of the articles go further in proposing fairly radical experiments in fieldwork techniques. Thus, both Amrit Srinivasan (1998) and Savyasachi (1998) feel that the emphasis in participant observation should shift from observation to participation. Both are influenced by Gandhian philosophy and suggest that fieldwork should entail a bodily engagement with the field that involves unlearning habitual practices that are intimately associated with bodily conceptions of the self so that the fieldworker is free to learn new ones in the field. Their work can also be read as a creative engagement with Bourdieu's concept of the "habitus" – the generative field that makes the structures of every day life possible. Bourdieu describes the habitus as embodied history that is forgotten because it has become second nature and says that this forgetting is crucial for the routinization of everyday life. Savyasachi responds to this conception of habitus by turning it on to himself – the anthropologist doing fieldwork by learning new modes of bodily care instead of using it as a tool for ethnographic representation as Bourdieu does.

The work of Das, Srinivasan, and Savyasachi all share a similar concern with the way fieldwork is embodied. However, it is Das who takes the next step by showing how new ways of constituting fieldwork experience can be translated into anthropological representation. In a recent work "Critical Events" (1995), she reflects on the relationship between contemporaneity and ethnographic writing by re-describing a series of significant events in modern India from the anthropological perspective. To this end, she looks at events around the time of the Partition of the Indian sub-continent in 1947, concentrating on the appropriation of issues that were traditionally the concern of social institutions by the nation-state. Thus, for instance, violence against women, typically thought of as an issue concerning the family, is transformed during the partition riots into a political event that concerns the newly independent nations of India and Pakistan. Until recently, it was the stable institutionalized aspects of society that anthropologists focused on. Increasingly, South Asian scholars are beginning to question this. Das' own contribution is to look at the everyday not from the perspective of the routine but from the shadow cast upon it by the extraordinary event. In her conception of the everyday, she includes the discourse of anthropology, which it surely must be for the academic anthropologist. She describes the appearance of the English translation of Dumont's great work Homo Hierarchicus as a rupture in the anthropological discourse on Indian society and revisits the debate between Louis Dumont and his Indian counterpart A.K. Saran. But for me, the most exciting part of the book is the chapter on pain and anthropological representation. She uses the conception of pain to mediate between "voice" and "culture" and in this way is able to configure the emergent quality of social life. She says that persons are not merely born into culture, the structures of which become knowable through the course of their lives, they also give birth to culture through the ordinary events and activities of daily life. Cultures bear the imprint of our voices, we authors culture through the uniqueness of our being (Das 1995).

Das has been influenced in her work on voice and the birth of culture by the philosophical writings of Stanley Cavell. The concept of voice has another disciplinary location – in the work of the subaltern historians. They depict the voices of their subaltern subjects at the moment of rupture. Their authentic voice is the voice of resistance articulated at the moment of conflict (cf. Guha 1982; Das 1989). The paradox, however, is that this voice is only available through colonial documents that defined this moment as conflict, that is, as a breakdown of law and order. From this perspective then, resistance can only be of the moment because the restoration of order will suppress it, silencing the voice that made itself heard in the momentary event of resistance. Das, like the subaltern historians, correlates "voice" with "event" but for her the event acquires a different time dimension. It is not momentary but rather weaves itself into the temporal rhythm of everyday life. In contrast to the subaltern historians for whom the event or the rebellious moment is only available as a trace, a fragment of dead time, in Das' work it becomes present through the biographies of persons influenced by it. Thus, she uses the biography of one woman, Asha, a young widow from Lahore now in Pakistan. Asha was not directly affected by the violence of Partition but her conjugal family with whom she lived lost their fortune when they came to India as refugees.

In her discussion of Partition violence, Das deliberately "evokes a scene of ordinariness" to demonstrate the effect of a violent event. Asha who was acknowledged as the widow of a much loved brother became a liability after Partition, a drain on the family's resources, and a sexual being available for experimentation within her conjugal family. This "poisonous" knowledge was never openly expressed either by Asha or by other women in the family. They tried their best to keep it hidden, even though they acknowledged her suffering by accepting her remarriage, so as to repair the rupture in the family relationships.[4] Asha and her kinswomen created a community through suffering, through their common goal in nurturing relationships. Das calls this the "souling" of culture. Voice appears through the acknowledgment of vulnerability in relationships and of the individual's responsibility for their maintenance and for us as anthropologists to claim responsibility in finding our voice through them.

In Das' work, the event of Partition is not constituted as a violent moment as in the work of Guha and the other subaltern historians, rather it is a rupture, the effects of which are felt long after the event has occurred. But this event is "critical" to the extent that it destabilizes the lifeworld, creating alternate biographies that are hidden behind the cultural roles that society expects its members to play.

The event and the organization of time

For both Das and the subaltern historians, "voice" is used to reflect on the distance between persons in society and society itself. Critical reflection is only possible in this gap. But how is this gap to be articulated? The subaltern historians articulate it as a temporal gap. They reflect on the colonial period from their location in the present and with a perspective shaped by their critical concern with the modern Indian society. In the process, India becomes for them a post-colonial society, shaped by its colonial past, so that even the scholarly perspective with which it views itself is shaped by this past.

The Indian sociology that was created by pioneers like M.N. Srinivas and Ramkrishna Mukherjee took a view that was diametrically opposed to that of the subaltern historians. Their focus was contemporary India and they were critical of pre-Independence Indian anthropology for its distancing gaze that focused on "primitive society." For them, independence marked the critical break between tradition and modernity. They distanced themselves both from the textual studies carried out by sociologists like B.K. Sarkar (1926) that were influenced by the Orientalist view of Indian civilization and also from anthropologists who used fieldwork techniques adopted from colonial anthropology (cf. Asad 1973).[5]

Srinivas, Madan, and other sociologists of their generation retained the anthropological method of intensive fieldwork through participant observation, but with the full awareness that they could never be complete outsiders to their fields. They were studying their contemporaries to the extent that the rapid changes brought about by the fall of colonialism effected the societies that they studied as much as it effected them. But by explicitly aligning themselves with a particular time and space were they perhaps too close to the nationalist project of the Indian state, a project that the subaltern historians have been able to critique precisely because they study the past? (cf. Chakravarty 1998; Guha 1998). Perhaps, sociologists of Srinivas' generation were too committed to the idea of the nation and were therefore unable to reflect on it from a disciplinary perspective.

It is only in the last decade that sociologists/anthropologists of India have been able to engage with this concept and only with the mediation of the subaltern historians. Thus, van der Veer (1994) shows how the so-called "communal" politics of the modern Indian state is a re-incarnation of the Orientalist essentialization of the Hindu/Muslim divide in India. Appadurai (1994), following other Indian scholars writing on the Indian census, shows how colonial representations of caste for administrative purposes is used for identity politics in modern India (see Pant 1987). Sociologists also use the idea of the postcolonial to study the way in which people experience global discourses – of governmentality, development, or nationalism. Gupta (1999) studies the discourse of modernization and development by examining what development has meant for people living in one village in North India. He says that these people experience themselves as being underdeveloped and that this identity as the underdeveloped co-exists with other identities like that of caste, class, region, gender, and nationality. By categorizing discourses like modernity and development as postcolonial, Gupta problematizes them. For the villagers that he studies, development is experienced as a lack, as a temporal, and as spatial marginality.

Clearly, it is the anthropological model of time that is at issue here. To understand the contribution of the post-colonial perspective we need to make a brief detour away from Indian sociology/anthropology to examine the temporal models implicit in our representations of society. Since Fabian's seminal work *Time and the Other* (1983) we are aware that the privileging of the present in most anthropological writings is a way of denying coevality with the societies being studied. An exclusive focus on the present prevents us as anthropologists from developing social critiques that would articulate our stake in these societies. The models we use are either teleological ones based on the notion of empty time or those based on the practices of everyday life. Thus Bourdieu includes time as a strategy in everyday life. Habitus is embodied history, objectified in things and in bodies, "in durable dispositions to recognize and comply with the demands immanent in the field" (1990: 58). But precisely because habitus is forgotten history, everyday temporality for Bourdieu requires a kind of misrecognition of the teleological model of time that anthropologists have posited. Thus, for instance, the gift may demand its return according to the formal principle of reciprocity on which social exchange is modeled (see Mauss 1990), but by controlling the timing of the return gift the social actor has the illusion that she/he has control over the cycle of gift exchange. The rhythm of social time must transcend the experience of individual actors and it is important that they be unconscious of this for everyday life to regain its ongoing character.

Even though Bourdieu introduces individual agency into anthropological writing by looking at lived time, his representation of Kabyle society in Morocco shares certain fundamental assumptions with those represented by the anthropologists he criticizes. Critical voices from within the field are absent. Bourdieu assumes a fantastic stability in Kabyle society. Any experience of uncertainty in everyday life can be made intelligible by the dispassionate anthropologist using the totalizing model of social structure unavailable to the native member of the society.

In this regard, Das (1995) as we have seen, introduces a very different model of social time by focusing on the "critical event." In this formulation, she is perhaps influenced by the great American sociologist G.H. Mead who said that it was the emergent event that allowed social actors to experience time as being organized socially into a past, a present, and a future. For Mead, social actors live in the spacious present, that is, the present that is encapsulated by the event that thrusts out of the temporal flow and organizes time into a past and a future (cf. Joas 1985). Das looks at time through the everyday work of care, through the process by which social actors, especially women, repair relationships ruptured by violent social events. A focus on events allows critical voices to emerge from the field – voices that express a concern with particular societal goals and with choices that individual actors make while carving out autobiographies for themselves. It also demystifies the anthropologist's own voice by positioning it vis-à-vis those of others from the field.

In the work that I am doing with a colleague, Deepak Mehta, on the narratives of violence, we have used the concept of event to construct overlapping perspectives on the violent events being narrated as well as the event of narration itself. We have studied the riots that took place in Bombay in 1992–3 through the narratives of the survivors. In these narratives, the incidents of violence were set in a time apart – a discrete and extraordinary time of the event and was not experienced as a continuous time of everyday life. Thus, the memories of the violence could not be placed in the same relationship as other past events. Rather, the riot was experienced as effect – bodily memories that gave rise to feelings of dread when the date 6 December came around. This is the date on which the Babri mosque was demolished by some Hindu fanatics, an event that directly preceded the riots in Bombay. The riot had the quality of a "critical event" as it reorganized the way in which the survivors now experience time. It continues to exist as a trace in their present.

The act of narration, the actual recounting of the incidents that made up the riot, became another event with its own temporal dimensions that shaped the way the riot was objectified for our benefit. The riot and narratives about it were inextricably interwoven so that in some parts of the shanty town in which we were doing our fieldwork, we heard narratives only in a group context, sitting in a community space listening to people reminiscence about how the violent mob suddenly appeared on the boundary of their neighborhood. In other neighborhoods, it was only by walking around with a few survivors, traversing the path of the violence, that we were able to get the narratives of the event.[6] It is as if the form the violence took and the trajectory that it followed also shaped the way in which it could be narrated.

In this chapter, I have used certain key terms like voice, event, and time to give shape to what an Indian sociology or anthropology might look like eschewing a thematic review. A conventional review is impossible given the diverse concerns even within one university department not to speak of India as a whole. However, what draws most anthropologists/sociologists together is the fact that most of them study in India. Even though this is largely the outcome of external constraints like the unavailability of funds to do overseas research, this has led to the articulation of a somewhat different relationship between the anthropologists' self and the other that is the object of study. Madan (1994) who studied his own community talks of the stranger within while discussing his fieldwork experiences and Srinivas articulates the self–other relationship as a continuous one in which each partakes of the other.

Both Madan and Srinivas were writing about societies that were familiar. Differences were a result of class position and rural location rather than of culture. Recent writings on anthropological fieldwork in India have tried to achieve this reflexivity even with fields that could be labeled as exotic. Thus, Savyasachi (1998) who studied the Koitor, a forest dwelling people in Central India, describes fieldwork as a process of "unlearning," that begins with bodily habits which includes a regime of hygiene, food habits, and so on and then moves on to cognitive categories that label certain forms of life as "tribal" or "underdeveloped." Much of what Savyasachi says echoes the recent writing on reflexivity in anthropology. Where it stands out is in the extent to which the field is constituted as intersubjective space. Other anthropologists working in conditions similar to that of Savyasachi are confronted with the same problems. A case to point is Jean Paul Dumont's ethnography of the Panera in Venezuela, which is built on self conscious representations of his face-to-face interactions with particular persons in the field (Dumont 1978). He, like Savyasachi, found that an ethnography of a "tribal" world in contemporary times only made sense if one was sensitive to its location vis-à-vis several other groupings like the nation state, the global economy, or anthropology in the person of Dumont that coloured his relationships in the field. Dumont also constitutes his field as intersubjective space but to do so he had to learn how to build an identity that was acceptable to his informants. This led him to construct a fictitious kinship universe that was intelligible to them. Dumont was able to do this because he knew that the terms of the relationship were set by him. He had sought contact with the Panera people and it was improbable that they would ever contact him once he left Venezuela. Even though Savyasachi's field was a classic anthropological field – a tribe practicing shifting cultivation – Delhi is not as far away as the United States or France. Savyasachi's contact with the Koitor could be mediated by persons like government officials, who participate in the same social world that he does. Savyasachi could become cognizable to the Koitor by trying to share their life world by not building a classificatory universe that was fictive though "meaningful." Savyasachi's location in Delhi made him more accessible, his world more verifiable. He could not take recourse to an alternate identity, only remake his by own learning Koitor ways, living in a Koitor household in which he was assigned specific tasks and asking questions not so much to gather anthropological information but to carry on the routine of everyday life.

Lévi-Strauss' critical reflections on the philosophical roots of anthropology are pertinent for this discussion. In an amplification of Rousseau's statement that knowledge of other societies would give the scholar a necessary distance from his or her own society, Lévi-Strauss says that action within one's society precludes the understanding of other societies. A striving for universal understanding must involve a detachment from one's own society, the only one from which we have a duty to be free because it is the only one to which we can ever belong (cf. Lévi-Strauss 1964). However, as Friedlander (1992) argues, for Rousseau, compassion is what allows individuals to relate to each other – compassion that must pre-exist any idea of human sociality. When natural compassion is displaced on to a universal principle there is a danger that we will be unable to relate to the particular event or incident. Without compassion, is it possible to relate to the other at all?

For both Dumont and Savyasachi, the fieldwork experience constitutes their anthropological "voice." Their claim to author anthropological scholarship emerges from their reflexive relationship to the fieldwork experience; that is, it becomes part of their anthropological voice to the extent that for both skepticism regarding their scholarly projects from the people in their fields shape the way they constitute anthropological reality. The difference lies in the way the people related to them. The Panera in Dumont's field related to him through the objects that he had with him – his knife, his radio, the medicines that he had brought with him, and so on. Savyasachi had to throw his away before he could get accepted. As an Indian from Delhi, he had to prove that he was different from the bureaucrats from the city – a generic label that the Koitor use to categorize most non-Koitor people. Dumont's relationship with his field operates with a fore knowledge of closure in a way that Savyasachi's cannot.

Up till now, I have tried to discuss the manner in which voices from the field destabilize our own perceptions of society and culture and our place within them. But now, we must turn to the anthropological voice – by whom is it heard and what influence does it have on the societies it is supposed to represent? The anthropological voice objectified in ethnographic texts is heard and addressed by tribal theologians in Central India, for instance. Beginning with the work of Hoffman and von Emelen (1950) and van Exem (1982), there is a movement that looks to the anthropology of religion to articulate the "tribal community" as a natural home for a tribal church informed by the true spirit of the Gospels (cf. van den Bogaert 1993). Similarly, in India as in other parts of the world, anthropological classics are used as resources by communities trying to hold on to the scattered remnants of their traditions in the face of rapid change. Thus Ghosh (1998) in a paper on the religious system of the Oraon tribe of Central India describes a situation in which the *pahan* (religious practitioner) had died without passing on his knowledge to his son. His son had to cull out this knowledge from a variety of sources including from a college text book on Oraon religion. In fact, Ghosh himself became a resource person for the *pahan* by supplying him with some of the anthropological classics on the tribe. These texts allowed the *pahan* to strengthen his position within the power structure of the village. There were complaints from other tribal elders that the material supplied by Ghosh was not being circulated to them. It is interesting to note that even though anthropological knowledge is operating here as a substitute for traditional knowledge, it is not thought to have the same status as the latter. Exclusive knowledge, passed down from father to son is perfectly acceptable within the traditional system but there seems to be an implicit understanding that anthropological knowledge, derived from a variety of different sources, available in book form, should be more accessible. So, treating anthropological knowledge like traditional knowledge is illegitimate.

From these cases, we see that anthropology allows the societies that it studies a certain perspective on their culture. Culture begins to be perceived as a resource that can be used to participate in more global discourses – for instance, anthropological knowledge becomes a powerful tool in the movement for declaring the tribal groups of central India "indigenous people" and allows them to participate in the global discourse on this theme. In my own work on performative traditions in the Purulia district of West Bengal, I show how scholarly discourses on the folklore of this region helps to reify open-ended and fluid dance forms, so that they conform to artificial standards set by scholarly demands for authenticity (Chatterji 1995). Thus, in the tribal belt that stretches from east to central India, the search for syncretic symbols that can unify the disparate tribal groups living in this region turns living cultural forms into deracinated symbols of an "authentic cultural community." Paradoxically, anthropological representations of cultures as readerly texts have been transformed into objects to be used in the politics of ethnicity. Therefore, in the light of this discussion would one still agree with Lévi-Strauss' statement that as anthropologists we must choose to distance ourselves from all societies, for only thus can we acquire the dispassionate voice of scholarship (cf. Lévi-Strauss 1964). For Indian anthropologists, this does not seem possible, not even desirable.

This brings me to the last point that I want to make in this chapter – the repeated slippage between the two terms "sociologist" and "anthropologist" when referring to the scholars whose work has been discussed here. In India, one often finds that scholars who occupy positions as sociologists in university departments in India refer to themselves as "anthropologists" when addressing issues relating to reflexivity (see Das 1995; Thapan 1998). It is as if these labels indicate different subject positions through which scholars who write on India have to move. In a previous section, I have said that sociologists writing in the 1950s self consciously focused on India's present, dissociating themselves from what they thought was a normative and textual view of traditional India.[7] For them, the present was open ended. It looked to the future and part of their work as sociologists was "diagnostic" – to suggest the direction that Indian society might take (cf. Mukherjee 1979). For my generation of sociologists/anthropologists perhaps this confidence is more muted. We still look to the present, continue the tradition of intensive fieldwork but the present that we study, under the influence of the subaltern historians, is inflected with a sense of history. An ordinary, everyday sense of history that highlights the role contingency plays in everyday life.

Acknowledgments

Rajendra Pradhan, Sanjib Dutta Chaudhury, and I did fieldwork in the Netherlands from 1986 to 1987 for a project titled "The Welfare State from the Outside. The Study of Aging and Care Institutions in the Netherlands." The project was funded by the Indo-Dutch Program for Alternatives in Development.

I would like to thank Jan van Bremen for suggesting that I write this chapter and for the patience with which he has borne the delay in submission, and Deepak Mehta for his critical comments.

Notes

1 According to Feuchtwang (1973), social anthropology received official encouragement in African colonies governed by the system of Indirect Rule. However, the relationship between British social anthropology and colonial rule is complex. Henrika Kuklick shows that Evans-Pritchard's somewhat idealized depiction of the Nuer as a stateless society was as much a "paean to the merits of egalitarian democracy than an apology for colonialism" (Kuklick 1984: 72).
2 Madan's designation of himself in his writing on fieldwork as an anthropologist is significant. His institutional designation as well as his self-designation in some of his other writing is as a sociologist. We will notice the same movement between the two terms in the work of Veena Das. They indicate different sorts of ethical engagement with society and with the discipline of sociology/anthropology and reflect the particular historical trajectory that these two disciplines have taken in India.
3 Viewing the archival document as a fragment is not so much a question of the contents of the documents – that is, historical information – but rather a perspective which asserts that often what we call history is gleaned from texts generated by the "oppressive contract" that certain groups were forced to make with modern institutions of the state and cannot be viewed outside a field of power (cf. Das 1989).
4 Widow remarriage was socially unacceptable in Asha's community at the time when Das did her fieldwork.
5 However, this picture is complicated by sociologists like D.P. Mukherji and J.P.S. Uberoi. Mukherji, a sociologist from one of India's first departments of sociology, thought of India's modernity as emerging from her tradition. He thought that her traditional cultures would allow her to choose between alternate trajectories to modernity (cf. Madan 1994). Uberoi, an anthropologist by training, though a teacher of sociology in the Delhi School of Economics, thought that *swaraj* (self governance) in Indian sociology would only come about in Indian sociologists who studied Europe and explored alternative European traditions of science and modernity (1984).
6 The violence is always spoken of as a force independent of peoples' agency.
7 This, however, did not prevent Srinivas from addressing issues relating to tradition like "sanskritisation," but he always focused on the "field view."

References

Amin, Shahid (1995) *Event, Metaphor, Memory: Chauri Chaura, 1922–1992*, Delhi: Oxford University Press.
Appadurai, Arjun (1994) "Number in the colonial imagination," in C.A. Breckenridge and P. van der Veer (eds), *Orientalism and the Postcolonial Predicament: Perspectives on South Asia*, Delhi: Oxford University Press, pp. 23–44.
Asad, Talal (ed.) (1973) *Anthropology and the Colonial Encounter*, Atlantic Highlands, NJ: Humanities Press.
Bourdieu, Pierre (1990) *The Logic of Practice*, Stanford, CA: University of Stanford Press.
Cavell, Stanley (1997) "Comments on Veena Das' essay 'Language and body: transactions in the construction of pain'," in A. Kleinman, V. Das, and M. Lock (eds), *Social Suffering*, Berkeley, CA: University of California Press, pp. 93–8.

Chakravarty, Dipesh (1998) "Postcoloniality and the artifice of history: who speaks for 'Indian' pasts?" in Ranajit Guha (ed.), *A Subaltern Studies Reader 1986–1995*, Delhi: Oxford University Press, pp. 263–94.

Chatterji, Roma (1995) "Authenticity and tradition: reappraising a 'Folk' form," in V. Dalmia and H. von Stietencron (eds), *Representing Hinduism: The Construction of Religious Traditions and National Identity*, Delhi: Sage, pp. 420–41.

Chatterji, Roma and Deepak Mehta (1995) "A case study of a communal riot in Dharavi, Bombay," *Religion and Society*, 42(4): 5–26.

Das, Veena (1989) "Subaltern as perspective," in R. Guha (ed.), *Subaltern Studies VI: Writings on South Asian History and Society*, Delhi: Oxford University Press, pp. 310–24.

——(1995) *Critical Events: An Anthropological Perspective on Contemporary India*, Delhi: Oxford University Press.

——(1997) "Language and body: transactions in the construction of pain," in A. Kleinman, V. Das, and M. Lock (eds), *Social Suffering*, Berkeley, CA: University of California Press, pp. 67–92.

——(1998a) "Anthropological knowledge, alterity and the autobiographical voice," in M. Thapan (ed.), *Anthropological Journeys: Reflections on Fieldwork*, Delhi: Orient Longman, pp. 41–53.

——(1998b) "Wittgenstein and anthropology," *Annual Review of Anthropology*, 27: 171–95.

——(2000) "The act of witnessing: violence, poisonous knowledge and subjectivity," in V. Das, A. Kleinman, M. Ramphele, and P. Reynolds (eds), *Violence and Subjectivity*, Berkeley, CA: University of California Press, pp. 205–25.

Dumont, Jean-Paul (1978) *The Headman and I: Ambiguity and Ambivalence in the Fieldworking Experience*, Austin, TX: University of Texas Press.

Fabian, Johannus (1983) *Time and the Other*, New York: Columbia University Press.

Feuchtwang, Stephan (1973) "The discipline and its sponsors," in T. Asad (ed.), *Anthropology and the Colonial Encounter*, Atlantic Highlands, NJ: Humanities Press, pp. 71–102.

Friedlander, Eli (1992) "Expressions of Judgement," PhD thesis submitted to Harvard University.

Ghosh, Abhik (1998) "Polarization of knowledge among the Oraons," *South Asian Anthropologist*, 19(2): 79–85.

Gould, Timothy (1998) *Hearing Things: Voice and Method in the Writing of Stanley Cavell*, Chicago, IL: University of Chicago Press.

Guha, Ranajit (1982) "Introduction," in R. Guha (ed.), *Subaltern Studies 1*, Delhi: Oxford University Press, pp. 1–6.

——(1987) "Chandra's death," in R. Guha (ed.), *Subaltern Studies V*, New Delhi: Oxford University Press, pp. 135–65.

——(1998) "Introduction," in R. Guha (ed.), *A Subaltern Studies Reader 1986–1995*, Delhi: Oxford University Press, pp. ix–xxii.

Gupta, Akhil (1999) *Postcolonial Developments: Agriculture and the Making of Modern India*, Delhi: Oxford University Press.

Hoffman, John and Arthur von Emelen (1950) *Encyclopedia Mundarica*, Patna: Government Printing.

Joas, Hans (1985) *G.H. Mead: A Contemporary Re-Examination of his Thought*, Cambridge, MA: Polity Press.

Kulick, Henrika (1984) "Tribal exemplars: images of political authority in British anthropology, 1885–1945," in G.W. Stocking, Jr (ed.), *Functionalism Historicized: Essays on British Social Anthropology*, Madison, WI: University of Wisconsin Press.

Last, Murray (1995) "Violence in Northern Nigeria and the processes of social healing," paper presented at a conference on *Violence, Political Agency and the Construction of the Self*, Rajiv Gandhi Institute for Contemporary Studies, New Delhi and Social Science Research Council, New York.

Lévi-Strauss, Claude (1964) *Tristes tropiques: An Anthropological Study of Primitive Societies in Brazil*, New York: Atheneum.

Madan, T.N. (1994) *Pathways: Approaches to the Study of Society in India*, Delhi: Oxford University Press.

Mauss, Marcel (1990) *The Gift: The Form and Reason for Exchange in Archaic Societies*, London: Routledge.

Mukherjee, Ramkrishna (1979) *What Will It Be? Explorations in Inductive Sociology*, Bombay: Allied Publishers.

——(1986) "The sociologist and the social reality," in T.K. Ooman and Partha N. Mukherji (eds), *Indian Sociology Reflections and Introspections*, Bombay: Popular Prakashan, pp. 73–100.

Pant, Rashmi (1987) "The cognitive status of caste in colonial ethnography: a review of some literature of the North West Provinces and Oudh," *Indian Economic and Social History Review*, 24(2): 145–62.

Sarkar, Benoy Kumar (1926) *Positive Background of Hindu Sociology*, Allahabad: The Panini Office.

Savyasachi (1998) "Unlearning fieldwork: the flight of the artic tern," in M. Thapan (ed.), *Anthropological Journeys: Reflections on Fieldwork*, Delhi: Orient Longman, pp. 83–112.

Schutz, Alfred (1970) *Phenomenology and Social Reality*, The Hague: Nijhoff.

Srinivas, M.N. (1987) "Practicing social anthropology in India," *Annual Review of Anthropology*, 26: 1–26.

Srinivas, M.N. and M.N. Panini (1986) "The development of sociology and social anthropology in India," in T.K. Oomen and Partha N. Mukherji (eds), *Indian Sociology. Reflections and Introspections*, Bombay: Popular Prakashan, pp. 16–55.

Srinivasan, Amrit (1998) "The subject in fieldwork: Malinowski and Gandhi," in M. Thapan (ed.), *Anthropological Journeys: Reflections on Fieldwork*, Delhi: Orient Longman, pp. 54–82.

Thapan, Meenakshi (1998) *Anthropological Journeys: Reflections on Fieldwork*, Delhi: Orient Longman.

Uberoi, J.P.S. (1984) *The Other Mind of Europe*, Delhi: Oxford University Press.

van den Bogaert, Michael (1993) "Communication, community and tribals," *Sevartham*, 3: 43–55.

van der Veer, Peter (1994) "The foreign hand: orientalist discourse in sociology and communalism," in C.A. Breckenridge and Peter van der Veer (eds), *Orientalism and the Postcolonial Predicament: Perspectives on South Asia*, Delhi: Oxford University Press, pp. 23–44.

van Exem A. (1982) *The Religious System of the Munda Tribe: An Essay in Religious Anthropology*, St. Augustin 1: Haus Volker und Kulturen.

Part V

South-East Asia

9 From *Volkenkunde* to *Djurusan Antropologi*

The emergence of Indonesian anthropology in postwar Indonesia

Michael Prager

Introduction

More than 40 years ago, the Indonesian anthropologist Koentjaraningrat remarked that one of the laudable results of the development of post-colonial anthropology is the "increasing number of non-European anthropologists" who will probably soon "dominate the anthropological activity" in their own countries (1964: 295). Koentjaraningrat's self-conscious assessment that most of the previously colonized countries "now have their have own national anthropologists" (ibid.) was influenced, of course, by the memories of the academic developments in his own country, where an anthropology of Indonesia dominated by Indonesian scientists only became possible after the Dutch scholars had been forced to leave the country in the late 1950s. During these years, for the first time after independence, the opportunity had developed to appoint Indonesian scholars to the vacant university positions, and thereby to make an attempt to decolonize and Indonesianize the Dutch scientific heritage.

The overall process of the decolonization of Indonesia, however, which necessarily affected the domain of the sciences too, including anthropology, should be evaluated at different levels. The notion of "decolonization" usually refers to a historical period during which former colonies gained their independence, mostly in the years following the Second World War. Indonesia achieved its independence in 1949, after having fought a war against the Dutch which has become engraved in the country's memory as the "Indonesian revolution." By the revolution, as the national self-esteem wants it, the Dutch overlords had been finally expelled from the country, leading to the decolonization of what once had been called the "Netherlands–Indies," and later on, to the nationalization of the remnants of the former colonial system.

It remains an interpretative problem, however, to delineate the point at which a country or society can be considered as being truly "decolonized," since the removal of the former colonial personnel and the abolishment or national incorporation of the former colonial institutions does not necessarily coincide with the decolonization of thought and ideology. The latter aspect has proved to be a difficult one in the development of many of the post-colonial states, since the new political elites usually were trained within the educational systems which had been erected by the colonizers themselves. Whereas many of the post-colonial states outwardly accentuated a strong anti-Western attitude, often proclaiming the necessity of an invigoration of pre-colonial forms of culture and society, the political rhetoric and the overall conceptualization of the state, however, inevitably remained being moulded by the ideological heritage of the West.

With regard to the ideological heritage of Dutch colonialism in Indonesia, Benedict Anderson (1983) has drawn a provocative line from Jan Pieterzoon Coen, who established Dutch power in Indonesia in the seventeenth century, to the New Order state under Suharto. More recently, Robert Cribb has put forward a similar view, by arguing that "many structures of the contemporary [Indonesian] state bear a strong resemblance to the institutions which took shape in the final century of colonial rule" (Cribb 1994: 1). Such continuities between the colonial and the post-colonial state apply in a certain sense also to the domain of the sciences, among them Indonesian anthropology. The fact that the Dutch scholars left the country in the 1950s is not necessarily identical with the decolonization of Indonesian scientific thought and discourse, the more so since the first generation of the Indonesian scholars was trained within the framework of the educational system created by the Dutch.

The present chapter analyzes the process which led to the emergence of one of the scientific disciplines in post-colonial Indonesia, the subject of anthropology, a process culminating in an attempt of the "sons" to dissociate themselves from the ideological heritage of their "fathers." In the framework of the following analysis, I shall first focus on the educational structures established by the Dutch, in order to assess the then existing possibilities for Indonesian students to become acquainted with that type of science. Moreover, the question must be posed whether Dutch ethnologists during the colonial period made concrete offers to Indonesian students for a scientific collaboration, and in terms of which topics they were trying to win the interest of the nationalist and modernist oriented Indonesian intellectuals. Finally, an assessment shall be reached whether Indonesian anthropologists managed at all to emancipate themselves from the ideological heritage of their "fathers," or whether in the context of early indigenous Indonesian anthropology one rather has to acknowledge an overt, although involuntary, continuity of Dutch colonial ethnology.

Educating natives about themselves: from "ethical policy" to the Japanese occupation period (1898–1945)

Over a period of more than 100 years, the undertaking of researches on the languages and cultures of Indonesia was basically an affair of the Dutch. At the beginning of the twentieth century, the Netherlands could proudly look back at a long-standing tradition of Oriental scholarship which had been mainly concerned with the study of the history, the languages and the cultures of the *Netherlands–East Indies* (*Nederlandsch–Indië*) as the Dutch colony in Island-Southeast Asia was called. Ethnographic knowledge in the widest sense had been laid down in the countless accounts of travelers, explorers, geographers and missionaries, and in the various journals and proceedings published by the major scientific institutions which had been founded from the eighteenth century onwards to promote the knowledge of the Netherlands–East Indies. The oldest of these institutions was the *Bataviaasch Genootschap van Kunsten en Wetenschappen* (Batavian Society for the Arts and Sciences) founded in Batavia (Jakarta) in 1778. In the following year the *Verhandelingen* (proceedings) of the *Bataviaasch Genootschap* began to appear. Some decades later, the same institution issued the *Tijdschrift voor Indische Taal-, Land- en Volkenkunde*, with the first volume being published in 1853.

Another important institution was (and still is) the *Koninklijk Instituut voor de Taal-, Land- en Volkenkunde*, established in The Hague in 1850. Its journal *Bijdragen tot de Taal-, Land- en Volkenkunde van Nederlandsch–Indië* appeared from 1853 onwards and was soon to become the most important publishing organ for Dutch anthropologists. Generally, the collection and presentation of ethnographic data in the journals and proceedings mentioned was not only nurtured by pure scientific motives, but the research institutes were expected to produce knowledge which would be of relevance for the colonial administration in order to facilitate the implementation of Dutch colonial rule.

The close connection between the scientific production of ethnographic knowledge and the more practically oriented interests of the colonial administration had become already manifest by the fact that Dutch ethnology, or *Land- en Volkenkunde* as it was called in the Netherlands, was for a long time only taught at the training academies for prospective colonial civil servants and military officers. Such training courses were first established in Surakarta (1832) and Breda (1836), and later also in Delft (1843) and Leiden (1864). In 1877, a chair of anthropology was attached to the University of Leiden, which made anthropology for the first time an academic subject. In 1902 Leiden University obtained the sole right to educate colonial civil servants in the framework of the multi-disciplinary study program of *Indologie* (Indonesian studies) in which the subject of anthropology was firmly embedded. Nurtured by these interests and institutional developments, by the end of the nineteenth century, the Dutch had assembled a vast amount of ethnographic data, which in most cases, however, were lacking any approach to arrive at some sort of theoretical interpretation.

This is not the place to analyze the nature of nineteenth and early twentieth century Dutch anthropology.[1] It is more important to stress the fact that within all the attempts to study the languages and cultures of Indonesia, Indonesians themselves were only rarely involved. This of course was due to the lack of educational facilities for Indonesians in the Dutch colony. Whereas the Dutch had created a *Hogere Burgerschool* (HBS) for their own children in Batavia in 1860, education for Indonesians was mainly available at the elementary level in primary schools run by the colonial government and private organizations. The fact that the question of higher education for Indonesians became an issue at all followed from the so-called "ethical policy" which was introduced around the beginning of the twentieth century. In 1898, the idealistic lawyer Van Deventer had published an essay in which he argued that the Netherlands had a moral and financial obligation toward the Netherlands–East Indies, because the wealth of the Netherlands had been largely achieved by draining the colony. In political circles, the essay soon became very influential and in the beginning of the twentieth century the "ethical policy" was officially adopted by Queen Wilhelmina and Dutch colonial politics. Apart from plans to improve the social welfare in the colony, one of the ideals of the new policy was to give Indonesians better access to higher education.

In the Netherlands–East Indies the new educational spirit led to the founding of various schools for native administrators, known as Opleidingsscholen voor Inlandse Ambtenaren (*OSVIA*), and to the establishment of a higher training school for native teachers (*Hogere Kweekschool*) which was founded in Central Java in 1914. In addition, schools for native doctors were founded in 1900 and 1914 respectively (School tot Opleiding voor inlandsche Artsen (*STOVIA*) and Nederlands Indische Artsen School (*NIAS*)), and by 1919 the colonial government had created a General Middle School for Indonesians, the so-called "Algemene Middelbare School" (AMS) in Jogyakarta which offered an educational program in the natural sciences. One year later, a second AMS was established in Bandung, offering a Western classical program, and in 1926 the city of Surakarta witnessed the founding of a third AMS which specialized in Oriental Languages and Literature. The graduates of these General Middle Schools were given the right to become university students at one of the institutions of higher education, such as the Technical College of Bandung, the Medical College, and the Batavia Law School.[2]

Before such institutions were founded between 1920 and 1927, however, Indonesians who had obtained a secondary high school education and wished to study at the university were compelled to go to the Netherlands. After the First World War, the Dutch government had made available several scholarships for Indonesian students to study at one of the Dutch universities. Most of these students studied at the University of Leiden, with Law, Economy, and *Indologie* being the preferable subjects. Other students were inscribed at the Universities of Utrecht and Amsterdam, the Technical College of Delft, the College of Agriculture at Wageningen, and the School of Economics at Rotterdam (Koentjaraningrat and Bachtiar 1975: 3). In the year 1924, there were 131 Indonesian students in the Netherlands, of which 40 were studying Law at the University of Leiden (Fasseur 1993: 410). There were also a few students studying *Indologie*, the multi-disciplinary study program in which prospective colonial officers were trained for the colonial service. The Indonesian students, however, who had inscribed for *Indologie*, found themselves in the strange situation that they were allowed to follow the courses and obtain their degree, but were hampered from entering the higher (Western) colonial administration (ibid.: 387). In the framework of the *Indologie* program, the Indonesian students could have also become acquainted with the subject of ethnology. Actually, however, they did not seem to have shown a great interest in this subject, the more so as A.W. Nieuwenhuis, the former explorer and medical officer, who held the Leiden ethnology chair from 1904 to 1934, is reported to have been a bad teacher (ibid.: 364).

The academic domains in which Indonesian students could truly make their mark were the fields of Javanese history and philology, and even more important – in the so-called "adat"-law studies. In the field of philology, mention should be made of scholars like Hoesein Djajadiningrat[3] and R.Ng. Poerbatjakara. Djajadiningrat (1896–1960) was a student of the famous Leiden professor of Islamic studies Snouck Hurgronje and obtained his PhD in 1913 with a study on the *Sejarah Banten* (History of Banten). In 1911, he had already published an article in the earlier mentioned journal *Bijdragen* for which he was awarded a medal by the University of Leiden. Later, he became professor at the Law School in Batavia (1924–35) and was thus the first Indonesian to be appointed at an institution of higher education. In 1919, he founded the *Java-Institute* and acted for many years as the general secretary of the *Bataviaasch Genootschap van Kunsten en Wetenschappen*; in 1935, he was elected as a member of the Council of the Netherlands–Indies (*Raad van Nederlandsch–Indië*).[4]

Poerbatjakara (1884–1964) also obtained his PhD from the University of Leiden in 1926 under Professor N.J. Krom. Later, he became curator of the Javanese manuscripts in the collection of the *Bataviaasch Genootschap*, and after the war he was appointed professor of Javanese at Gajah Mada University in Jogyakarta and the University of Indonesia in Jakarta.[5] Djajadiningrat and Poerbatjakra belonged to the few Indonesians who published articles in the journal *Bijdragen* during the colonial period,[6] and both were the only Indonesian scholars to contribute to the two commemorative volumes of the *Bataviaasch Genootschap* which were published in 1929 to celebrate the 150th year of the Society's existence (Djajadiningrat 1929; Poerbatjakara 1929).

Often, Indonesian scholars like Djajadiningrat were considered as a kind of "guinea-pig" by the supporters of the ethical policy, proving their point that Indonesians were well capable of successfully mastering a higher education (Pieper 1961: 403). Many of the exemplary Indonesian students became less popular in Dutch circles, however, when at the beginning of the 1920s they increasingly transformed into radical nationalists and renamed their hitherto harmless *Indische Vereeniging* (founded in 1908) into *Perhimpunan Indonesia* (1924), whereas their journal *Hindia Poetra* was renamed *Indonesia Merdeka*. Prospective famous nationalists like Hatta and Sjahir evolved from that nationalist circle of Indonesian students in the Netherlands.

The other field of qualification for Indonesian students was the already mentioned *adat*-law studies, of which the Leiden Professor Cornelis van Vollenhoven undeniably was the doyen. Van Vollenhoven, a glowing supporter of the ethical policy, devoted his whole academic career to the documentation and classification of the various traditional *adat* (customary law) practices which were thought to be prevalent among the various ethnic groups of the Indonesian archipelago. In his magnum opus *Het adatrecht van Nederlandsch–Indië* (1918–33), he divided Indonesia into nineteen law provinces (*adatrechtskringen*), each of which being characterized by a special type of *adat* law. By arguing that the various forms of *adat* law were more than just a collection of non-codified rules, but a *Weltanschauung* of which the social and cosmological background had to be taken into account, Van Vollenhoven strongly recommended the colonial government to acknowledge such indigenous forms of *adat* law and to refrain from the idea of imposing on the colony a system of common state- and private law based on Western legal ideas.[7]

During the period of Van Vollenhovens' professorship (1901–33), several Indonesian students obtained their PhD with studies on Indonesian *adat* law, among them Gondokoesomo (1922), Kusumah Atmadja (1922) who became President of the Supreme Court of Indonesia after independence, Enda Boemi (1925), Soepomo (1927), the later professor of *adat* law at the Batavia Law School and "father" of the 1945 Indonesian Constitution, Soeripto (1929), and Soumokil (1933), the prospective tragic hero of the short-lived Republic of South Maluku in 1950.[8] Whereas the Dutch graduates of the Leiden Faculty of Law quickly occupied high positions in the colonial hierarchy, for their Indonesian fellow-graduates the colonial system "evidently did not constitute an environment favoring Indonesian success" (Pompe 1993: 73). Notable exceptions are the already mentioned Soepomo and Atmadja, the latter being appointed a judge at the court for indigenous affairs in 1926, who three years later was transferred as judge to the court for Europeans in Padang (ibid.).

The fact that Indonesian students had successfully completed their education with a PhD dissertation, and that some of them were even trying to get a foothold in the field of science, was not unanimously welcomed in the Netherlands or in the colony, let alone that they were self-evidently considered as equal scholars. A publication from the mid-1930s, which was supposed to summarize the hitherto existing knowledge on the Netherlands–East Indies, may elucidate the arrogant attitude that now and then came to the fore on the side of the Dutch academic establishment:

> while some natives may have defended a meritorious scholarly dissertation... their intellectual contributions have no significance, and as soon as their academic studies are behind them, they rarely engage in further research.
> (Hasselman 1935: 42; quoted from Gouda 1995: 222)

A remarkably different attitude was displayed by the Dutch anthropologist J.P.B. de Josselin de Jong, when he took over the Leiden chair of anthropology of the Netherlands–Indies in 1935, and concluded his inaugural lecture by directly addressing the Indonesian students and expressing his hope that they would actively participate in the establishment of an indigenous anthropology of Indonesia:

> Finally some words addressed especially to you, Indonesian students! Up till now I have had no students among you. Initially, I have been somewhat surprised about the lack of interest on your side for precisely this branch of science. But later it has become clear to me what is the main reason. You are inclined to consider the old Indonesian culture, which you think to have out-grown, and archaic forms of culture in general, as curiosities, the study

of which cannot contribute to your understanding of the problems of the modern world with which you prefer to concern yourself. Apparently you do not realize sufficiently that the ethnological study of archaic forms of culture serves not as an aim but as a means – often the only means – not to get completely lost in the infinitely complex labyrinth of modern civilization. In most eastern countries indigenous and European ethnologists nowadays cooperate in performing a gratifying communal task; the Netherlands Indies, however, constitute one of the few exceptions, which is detrimental both to Indonesian ethnography and to general ethnology which badly need your cooperation. I take the liberty to appeal to your intellectual insight and to your patriotism as well, because I am convinced that you cannot serve your home country better than by expanding and deepening your knowledge in all directions, particularly concerning the basic foundations of your own culture. May this appeal not be in vain!

(De Josselin de Jong 1935: 24)

From this strikingly long address to the Indonesian students emerges clearly that De Josselin de Jong did not consider them as "natives" who should be content only because they were granted the privilege of receiving a higher education from the West, but as equal prospective counterpart researchers. Moreover, his emphasis on the role of anthropology as a "service to the home country" elucidates that he was trying to convince the Indonesian intellectuals that anthropology had to offer more than the study of remote island populations, that anthropology could yield answers to the problems of modernity. Despite this appeal, De Josselin de Jong could attract only a few Indonesian students during the years to come.

Meanwhile, in Batavia a Law College had been founded in 1924, offering Indonesian and Dutch students the opportunity to combine the study of law with courses on the social sciences. The Law School offered a four-year (later five-year) interdisciplinary curriculum which comprised among other subjects courses in *adat* law (taught by B. ter Haar), Interracial Law (R.D. Kollewijn), Islamic Law (H. Djajadiningrat), State- and Administrative Law (J.H.A. Logeman), Economy (J.H. Boeke), and Sociology (taught by B.J.O. Schrieke from 1924 to 1930, and by F.D. Holleman from 1930 to 1934). Until 1938, the one-year course in anthropology was taught by Ter Haar as a kind of subsidiary subject to his courses on *adat* law. As in Leiden, there were several Indonesian students at the Batavia Law School who wrote PhD dissertations on Indonesian *adat* law, such as Hazairin (1936) who did a study on the *adat* law of the Rejang of Sumatra and who later became Ter Haar's assistant, and M.M. Djojodiguno and Tirtawinanta who compiled a comprehensive study of the *adat* law of Central Java (1940).

The Batavia Law School was not only exceptional in that during the time of its existence (from 1924 to the Japanese occupation of Indonesia), the teaching staff included Indonesian scholars (the already mentioned Hoesein Djajadiningrat and Raden Soepomo who succeeded Ter Haar at the chair of *adat* law in 1941); it was also famous for the political liberalism of the Dutch professors. G.J. Resink, one of their students, later recalled that many of the Dutch scholars consequently used the terms "Indonesia" and "Indonesians" in their courses – at a time, as Resink ironically remarked, when intellectuals were already suspected as being leftist if they preferred to employ the word "Inheemsen" (Indigenous) instead of "Inlander" (1974: 431). The students were also surprised that they had to follow a two-year course in the Malay or Javanese language, and that they were taught subjects such as Islamic Law and were confronted with the theoretical (and practical) problems of reconciling Dutch Colonial Law with the various indigenous forms of *adat* law.

The political liberalism of the Batavia Law School also became manifest when some of the Dutch professors co-founded the "Society for the promotion of the social and political development of the Netherlands–Indies" in 1930, of which the journal *De Stuw* was to serve as the mouthpiece (1930–4). The "radicalism" put forward in this journal impressed above all the Indonesian students and intellectuals, for the *Stuw*-members were frankly arguing that the final aim of Dutch colonial politics should be the formation of an independent Indonesian polity (Resink 1974: 434; Locher Scholten 1981).

Many of the Indonesian students of the Batavia Law School soon became involved in the nationalist movement. According to Resink, it was mainly the law students from Batavia, such as Soegondo Djojopoesito and (the prospective famous nationalist) Muhamad Yamin, who dominated the political spirit of the famous Indonesian Youth congress at Bandung in October 1928, where the students enthusiastically formulated the three ideals of "one fatherland, Indonesia," "one nation, Indonesia," and "one language, Bahasa Indonesia." Moreover, at the end of the congress the students proclaimed that the unity of Indonesia could only be achieved by taking into account the principles of *kemuan* (communal will), *sejarah* (history), *bahasa* (language), *hukum adat* (adat law), and *pendidikan* (education). As Resink emphasized, it was in particular in the domain of *adat* law and history that the law students were heavily influenced by their teachers at the Batavia Law School (1974: 433). Resink thus saw a close connection between the liberal teaching in the Batavia Law School and several political issues which were discussed in the Indonesian nationalist movement, in particular the question whether *hukum adat* could serve as a common denominator for an all-Indonesian identity.

There can be no doubt that Indonesian nationalists, during this period, were searching for ideological concepts which would enable them to transcend the cultural heterogeneity of the various Indonesian islands and peoples. When Sukarno founded the Indonesian Nationalist Party in 1927, it was the first political association in Indonesia which had neither religious nor regional connotations. The goal was simply to achieve political independence and to ensure that the future independent Indonesian state would encompass the then present boundaries of the Netherlands–Indies. By the end of the 1920s, "the idea of a national Indonesian identity devoid of specific religious or regional ties" had already begun to be widely accepted among Indonesian nationalists (Ricklefs 1993: 185). Since the colonial power, however, had argued for decades that the only force to knit the archipelago together was the colonial order itself, one of the focal problems for Indonesian nationalists was, of course, the question as to what would constitute the common denominator for an independent state.

Whether the concept of *adat* law may have, or even has, served as such a culturally unifying concept is rather questionable. On the one hand, the notion of *adat* law could have provided the Indonesian intellectuals with a concept that vaguely implied a common and distinctive cultural inheritance. On the other hand, with its connotations of regionally autonomous *adat* communities and diverging legal and cultural practices, it was too specific and limited to provide an overall frame of Indonesian culture and nationhood. By over-emphasizing the role of *adat* "the Indonesian advocate of adat would have ended up defending the details of his own regional usages rather than the enduring unity of national culture" (Burns 1989: 2). Moreover, in the perception of the modernist Indonesian intellectuals, the concept of *adat* law had clear overtones of backwardness (Lev 1972: 255).

Later, when Soepomo, the professor of *adat* law at the former Batavia Law School, became involved in the 1945 preparations for the provisional Indonesian constitution and outlined his visions of an "integralist" state by rejecting Western liberalism and individualism as being alien and unfitting to Indonesian society, some of his ideas were clearly predicated on ideological concepts which he had borrowed from the terminology of *adat* law. According to Soepomo, the President of the state and the council should work together on the basis of *musyawarah* (mutual consultation) and *mufakat* (consensus), reverberating the collective decision making processes of traditional *adat* communities. However, in order to define the unity of the state in terms of the relation between the president and the people, which was the essential purpose of his speech, Soepomo was not referring to *adat* law but to the German "Führer-Prinzip" and to aspects of Japanese Shintoism as forming a suitable model for the Indonesian state (Bahar *et al.* 1999; Drooglever 1997: 66).[9] Maybe Sukarno was influenced by Soepomo when he declared the concept of *musyawarat* as one of the five principles in his famous 1945 *pancasila* speech, which were to serve as the philosophical foundation of the independent state. But seen as a whole, the possible connections between *adat* law and modern Indonesian politics are too superficial as to argue for the existence of a penetrating influence exerted by the former on the latter.

After independence, some of the former Indonesian students of the Batavia Law School were appointed as ministers in various cabinets or took over professorships at the Universities of Jakarta and Yogyakarta. There were a few Indonesian scholars who tried to keep up an academic interest in *adat* law, but in the late 1950s the study of *adat* law in Indonesia was clearly declining (Resink 1974: 442; Koentjaraningrat 1975: 233). Sometimes, the notion of *adat* was politically paid lip-service, but generally legal diversity became an anathema for the Jakarta government since it reflected social and cultural fragmentation (Lev 1972: 393).

Whereas in the 1930s there existed thus at least some slight connections between the study of *adat* law and the contemporary political situation in Indonesia, the subject of anthropology eked out an existence at the fringes. As already mentioned, anthropology at the Law School was taught by Ter Haar as a subsidiary subject to his courses on *adat* law. Ter Haar never assigned anthropology an independent identity or task. Accordingly, Indonesian students seemed to have shown no great interest in this subject.

The teaching of anthropology became more sophisticated, however, when at the Law School a chair for ethnology was established to which J.Ph. Duyvendak (1897–1946)[10] was appointed in 1938. The topics which he discussed in his inaugural speech were geared entirely to the possible interests of the modernist Indonesian intellectuals. Duyvendak observed that anthropology could no longer be considered as a European science only, for the expansion of European culture had led to the situation that the former "objects" of Western anthropology were turning more and more into the practitioners of that very discipline (1938: 3). Since anthropology, as Duyvendak further remarked, was now taught "in the midst of her field of research" it is by no means a matter of indifference to anthropology about who it is and who practices it. "Here we do not think of differences between individuals, but of differences resulting from the cultural milieu from which the researcher stems" (ibid.).

Duyvendak was fully aware of the ironies connected with the strange task of teaching the "natives" their own culture. Often, the indigenous students commanded more cultural common sense knowledge than their Western teacher, while ethnographic facts which for the European audience appear as "charmingly exotic" amount to "pale descriptions of the ordinary and profane" for the Indonesian listener (ibid.: 4). Indonesian intellectuals were thus often of the opinion that anthropology is an unimportant – if not compromising – science, mainly concerned with the study of outlived forms of culture (ibid.: 3). In order to get rid of this "touch of ridicule," anthropology must offer above all something to the Indonesian intellectual (ibid.: 4).

In line with these observations, Duyvendak took great pains in trying to demonstrate that anthropology, rather than being a naive form of butterfly-collecting, addresses questions which are of social and political relevance for the study of modern Indonesia. Referring to Max Scheler, Duyvendak announced that also for Indonesia, the hour of the "cosmopolitism of culture areas" had finally come, which meant that due to the increasing Europeanization of the world the so-called "traditional" cultures could no longer be saved. The more such cultures were in the process of vanishing, the more the Indonesian intellectual must ponder about the concept of "culture." According to Duyvendak, Indonesia was already subject to an advanced process of acculturation which made both the study of Indonesian and that of European culture an intellectual necessity (ibid.: 18).

When Duyvendak was appointed in 1938, the Batavia Law College had 412 students, of whom 264 were Indonesians, 69 Chinese, and 54 Europeans (Koentjaraningrat and Bachtiar 1975: 5). How many of them followed Duyvendaks's courses is difficult to assess. Under the new professorship, anthropology was still a subsidiary subject for the law students, which meant that in contrast to Ter Haar and the other law professors, Duyvendak had no students of his own. But, reportedly, he was highly respected among the Indonesian students since he organized his courses in a very unorthodox manner (De Josselin de Jong

1946: 174). Although his teaching obligation was basically confined to the ethnology of Indonesia, he taught his students European cultural history as well, not to demonstrate the intellectual superiority of the West but in order to show the relativity of European cultures as well and to subject them to a comparative ethnological perspective (Bernet-Kempers 1946: 255). It is probably more than conjecture to assume that these views of European cultural values must have deeply impressed his Indonesian students.

Another unorthodox method of Duyvendak's teaching, vividly remembered by the students in later times, was to let the students, who came from different ethnic contexts, write essays in which they had to document their own life history. Later on, it was discussed in the courses to what extent the different cultural backgrounds had shaped the life histories of the respective students (Bernet-Kempers 1946: 256; De Josselin de Jong 1946: 176).[11] This type of teaching was surely influenced by Duyvendak's reception of the American Culture and Personality school and shows that he was trying to convey to his students contemporary theories and methods of anthropology. Especially by relativizing his own culture against that of his students, Duyvendak can be considered as a forerunner in the decolonization of Dutch ethnology, which – at this time – was far from being on its way.

In the meantime, plans had been made to establish a University of Batavia. To that end, the Colonial Government created a Faculty of Letters and Philosophy in 1940, followed by the establishment of a Faculty of Agriculture in 1941. Duyvendak's anthropology chair was anchored at the Faculty of Letters, but due to illness he had to drop out of the university in 1941. His courses were taken over by Gerrit Jan Held (1906–55) who, like Duyvendak, had studied under J.P.B. de Josselin de Jong in Leiden.[12] Held, however, taught only for a short time, for in the spring of 1942 Japanese troops began to invade Indonesia. After a short period of military resistance, the Netherlands–East Indies were fully occupied by Japan and most of the Dutch academics and colonial officers including their families were interned in Japanese prison camps. Many of them did not survive the period of imprisonment. Duyvendak, for instance, after having been released, died in January 1946, just returned to the Netherlands, from the mental and physical strains which followed from the time of his internment.

During the Japanese occupation period, academic life in the field of law and social sciences had come to a complete standstill. Since the Dutch language and Western textbooks were banned, higher education became almost impossible. Moreover, the university was closed by the Japanese, and only the Medical College and the Technical College remained open. In order to outweigh former Western influences, the Japanese created a College of Civil Administration in 1944 and an Islam College in 1945, shortly before they surrendered to the Allied Forces.

When, after the three years of internment, the Dutch academics were finally released from their prisons, the Indonesia they knew had changed tremendously. These changes would leave their mark on the development of the cultural sciences in Indonesia.

The political impasse of anthropology in the postwar period (1945–9)

After the war, Dutch anthropologists in Indonesia found themselves exposed to a radically altered political situation. During the period of the Japanese surrender (August 15, 1945) and the landing of the Allied Forces, Sukarno and Hatta had proclaimed the Independence of Indonesia on August 15, 1945. In Jakarta, a Republican government was quickly established, with Sukarno being appointed as President and Hatta as Vice-President. With the help of the Allied forces, however, the Dutch colonial army succeeded in reoccupying Jakarta, the western part of Java, and practically all of the outer islands. The Indonesian Republican Forces who were trying to defend the newly founded "Independent State" moved to East Java, with Yogyakarta being proclaimed the seat of the Republican Government in January 1946. These incidents led to what in Indonesia has been (and is still) called the "Indonesian Revolution" by which independence was finally gained in 1949.

The 1946 division of Indonesia into a Dutch-controlled and a Republican part was also reflected in the field of academic education. In Yogyakarta, the Revolutionary Gajah Mada University had been founded in 1946. Right from the start, this university was established to form a prospective center for "national culture" and to offer a form of education which would run counter to Dutch (imperial) ideology. The university was to have its roots in *Indonesian* society and was expected to provide for an *Indonesian* education, rendered by *Indonesian* scholars in the *Indonesian* Language (Knoppers 1949–50: 57). Anthropology and Sociology were taught by M.M. Djojodigeno, a former student of Ter Haar at the Batavia Law School. The Indonesian anthropologist Koentjaraningrat later recalled that the teaching at this university became possible only because students from Jakarta had smuggled hundreds of books to Yogyakarta while Jakarta was surrounded by Dutch troops (Visser and Koentjaraningrat 1988: 750).

In the Dutch-controlled Jakarta a so-called "Nood-Universiteit" had been founded in 1946 which one year later was renamed the University of Indonesia. The chair of anthropology, which was anchored in the Faculty of Law and Social Sciences, was given to Held since Duyvendak had died in 1946. Held was also appointed head of the newly founded Research Institute for Language and Culture (after independence: Lembaga Bahasa dan Budaja) which was attached to the Faculty. In the beginning, Indonesian students seemed to have been rather reluctant to study at the University of Indonesia, for it was an institution founded and controlled by the former colonial power. Furthermore, due to the repatriation of Dutch scholars who had preferred to return to the Netherlands after Japanese imprisonment, the University was heavily understaffed (Knoppers 1949–50: 56). In 1947, however, the frustrating situation of the Dutch lecturers seemed to have somewhat improved. In 1948, the Faculty of Law and Social Sciences had 139 students: 64 Indonesians, 53 Chinese, and 22 Dutch (ibid.: 45). How many of them were studying anthropology is not known. In particular, the Indonesian students were probably suspicious about that subject, given its long-standing institutional relationship with the colonial office (De Josselin de Jong 1956: 52).

For Dutch anthropologists in Indonesia the postwar period therefore posed the problem, so that many Indonesian intellectuals considered ethnology – due to its embeddedness in the colonial *Indologie* program – as a highly imperialistic science. With what arguments could a discipline be legitimized in a region where the indigenous intellectuals increasingly conceived of ethnologists as the handmaidens of colonialism and disqualified their traditional object of study as "primitivology" (De Josselin de Jong 1946: 22)? To put it shortly, in the postwar period Dutch ethnologists were more and more accused of having cultivated a scientific attitude which Edward Said would later come to label as "Orientalism."

Given these negative assessments from the Indonesian side, Dutch anthropology could hardly proceed with the unproblematic study of remote island societies. Some of the Dutch anthropologists[13] tried to find a way out of this impasse by redefining the theoretical contents and tasks of an anthropology of Indonesia. Nooteboom, for instance, one of De Josselin de Jong's former students, published an article in 1947–8 in which he expressed his understanding that the participants of the cultures which anthropologists traditionally had studied felt increasingly discriminated by that very science (1947–8: 43). In order to prevent anthropology from becoming merely considered as a kind of "archaeology," Nooteboom pleaded for studying processes of acculturation and focusing the research on the populations of the new urban centres and their political and religious organizations (ibid.: 45, 51). By concentrating on the rapid developments of modernization, as Nooteboom hoped, even the "new Indonesian authorities" might become convinced of the undeniable value of anthropology for the understanding of modern Indonesian culture (ibid.: 45).

Before such studies on the new urban centers could materialize, however, Indonesia had won its independence from the Netherlands. The suspicion against the colonial background of anthropology was to remain strong in the years to come, so that the position of the Dutch ethnologists who had stayed at the University of Indonesia was far from being promising. It was the time when the sons became prepared to replace their fathers.

From *Volkenkunde* to *Djurusan Antropologi*: the post-independence period (1950–8)

After several futile attempts to establish a federal United States of Indonesia and as a consequence of two so-called "police actions" by which the Dutch had tried to conquer the Republican territory, the Netherlands finally had to acknowledge the independence of Indonesia in November 1949 at the Round Table Conference in The Hague. One month later, on December 27, the Netherlands officially transferred sovereignty to Indonesia, with the exception of Irian (West New Guinea) which remained under Dutch control.

The University of Indonesia was handed over to the new Ministry of Education and was renamed *Universitas Indonesia*. In 1950 President Sukarno announced that the education system which had been prevalent in the former Dutch controlled regions was to be fully nationalized. Many of the Dutch professors refused to teach under the new conditions and returned to the Netherlands. In the same year, the Dutch Government announced that the study of *Indologie* was to be abandoned, since Dutch colonial officers were of course no longer needed. From the institutional remains of the once multi-disciplinary and mighty *Indologie*-program emerged a new discipline in 1952, the Sociology of Non-Western Societies, with anthropology in the Netherlands becoming again an independent subject (Kloos 1988).

The independence of Indonesia, however, did not result in the immediate withdrawl of the Dutch scholars. As far as anthropology was concerned, the Dutch teaching staff of the University of Indonesia could retain their position for a couple of years. Held remained at his professorship until 1955 and was assisted by the Dutch lecturers F.A.E. van Wouden and Elisabeth Allard. Naturally, the situation of the Dutch scholars had deeply changed. The university was headed and administered by Indonesians, the former Literary Faculty had been renamed *Fakultas Sastra*, and the official language had changed from Dutch to Bahasa Indonesia. Moreover, as had become already virulent in the postwar period, the subject of anthropology – as embodied by the Dutch – was increasingly considered as being politically suspect.

Accordingly, in the post-independence period, the Dutch anthropologists in Indonesia were wrestling ever stronger with the problem of the political legitimation of their discipline. As Held put it in:

> Anthropology...is to a degree suspect for its presumed advocacy of the cultural status quo and is even considered as "colonialistic" in its type of thought. The interest in *primitive* societies, as exhibited even by the most modern and progressive anthropology, can hardly be expected to harmonize with the interests of a young and fervent nationalism.
>
> (1953a: 877)

Such a critical attitude toward anthropology had been already put forward in 1950 by the Indonesian sociologist T.S.G. Moelia, shortly after the latter had taken over the professorship of Sociology at the University of Indonesia. In a polemical article, he accused Western anthropology of having been basically interested in the "primitive" and "static" aspects of society, thus being more or less unsuited to provide for the impulses which were deemed necessary for the future development of the nation: "In Indonesia there is a new society emerging, being radically different from those which are still bound by tradition and which anthropology preferably has chosen as its objects of study" (Moelia 1951: 32). "New groups, new political and social institutions have developed which are based on political and societal ideals" (ibid.: 31). As Moelia argued, in order to study such processes and to deduce from them the practical instructions which are needed for the development of the state, the impact of sociology should be academically strengthened whereas the role of anthropology had better be diminished.

Noteworthy in this respect is that the cultural conservatism, of which Moelia had so strongly accused Dutch anthropology, was reproduced in his own discourse concerning Indonesia's cultural differences in an amazingly naive manner: "Between the culture of the Javanese and that of the Papuas of Irian there is a gap of thousand years" (ibid.: 28). In the same year Moelia was appointed Minister of Education; he was succeeded by Ismael, the second Indonesian who had written a PhD dissertation under J.P.B. de Josselin de Jong in Leiden (1949) (see later). Ismael in turn soon took over a political office himself and was replaced by the Dutch sociologist H.J. Heeren who lectured from 1954 to 1957.

Despite the critical tones from the side of Indonesian sociology, the Indonesian authorities did not seriously consider abolishing the subject of anthropology. Held, who was on leave in Europe and the United States from 1951 to 1952 and was not sure whether he should return to Indonesia, was explicitly assured from the Indonesian side that his presence at the university was more than welcomed, whereupon he returned to Jakarta. Held was also promised that he was completely free in choosing the topics of his lectures and that he could do fieldwork wherever he wanted (de Josselin de Jong 1956: 552).

Held indeed received permission to undertake fieldwork on the island of Sumbawa from 1954 to 1955. In this context, it is interesting to note how the scientific rhetoric of the Dutch scholars in Indonesia had changed whenever they wanted to do research under the new political conditions. In present terms, Dutch anthropologists had to employ a terminology of "political correctness." Held's own research proposal to the President of the University of Indonesia may serve as an example here. The overall tone of the proposal shows clearly that under the new conditions, Held was compelled to synthesize his research questions with the national interests of the government and to assure the authorities that the whole style of the research project differed clearly from Dutch pre-war anthropology.

In order to acquit himself from the possible suspicion that his research project might have anything in common with the old colonial circumstances, Held right from the start made clear that his project would not amount to an investigation into the rationalization of the local administration; that is, a project which possibly aimed at scrutinizing the local political system in order to facilitate indirect rule. By contrast:

> It is absolutely necessary to emphasize that I am not a colonial officer and that the planned research project is solely based on an interest of the university as a center of science. This research is not so much concerned with the local circumstances on Sumbawa than with the *national culture of Indonesia* as it is reflected on this island.
>
> (Held 1953b: 6, italics added)

This passage demonstrates that Held was at pains to link his own research questions with the interests of the Indonesian state in forging a national culture.

Just as new was Held's concession that the research project could only be successfully implemented if the local authorities and the inhabitants of Sumbawa would give their agreement to the project. As Held remarked, the times had finally gone in which the consent and cooperation of the local officials could be ordered from "above." Should there be any reservations from the local side, the project would have to be abandoned. Moreover, this time it was planned to involve Indonesian counterpart researchers right from the start (1953b: 7).[14] Obviously, the preconditions for undertaking anthropological field researches had changed tremendously: anthropologists should no longer be concerned with the study of singular cultures, but with the national culture of Indonesia as a whole; local authorities could no longer be bypassed, and Indonesian counterpart researchers should be involved.

Possibly, by taking into account the necessary preconditions, a fruitful cooperation of Dutch and Indonesian anthropologists might have evolved, just as it had been envisaged by J.P.B. de Josselin de Jong in 1935 (see previous section). The political tensions between the Netherlands and Indonesia resulting from the Irian-conflict, however, put an early end to such efforts. Due to these tensions, the Dutch scholars were finally compelled to leave the country. Held had already accepted a professorship at the Royal Tropical Institute in Amsterdam, but died unexpectedly in 1955 before he could leave for the Netherlands. Van Wouden had been on leave in the Netherlands in 1954 and never returned to Indonesia (Roolvink 1989: 422). From the old anthropology staff, there was only Elisabeth Allard left who taught until 1958.

Due to the retreat of the Dutch lecturers, the vacant teaching positions could more and more be occupied by Indonesian anthropologists who were striving to establish an indigenous form of Indonesian anthropology, whatever that would mean in praxis. Held, being insecure about the future role of Dutch anthropologists in Indonesia, was not sure whether he would find interested Indonesian students:

> It is still an open question whether Holland will be in a position to give Indonesian anthropology further guidance and assistance ... Holland now has a number of young anthropologists but lacks the funds to give them a start in practical research. Indonesia needs anthropologists but lacks the experience which could make it conscious of this need.

> (1953a: 877)

In the mid-1950s, there were some Indonesian students who had become conscious of this need, but they resolved to put it into practice without the Dutch. In the Netherlands, there were a few Indonesian students who had obtained a degree in anthropology in the postwar period. In Leiden, three Indonesian students, Koes Sardjono, J. Ismael, and J. Avé, had been trained by J.P.B. de Josselin de Jong. Two of them had completed their study with a PhD dissertation (Sardjono 1946; Ismael 1949). In Utrecht, the Indonesian anthropology student Ph. Tobing had obtained his PhD in 1956 under H.Th. Fischer.[15] Most of them were now available to replace the Dutch lecturers.

Avé (born, 1923) was the first to be appointed lecturer at the *Fakultas Sastra* of the University of Indonesia in 1955.[16] As Avé recalled proudly, officially there existed no *Djurusan Antropologi* at this time, "it had to be established by the Indonesians themselves" (Avé 1995: 4). This happened eventually in 1956 when under the name *Djurusan Antropologi budaja*, the first Indonesian Chair for Anthropology was established at the Fakultas Sastra. Two years later, the anthropologist Koentjaraningrat (1923–99) who had written his MA thesis at Yale University (1954) and a PhD dissertation under E. Allard was appointed to the chair. He became one of Indonesia's most distinguished scholars. Also, the subject of sociology became fully "indonesianized" with Harsia W. Bachtiar being appointed to the Chair of Sociology in 1958. Bachtiar had obtained his MA from Cornell University in 1956 with a thesis on "Twelve Sumatran Villages."

The fact that both Koentjaraningrat and Bachtiar had obtained their MA from American universities points to another aspect which was linked to Indonesia's problem of decolonizing the Dutch scientific heritage. In order to distance themselves from their Dutch "fathers," Indonesia's anthropology and sociology students were frequently sent to academic institutions in the United States where during the postwar period several centers for Southeast Asian studies had been established (Yale, Cornell, MIT).[17] This was one of the ways to diminish the impact of the Dutch heritage. Another strategy was to send "loyal" Republican students from Yogyakarta to Jakarta in order to achieve the full nationalization of the University of Indonesia. The intellectual transmigrants from Yogyakarta should "form a national student force to counterbalance the Jakarta students, who had studied under the Dutch" (Visser 1988: 750). Possible traces of Dutch-bred academic thought should in this way swiftly be Indonesianized.

The inexorable trend toward the Indonesianization of the remnants of the Dutch anthropological institutions had also become manifest when the venerable *Bataviaasch Genootschap* embodying more than 150 years of Dutch Oriental scholarship was renamed in *Lembaga Kebudajaan Indonesia* (1951). The last two volumes of the Society's journal *Tijdschrift voor Indische Taal-, Land- en Volkenkunde* appeared under the name *Madjalah untuk Ilmu Bahasa, Ilmu Bumi dan Kebudajaan Indonesia* in 1957 and 1958.

At the end of the 1950s, the decolonization of the Dutch academic heritage was thus more or less completed at the level of institutions. This did not mean, however, that the Dutch impact could be immediately neutralized in the ideological sense. Until the 1960s, Duyvendak's introductory textbook from 1935 was still used in Indonesian classrooms due to the lack of suitable textbooks in the Indonesian language. Fischer's 1940 introduction was used merrily as well. There were also scripts copied from Held's lecture notes, which circulated among the Indonesian anthropology lecturers (Koentjaraningrat 1975: 242). Obviously, Dutch anthropology took revenge for its expulsion by subversively infiltrating the Indonesian academe for a long time.

Other academic continuities shook the national image of a fully Indonesianized scientific system as well. In the 1990s, the sociologist Bachtiar conceded that many of the senior Indonesian academics still clung to the Dutch academic tradition and that the academic hierarchy as a whole was still based on the old Dutch system (Bachtiar 1999). Also, with regard to the role attributed to anthropology in the context of the problems of national integration, some remarkable ideological continuities can be observed. In an interview at the occasion of his retirement in 1988, Koentjaraningrat argued that the main purpose of anthropological studies in Indonesia was, and still is, the national integration of the multiethnic nation-state[18] which may be promoted by mutual understanding and tolerance among the component ethnic units:

> The anthropology of Indonesia is part of almost every curriculum in our vocational schools, schools of public administration, military schools, police academies, etc. The reason is that, if, let's say, an Indonesian military officer or civil servant is appointed to an area different from his own, he needs to know the different ethnic groups in the area he lives. This education therefore serves to bring about a sort of theoretical unity.
>
> (Visser 1988: 752)

The civil servant's or military officer's "need to know the ethnic groups": with this type of argumentation Dutch anthropologists and supporters of *Indologie* for decades had argued for the promotion of their science. It thus seems that in the 1980s, the decolonization of Dutch ethnology in Indonesia was still on its way. The main difference is of course that while the Dutch anthropologists could easily acknowledge the ethnic heterogeneity of the archipelago – an attitude for which they were later accused as having overstressed cultural diversity and therefore underpinning the colonial ideology of "divide and rule" (Ellen 1976) – their Indonesian successors were in a quite different position. Not long after its foundation, the Indonesian state was repeatedly shattered by a series of regional conflicts, Maluku, West-Sumatra, and North-Sulawesi being the most prominent cases. Avé aptly describes the ideological consequences to which Indonesian anthropology was increasingly exposed:

> Indonesian anthropology developed in a milieu in which – due to the political developments – federal ideas were considered as threatening the state. Regional autonomy was interpreted as the beginning of separatism, as a falling apart of the state. This anxiety was not only prevalent among the military, but also the president was prepossessed by such ideas.... Officially the existence of different ethnic identities in the country was completely denied. The 1960 census registered inhabitants in all of the different provinces... but no mention was made of suku bangsa (ethnic groups).
>
> (1995: 8)

Nourished by the national anxiety concerning ethnic diversity and regional identity, Indonesian anthropology developed mainly into an applied science, which was supposed to sustain the national ideology of pempangunan (development). The thematic correlations between Indonesian anthropology and the ideology of the nation-state, however, are discussed elsewhere in this volume.

Notes

1 For an analysis of nineteenth and early twentieth-century Dutch ethnology see De Josselin Jong and Vermeulen (1989), Platenkamp and Prager (1994); the linkages between Dutch anthropology and colonialism are described by Ellen (1976), and Prager (1996, 1999).

2 On the general development of higher education in Indonesia during the period from 1900 to 1950, see Murray (1973), and van der Wal (1963).

3 Throughout this chapter, I will use the old spelling of Indonesian personal names.

4 An account of Djajaningrat's life and work is given by Pieper (1961).

5 On Poertbatjakara see Pigeaud (1966).

6 Knaap (1994: 641) observes that during the colonial period, articles written by Indonesian authors constituted only 1 percent of the total number of the contributions to the journal Bijdragen. Knaap attributes this lack of Indonesian contributions to "the tremendous gap that existed between the worlds of colonizers and the colonized" (ibid.).

7 On van Vollenhoven and Dutch *adat*-law studies, see the critical but sympathetic account of Burns (1989).

8 Pompe (1993: 89–98) gives a list with the titles and topics of the PhD theses of the Indonesian Law students.

9 On the political afterlife of Soepomo's model of the integralist state in the New Order Indonesia under Suharto, see the interesting analysis of Bourchier (1997).

10 Duyvendak (1897–1946) had obtained his PhD in 1926, under De Josselin de Jong in Leiden. In 1929, he was appointed as a teacher to the General Middle School in Surakarta; later he was teaching at the General Middle Schools of Yogyakarta and Batavia. In 1935, he published an introductory textbook on the anthropology of Indonesia.

11 A list with the titles and the names of the Indonesian authors of such scripts can be found in Niessen (1982: 114–16).

12 Held had obtained his PhD in 1935. Before taking over Duyvendak's lectures at the Faculty of Letters, he had worked for the Dutch Bible Society in Dutch New Guinea from 1935 to 1940, and from 1940 to 1941 he was employed as a Language Officer by the Dutch colonial service.

13 For an evaluation of the general (anti-)colonial attitude of the Leiden anthropologists and contemporary discussions about the relation between anthropology and acculturation, see Prager (1999).

14 On the issue of involving Indonesian counterpart researchers and Indonesian doctoral students, see also Held (1953c, 1954).

15 Fischer had another Indonesian PhD student, M.M. Nasoetion, who wrote a thesis on the role of women in the Batak society of Sumatra in 1943 (Nasoetion 1943).

16 Avé had studied anthropology from 1948 to 1954 under J.P.B. de Josselin de Jong in Leiden. After the military coup of 1965, he left Indonesia to work as curator at the Leiden Ethnological Museum from 1968 to 1986.

17 For an overview of the theses written by Indonesian students in the United States, see Koentjaraningrat (1975).

18 On the relationship between national integration and the social sciences in Indonesia, compare also Bachtiar (1993).

References

Anderson, B. (1983) "Old state, new society: Indonesia's new order in comparative perspective," *Journal of Asian Studies*, 42: 477–96.

Avé, J. (1995) "De groei van een tropische variëteit: culturele antropologie in Indonesia," in G.D. van Wengen, R.S. Wassing, and A.A. Trouwborst (eds), *Waar dromers ontwaken*, Leiden: P.E. Bijvoet, pp.1–15.

Bachtiar, Harsja (1993) "Developing universities in multi-ethnic Indonesia: a problem of national integration," in J.B. Balderston and F.E. Balderston (eds), *Higher Education in Indonesia: Evolution and Reform*, Berkeley, CA: Center for Studies in Higher Education, University of California, pp. 63–82.

Bachtiar, Harsja (1999) *Universities in Indonesia: An Assessment*, unpublished paper, Leiden: KITLV Press.

Bahar, S., A.B. Kusuma, and N. Hudawati (eds) (1999) *Risalah Sidang Badan Penyelidik Usua-Usua Persiapan Kemerdekaan Indonesia (BPUPKI), Panitia Persiapan Kemerdekaan Indonesia (PPKI)*, Jakarta: Sekretariat Negara Republik Indonesia.

Bernet-Kempers, A.J. (1946) "In memoriam Professor Dr J.Ph Duyvendak," *Tijdschrift van het Nederlands Aardrijkskundig Genootschap*, 63: 253–6.

Bourchier, D. (1997) "Totalitarianism and the 'National Personality': recent controversy about imagining Indonesia: cultural politics and political culture," Athens: Ohio University Center for International Studies, Southeast Asia Series, 97: 157–85.

Burns, P. (1989) "The myth of adat," *Journal of Legal Pluralism and Unofficial Law*, 28: 1–125.

Cribb, R. (1994) "Introduction: the late colonial state in Indonesia," in R. Cribb (ed.), *The Late Colonial State in Indonesia: Political and Economic Foundations of the Netherlands Indies, 1800–1942*, Leiden: KITLV Press.

Djajadiningrat, H. (1929) "Toepassing van het Mohamedaansche slavenrecht," in *Feestbundel uitgegeven door het Koninklijk Bataviaasch Genootschap van Kunsten en Wetenschappen ter gelegenheid van zijn 150 jaring bestaan, 1787–1928, Vol. I*, pp. 87–92.

Djojodigoeno, M.M. and R. Tirtawinanta (1940) *Het Adatprivaatrecht van Middel-Java*, Batavia: Soekamiskin, Dept. v. Justitie.

Drooglever, P.L. (1997) "The genesis of the Indonesian constitution," *Bijdragen tot de Taal-, Land- en Volkenkunde*, 153: 65–84.

Duyvendak, J.P. (1935) *Inleiding tot de ethnologie van de Indische Archipel*, Groningen/ Batavia: Wolters.

——(1938) *Ethnologische Belangstelling*, Inaugural Lecture, Batavia Law School, Groningen/Batavia: Wolters.

Ellen, R. (1976) "The development of anthropology and colonial policy in the Netherlands, 1800–1960," *Journal of the History of the Behavioral Sciences*, 12: 303–24.

Fasseur, C. (1993) *De Indologen: Ambtenaren voor de Oost, 1825–1950*, Amsterdam: Uitgeverij Bert Bakker.

Gouda, F. (1995) *Dutch Culture Overseas. Colonial Practice in the Netherlands Indies, 1900–1942*, Amsterdam: Amsterdam University Press.

Hasselman, C.J. (1935) "Karakter van ons koloniaal beheer," in D.G. Stibbe (ed.), *Neerlands-Indië. Land en volk; geschiedenis en bestuur; bedrijf en samenleving*, 2 vols, Amsterdam: Elsevier.

Hazairin (1936) *De Redjang. De volksordening, het verwantschaps-, huwelijks- en erfrecht*, Bandung: A.C. Nix & Co.

Held, G.J. (1953a) "Applied anthropology in government: The Netherlands," in A.L. Kroeber (ed.), *Anthropology Today*, Chicago, IL: University of Chicago Press, pp. 453–72.

——(1953b) "Toelichting op het voorstel tot antropologisch onderzoek in opdracht van den President der Universiteit Indonesia in te stellen op het eiland Sumbawa" Unpublished paper, Held Collection, HR 1220, Leiden: KITLV Press, 2 June.

——(1953c) "Penjelidikan di Sumbawa dari Universitet Indonesia," unpublished paper, Held Collection, HR 1220, Leiden: KITLV Press, 26 October.

——(1954) "Penjelidikan sosiologi di Sumbawa dari Universitet Indonesia," unpublished paper, Held Collection, HR 1220, Leiden: KITLV Press, 3 November.

Ismael, J. (1949) *De immigratie van Indonesiërs in Suriname* (PhD dissertation, University of Leiden), Leiden: Luctor et Emergo.

Josselin de Jong, J.P.B. de (1935) *De Maleische Archipel als ethnologisch studieveld*, Leiden: Ginsberg (Inaugural Lecture, University of Leiden).

——(1946–7) "Herdenking van Johan Philip Duyvendak," *Jaarboek der Koninklijke Akademie van Wetenschappen*, pp. 170–7.

——(1956) "Herdenking van Gerrit Jan Held," *Bijdragen tot de Taal-, Land- en Volkenkunde*, 112: 344–54.

Josselin de Jong, P.E. de and H. Vermeulen (1989) "Cultural anthropology at Leiden University: from encyclopedism to structuralism," in W. Otterspeer (ed.), *Leiden Oriental Connections, 1850–1940*, Leiden: Brill, pp. 280–316.

Kloos, P. (1988) "Het ontstaan van een discipline: de Sociologie der Niet-Westerse Volken," *Antropologische Verkenningen*, 7: 123–46.

Knaap, G. (1994) "One hundred fifty volumes of Bijdragen," *Bijdragen tot de Taal-, Land- en Volkenkunde*, 150: 637–52.

Knoppers, B.A. (1949–50) "Het Hoger Onderwijs in Indonesië," *Indonesië*, 3: 36–60.

Koentjaraningrat, R.M. (1964) "Anthropology and non-Euro-American anthropologists: the situation in Indonesia," in W.H. Goodenough (ed.), *Explorations in Cultural Anthropology*, pp. 293–308.

——(1975) *Anthropology in Indonesia: A Bibliographic Review*, The Hague: Nijhoff.

Koentjaraningrat, R.M. and H.W. Bachtiar (1975) "Higher education in the social sciences in Indonesia," in R.M. Koentjaraningrat (ed.), *The Social Sciences in Indonesia*, Jakarta: LIPI, pp. 1–42.

Lev, D.S. (1972) "Judicial institutions and legal cultures in Indonesia," in Claire Holt (ed.), *Culture and Politics in Indonesia*, Ithaca, NY: Cornell University Press, pp. 246–318.

Locher-Scholten, E. (1981) *Ethiek in fragmenten. Vijf studies over koloniaal denken en doen van Nederlanders in de Indonesische Arcipel*, Utrecht: HES.

Moelia, T.S.G. (1951) "Indonesische Sociologie," *Cultureel Nieuws Indonesië*, (11): 28–32.

Murray, T.R. (1973) *A Chronicle of Indonesian Higher Education: The First Half Century, 1920–1950*, Singapore: Chopmen Enterpises.

Nasoetion, M.H. (1943) *De plaats van de vrouw in de Batakse maatschappij*, Utrecht: Kemink en zoon.

Niessen, S. (1982) *De Leidse Richting, toen en thans*, Leiden: ICA publicatie No. 49.

Nooteboom, C. (1947/8) "Het belang van socio-ethnologisch onderzoek in het nieuwe Indonesië," *Indonesië*, 1: 43–52.

Pieper, G.F. (1961) "Professor Dr Pangeran Ario Hoesein Djajadiningrat," *Bijdragen tot de Taal-, Land- en Volkenkunde*, 117: 401–9.

Pigeaud, Th. (1966) "In memoriam Professor Poerbatjakra," *Bijdragen tot de Taal-, Land- en Volkenkunde*, 122: 405–12.

Platenkamp, J.D.M. and M. Prager (1994) "A mirror of paradigms: nineteenth and early twentieth-century ethnology reflected in Bijdragen," *Bijdragen tot de Taal-, Land- en Volkenkunde*, 150: 703–27.

Poerbatjakara, R.Ng. (1929) "Mengeling," in *Feestbundel uitgegeven door het Koninklijk Bataviaasch Genootschap van Kunsten en Wetenschappen ter gelegenheid van zijn 150 jaring bestaan, 1787–1928, Vol. II*, pp. 291–8.

Pompe, S. (1993) "A short review of doctoral theses on the Netherlands–Indies accepted at the Faculty of Law of Leiden University in the Period 1850–1940," *Indonesia*, 56: 67–98.

Prager, M. (1996) *Strukturale Anthropologie in Leiden, 1917–1956: Ursprung und Entwicklung eines wissenschaftlichen Forschungsprogamms* (PhD dissertation, University of Heidelberg) [English translation forthcoming].

Prager, M. (1999) "Crossing borders, healing wounds: Leiden anthropology and the colonial encounter, 1917–1949," in J. van Bremen and A. Shimizu (eds), *Anthropology and Colonialism in Asia and Oceania*, Richmond: Curzon, pp. 326–61.

Resink, G.J. (1974) "Rechtshoogeschool, jongereneed, 'Stuw' en gestuwden," *Bijdragen tot de Taal-, Land- en Volkenkunde*, 130: 428–49.

Rickleffs, M.C. (1993) *A History of Indonesia*, London: MacMillan.

Roolvink, R. (1989) "In memoriam F.A.E. van Wouden," *Bijdragen tot de Taal-, Land- en Volkenkunde*, 145: 420–3.

Sardjono, K. (1947) *De botjah-angon (herdersjongen) in de Javaanse cultuur* (PhD dissertation, University of Leiden).

Visser, L.E. (1988) "An interview with Koentjaraningrat," *Current Anthropology*, 29(5): 749–53.

Wal, S.L. van der (1963) *Het Onderwijsbeleid in Nederlandsch–Indië, 1900–1940 (Een Bronnenpublicatie)*, Groningen: Wolters.

10 Anthropology and the nation state

Applied anthropology in Indonesia

Martin Ramstedt

Between localised, indigenous and intercultural anthropology

Why do I, a German anthropologist working in the Netherlands, want to write about the history, the socio-political context and the perspectives of Indonesian anthropology? Am I just another contributor to 'hegemonic Northern anthropology' who is going to silence the voices of 'Southern' colleagues by attempting to assess 'them' or, even worse, to speak 'for them'?[1] With regard to the critique of Western 'orientalism'[2] and the concurrent deconstruction of Western strategies of 'othering',[3] my attempt to describe the function of anthropology in modern Indonesia demands a clarification or even justification, since indigenous anthropologists are likely to be much more conversant with the national history of their discipline.

I have derived my motivation[4] for discussing dominant aspects of the Indonesian anthropological discourse[5] in its socio-political context from co-operating with different Indonesian scientific institutions and colleagues over the course of many years.[6] In the context of this co-operation, it has been imperative to determine the 'localised' and the 'indigenous' elements of the Indonesian anthropological discourse in order to establish a communication with the 'Other' which is 'meaningful' to both 'sides'. Investigating the socio-political parameters of anthropology in Indonesia, especially at a time when ex-President Soeharto was still in power, has for me been tied up with the quest for a truly 'intercultural' anthropology. However, the process of establishing an intercultural dialogue between anthropologists of different national or ethnic background, which is based on mutual respect, also requires an appreciation of those *différances* (Jacques Derrida) which are not mere differences, but incompatibilities.

For me as a German anthropologist who was brought up to condemn the instrumentalisation of science by the Nazi- and the Stasi-regime, it was hard, for instance, not to demur at the duty assigned to Indonesian anthropology and anthropologists by the government of ex-President Soeharto ([1965] 1968–98), to foster the 'building of the Indonesian nation'. I was often tempted to speak of the *gleichschaltung* of anthropology – or of science in general for that matter – in Indonesia, whereas the development of Indonesian anthropology could just as well – and justifiedly so – be described as a kind of indigenisation of Western anthropology, since Indonesian anthropologists have amalgamated Western anthropological theory and method with the tenets of the Indonesian state-philosophy.[7]

Moreover, it does not suffice to reduce the intrinsic complexity of the discourse of Indonesian anthropologists during the reign of Soeharto by suggesting its total dependence on governmental directives. The influence of emancipatory strands of Western – especially American – anthropology or 'cultural studies', apparent in Indonesian anthropological textbooks and other publications of that period, reflects the growing orientation of an increasing part of the modern Indonesian intellectual elite towards Human Rights (*Hak Asasi Manusia*); that is, the values of a 'civil society' (*masyarakat madani*), an orientation which finally resulted in the recent downfall of the Soeharto-regime and the subsequent reformation of Indonesian politics. Those intellectuals and anthropologists who were the strongest supporters of an emancipatory anthropology in 'new order' Indonesia,[8] such as for instance George Aditjondro, and who were consequently prevented from getting an academic position by the Soeharto-regime, or who – even worse – had to go into exile, are now having an impact on the development of anthropological discourse in post-Soeharto Indonesia. Moreover, the indigenisation of anthropology in Indonesia will surely get a boost from the intent of the present Indonesian government, to focus more on exchange with other Asian countries.

At this point, it might be important to state that in contrast to Michael Prager I hesitate to consider Indonesian anthropology as not yet being 'de-colonised'. It is true that a dependence on 'Western' theoretical frameworks as well as methodologies is apparent in every Indonesian project and publication. It is also true that an emancipated 'Southern', that is, Indonesian corrective of 'Northern' anthropology or even 'Northern' culture,[9] which would help to achieve a truly intercultural discipline has not yet been put forward.[10] But I would suggest that it was the educational and cultural policy of Soeharto's 'new order' government that stifled the intellectual climate in Indonesia and prevented Indonesian anthropologists from developing a truly indigenised theoretical discourse. However, as I have already alluded to, even during the Soeharto-period a growing number of indigenous anthropologists took sides with 'local voices' against issues of government policy by using the official rhetoric to a local end. At present, discussions among Indonesian anthropologists as well as some of their latest publications show a growing self-reflexivity and a greater willingness to re-examine Western anthropological concepts.[11] This process is boosted by the fact that since a few years ago, the shelves of the academic bookshops in Indonesia, such as Gramedia and others, display many copies of books by representatives of those Western intellectual strands that were suppressed by the Soeharto-regime, including books by Marx and other classics of leftist social and political science.

Since the recent reformation, democratisation and decentralisation of the Indonesian bureaucracy and political system, the intellectual and the academic life in Indonesia has definitely changed for the better. That means the stifling intellectual climate that did not encourage emancipatory – indigenous or otherwise – theoretical approaches in Indonesian anthropology has vanished. As

Indonesian universities are entitled to independently develop, formulate and implement their academic programmes and curricula, co-operation with Western scientific institutions have become more frequent. Due to the fact that such a co-operation often entails financial benefits as well as a rise in intellectual prestige, there is – alas – the danger that Indonesian anthropologists will be more inclined to submit to hegemonic Western meta-theoretical discourses than to really develop independent concepts and approaches, which would provide deeper insights into local affairs. Moreover, Indonesian anthropology is still very much 'applied anthropology' which is called to contribute towards solving the over-whelming social, political, economic and ecological problems of the country. Yet, applied Indonesian anthropology less and less reflects Sukarno's and Soeharto's rhetoric of nationalisation. In order to fully emancipate Indonesian anthropology from government interests, though, Indonesian anthropologists have to be wary of getting entangled in local politics, sacrificing scientific interests for individual gain, as the recent implementation of the legislation on decentralisation and regional autonomy has empowered the local governments, resulting in the estab-lishment of new and powerful local bureaucracies and elites ready to pursue their own agenda.

Coming from a country with an unfortunate history of totalitarian regimes, in which science was blatantly instrumentalised for political ends, I have academic-ally positioned myself in a paradigm geared to deconstruct entangled 'logics' of politics and hermeneutics, knowing, however, that power and knowledge are inherently related categories of social action. Being interested in the chances for emancipatory thinking in the social sciences in general as well as in future co-operation with Indonesian colleagues, I am of course interested in the chances for emancipatory thinking in Indonesian anthropology. This interest necessitates – for me at least – reflecting on the historical development of Indonesian anthropology since Independence.

Since Indonesian anthropology has indeed mostly been 'applied anthropology', which has had a considerable impact on the socio-cultural development of vari-ous segments of Indonesian society, reflecting upon the development of anthro-pology in Indonesia can effect a better understanding of the development of Indonesian society, in general, and the nationalisation process, in particular. While elaborating some of the points, Michael Prager has already briefly addressed in his contribution, I will particularly focus on the development of Indonesian anthropology from the beginning of Soeharto's 'new order' government until now.

Imagining a nation[12]

It is a well-known strategy of the political elite of a multi-ethnic country like Indonesia to 'imagine' a common culture by rediscovering a common past of the various local traditions with the help of history, anthropology, ethnography and folklore studies, respectively.[13] The history of these interrelated disciplines has often intersected with the nationalisation process in various geographic areas of the globe. In Indonesia, however, the contribution of the humanities to the development of a national culture has been very explicit due to the fact that 'building the Indonesian nation' on the fundament of 931 different local traditions[14] has been a somewhat Sisyphean task in the face of continuous separatist tendencies in various parts of the country.

In order to appreciate the function of anthropology within the Indonesian nationalisation process, it is helpful to recall the beginnings of the Indonesian state, the ideological currents within the independence movement and their impact on the creation of the Indonesian constitution. As Michael Prager has shown in his chapter, the leaders of the Indonesian independence movement were mostly men who had profited from a Dutch education either at home or in the Netherlands themselves. The Dutch image of 'Indonesian cultures' had, therefore, shaped in a rather inconsistent manner the self-image of 'young Indonesians' like Sukarno, Mohammad Hatta, Soepomo, Sanusi Pane, Soetomo, Muhammad Yamin, Poerbatjaraka, Ki Hadjar Dewantara Hajar or Sutan Takdir Alisjahbana, who all had their share in defining the future national identity when the Indonesian state was about to come into being.[15]

The Dutch image of the peoples and cultures of their colony *Nederlandsch–Indië* was largely shaped by the discourse of colonial *Indologie*, a kind of area study with the function to support the colonial administration in Indonesia.[16] At the heart of both the colonial administration as well as 'applied Dutch *Indologie*' were the so-called *adatrechtstudiën* (study of *adat* law). The term *adat* is in fact an Arabic term which means 'custom'. It became a popular *terminus technicus* within the 'indological' discourse through the works of the late nineteenth-century Dutch scholar Christiaan Snouck Hugronje. Snouck Hugronje had used the Arabic word *adat*, signifying 'custom', in order to discriminate between the Islamic law (*shariah*) and the 'customary law' (*adat*) in Aceh (North Sumatra). Since he was also an important adviser of the Dutch colonial administration, the term *adat* soon became a well-known 'common denominator' for the mostly unwritten local customary law, embedded in a sacred cosmology, and the customary routines of all ethnic groups in the archipelago. As a 'common denominator' *adat* suggested a basic 'Old Indonesian' cultural stratum shared by all local traditions in the archipelago in spite of their myriad idionsyncrasies which were thus reduced to mere versions of a basically common set of customs, values and beliefs. Concurrently, the Dutch instigated a homogenisation of divergent *adat* by classifying the myriad idiosyncrasies into nineteen different '*adat* law areas' (*adatrechtskringen*) and by introducing significant administrative changes to the local organisation of community life.[17]

When, in October 1928, several 'young Indonesians' gathered at a conference in order to envisage a future 'Indonesia', they decided on what was to become known under the slogan 'Oath of the Indonesian Youth' (*Sumpah Pemuda Indonesia*), claiming a unified Indonesian territory, a unified Indonesian nation and the Indonesian language (*Bahasa Indonesia*) as national language. They justified their claim to unification with the explicit will (of the people), the common history of the various ethnic groups within the boundaries of a common territory, the existence of an Indonesian language, the *adat* law as the basis of a common identity, as well as the need for education and political guidance on the basis of democracy. Thus, the 'indological' concept of *adat* helped to legitimise the existence of an Indonesian nation postulated by the Indonesian independence movement.[18]

However, the equivocal term '*adat*' eventually proved to be rather unsuitable as a unifying core concept for the development of a new national identity. The Muslim strand of the Indonesian independence movement rejected the term because the sacred cosmologies, in which *adat* is embedded, have been associated with animism, polytheism, ancestor worship and other 'repulsive' customs, such as head hunting and the keeping of pigs. For the modernists among the secular nationalists as well as for the communists, *adat* connoted a primitive stage of culture which was to be overcome rather than to be identified with. The 'Unitarians' among the nationalists, who consisted mostly of law scholars, rejected the term on the grounds that it was unsuitable as a unifying concept, since the Dutch colonial administration discriminated between nineteen different *adat* law areas.[19] *Adat* in the sense of local tradition was compromised by the fact that many local 'guardians of tradition' like village heads and local kings throughout the archipelago had collaborated with the Dutch.[20] Let us remember that it was only very rarely the indigenous nobility *per se*, but mostly the Dutch, educated intellectuals that mobilised people against the colonial regime. *Adat*, in the sense of local identity, was further discredited because of the continuous outbreaks of separatist upheavals once national independence was achieved.

Eventually, the indological concept of *adat* only obliquely influenced the content of the national constitution of 1945 (*Undang–Undang Dasar 1945*). The term *adat* itself was even nowhere explicitly mentioned, not in the least because it conflicted with the foremost unifying factor mentioned in the preamble of the constitution, the 'Belief in One God', that is, 'religion' (*agama*) as defined by the Ministry of Religion. According to the Muslim dominated Ministry of Religion, *agama* is 'a universal monotheistic creed based on a holy book which was received by a holy prophet in divine revelation'. Hence, *agama* is the exact anti-thesis to *adat*; that is, traditional, polytheistic cosmological systems linked to certain customary laws and regulations which were conceived at best as areligious, if not irreligious, by devout Muslims (and Christians).[21] The only influence from the sphere of *adat* was apparent in the fourth of the 'five (core) principles (i.e. "Belief in the One God," "Humanity," "National Unity," "Democracy led by the Wisdom of the Unanimous Decision Evolving from the Discussion of the Representatives of the People," "Social Justice")' or *panca sila*[22] of the Indonesian Constitution of 1945 advanced by Sukarno, the president of the newly proclaimed, but not yet internationally acknowledged, Republic of Indonesia: Indonesian democracy was to be based on the traditional mechanism of collective decision making so widespread among Indonesian village or *adat* communities, that is, unanimous decision (*mufakat*) of the village members after common discussion (*musyawarat*).[23] The application of the principles of traditional decision making to the political decision making of the new Indonesian government thus suggested that Indonesian democracy was to be fashioned after the 'democratic' tradition of local village communities. This is a strange reverberation of the romantic image of the local *dorpsrepublieken* (village republics) nurtured by some colonial administrators and their special strand of 'indological' research.[24]

Whereas the sacred component of traditional *adat* was irreconcilable with the new Indonesian identity, its supposedly 'neutral' and 'material' aspects like traditional decision making, neighbourly co-operation (*gotong royong*) and traditional material culture (cooking, dancing, music, painting, costumes, architecture, etc.) were found suitable as ingredients of the 'new Indonesian culture' by most 'fathers' of the Indonesian constitution. These aspects were not called '*adat*', though, but they were classified as '*budaya*' or '*kebudayaan*', the Indonesian translation of the Western concept of 'culture'. The term 'culture' served as a supplement to 'religion' or *agama* and covered also all the value orientations[25] which were not 'religious' in the sense of the narrow definition of the Ministry of Religion.

Hence, the paragraph 32/XIII of the Constitution of 1945 demands that the government is to promote the development of the national Indonesian culture; and the official commentary to this paragraph (*Penjelasan Undang–Undang Dasar 1945 Faisal 32 Bab XIII*) lists the highlights of the various traditional cultures among the components of the new Indonesian culture,[26] next to useful foreign elements which would advance the development of the 'integral Indonesian state'. The principle of integrating the 'best' elements of the diverse traditional cultures in Indonesia into the new Indonesian culture was also formulated in what became the national motto of Indonesia: 'unity in diversity' (*Bhineka Tunggal Eka*). The concept of the 'integral state' or of the 'highlights of the plural local cultures of the archipelago being integrated into the organic unity of the Indonesian nation' had been put forward in the commentary by Soepomo, a Dutch trained scholar of law and one of the founding fathers of the constitution of 1945.[27]

The Sukarno-era

When the Republic of Indonesia finally achieved full independence as an internationally recognised and unified nation state in 1950, the various ideological groupings were, however, not easily harmonised or integrated on a permanent scale. Separatist upheavals in West Java, the Moluccas, West Kalimantan, South Sulawesi and Aceh threatened the newly achieved unity, causing President Sukarno to reinforce national unity by propagating the policy of *Nasakom* in 1957. The slogan *Nasakom* was a contraction of *nasionalisme* (nationalism), *agama* (religion) and *komunisme* (communism) and demanded the integration of these ideological factions into a national front. These three ideological currents, which had also been the main ideological strands of the independence movement,[28] were represented by the five most influential political parties which had emerged from the first common election in 1955: the *Partai Nasional Indonesia* or National Party of Indonesia (*PNI*), the *Partai Sosialis Indonesia* or Socialistic Party of Indonesia (*PSI*), the *Partai Komunis Indonesia* or Communist Party of Indonesia (*PKI*) and the two Islamic parties *Masjumi* and *Nahdlatul Ulama*. When *Nasakom* could not prevent further upheavals in West Sumatra and North Sulawesi, Sukarno abolished the original parliamentary democracy by introducing a new political manifesto in 1959. This political manifesto covered another set of five principles abbreviated by the acronym USDEK:

1   confirmation of the constitution of 1945 (*Undang–Undang Dasar 1945*) and its preamble (*Panca Sila*);
2   Indonesian socialism (*Sosialisme Indonesia*) which is to be promoted with the help of the *PKI*;[29]
3   guided democracy (**Demokrasi** *Terpimpin*) under the leadership of Sukarno;
4   guided economy (**Ekonomi** *Terpimpin*) in order to achieve the complete autarchy of the country;
5   and reinforced development of a national identity (**Kepribadian** *Indonesia*).

Both *Nasakom* and *Manipo*[30]–USDEK displayed the increasing influence of communism as well as anti-traditionalist or 'modernist' thinking on Sukarno's policy, which was probably caused by the president's need to strengthen his position against rival military leaders, who were strongly anti-Communist in orientation,[31] and to prevent further separatist upheavals motivated by ethnic or religious issues.[32]

'Anti-traditionalist' or 'modernist' tendencies were especially manifest in the new interpretation of 'national identity' or 'national culture', which significantly differed from the one advanced in the official commentary on the constitution of 1945 (*Penjelasan Undang–Undang Dasar 1945*). The new interpretation now called for a totally new culture, which would be free from any feudal, colonial, tribalist or ethnocentric traits.[33]

The rejection of the term *adat* as a core concept for the development of an Indonesian identity and the debate between 'modernists' and 'integrationalists' provided a backdrop for an academic discussion concerning the introduction of a supplementary course in anthropology at the Faculty of Law (*Fakultas Hukum*) and the Faculty of Letters (*Fakultas Sastra*) at the University of Indonesia (*Universitas Indonesia* or *UI*) in the national capital Jakarta shortly after independence. There was a rather strong lobby of Indonesian academics, led by the prominent sociologist T.S.G. Moelia, who opposed the introduction of what they thought was a 'colonial' and supposedly backwards oriented discipline. As nationalists with a modernist orientation, they argued in favour of a course in sociology that was to replace the anthropological one. The supporters of anthropology, however, successfully argued that a country with so many different ethnic groups like Indonesia required specialists in anthropological research in order to achieve 'unity in diversity'.

As Michael Prager has related in his article, the first supplementary anthropological courses at the *UI* were taught by a Dutch professor (Gerrit Jan Held) and two Dutch lecturers (F.A.E. van Wouden, Elisabeth Allard), whereas at the Gajah Mada University in Yogyakarta or *Universitas Gajah Mada* (*UGM*) – the only other university in Indonesia that had an academic prestige similar to that of the *UI* – a predominantly Indonesian staff had taken over the teaching in anthropology (and sociology), already in the first years after independence. Due to the increasingly strained relations between the Netherlands and Indonesia over the issue of West New Guinea (Irian Barat), however, the Dutch staff at the *UI* soon diminished considerably. Van Wouden, for instance, left Indonesia in 1955. In the same year, Held passed away, and Allard was appointed professor of anthropology. By 1958, Elisabeth Allard too had to finally leave Indonesia.

Already a year earlier; that is, in 1957, a department of cultural anthropology (*jurusan antropologi budaya*) had been set up at the Faculty of Letters at the *UI*. The name of the department, which highlighted 'cultural anthropology' rather than just 'anthropology', pointed to the fact that, from now on, the American tradition of the discipline was to have predominant impact on the development of anthropology in Indonesia; at the same time, American sociological theory influenced the development of the other social sciences in Indonesia.

In spite of their initial differences, Indonesian anthropologists and sociologists have worked closely together from the start. They have investigated similar problems – often in joint projects – such as national integration, social adjustment, accommodation of ethnic and cultural diversity, the transformation of the peasant economy, urbanisation or illiteracy, both using qualitative as well as quantitative methods. The most prominent books, which have resulted from these studies, were co-authored by Koentjaraningrat and Harsia W. Bachtiar. Koentjaraningrat had studied on a Fullbright scholarship at Yale University from 1954 to 1956, whereas Harsia W. Bachtiar had studied at Cornell University in the same years. Among their best known books is *Penduduk Irian Barat* ('The Inhabitants of West Irian'), which was published in 1963, at the peak of the Irian crisis aggravating relations between Indonesia and the Netherlands. This book shows that Koentjaraningrat, the undisputed 'father' of Indonesian anthropology who passed away on 23 March 1999,[34] had tried to make anthropology respond to the needs of the nation as soon as he had become professor of the anthropological department at the *UI*, in 1962. Under his direction, Indonesian anthropology developed very much as 'applied anthropology'.

At Yale, Koentjaraningrat had been invited to contribute to the Human Relations Area Files (HRAF) by G.P. Murdock. The HRAF project inspired him to promote a similar project back home that would, however, only cover the cultures of Indonesia. The theoretical concept of 'value orientation', developed by Florence R. Kluckhohn and Fred L. Strodtbeck on the basis of Clyde Kluckhohn's action theory and the concept of value connected to it, were to also exert a great influence on Koentjaraningrat.[35] It has to be borne in mind, though, that both the project of writing an encyclopaedia of all Indonesian cultures and the concept of 'value orientation' were to serve the process of nation building. It was one of Koentjaraningrat's major goals to rouse the awareness of the Indonesian Government regarding the important role anthropology could play in this process.

And he was in a very apt position to achieve this goal, since in 1964 he was appointed as Director of the Institute for Research on the National Culture (*Direktur Lembaga Riset Kebudayaan Nasional*) within the Indonesian Institute of Science or *Lembaga Ilmu Pengetahuan Indonesia (LIPI)*, a position which he held until 1967. From 1967 until 1977, he was deputy chair of *LIPI*. Moreover, he was Dean of the Faculty of Letters at the *UI* from 1965 to 1966.

After the Dutch staff had left Indonesia, Indonesian anthropology suffered from a lack of text books in the Indonesian language as well as capable lecturers. In spite of this handicap, the anthropological department at the *UI* was assigned the task of establishing and developing anthropological departments at state universities in other provinces of the country, sharing both staff and resources with these new departments. Koentjaraningrat tried to meet this challenge with relentless personal teaching at various universities in Indonesia by preparing specially gifted students for the task of promoting anthropology throughout the academic institutions of the country and by beginning to publish the revised preparations for his various courses as academic text books.

Apart from the anthropological department at the *UI*, anthropology was continued to be taught at the *UGM* in Yogyakarta. The anthropology lecturer at the *UGM* was the philologist Prof. Prijohutomo, while sociology was taught by the scholar of law Prof. M.M. Djojodigoeno. Djojodigoeno had served as civil servant under the Dutch, doing research on *adat* law. He stimulated the creation of a committee for social research at his university which was soon transformed into the Institute for Sociography and Adat Law (*Lembaga Sosiografi dan Hukum Adat*). One of its staff members, Soedjito Sosrodihardjo, received an MA degree from the University of London, his thesis bearing the title *A Sectarian Group in Java with Reference to a Midland Village: A Study in the Sociology of Religion* (1959). On his return to the *UGM* in 1960, he started to teach at the Faculty of Political Science. Masri Singarimun, another staff member of the Institute for Sociography and Adat Law, received a graduate fellowship from The Australian National University (ANU) and returned to teach at the *UGM* in 1973.

Despite the comparatively good facilities at the *UGM*, the task of establishing anthropological departments at state universities of other provinces burdened mainly the anthropological department at the *UI*, probably because it was Indonesia's national university. In 1962, an affiliated anthropological department was established at the *UGM* in Yogyakarta, which was quite independent from the Institute of Sociography and *Adat* Law, and another one was established at the *Universitas Cendrawasih* in Jayapura (Irian). Two years later, a further one was established at the *Universitas Sam Ratulangie* in Manado (North Sulawesi). When a sister university, called Hasanudin University, was founded in Makassar[36] (South Sulawesi), Utrecht trained Ph.L. Tobing became the professor of anthropology there. Another sister university, the Airlangga University, was established in Surabaya (East Java), which in turn helped to establish the Udayana University in Denpasar (Bali).[37] Anthropology departments were among the earliest departments that were established at both universities. Besides, courses on anthropology were set up at departments and faculties of universities throughout the country, for instance, at departments of political science, departments of public administration, departments of sociology or faculties of psychology, faculties of public health etc., as well as at law schools, teachers colleges, institutes for Islamic theology, catholic seminaries and divinity schools. These anthropological courses were meant to provide lawyers, teachers, psychologists, public health officers or priests with some insight not only into the diversity of local traditions in Indonesia but also into the peculiarities of the local culture they were living in.

Although regular students of anthropology received theoretical training in various branches of anthropology (e.g. medical anthropology, physical anthropology, anthropology of law, social anthropology, linguistics etc.), the focus of ethnographic study and research was on the cultures of Indonesia with field work being carried out exclusively in the archipelago. The main reason for this was the fact that anthropologists who graduated from the earlier-mentioned departments of anthropology were required to study the various problems of nation building. Hence, anthropologists began to participate in interdisciplinary projects organised by governmental institutions, such as the Ministry of Education and Culture (*Departemen Pendidikan dan Kebudayaan*), the Ministry of Information (*Departemen Penerangan*), the Ministry of Public Health (*Departemen Kesehatan Umum*), the Ministry of Higher Education (*Departemen Perguruan Tinggi*) or the Ministry of Religion (*Departemen Agama*).[38]

Apart from anthropology and sociology, other academic disciplines had to contribute to the study of nation building too. In an effort to de-colonise the historiography of Indonesia largely written by the Dutch, the vehemently nationalistic historian Muhammad Yamin, for instance, imagined a national history suggesting a teleological progress from the pre-historic past of the archipelago to the golden era of the Hindu–Javanese period to the modern Indonesian state.[39] Yamin, who was Sukarno's Minister for Education and Culture in 1958, regarded the glorious Hindu–Javanese empire Majapahit as the direct predecessor of the Republic of Indonesia. Majapahit's highest military commander Gajah Mada, who had considerably enlarged Majapahit's realm of rule by military operations in the fourteenth century, was in Yamin's opinion a national hero, and his conquests were regarded as antecedents of the Indonesian nationalisation process (*Gajah Mada – pahlawan persatuan nusantara*). Yamin also investigated the history of the red-and-white banner of the modern Indonesian state, which – to him – covered a period of 6,000 years, assuming that the colours red and white have held symbolic meaning in various Indonesian cultures since pre-historic times.[40]

The new order

By 1965, Sukarno's policy of *Manipol–USDEK* had clearly failed as became evident in the attempted coup d'état of 30 September–1 October Gerakan September Tiga Puluh (*GESTAPU*). Sukarno's rejection of foreign investment, the general maladministration of his government, his disapproval of family planning at a time of rapid decline in food supplies, the deterioration of the public health system and continuous ideological battles between the different political groupings had pushed the country towards economic and social disaster. The putsch, which was afterwards attributed to the *PKI* and the contrivance of the People's Republic of China (PRC), was quelled by the Indonesian military under the leadership of General Soeharto. Subsequently, the *PKI* was banned and the country reorganised, while thousands of communists were being killed in the process.

In 1968, Soeharto was officially appointed as President of Indonesia. His government established a 'new order' (*orde baru*) which propagated the de-ideologisation of society, the dual function (*dwifungsi*) of the military, social harmony and the economic development of the country.

'De-ideologisation' meant restraining the influence of the remaining political parties, creating non-ideological or 'functional groups' (*golongan karya*) that would represent all segments of society, and appointing soldiers to both military and civil functions (*dwi fungsi*). Related to this was Soeharto's effort to promote 'social harmony' by returning to the guidelines of the constitution of 1945 – that is, abolishing *Manipol–USDEK* – and thereby to the five principles of the preamble (*panca sila*) as well as to Soepomo's concept of 'national integration'. The former Minister of Education and Culture, Muhammad Yamin, reinvigorated the notion that the *panca sila* were an intrinsic part of the Indonesian culture and history, developing them into a kind of state philosophy (*filsafat pancasila*)[41] for the 'New Order'.

In 1978, that is, at a time when there were fears that the Khomeini revolution in Iran might give boost to Islamic fundamentalism in Indonesia, the Ministry of Education and Culture (*Departemen Pendidikan dan Kebudayaan*) introduced a *pancasila*-indoctrination program called *Pedoman Penghayatan dan Pengamalan Pancasila (P4)*. This program was to foster the revitalisation (*penghayatan*) and application (*pengamalan*) of the *pancasila* in all public institutions. The application of this program was financed and organised with the help of the UNESCO and the American Ford Foundation.[42] In 1983, the *pancasila*-philosophy was made the sole philosophical base (*asas tunggal*) for all socio-political organisations, including political parties and religious organisations.

The *pancasila*-philosophy was in fact a new interpretation of Sukarno's five pillars of the Indonesian state, entailing the following deviations. The principle 'Belief in One God,' which had been the basis for the recognition of a religious community under Sukarno, was now to be a stronghold against atheism and therefore communism. Hence, it was now compulsory for every citizen to join one of the five 'religions' (Islam, Protestantism, Catholicism, Hinduism, Buddhism) acknowledged by the Ministry of Religion (*Departemen Agama*). With the beginning of the 'new order', the principle of 'National Unity' implied a concept of 'national culture' which was a compromise between the 'traditionalist' and the 'modernist' approach. Hence, the Indonesian culture was conceived to consist of the highlights of the local cultures as well as of useful foreign values such as those of the Protestant work ethics or the Japanese *bushido*.[43] Apart from religion (*agama*), useful traditional values like co-operation among members of a village community (*gotong royong*) or familial relationships (*kekeluargaan*) were to counter any destructive foreign – that is, communist – influence. However, separatist tendencies, based on ethnicity or religious fundamentalism, should not be encouraged. The motto was to revitalise traditional values without a tradition-alist attitude (*membangun tradisi tanpa sikap tradisional*[44]). Hence, the 'new Indonesian' (*manusia Indonesia seutuhnya, manusia pembangunan, manusia pancasila*) should have faith in God, be a useful member of society, work hard and be honest'.[45] This concept linked up very well with the new interpretation of the fifth principle 'Social Justice', which now contained a liberal-capitalist rather than a socialist rendering. Accordingly, 'social justice' was conceptionally linked to economic progress as the core of national development (*pembangunan*). It was to be the major concern of Soeharto's regime and an important source of its legitimation (see also Suparlan 1986: 85).[46]

Abolishing Sukarno's concept of economic autarchy, Soeharto succeeded in attracting foreign investment which greatly helped to develop the infrastructure of the country. Soeharto's 'green revolution' achieved self-sufficiency in rice by the mid-1980s, and the Indonesian model of familiy planning received worldwide recognition. The new order's emphasis on development accelerated industrialisa-tion and improved housing, the school system, health clinics and communication. In the beginning of the 1980s, Indonesia was recommended as a model for the other Organization of the Petroleum Exporting Countries (OPEC) members, because the country had re-invested its oil revenue gains effectively and had quickly adjusted to the declining oil prices. One of Indonesia's strategies to alleviate the economic losses, resulting from the declining oil prices, was the promotion of tourism. The tourist industry in turn created a market – at least to a certain extent – for local agricultural products, for traditional handicraft and local art forms.[47]

In conformance with the priorities of Soeharto's rule, anthropology was now explicitly assigned an important function in the implementation of government policies. It was to promote national integration, *pancasila* and economic progress. More departments of anthropology were established at provincial universities with the help of the department of anthropology at the *UI* in Jakarta. The close political and military relation between the 'new order' government and the United States intensified academic co-operation between Indonesia and the States which gave boost to the already strong orientation towards American cultural anthro-pology within the Indonesian anthropological departments. Eventually, the department of anthropology at the *UI*, where American influence has perhaps been the strongest, was moved from the Faculty of Letters to the Faculty of Social and Political Sciences in 1983.[48] This move, however, was not followed by all of the other departments of anthropology in Indonesia. While at the Airlangga University in Surabaya, for instance, the department of anthropology is also part of the Faculty of Social and Political Sciences, at the Udayana University in Denpasar it still belongs to the Faculty of Letters.[49] Today, every state university of Indonesia's twenty-six[50] provinces has an anthropological department, and anthropological courses are offered in many private universities, too.[51] Besides, just like during the 'old order' (*orde lama*) under Sukarno, anthropological courses have been taught also in other departments, where an understanding of the local cultures of Indonesia is imperative for the successful application of their scientific models. Doctoral programmes, however, are even until now not available at every university due to the lack of adequately trained staff especially in the so-called 'outer islands' of Eastern Indonesia.

During the Soeharto-era, the chance of future employment was comparatively high, given the variety of jobs provided by the Indonesian government. In order to be able to cope with the diversity of concrete problems in their future jobs, graduate students could enrol for a number of anthropological sub-disciplines such as physical anthropology, medical anthropology, psychological anthropology, religious anthropology, urban anthropology, rural anthropology, cognitive anthropology, political anthropology, the anthropology of education, the anthropology of law, economic and population anthropology or anthropological ecology.[52]

The number and standard of anthropological studies has been the highest to date at the state universities of Java, especially at the *UI*. Koentjaraningrat, who remained the strongest protagonist of Indonesian anthropology until his retirement in 1988, seized the opportunity to enhance the status of anthropology by fully supporting the development policy of the government. When, from the beginning of the 1970s onwards, investors from Japan and the neighbouring ASEAN countries were increasingly attracted to Indonesia, Koentjaraningrat sought the co-operation with academic institutions in Japan, Malaysia, Thailand and Singapore. After the return of the students, whom he had sent to those countries in order to study the local language and culture, the study of Southeast Asian and East Asian cultures was integrated into the anthropological curriculum. Today, it is an integral part of the studies pursued at the *UI* anthropological department as well as at some anthropological departments of other universities in Java, such as the *UGM*. With the increasing importance of Australia as an economic partner, academic relations were established with Australia, too. These relations have somewhat suffered, though, due to the tensions between Indonesia and Australia that arose in connection with the referendum for independence in East Timor in 1999.

When 'cultural tourism' was designed to promote the economic development of the country, Koentjaraningrat immediately responded by promoting the study of tourism by Indonesian anthropologists. One of his students, I Gusti Ngurah Bagus, who became professor of anthropology at the Udayana University in Depasar in the beginning of the 1970s, meticulously monitored the development of tourism in Bali, until his premature death in 2003. Tourism studies are by now well established at every anthropological department throughout the country.[53]

From 1984 until the mid-1990s, Koentjaraningrat sent many students to the Netherlands, promoting the study of pre-independence 'Indonesia' (i.e. the Netherlands' Indies) by having them study the language of the former colonial power as well as the 'Indonesian cultural heritage' in the Dutch archives and museums. He himself was also personally concerned with Europe at that time (1987–8), for he investigated the issue of ethnicity in Yugoslavia and Belgium in order to obtain comparative data for the case of Indonesia. Until now, Koentjaraningrat has been the only Indonesian anthropologist who has chosen 'the West' as a field of study.[54]

The research domain of most Indonesian anthropologists has to date been the villages (*desa*), the rural ecology and the diverse ethnic groups (*suku bangsa*) of Indonesia. During the Soeharto-era, a major task for anthropologists was to contribute to harmonious community development by educating the members of local communities in accordance with the government policies. Thus, the function of anthropology in the 'New Order' Indonesia largely consisted of mediating between tradition and an 'Asian' – that is, Indonesian – variety of modernity. This mediation by Indonesian anthropologists was grounded in the study of the socio-cultural problems caused by transmigration projects, agricultural innovation, family planning and other governmental projects. Moreover, anthropologists investigated the potential of local value-systems for developing local economic conditions.[55] Indonesian folklorists tried to introduce innovations to the villages through traditional media such as folk drama or other folklore genres,[56] and psychological anthropologists studied the psychological effects of socio-cultural change in local communities.[57] Anthropological research and consultancy was carried out in connection with the various government institutions. Indonesian anthropologists, for instance, participated in projects which were under the tutelage of the Ministry of Education and Culture (*Departemen Pendidikan dan Kebudayaan*) and its regional offices (*Kantor Pendidikan dan Kebudayaan Daerah*), the Indonesian Institute of Science or (*LIPI*), the Institute for the National Language (*Lembaga Bahasa Nasional*), the Ministry of Religion (*Departemen Agama*), the Ministry of Agriculture and Forestry (*Departemen Pertanian dan Kehutanan*), the Ministry of Tourism (*Departemen Pariwisataan*), the Ministry of Public Labour (*Departemen Pekerjaan Umum*), the Ministry of Public Health (*Departemen Kesehatan Umum*), the Bureau of Familiy Planning (*Kantor Berencana Keluarga*) and other institutions. Already in 1980, there were 364 research institutions jointly managed by Indonesian universities and government institutions; 153 of them were centres of the social sciences employing 3,633 researchers.[58] Anthropologists like Koentjaraningrat complained, though, that they were only consulted when definite problems emerged in connection with the application of certain development programmes. Anthropologists were, however, not given the chance to contribute to the planning of the programmes themselves.[59]

Similar complaints were put forward by the comparatively few Indonesian scholars of *adat* law, who had graduated either in anthropology or law. From 1980 onwards, the Indonesian government intensified its promotion of the development of a national law to the disadvantage of the various *adat* law, in order to accelerate the economic development of the country.[60] The rigorous modernisation caused severe problems in various localities. Scholars of *adat* law frequently tried to remind the government of the local cultural values which would have to be taken into account when trying to implement new policies.[61] Some scholars even suggested in private that Soeharto and his 'cronies' tried to abolish *adat*, so that they could easily take over unoccupied land (such as forests or coastlines), which is traditionally owned by *adat* communities. Yet, in spite of several laudable efforts,[62] the scholars of *adat* law were not very successful in re-introducing *adat* as a respected category.

Apart from the ludicrously high degree of corruption, it was mainly the brutal silencing of regime opponents and the heavy indoctrination which prevented scholars from effectively speaking up against directives from above. Like in other totalitarian countries, national museums were not so much scientific institutions as state organs propagating the glory of the Soeharto-regime as well as its view of 'national history'. The ethnographical museums mostly represented local culture as folkloristic attraction for the tourist market, and not as a vital value orientation for a potentially disruptive society.[63] Indoctrination entailed that the undergraduate programmes at the universities provided for both the moral and the scientific education of the students. At the *Universitas Airlangga*, for instance, undergraduate students of anthropology had to enroll for courses which were compulsory at every other educational institution too: '*pancasila*', 'heroism' (*kewiraan*), 'religion' (according to the religious affiliation of the student) and 'basic cultural science' (*ilmu budaya dasar*), teaching the national history as well as the national ethics of development.[64] This practice continued even under Soeharto's successor Habibie until October 1999.[65]

Anthropology in post-'New Order' Indonesia

The success of the recent student revolution and the subsequent legitimate election of a democratic government in October 1999, has had many consequences for the anthropological discourse in Indonesia. The universities, for instance, have become autonomous institutions; that is, they are no longer under the direct control of the Ministry of Education and Culture. The *pancasila* indoctrination programme *P4* was abolished as soon as Abdurrahman Wahid, the successor of Habibie, was elected as Indonesia's new president. Dialogue with both Asian and Western colleagues is encouraged, and books to support this dialogue have become available. Wahid's liberalisation policy has been continued by his successor, Megawati Sukarnoputri, who was appointed president in July 2001. In the anthropological departments, Indonesian anthropologists have started to rethink the role of anthropology. There are some indications that 'applied anthropology' might soon be balanced by indigenised 'action anthropology'.[66] Moreover, the current decentralisation process provides ample opportunity for Indonesian anthropologists to help emancipate hitherto repressed 'local voices'. This is, I think, a promising outlook in spite of the serious financial problems which all Indonesian universities face due to the ongoing economic crisis. The rethinking of the role of anthropology in Indonesia, furthermore, takes place within a conducive context, for issues such as nationalism, democracy and autonomy are reflected upon on all levels of Indonesian society. This should give a boost to the democratisation as well as indigenisation, and hence emancipation, of anthropology in Indonesia.

Notes

1 Cf. Krotz 1997: 240–2.
2 Cf. Said, Edward (1978) *Orientalism: Western Conceptions of the Orient*. London: Routledge & Kegan.

3 Cf. for instance Corbey Raymond and Joep Leerssen (1991) 'Studying alterity: backgrounds and perspectives', in Raymond Corbey and Joep Leerssen (eds), *Alterity, Identity, Image*, Amsterdam, Atlanta, GA: Editions Rodopi, pp. vi–xviii; Fuchs, Martin and Eberhard Berg (1993) 'Phänomenologie der Differenz: Reflexionsstufen ethnographischer Repräsentation', in Eberhard Berg and Martin Fuchs (eds), *Kultur, soziale Praxis, Text: die Krise der ethnographischen Repräsentation*, Frankfurt am: Suhrkamp, pp. 69–96; Ramstedt, Martin (1996) 'Das "weibliche" Asien', in Margret Jäger and Siegfried Jäger (eds), *Baustellen: Beiträge zur Diskursgeschichte deutscher Gegenwart*, Duisburg: DISS, pp. 238–57.

4 The anthropological discourse in Indonesia has been a recurrent topic of interest to me since 1991. In an earlier publication in the German language, my starting point for a discussion of applied anthropology in Indonesia was the discourse on ethics in the social sciences and its special attention to the role of science in colonial and totalitarian states (Ramstedt 1994: 210–11).

5 I use the term 'discourse' as it has been put forward by representatives of 'discourse analysis' in the wake of Foucault who defines 'discourse' as 'an institutionalised way of speaking about things which supports certain interests, induces certain actions and thus exerts power' (cf. for instance Siegfried Jäger (1993) *Kritische Diskursanalyse. Eine Einführung*, Duisburg: DISS, 152).

6 Three research projects which I carried out in Indonesia in 1986–7, in 1989–90 and in 1998–2000 were supported by various Indonesian academic institutions (i.e. the Indonesian Institute for Science (*Lembaga Ilmu Pengetahuan Indonesia*) in Jakarta, the Academy for Indonesian Dance and Music (*Akademi Seni Tari Indonesia*) in Denpasar, the Udayana University (*Universitas Udayana*) in Denpasar, the Indonesian Hindu University (*Universitas Hindu Indonesia*) in Denpasar, and the Police University (*Universitas Bhayangkara*) in Surabaya), which I have come to know quite well in the course of our co-operation. I was asked to become academic adviser of the Police University in 1998. In 2000, I was honoured by the State School of Hindu Theology (*Sekolah Tinggih Agama Hindu Negeri*) in Denpasar by a similar request. I have been fortunate to have closely cooperated with renowned Indonesian anthropologists, musicologists and scholars of *adat* law (i.e. the customary law of the various ethnic groups in Indonesia), of whom I want to especially mention here the late Prof. Dr Koentjaraningrat, the late Prof. Dr I Gusti Ngurah Bagus, the late Prof. Dr Mohammad Koesnoe, Prof. Dr Amri Marzali, and Dr I Made Bandem. At the moment, Dr Coen Holtzappel and I are co-editing the book *Dynamics of Decentralization and Regional Autonomy in Indonesia: Implementation and Challenge*, to which leading social scientists, representing important research institutions in contemporary Indonesia (such as the Indonesia Rapid Decentralization Appraisal programme or IRDA at The Asia Foundation in Jakarta, the Center for Asia and Pacific Studies at Gadjah Mada University in Yogyakarta, the SMERU Research Institute in Jakarta, and others), have contributed.

7 Cf. for instance Kleden 1987: 22: 'Dari perspektif ini indigenisasi berarti menyesuaikan asumsi dasar teori ilmu sosial dengan sistem nilai lokal (atau nasional) serta merekonstruksikan isi teori tersebut atas dasar sistem kognitif lokal (atau nasional)'. ('From this perspective, indigenisation means to adjust the basic assumption of scientific theory to the local (or national) value system and to reconstruct the content of this theory on the basis of the local (or national) cognitive system'.)

8 Cf. Aditjondro 1997: 43, 48, 50.

9 Cf. also Das 1993: 419–20, 422.

10 Cf. also Budiman 1983: 1.

11 Cf. for instance *Wacana Antropologi* 3(1) (Juli–Aug. 1999): 4–13; Marzali 1998a; Marzali 1998b.

12 This heading is of course a variation of the title of Anderson, Benedict (1996) *Imagined Communities: Reflections on the Origin and Spread of Nationalism*. London, New York: Verso.

13 See also Rothermund 1997: 13; Sutherland 1997: 85.

14 Cf. Koentjaraningrat 1997: 104.

15 Cf. Alisjahbana 1966: 2, 24–8; Harsojo 1988: 260; Koentjaraningrat 1982c: 411–17; Rahardjo, M. 1996: xv–xvi.

16 The 'indological' discourse of the Dutch colonial government was generated in the institutions already mentioned in detail by Michael Prager.

17 Cf. Alisjahbana 1966: 70–7; Hooker 1978: 1, 16; Koesnoe 1992: 1, 4–5, 10–20; Warren, Carol (1993) *Adat and Dinas. Balinese Communities in the Indonesian State*, New York: Oxford University Press, pp. 3–5; Guinness 1994: 268; Astiti 1995: 99–102; Koesnoe 1996: 2–3.

18 Cf. for example, Koesnoe 1988: 29–31; see also Kartodirdjo 1997: 78–80.

19 Cf. Hooker 1978: 1, 20–3.

20 See also Kartodirdjo 1997: 75.

21 See also M. Ramstedt (2004) 'Introduction: negotiating identities – Indonesian "Hindus" between local, national, and global interests', in Martin Ramstedt (ed.), *'Hinduism' in Modern Indonesia: A Minority Religion between Local, National and Global Interests*, London: RoutledgeCurzon (IIAS Asian Studies Series).

22 The so-called 'Jakarta-Charter' (*Piagam Jakarta*).

23 Cf. Koesnoe 1969: 5.

24 Cf. for instance Henk Schulte Nordholt (1988) *Een Balische Dynastie. Hiërarchie en Conflict in de Negara Mengwi 1700–1940*, Amsterdam: Vrije Universiteit, pp. 218–20.

25 Cf. for example, Marzali 1998b.

26 '*Kebudayaan bangsa ialah kebudayaan yang timbul sebagai usaha budinya rakyat Indonesia seluruhnya*'; see also, for instance, Hassan 1993: 17.

27 Cf. Bachtiar 1986: 66, 69, 72–3; Kleden 1987: 220; Wandelt 1989: 35–6; Hassan 1993: 17, 22, 34; Bachtiar 1994: 12, 19–20, 27–9, 42, 52; Koesnoe 1996: 6, 11, 19; Koesnoe, Mohammad (1997) *Undang–Undang Nomor 14/1970 dan Pasal 24 dan 25 Undang–Undang Dasar 1945*, Surabaya: Temu Ilmiah Guru Besar dan PAKAR Ilmu Hukum dan Ketatanegaraan, Universitas Bhayangkara, 10–11 April, pp. 58–9.

28 See also Bachtiar 1994: 30–2; Kartodirdjo 1997: 78.

29 The *PSI* was banned because of its involvement in the separatistic upheavals in West Sumatra and North Sulawesi.

30 A contraction of *Manifesto Politik*.

31 Cf. a.o. Rex Mortimer (1980) 'The place of communism', in James J. Fox, Ross Garnaut, Peter McCawley and J.A.C. Mackie (eds), *Indonesia: Australian Perspectives*, Canberra: Research School of Pacific Studies, The Australian National University, p. 620.

32 Cf. Alisjahbana 1966: 147–55; Koentjaraningrat (1984) 'Migrasi, Transmigrasi dan Urbanisasi', in Koentjaraningrat (ed.), *Masalah–Masalah Pembangunan: Bunga Rampai Antropologi Terapan*, Jakarta: LP3ES, pp. 255–7; Sjamsuddin 1989: 1, 16–21, 49–69, 110, 113, 132–3; Wandelt 1989: 20–1; Koentjaraningrat 1993: 20–5.

33 Cf. for example, Rahardjo 1983: 43.

34 Cf. *Wacana Antropologi*, 2(5) (Maret–April 1999): 1.

35 Cf. Marzali 1998b.

36 During the Soeharto regime, Makassar's name was changed to Ujung Pandang. In 1999, the old name Makassar was re-introduced.

37 Cf. for example, *Buku Panduan Studi*, Denpasar: Fakultas Sastra Universitas Udayana, 1998: 2.

38 Cf. Alisjahbana 1966: 74–5; Koentjaraningrat 1975: 217–53; Koentjaraningrat 1987: 219, 222–4, 227; Danandjaya 1994: 26; Dharmaperwira-Amran 1997: 19, 24, 25, 33–42; Marzali 1998b: 13. See also: 'Obituari: in memoriam Prof Koentjaraningrat (15 Juni 1923–4 Maret 1999)', *Antropologi Indonesia*, 57, Th. XXII (Sept.–Des. 1998; the issue was published belatedly in spring 1999), pp. 1–12; Martin Ramstedt (1992) 'Indonesian cultural policy in relation to the development of Balinese performing arts',

in Danker Schaareman (ed.), *Balinese Music in Context. A Sixty-fifth Birthday Tribute to Hans Oesch*, Winterthur: Amadeus, pp. 68–71.

39 See also Ali 1981: 5, 7, 13–5, 22–3.

40 Cf. Yamin 1951: 1–10; Yamin 1974: 5, 15, 16, 91–102; Kleden 1987: 12–3; Wandelt 1989: 22–5.

41 In the context of the *orde baru*, the *panca sila* are contracted into *pancasila*, the contraction signifying the Indonesian state-philosophy of the Soeharto-era. See also Wandelt 1989.

42 Cf. Wandelt 1989: 205.

43 *Bushido* signifies the 'way of the *samurai*'. During the Second World war, the slogan 'bushido means death' encouraged Japanese soldiers to throw themselves into desperate battles and thus became known to Indonesian recruits, too. Cf. Ikegami, Eiko (1995), *The Taming of the Samurai: Honorific Individualism and the Making of Modern Japan*. Cambridge/MA, London: Harvard University Press; pp. 285–6. See also Sutherland 1997: 89.

44 Cf. Kleden 1987: 214–47.

45 Cf. Suparlan 1986: 85.

46 See also Kleden 1997: 10, 11.

47 Cf. Koentjaraningrat 1982b: 351–2, 355; Koentjaraningrat 1982c: 428; Rahardjo 1983: 43; Bachtiar 1986: 71, 72; Suparlan 1986: 82–3, 85, 88; Widjaja 1986a: 18, 20; Widjaja 1986b: 50–1; Wandelt 1989: 22–5, 27, 64, 77, 97–8, 110–17, 121, 132, 153–4, 161–5, 172–93, 249; Hassan 1993: 22, 26, 29–30, 31–5, 77–8, 100, 108; Bachtiar 1994: 19, 42; Guiness 1994: 269, 270, 271, 272, 273, 276, 279, 281, 286, 295–7; Hatley 1994: 224; Hill 1994: 54–5, 63, 68, 72, 74, 77, 87; Hill and Mackie 1994: xxiii, xxiv, xxix–xxx; Mackie and McIntyre 1994: 2, 3, 7, 11, 12, 15, 23, 24, 26, 27, 31; Anggoro 1996: 208, 212–4, 229.

48 Cf. Koentjaraningrat 1987: 223; *Pedoman Pendidikan Sarjana Strata 1*, Jakarta: Fakultas Ilmu Sosial & Ilmu Politik, 1999–2000: 2.

49 Cf. Buku Panduan Studi. Denpasar: Fakultas Sastra Universitas Udayana, 1998: 2.

50 Since East Timor became independent in 1999, there are only 26 instead of 27 Indonesian provinces.

51 With the exception of a very few like, for example, the Tri Sakti University in Jakarta, private universities in Indonesia usually have a lower standard than the state universities.

52 Cf. for example, Buku Panduan Studi. Denpasar: Fakultas Sastra Universitas Udayana, 1998: 68–71; Departemen Pendidikan dan Kebudayaan (1985–6) *Buku Pedoman Pendidkan Program studi Antropologi*, Surabaya: Fakultas Ilmu Sosial dan Ilmu Politik, Universitas Airlangga, p. 5; Koentjaraningrat 1987: 224.

53 See also Budihardjo 1997; Matullada 1997; Martin Ramstedt (1993) 'Indonesian Cultural Policy in Relation to the Development of Balinese Performing Arts', in Danker Schaareman (ed.), *Balinese Music in Context. A Sixty-fifth Birthday Tribute to Hans* Oesch, Winterthur: Amadeus; Rata 1997; Research Team of the State University of Udayana (1975), *The Impact of Tourism on Village Community Development*, Denpasar: Universitas Udayana; Sedyawati 1997; Soedarsono 1999; Yoety, Oka A (1985), *Komersialisasi Seni Budaya dalam Pariwisata*, Bandung: Angkasa.

54 Cf. Koentjaraningrat 1993: iv–v, 52–7, 61–8, 69–148; Dharmaperwira-Amran 1997: 48–61, 120, 122–4; Kleden 1997: 35; Koentjaraningrat 1997; 'Obituari: in Memoriam Prof. Koentjaraningrat (15 Juni 1923–4–Maret 1999', *Antropologi Indonesia*, No. 57, Th. XXII (Sept.–Des. 1998; the issue was published belatedly in spring 1999), pp. 6–7; *Pedoman Pendidikan Sarjana Strata 1*, Jakarta: Fakultas Ilmu Sosial & Ilmu Politik, 1999–2000: 129, 131–40.

55 Cf. Danandjaya 1994: 27.

56 Cf. Danandjaya 1987: 237.

57 Cf. for instance, Danandjaya 1994: 23–4.

58 Cf. for example, Kleden 1997: 22.

59 Cf. Koentjaraningrat 1982a: 7, 8–9; Koentjaraningrat 1984: 3–4; Koentjaraningrat 1987: 223–4; Harsojo 1988: 243–59, 265–7; Wandelt 1989: 185; Danandjaya 1991: 17; Koentjaraningrat 1993: 222–8.
60 Cf. Rahardjo 1998: 164.
61 See for instance, Rahardjo 1998: 168; Sostrodihardjo 1998: 198.
62 See for instance, the works of Koesnoe mentioned in the bibliography as well as Masduki 1998; Wignjosoebroto 1998.
63 Cf. for example, Schreiner 1997.
64 Cf. Departemen Pendidikan dan Kebudayaan (1985/86) *Buku Pedoman Pendidkan Program studi Antropologi*, Surabaya: Fakultas Ilmu Sosial dan Ilmu Politik, Universitas Airlangga, p. 3; Mustopo 1983.
65 Cf. for example, Buku Panduan Studi. Denpasar: Fakultas Sastra Universitas Udayana, 1998: 68–9; *Pedoman Pendidikan Sarjana Strata 1*. Jakarta: Fakultas Ilmu Sosial & Ilmu Politik, 1999–2000: 36–42.
66 Cf. for example, *Nuansa Pemberdayaan*, Vol. 1/I/1999.

Bibliography

Aditjondro, George J. (1997) 'Implikasi Pergeseran Ilmuwan Sosial dari "Pro-Negara" ke "Pro-Masyarakat" ', in Nico G. Schulte Nordholt and Leontine E. Visser (eds), *Ilmu Sosial di Asia Tenggara: dari partikularisme ke universalisme*, Jakarta: LP3ES, pp. 41–50.

Ali, R. Moh (1964, 1981) *Pandangan Tentang Sejarah Indonesia Yang Bersifat Serba-Dua Dan Yang Bersifat Serba Tunggal*, Jakarta: Bhratara Karya Aksara.

Alisjahbana, Sutan Takdir (1966) *Indonesia. Social and Cultural Revolution*, Singapore, Oxford, New York: Oxford University Press.

Anderson, Benedict (1996) *Imagined Communities: Reflection on the Origin and Spread of Nationalism*, London, New York: Verso.

Anggoro, Kusnanto (1996) 'Rekonstruksi dan Reorientasi Budaya Politik', in J. Soedjati Djiwandono and T.A. Legowo (eds), *Revitalisasi Sistem Politik Indonesia*, Jakarta: Centre for Strategic and International Studies, pp. 207–31.

Astiti, Tjokorda Istri Putra (1995) 'Benarkah Bali Berdiri Di Antara Adat dan Agama?', in Usadi Wiryatnaya and Jean Couteau (eds), *Bali Di Persimpangan Jalan, Jilid 2 (Sebuah Bunga Rampai)*, Denpasar: Nusa Data Indo Budaya , pp. 97–107.

Bachtiar, Harsja W. (1986) 'Puncak-Puncak Kebudayaan Daerah Dan Kebudayaan Bali', in I. Gusti Ngurah Bagus (ed.), *Sumbangan Nilai Budaya Bali Dalam Pembangunan Kebudayaan Nasional*, Denpasar: Proyek Penelitian Dan Pengkajian Kebudayaan Bali, Direktorat Jenderal Kebudayaan, Departemen Pendidikan dan Kebudayaan, pp. 66–73.

——(1994) 'Integrasi Nasional Indonesia', in *Wawasan Kebangsaan Indonesia. Gagasan dan Pemikiran Badan Komunikasi Penghayatan Kesatuan Bangsa*. Jakarta: Bakom PKB Pusat, pp. 7–55.

Budihardjo, Eko (1997) 'The Role of the Market as a Heritage Revitalizer', in Wiendu Nuryanti (ed.), *Tourism and Heritage Management*, Yogyakarta: Gajah Mada University Press, pp. 221–5.

Budiman, Arief (1983) 'Ilmu-Ilmu Sosial dan Perubahan Masyarakat di Indonesia', in Nurdien (ed.), *Perubahan Nilai–Nilai di Indonesia*, Bandung: Alumni, pp. 1–9.

Corbey, Raymond and Joep Leerssen (1991) 'Studying allterity: backgrounds and perspectives', in Raymond Corbey and Joep Leerssen (eds), *Alterity, Identity, Image*, Amsterdam, Atlanta, GA: Editions Rodopi, pp. vi–xviii.

Danandjaya, James (1987) 'Manfaat Media Tradisional untuk Pembangunan', in Nat J. Coletta and Umar Kayam (eds), *Kebudayaan dan Pembangunan: Sebuah Pendekatan*

Terhadap Antropologi Terapan di Indonesia. Jakarta: Yayasan Obor Indonesia, pp. 229–39.

Danandjaya, James (1991) *Folklor Indonesia: Ilmu gosip, dongeng, dan lain-lain*, Jakarta: Pustaka Utama Grafiti.

——(1994) *Antropologi Psikologi: Teori, Metode dan Sejarah Perkembangannya*, Jakarta: Raja Grafindo Persada.

Das, Veena (1993) 'Der anthropologische Diskurs über Indien. Die Vernunft und ihr Anderes', in Eberhard Berg and Martin Fuchs (eds), *Kultur, soziale Praxis, Text. Die Krise der ethnographischen Repräsentation*, Frankfurt aM: Suhrkamp, pp. 402–22.

Dharmaperwira-Amran, Frieda (1997) *Corat-coret Koentjaraningrat*, Jakarta: Asosiasi Antropologi Indonesia bekerjasama dengan Yayasan Obor Indonesia.

Fuchs, Martin and Eberhard Berg (1993) 'Phanomenologie der Differenz: Reflexions-stufen ethnographischer Repräsentation', in Eberhard Berg and Martin Fuchs (eds), *Kultur soziale Praxis, Text: die Krise der ethnographischen Repräsentation*, Frankfurt, aM: Suhrkamp, pp. 69–96.

Guiness, Patrick (1994) 'Local society and culture', in Hal Hill (ed.), *Indonesia's New Order: The Dynamics of Socio-Economic Transformation*, St. Leonards: Allen & Unwin, pp. 267–304.

Harsojo (1988) *Pengantar Antropologi*, Bandung: Binacipta.

Hassan, Fuad (1993) *Renungan Budaya*, Jakarta: Balai Pustaka.

Hatley, Barbara (1994) 'Cultural expression', in Hal Hill (ed.), *Indonesia's New Order: The Dynamics of Socio-Economic Transformation*, St. Leonards: Allen & Unwin, pp. 216–66.

Hill, Hal (1994) 'Economy', in Hal Hill (ed.), *Indonesia's New Order: The Dynamics of Socio-Economic Transformation*, St. Leonards: Allen & Unwin, pp. 54–122.

Hill, Hal and Jamie Mackie (1994) 'Introduction', in Hal Hill (ed.), *Indonesia's New Order: The Dynamics of Socio-Economic Transformation*, St. Leonards: Allen & Unwin, pp. xxii–xxxv.

Hooker, M.B. (1978) *Adat Law in Modern Indonesia*, Kuala Lumpur, Oxford, New York, Jakarta: Oxford University Press.

Ikegami, Eiko (1995) *The Taming of the Samurai: Honorific Individualism and the Making of Modern Japan*, Cambridge, MA and London: Harvard University Press.

Kartodirdjo, Sartono (1987) *Kebudayaan Pembangunan dalam Perspektif Sejarah*, Yogyakarta: Gajah Mada University Press.

——(1997) 'From ethno-nationalism to the "Indonesia Merdeka" movement 1908–1925', in Sri Kuhnt-Saptodewo, Volker Grabowsky and Martin Großheim (eds), *Nationalism and Cultural Revival in Southeast Asia: Perspectives from the Centre and the Region*, Harrassowitz, pp. 75–81.

Kleden, Ignas (1987) *Sikap Ilmiah dan Kritik Kebudayaan*, Jakarta: LP3ES.

——(1997) 'Ilmu Sosial di Indonesia: Tindakan dan Refleksi dalam Perspektif Asia Tenggara', in Nico G. Schulte Nordholt and Leontine E. Visser (eds), *Ilmu Sosial di Asia Tenggara: dari partikularisme ke universalisme*, Jakarta: LP3ES, pp. 10–40.

Koentjaraningrat, R.M. (1975) *Anthropology in Indonesia. A Bibliographical Review*, 's-Gravenhage: Martinus Nijhoff (KITLV Bibliographical Series 8).

——(1982a) 'Arti Antropologi Terapan dalam Pembangunan Nasional', in R.M. Koentjaraningrat (ed.), *Masalah-masalah Pembangunan: Bunga Rampai Antropologi Terapan*, Jakarta: LP3ES, pp. 3–10.

——(1982b) 'Lima Masalah Integrasi Nasional', in R.M. Koentjaraningrat (ed.), *Masalah-masalah Pembangunan: Bunga Rampai Antropologi Terapan*, Jakarta: LP3ES, pp. 345–70.

——(1982c) 'Ikhtisar Sejarah Pendidikan di Indonesia dan Perubahan Orientasi Nilai-Budaya Indonesia', in R.M. Koentjaraningrat (ed.), *Masalah-masalah Pembangunan: Bunga Rampai Antropologi Terapan*, Jakarta: LP3ES, pp. 409–29.

——(1984) *Kebudayaan Mentalitas dan Pembangunan*, Jakarta: Gramedia.

——(1987) 'Anthropology in Indonesia', *Journal of Southeast Asian Studies*, XVIII(2): 217–34.

——(1993) *Masalah Kesukubangsaan dan Integrasi Nasional*, Jakarta: Penerbit Universitas Indonesia.

——(1997) 'Anthropological aspects of cultural tourism', in Wiendu Nuryanti (ed.), *Tourism and Heritage Management*, Yogyakarta: Gajah Mada University Press, pp. 101–4.

Koesnoe, Mohammad (1969) *Musjawarah: Een Wijze van Volksbesluitvorming volgens Adatrecht*, Nijmegen: Katholieke Universiteit te Nijmegen.

——(1988) *Enam Puluh Tahun Sumpah Pemuda*, Malang: Sekolah Tinggi Ilmu Hukum Sunan Giri.

——(1992) *Hukum Adat Sebagai Suatu Model Hukum, Bagian I (Historis)*, Bandung: Mandar Maju.

——(1996) *Hukum Adat (Dalam Alam Kemerdekaan Nasional Dan Persoalannya Menghadapi Era Globalisasi)*, Surabaya: Ubhara Press.

—— (1997) *Undang-Undang Nomor 14/1970 dan Pasa/24 dan 25 Undang-Undang Dasar 1945*, Surabaya: Temu Ilmiah Guru Besar dan PAKAR Ilmu Hukum dan Ketatanegaraan, Universitas Bhayangkara, 10–11 April.

Krotz, Esteban (1997) 'Anthropologies of the South: their rise, their silencing, their characteristics', *Critique of Anthropology*, 17(3): 237–51.

Mackie, Jamie and Andrew MacIntyre (1994) 'Politics', in Hal Hill (ed.), *Indonesia's New Order: The Dynamics of Socio-Economic Transformation*, St. Leonards: Allen & Unwin, pp. 1–53.

Marzali, Amri (1998a) 'Konsep Peisan dan Kajian Masyarakat Pedesaan Di Indonesia', *Antropologi Indonesia*, No. 54, Th. XXI (Des. 1997–April 1998), pp. 85–97.

——(1998b) 'Pergeseran Orientasi Nilai Kultural dan Keagamaan di Indonesia: Sebuah Esei dalam Rangka Mengenang Almarhum Prof. Koentjaraningrat', *Antropologi Indonesia*, No. 57, Th. XXII (Sept.–Des. 1998), pp. 13–22.

Masduki, Achid (1998) 'Peranan Hukum Adat dalam Mengatasi Masalah Pemilikan pada Masyarakat Industri', in M. Syamsuddin, Endro Kumoro, Aunur Rachiem F. and Machsum Tabrani (eds), *Hukum Adat Dan Modernisasi Hukum*, Yogyakarta: Fakultas Hukum, Universitas Islam Indonesia, pp. 225–38.

Matullada, H.A. (1997) 'Heritage and living culture in the eastern islands of Indonesia', in Wiendu Nuryanti (ed.), *Tourism and Heritage Management*, Yogyakarta: Gajah Mada University Press, pp. 404–24.

Mortimer, Rex (1980) 'The place of communism', in James J. Fox, Ross Garnaut, Peter McCawley and J.A.C. Mackie (eds), *Indonesia: Australian Perspectives*, Canberra: Research School of Pacific Studies, The Australian National University, pp. 615–32.

Mustopo, M. Habib (1983) 'Pendahuluan', in M. Habib Mustopo (ed.), *Ilmu Budaya Dasar: Kumpulan Essay Manusia dan Budaya*, Surabaya: Usaha Nasional, pp. 13–23.

Rahardjo, M. Dawam (1996) 'Cendekiawan Indonesia; Masyarakat dan Negara: Wacana Lintas-Kultural', in Tim Editor Masika (ed.), *Kebebasan Cendekiawan: Refleksi Kaum Muda*, Yogyakarta: Yayasan Bentang Budaya, Pustaka Republika, pp. vii–xix.

Rahardjo, Satjipto (1998) 'Relevansi Hukum Adat dengan Modernisasi Hukum Kita', in M. Syamsuddin, Endro Kumoro, Aunur Rachiem F. and Machsum Tabrani (eds), *Hukum*

Adat Dan Modernisasi Hukum, Yogyakarta: Fakultas Hukum, Universitas Islam Indonesia, pp. 161–8.

Rahardjo, Slamet (1983) 'Pendekatan Budaya Terhadap Integrasi Nasional', in Nurdien (ed.), *Perubahan Nilai–Nilai di Indonesia*, Bandung: Alumni, pp. 43–8.

Ramstedt, Martin (1993) 'Indonesian cultural policy in relation to the development of the Balinese performing Arts', in Danker Schaareman (ed.), *Balinese Music in Context* (Festschrift für Hans Oesch), Winterthur: Amadeus-Verlag, pp. 59–84.

—— (1994) 'Applied anthropology und nationaler Aufbau in Indonesien', in Matthias S. Laubscher and Bertram Turner (eds), *Völkerkunde Tagung München 91, Bd. 2: Afrika, Asien, Europa, Mittelund Südamerika*, München: Akademischer Verlag, pp. 207–23.

——(1996) 'Das "weibliche" Asien', in Margret Jäger and Siegfried Jäger (eds), *Baustellen: Beiträge zur Diskursgeschichte deutscher Gegenwart*, Duisburg: DISS, pp. 238–57.

——(1997) 'Interkulturelle Kommunikation – wozu?', in Andreas Disselnkötter, Siegfried Jäger, Helmut Kellershohn and Susanne Slobodzian (eds), *Evidenzen im Fluß: Demokratieverluste in Deutschland*, Duisburg: DISS, pp. 205–31.

——(2004) 'Introduction: negotiating identities – Indonesian "Hindus" between local, national, and global interests', in Martin Ramstedt (ed.), *'Hinduism' in Modern Indonesia: A Minority Religion between Local, National and Global Interests*, London: RoutledgeCurzon, p. xiv.

Rata, Ida Bagus (1997) 'The use of archaeological remains in the development of cultural tourism', in Wiendu Nuryanti (ed.), *Tourism and Heritage Management*, Yogyakarta: Gajah Mada University Press, pp. 357–64.

Rothermund, Dietmar (1997) 'Nationalism and the reconstruction of traditions in Asia', in Sri Kuhnt-Saptodewo, Volker Grabowsky and Martin Großheim (eds), *Nationalism and Cultural Revival in Southeast Asia: Perspectives from the Centre and the Region*, Harrassowitz, pp. 13–28.

Said, Edward (1978) *Orientalism: Western Conceptions of the Orient*, London: Routledge & Kegan.

Schreiner, Klaus H. (1997) 'History in the showcase: representations of national history in Indonesian museums', in Sri Kuhnt-Saptodewo, Volker Grabowsky and Martin Großheim (eds), *Nationalism and Cultural Revival in Southeast Asia: Perspectives from the Centre and the Region*, Harrassowitz, pp. 99–117.

Schulte Nordholt, Henk (1988) *Een Balische Dynastie. Hiërarchie en Conflict in de Negara Mengwi 1700–1940*, Amsterdam: Vrije Universiteit, pp. 218–20.

Sedyawati, Edi (1997) 'Potential and challenges of tourism: managing the national cultural heritage of Indonesia', in Wiendu Nuryanti (ed.), *Tourism and Heritage Management*, Yogyakarta: Gajah Mada University Press, pp. 25–35.

Sjamsuddin, Nazaruddin (1989) *Integrasi Politik di Indonesia*, Jakarta: Gramedia.

Soedarsono, R.M. (1999) *Seni Pertunjukan: Indonesia and Pariwisata*, Bandung: Masyarakat Seni Pertunjukan.

Sostrodihardjo, Soedjito (1998) 'Kedudukan Hukum Adat dalam Industrialisasi', in M. Syamsuddin, Endro Kumoro, Aunur Rachiem F. and Machsum Tabrani (eds), *Hukum Adat Dan Modernisasi Hukum*, Yogyakarta: Fakultas Hukum, Universitas Islam Indonesia, pp. 198–214.

Suparlan, Parsudi (1986) 'Penelitian bagi Menunjang Pembinaan dan Pengembangan Kebudayaan Nasional', in A.W. Widjaja (ed.), *Individu, Keluarga dan Masyarakat: Topik-topik Kumpulan Bahan Bacaan Mata Kuliah Olmu Sosial Dasar*, Jakarta: Akademika Pressindo, pp. 81–8.

—— (1998) 'Model Sosial Budaya bagi Penyelenggaraan Transmigrasi di Irian Jaya', *Antropologi Indonesia*, No. 57, Th. XXII (Sept.–Dec. 1998), pp. 23–47.

Sutherland, Heather (1997) 'Professional paradigms, politics and popular practice: reflections on "Indonesian national history"', in Sri Kuhnt-Saptodewo, Volker Grabowsky and Martin Großheim (eds), *Nationalism and Cultural Revival in Southeast Asia: Perspectives from the Centre and the Region*, Harrassowitz, pp. 83–98.

Wandelt, Ingo (1989) *Der Weg zum Pancasila-Menschen: Die Pancasila-Lehre unter dem P4-Beschlußdes Jahres 1978, Entwicklung und Struktur der indonesischen Staatslehre*, Frankfurt am, Bern, New York, Paris: Peter Lang.

Warren, Carol (1993) *Adat and Dinas: Balinese Communities in the Indonesian State*, New York: Oxford University Press.

Widjaja, A.W. (1986a) 'Manusia, Nilai Tradisional dan Lingkungan', in A.W. Widjaja (ed.), *Individu, Keluarga dan Masyarakat: Topik-topik Kumpulan Bahan Bacaan Mata Kuliah Olmu Sosial Dasar*, Jakarta: Akademika Pressindo, pp. 17–21.

—— (1986b) 'Integrasi Nasional, Bangsa dan Nasion Indonesia', in A.W. Widjaja (ed.), *Individu, Keluarga dan Masyarakat: Topik-topik Kumpulan Bahan Bacaan Mata Kuliah Olmu Sosial Dasar*, Jakarta: Akademika Pressindo, pp. 42–52.

Wignjosoebroto, Soetandyo (1998) 'Peranan Hukum Adat dalam Menata Hubungan Kerja Masyarakat Industri', in M. Syamsuddin, Endro Kumoro, Aunur Rachiem F. and Machsum Tabrani (eds), *Hukum Adat Dan Modernisasi Hukum*, Yogyakarta: Fakultas Hukum, Universitas Islam Indonesia, pp. 215–24.

Yamin, Muhammad (1951) *6000 Tahun Sang Merah-Putih*, Jakarta: Siguntang.

—— (1974) *Gajah Mada. Pahlawan Persatuan Nusantara*, Jakarta: Balai Pustaka.

Yoety, Oka A. (1985) Komersialisasi Seni Budaya delam Pariwisata, Bandung: Angkasa.

Part VI

Afterword

11 Indigenization

Features and problems

Syed Farid Alatas

Introduction

The discourse on the indigenization of the social sciences, particularly where anthropology, psychology and sociology are concerned, has been in existence for a little over twenty years. Indigenization was and continues to be a response to what many non-Western social scientists perceive as the inability of Euro-American social science to constitute a relevant and liberating discourse in the context of Asian, African and Latin American societies. This problem was exacerbated by the fact that much of such social science was assimilated uncritically outside of their countries of origin among students, lecturers, researchers and planners. While the problem of irrelevance and its concomitants raised in the discourse on indigenization had been recognized by non-Western scholars as early as the beginning of this century, the term 'indigenization' has only gained currency since the 1970s. It could be said that indigenization is a relatively new term that addresses a problem recognized quite some time ago.

The purpose of this chapter is to discuss the main features of indigenization, the context of its discourse, the criteria of indigenization as understood by its proponents, and the pitfalls of the indigenization project, in the course of reflecting on the chapters of this volume as well as a number of other works. The following section provides a brief sketch of the implantation of the social sciences during the colonial period and stresses that it was in this period that the same issues addressed in the discourse on indigenization since the 1970s had already been raised. This is followed by an account of various reactions seeking to create more relevant, autonomous and progressive social sciences, including the move to indigenize the social sciences. I then move on to a consideration of the variety of definitions of indigenization and identify a common theme. After this, I turn to an enumeration of some problems and obstacles facing the call to indigenization. The final section discusses, by way of conclusion, the prospects for the successful indigenization of anthropology and other social sciences.

The implantation of the social sciences

The formative period of the various disciplines of the social sciences and the institutions in which they were taught, in much of Asia and Africa, was initiated and sustained by colonial scholars and administrators since the eighteenth century, as well as by other Europeans directly and indirectly in vicariously colonized areas.

In Afghanistan, political economy, sociology, economic geography and political history have been taught since 1939 at Kabul University. While the foreign teaching staff were mainly Turkish (Rahimi 1984: 28), Turkish social science itself was very much influenced by the French and German traditions. In the Indian sub-continent the three presidency capitals of Bombay, Calcutta and Madras acquired universities in 1856 and were modelled after British centres of higher education (Dube 1984: 233). Dhaka University in Bangladesh was set up in 1921 based on the model of Calcutta University, and offered courses in economics, political science, sociology, anthropology and geography (Karim 1984: 84–7).

In Burma, the University of Rangoon was established in 1920 in the images of Oxford and Cambridge Universities, the first social sciences taught there being economics, history, political science, psychology, anthropology and sociology (Kyi 1984: 100–1). In Nepal, the first social science, economics, was introduced in 1943 at Tri Chandra College which was itself established by the British in 1918 (Rana 1984: 354–5).

In the Netherlands Indies, Dutch and Dutch-trained Indonesians have been teaching the social sciences since the 1920s (Bachtiar 1984: 253). In Malaysia and Singapore, social science disciplines were formally introduced with the formation of Raffles College in 1929, with the primary function being to produce second-level manpower for the colonial administration while serious research, especially in anthropology, history, law and linguistics, was conducted by colonial scholars and administrators (Chee 1984: 297). In 1949, Raffles College and King Edward VII College of Medicine, both in Singapore, were amalgamated to become the University of Malaya. In 1958, two autonomous divisions of the University of Malaya were established in Kuala Lumpur and Singapore. These eventually became two separate national universities, the University of Malaya and the National University of Singapore.

In the Philippines, the first social science to be taught, history, was introduced as early as the seventeenth century, with anthropology, economics, political science, psychology and sociology emerging during the American colonial period (Feliciano 1984: 469). The Philippine system was patterned after the American educational system. In the early part of this century, many Filipinos were sent to the United States for graduate studies, further strengthening the American influence in social science education (ibid.: 470).

In China and Japan, the social sciences were introduced from the West in the last century. Although not formally colonized, the mode of implantation of the social sciences in these societies was not very different from the colonies. The social sciences were introduced into Japan during the Meiji period (1868–1912) (Watanuki 1984: 283) and were influenced above all by the Germans and Americans. The social sciences began their career in China with a partial translation of Herbert Spencer's *Principles of Sociology* by Yen Fu, with a complete translation appearing in 1902 (Hsu 1931: 284; Huang 1987: 111–12).

The chronic lack of creativity and originality in the social sciences has no less been felt to be a general problem of knowledge in China and Japan than in many other non-Western academic communities that came under the colonial rule. This problem of originality is partly due to the fact that the social sciences were introduced from without. As a result, there was no continuity between the European tradition of knowledge and indigenous systems of ideas (Watanuki 1984: 283) and no organic relationship with the cultural history of the colony (Kyi 1984: 94). In the case of anthropology, what Ramstedt says of Indonesian anthropology as having been hegemonized three ways by colonial discourse, American anthropology and state nationalization agenda, is true of most countries (Ramstedt, Chapter 10, in this volume). The interesting thing about Japanese anthropology is that while it was introduced from the outside, its development received further impetus during the Japanese colonization of China in the nineteenth century, which saw a dramatic accumulation of ethnographic knowledge on China (Eades, Chapter 4, in this volume).

The introduction of the social sciences in general and anthropology in particular, in the context of colonial expansion, had defined the subsequent development of these disciplines during the post-colonial period in a number of ways, as follows:

(i) *The lack of creativity*. This refers to the inability of anthropologists outside of the Euro-American cultural area to generate original theories and methods (Sinha, Chapter 7, in this volume).

(ii) *Mimesis*. This refers to the uncritical adoption or imitation of Western anthropological models (Sinha, Chapter 7, in this volume). Eades provides an example of this, referring to the theorizing of a Chinese anthropologist well-grounded in Sahlins, Firth and Mauss as being largely irrelevant to the Chinese case as a result of the poor ethnography on which the work is based (Eades, Chapter 4, in this volume).

(iii) *Essentialism*. European discourses on non-Western societies tended to lead to essentialist constructions of these societies, 'confirming' that they were the opposite of what Europe represented, that is, barbaric, backward and irrational (Sinha, Chapter 7, in this volume). Essentialism was, therefore, a basic ingredient of Eurocentrism.

(iv) *The absence of subaltern voices*. Evans notes that in the multitude of materials gathered by Chinese, Vietnamese and Lao ethnographers, there is 'no tradition of recording minority "voices"' (Evans, Chapter 2, in this volume). Along similar lines, Chatterji notes how prominent Indian anthropologists have been too close to the nationalist project of the state (Chatterji, Chapter 8, in this volume). If we understand by 'minority' not just ethnic minorities but all other subaltern groups, then we may define such anthropology as being dominated by an elitist perspective.

(v) *Alignment with the state*. The role that anthropology played in the colonial period continues to define the present day anthropology. As such, anthropology is in the service of the state as far as the promotion of national integration, control over state policies and the creation of a national culture are concerned (Evans, Chapter 2, Ramstedt, Chapter 10 and Pieke, Chapter 3, in this volume).

As a result of such problems, a number of theories of social sciences emerged. These sought to theorize the state of the social sciences and humanities in post-colonial societies and include the theory of Orientalism (Said 1979, 1990), the theory of mental captivity (Alatas 1972, 1974), pedagogical theories of modernization (Al-e Ahmad n.d.; Freire 1970; Illich 1973), the colonial critique of Cesaire (1972), Memmi (1965) and Fanon (1968), and academic dependency theory (Altbach 1977; Garreau 1985; Altbach and Selvaratnam 1989; Alatas 1995).

While space does not permit a discussion of each of these theories, it would be pertinent to mention here that academic dependency theory has much in common with Kuwayama's world system of anthropology in which there is a dominance of the core over the periphery. The situation is characterized by ' "scientific colonialism," in which the centre of gravity for acquisition of knowledge about a people is located elsewhere' (Kuwayama and van Bremen 1997: 54; Kuwayama, Chapter 5, in this volume).

The understanding that the social sciences in Asia, Africa and Latin America has been plagued by problems such as the five listed earlier has led to intellectual reactions among both Western and non-Western scholars. What these reactions have in common is not just the critique of the Eurocentric, imitative, elitist and irrelevant social science they find in their societies but also the call for alternative discourses. We tend to be familiar with such calls originating in the second half of the twentieth century when in fact they began in the last century. The call to indigenization is merely a more recent manifestation of earlier efforts towards more relevant social science. As noted by Sinha, 'the by now commonplace critique of essentialist tendencies in "European"/"Western" Orientalist discourses about "other" peoples and places, launched by feminist, post-colonial, post-Orientalist and deconstructionist theorists, was in a very serious way already anticipated/prefaced/embedded in the discourse about "decolonizing" the social sciences' (Sinha, Chapter 7, in this volume). It would be accurate to say that the notion of indigenization appeared *avant la lettre* in the minds of those who in the last century came to be critical of the Orientalist language and culture studies.

The call to indigenization

Among the earliest to counter Eurocentric thinking was the Indian thinker and reformer, Rammohun Roy (1772–1833). Roy lived during a period of intense proselytization activities carried out by British missionaries among the Hindus and Muslims of India. Roy was critical of the derogatory attitude of the English missionaries towards Hinduism and Islam. Replying to British objections against the literary genres of the *Vedas*, *Puranas* and *Tantras*, Roy argued that the doctrines of the first were more rational than Christianity and that the teachings of the last two were not more irrational than what is found in Christianity (Roy 1906; cited in Sarkar 1937/1985: 622).

A little cited but very important early sociologist, Benoy Kumar Sarkar (1887–1949), systematically critiqued various dimensions of Orientalist

Indology. Writing in the early part of this century, Sarkar was well ahead of his time when he censured Asian thinkers for having fallen 'victim to the fallacious sociological methods and messages of the modern West, to which the postulate of an alleged distinction between the Orient and the Occident is the first principle of science' (Sarkar 1937/1985: 19). He attacked such Eurocentric notions as the inferiority of Hindus in matters of science and technology, the one-sided emphasis on the other-worldly and speculative dimension of the Hindu spirit, and the alleged dichotomy between Orient and Occident (ibid.: 4, 18 and 35). He was also critical of the methodology of the prevailing Indology of his times on three grounds: (i) it overlooked the positive, materialistic and secular theories and institutions of the Hindus, (ii) it compared the ancient and medieval conditions of India with modern and contemporary European and American societies, and (iii) it ignored the distinction between the existing institutions on the one hand and ideals on the other (ibid.: 20–1).

Sarkar was very explicit about his call for a new Indology that would function to demolish the *idolas* of Orientalism as they are found in sociology (ibid.: 28–9). Although Sarkar tended to be Hinducentric in some of his interpretations pertaining to the history of ideas in India, this does not detract from his critique of Orientalism.

As noted by Pieke, China in the 1930s and 1940s came close to establishing an anthropological tradition of its own. A case in point is the work of Fei Xiaotong who brought British functionalist anthropology to bear upon real villages and towns in China (Pieke, Chapter 3, in this volume). One of his findings, namely that 'the way the Chinese person defines him/herself is fundamentally different from Western individualism' (ibid.), attests to the need for a judicious application of Western theories to non-Western realities. The spirit of Fei's work can, of course, be understood in terms of his overall concern with the problem of relevance.

Speaking of the 1940s, Fei was critical of the way debates among sociologists were carried out in China.

> The positions taken by professors in their debates were for the most part based upon facts and theories derived from Western sociology. The various schools of Western sociology were each introduced into China by its followers. That which made Chinese sociology less identical with Western sociology lay in its relationship to the real society. Whatever the particular one, the various schools of Western sociology each reflected a portion of social phenomena, but when they were brought into China, they became empty theories divorced from social reality. This can be seen in the professors' debates at the time because their criticisms of each other always ended up in appeals to logic, and not in appeals to the facts.
>
> (1947/1979: 25)

What was laudable in Fei's view were the efforts to extend or revise existing theories. This went beyond making descriptive statements on Chinese society and the systematic application of Western concepts to Chinese realities. Rather, they attempted to apply Western theories to the observation and analysis of social life in China, with a view to generating explanations for problems in Chinese society (ibid.: 29).

Interest in the theme of relevance continued into the 1950s and 1960s, with the appearance of a number of papers and reports on academic colonialism and the tasks facing the Third World scholars. Syed Hussein Alatas referred to the problem of the 'wholesale importation of ideas from the western world to eastern societies' out of their socio-historical context as a more fundamental problem of colonialism (Alatas 1956). In 1968, the well-known Indian periodical, *Seminar*, devoted an issue to the topic of academic colonialism, which was understood in terms of two aspects. One referred to the use of academically generated information by overt and covert North American agencies, to facilitate political domination of Afro-Asian countries. The other refers to the economic, political and intellectual dominance that North American academics themselves exercise over academics elsewhere (Saberwal 1968: 10). It was recognized that the political and economic structure of imperialism had its parallels in the ways of thinking of the subjugated people (Alatas 1969).

The awareness of such a problem as academic imperialism was widely discussed, particularly after the Project Camelot affair of 1964–5, and led to various calls for endogenous intellectual creativity (Alatas 1981), the decolonization of knowledge (Khatibi 1967; Zghlal and Karoui 1973; ben Jelloun 1974; Zawiah 1994; Boehmer 1995), the globalization of knowledge (Hudson 1977; Taylor 1993; Bell 1994) and the indigenization of social sciences (Atal 1981). The implicit concern had been with addressing the problem of irrelevancy, assessing the progress made by various disciplines and prescribing an alternative discourse. It is in this context that the indigenization of anthropology projects must be seen.

Indigenization, however, is an amorphous term. It does not refer to a new paradigm or a theoretical perspective in the social sciences. Neither can it be referred to as an intellectual movement. 'Indigenization' is a category that subsumes the works of various authors from a wide variety of disciplines in the social sciences, most of which are concerned with the task of liberation from academic colonialism, the problem of the irrelevance of the Euro-American social sciences and the resulting need to create the conditions under which alternative discourses in non-Western societies may emerge.

The features of indigenized anthropology

The numerous works on indigenization including those cited earlier present a wide range of definitions of indigenization. These are useful to work through, with the aim of enumerating a list of traits which capture the essential features of the notion. Evans' Chapter 2, is appropriate to begin with because his discussion on indigenous and indigenized anthropology in Asia provides a definition of indigenization that is at odds with those that are presented in the other chapters of this volume as well as with the dominant thinking on the subject.

Evans suggests that communism in Asia indigenized anthropology. In Vietnam, for example, for a long time anthropological research was conducted largely by indigenous anthropologists, whose research agendas were defined by the developmental aims of the state. These anthropologists subscribed to an ideology according to which national minorities were backward and in need of development as defined by the state (Evans, Chapter 2, in this volume). Evans refers to the theoretical basis of this indigenized anthropology as being derived from a 'Stalinist-Maoist version of Marxism' (ibid.). Here, indigenized anthropology is defined in terms of having 'forced Marxism through their own (Chinese, Vietnamese, North Korean) cultural sieve, and rationalized this in all sorts of ways' (ibid.). Furthermore, because these anthropologists had aligned themselves to the state in its bid to exert control over the national minorities, Evans likens their work to a form of high colonial anthropology (ibid.).

Ramstedt is tempted to understand the amalgamation of Western anthropological theory with the Indonesian state philosophy (*pancasila*) as indigenized Western anthropology (Ramstedt, Chapter 10, in this volume). Although such anthropologists may see themselves as indigenizing Marxist or Western theories, this understanding of indigenization is antithetical to others that have been identified elsewhere.

'Indigenization has generally been understood to constitute a revolt against "intellectual imperialism" as a component of the revolt against politico-economic domination' (Bennagen 1980: 7). Pertierra recognizes the role of indigenized social sciences as a weapon in neo-colonial struggles as long as the social sciences 'act as the counter-point between the state and society' as opposed to becoming an 'instrument of the state's colonization of civil life' (Pertierra forthcoming).

Sinha views the call for indigenizing anthropology and the other social sciences as arising out of the need to ' "purge" the social sciences of Eurocentrism and thus register a crucial break from the hegemony of a colonial past...' (Sinha, Chapter 7, in this volume). She further elaborates this as a need to 'articulate and theorize global politics of academia and its complex role in perpetuating the traditional intellectual division of labor: non-Western scholars as gatherers of empirical material, which forms the grounding for theoretical arguments advanced by Western scholars' (ibid.). Thus, analysis of the problems presented by the structure of the world system of anthropology, in which the dominant discourse of the core social science powers of the United States, Great Britain and France result in conformity, imitation and lack of originality in the periphery (Kuwayama and van Bremen 1997: 54–5), is seen to be a central task of the indigenization of anthropology project.

Another feature of indigenized anthropology is its problematization of the epistemological and methodological underpinnings of the social sciences (Sinha, Chapter 7, in this volume). This would involve exposing the Eurocentrism and Orientalism that undergirds much of the social sciences.

But the indigenization of anthropology is not understood simply in negative terms, that is, in terms of a delinking from metropolitan, neo-colonialist control. It is also understood in a more positive way, in terms of the contribution of non-Western systems of thought to anthropological theory (Evans, Chapter 2, in this volume). Non-Western thought and cultural practices are to be seen as sources of anthropological theorizing, while at the same time Western anthropology is not to be rejected in toto. The indigenization of anthropology projects are not conceived to be a 'categorical rejection of all "Western" input in theorizing' and does not 'seek to replace "Eurocentrism" with "nativism" or any other dogmatic position' (Sinha, Chapter 7, in this volume). Here, there is an explicit claim that theories and concepts can be derived from the historical experiences and cultural practices of the various non-Western cultures, whether culture is defined to be co-terminous with the nation-state or otherwise (Moon, Chapter 6, in this volume; Lee 1979; Fahim and Helmer 1980; Alatas 1993; Enriquez 1994a).

Pieke suggests, with reference to China, that one can speak of an indigenous anthropology as matured only when it has generated a corpus of knowledge that is comparative and cross-cultural. The need for comparative and cross-cultural research is based on the idea that an indigenized anthropology 'autochthonously generates its own ideas, concepts, and debates that are informed by an ongoing hermeneutics between one's own and other cultures' (Pieke, Chapter 3, in this volume). In the absence of such a hermeneutics existing ideas would simply be recycled and new ones imported from the usual Western sources. While this point is well taken, the role of comparative and cross-cultural research can only have the desired effect of indigenizing anthropology if such research is carried out by people already conscious of the problems of academic imperialism, mental captivity and relevance. Only then would comparative research yield original ideas and concepts.

We could then formulate a definition of indigenous anthropology as that which is based upon indigenous historical experiences and cultural practices, in the same way that Western social sciences are. Indigenization requires the turn to indigenous philosophies, epistemologies, histories, art and other modes of knowledge, which are all potential sources of social science theories and concepts. Such activities are deemed to decrease intellectual dependence on the core social science powers of the North Atlantic. Nevertheless, most observers and proponents of indigenization, including those of this volume, do not understand indigenization as constituting a rejection of Western social science.

The generation and use of indigenous viewpoints can be approached in two broad ways, as nicely put by Enriquez. Indigenization from within refers to the process in which key indigenous concepts, methods and theories are semantically elaborated, codified, systematized and then applied. On the other hand, indigenization from without refers to the modification and translation of imported materials that are ultimately assimilated theoretically and culturally (Enriquez 1994: 22).

Atal, on the other hand, had made the distinction between indigenization and endogenous development:

> Taken literally, endogenous development signifies development generated from within and orthogenetically, which would, thus, have no place for any

exogenous influence.... Indigenization, by contrast, at least honestly alludes to outside contact by emphasizing the need for indigenizing the exogenous elements to suit local requirements; whether this is done by the 'indigenous' or by 'outsiders' is mere detail.

(1981: 193)

Generally speaking, what is meant by indigenization by Enriquez and by other authors, including those proponents referred to by the authors of this volume, includes both what Atal refers to as endogenous development and indigenization. It has been widely recognized and accepted that if serious efforts are to be made to bring about more 'relevant' social sciences, the selective assimilation of exogenous (western) elements should be considered a vital part of the endogenous intellectual activity.

(Alatas 1981: 462)

It should, therefore, be obvious that the indigenization of knowledge projects around the world for the most part seek to contribute to the universalization of the social sciences by not just acknowledging but insisting that all cultures, civilizations and historical experiences must be regarded as sources of ideas. Local scholars should contribute on an equal basis with their Western colleagues to international scholarship (Fahim 1970: 397). Referring to the indigenization of development thinking, Hettne suggests that the solution to academic imperialism is not to altogether do away with the Western concepts but to adopt a more realistic understanding of Western social sciences as reflecting particular geographic and historical contexts (Hettne 1991: 39). By and large, proponents of indigenization recognize that the Western social sciences are also indigenous in the sense that they arose in the context of concern with indigenous problems, developed on the basis of indigenously generated research agenda, and supported by indigenous academic institutions.

If we understand indigenization in this way, it becomes clear that it is the prerequisite to the universalization of the social sciences, to the maintenance of internationally recognized standards of scholarship. In fact, indigenization has been defined in precisely these terms. In Korea, for example, indigenization (*tochakhwa*) refers to proceeding from research on the historical development of Korean society to universal theory (Shin 1994: 21).

Returning to Evans' definition of indigenized anthropology, this raises a question that from time to time emerges in indigenization debates – to what extent is the indigenization of anthropology a project in service of the state? In fact, the vast majority of proponents of the indigenization of anthropology, in particular, and the social sciences, in general, would distance themselves from this political stance. This is not to stay that such scholars would be adverse to working with the state or to engaging in policy-related research. Nevertheless, they would not understand the indigenization of anthropology to mean the realignment of the discipline with the objectives of the state.

Problems with the call for indigenization

Nativism

The problem of academic imperialism, mental captivity and the uncritical adoption of Western concepts and research agendas had been perceived as having become so pervasive in the social scientific traditions of developing societies that there were, from time to time, reactionary calls among critics of Western social sciences. The result is a high degree of intolerance towards the Western social sciences in terms of theories, methodologies and the selection of problems. Consider the following viewpoint from a Muslim.

> The fact that concerns us here most is that all the social sciences of the West reflect social orders and have no relationship or relevance to Muslims, and even less to Islam. If we learn and apply Western social sciences, then we are not serious about Islam.
>
> (Siddiqui, n.d.)

This attitude can be captured under the notion of Orientalism in reverse or nativism. The idea of Orientalism in reverse was developed by the Syrian philosopher, Sadiq Jalal al-' Azm. He quotes from the work of a fellow Syrian, Georges Saddikni, on the Arabic notion of man (*insān*) which runs thus:

> The philosophy of Hobbes is based on his famous saying that 'every man is a wolf unto other men', while, on the contrary, the inner philosophy implicit in the word *insān* preaches that 'every man is a brother unto other men'.
>
> (Saddikni cited in al-' Azm 1984: 368)

Al-' Azm then continues with an assessment of the above:

> I submit that this piece of so-called analysis and comparison contains, in a highly condensed form, the entire apparatus of metaphysical abstractions and ideological mystifications so characteristic of Ontological Orientalism and so deftly and justly denounced in Said's book. The only new element is the fact that the Orientalist essentialist ontology has been reversed to favour one specific people of the Orient.
>
> (1984: 368)

Orientalism in reverse involves an essentialist approach to both Orient and Occident and is, therefore, a form of auto-Orientalism. This can be illustrated by the Japanese case. There is a tradition in Japanese sociology that is defined by *Nihonjinron* (theories of Japanese people), which is informed by essentialized views on Japanese society, with the stress on cultural homogeneity and historical continuity. This remains squarely in the tradition of Western scholarship on Japan with the difference that the knowing subjects are Japanese. Hence the term auto-Orientalism (Lie 1996: 5). This is parallelled in Korean anthropology where there are studies founded on the assumption of a monolithic Korean culture (Moon, Chapter 6, in this volume). Also relevant in this regard is Pieke's discussion of Chinese Occidentalism (Pieke, Chapter 3, in this volume) and Yanagita's cultural nationalism discussed by Kuwayama (Kuwayama, Chapter 5, in this volume).

In Chapter 7, Sinha notes that Indian scholars continue to 'reproduce the image of India as an exotic "other," and through the particular project of indigenizing anthropology, the image of India as an "exotic" self' (Sinha, Chapter 7, in this volume), thereby continuing the Orientalist tradition in the form of auto-Orientalism. Pertierra has similar concerns when he warns that indigenized social science in the Filipino context 'risks essentializing Filipinohood by reducing its differences' because of 'insistence on unproblematically using the nation as its referent point...' at the expense of the personal, global, local and other referents (Pertierra forthcoming).

The logical consequence of Orientalism in reverse and auto-Orientalism is nativism. This refers to the trend of going native among Western and local scholars alike, in which the native's point of view is elevated to the status of the criterion by which descriptions and analyses are to be judged. This entails a near total rejection of Western knowledge.

The type of anthropology that Evans wants to typify as indigenized but which is at odds with most definitions of indigenization of social science comes close to being nativistic. This is an anthropology that is informed by a problematic notion of indigeneity, as pointed out by Evans, and which makes claims such as 'only the Chinese can really understand Chinese culture and society', and so on (Evans, Chapter 2, in this volume). Similarly, van Bremen warns of the danger for scholarship of the 'reappearance in places of the idea that anthropological knowledge and scholarship is grounded in an ethnic membership, or even the property of a presumed race, as proclaimed by some anthropologists today' (Kuwayama and van Bremen 1997: 64).

Nevertheless, it has to be stressed that the various conceptions of indigenization, particularly in the fields of anthropology, sociology and psychology, are opposed to nativistic approaches to knowledge.

The nation-state as the basis of indigenization

The nationalization of the social sciences is a process that had been taking place *pari passu* with the indigenization of the social sciences. The case of the Sinicization of Marxist sociology in China presents us with an illustration of the nationalization of the social sciences as a project that, for example, legitimized the Chinese version of socialism and China as a nation (Alatas 1998: 75–6). Because of the nationalist connotations of the term Sinicization, many Taiwanese anthropologists and sociologists eventually dropped the term. They found it more acceptable to refer to their efforts as indigenization as their subject-matter was Taiwan and not China and the recontextualization of their disciplines was to be carried out vis-à-vis Taiwan and not China (Hsu 1991: 35). But in this case, indigenization appears to be synonymous with Taiwanization. It is, therefore, not surprising that many understand indigenization to refer to the development of the social sciences with the nation as the basis. As Pertierra notes, while there may be a quest to generate an indigenous Filipino psychology, there are no demands for an Ifugao one (Pertierra forthcoming). Indian anthropologists similarly lamented that the indigenization of anthropology had failed to take into account the social and cultural diversity of the country. It instead posited the possibility of an 'Indian' anthropology as if there was a homogeneous Indian viewpoint or way of thinking (Sinha 1998: 24).

The danger of anthropology aligning itself too closely with the interests of the state is all the more apparent when it is realized that in many developing societies, a great deal of anthropological research is funded by governments rather than private foundations, a point that Sinha notes for India. Competition for funds often results in anthropologists seeking to demonstrate their utility in policy formulation and programmatic change (Sinha, Chapter 7, in this volume). To the extent that indigenized anthropologies see themselves as liberating discourses, they may be compromised by too close an association with the state and by being defined at the level of the nation and glossing over internal diversities.

The paucity of examples of indigenized anthropology

I had earlier suggested that indigenized anthropology could be defined as anthropology that draws upon indigenous historical experiences and cultural practices for its concepts and theories. The indigenization of anthropology would require the turn to local philosophies, epistemologies and historical experiences. While there have been decades of discourse on the need for indigenized anthropology and other social sciences as well, as some attempts to do indigenized anthropology as noted in the chapters of this volume, there has been little by way of indigenized anthropological theories and concepts. An exemplar for indigenized anthropology would be Khaldunian political anthropology. While ibn Khaldun has, since the last century, been recognized as a precursor of many modern disciplines in the social sciences, there have been practically no attempts to develop Khaldunian or neo-Khaldunian theory. An exception is the work of Ernest Gellner who offered a model of traditional Muslim civilization based on a fusion of ibn Khaldun's political sociology with David Hume's oscillation theory of religion (Gellner 1981: chapter 1). This is an example of indigenization because it regards non-conventional, non-Western sources as legitimate and attempts to develop an integrated model by bringing in Western thought as well. The inclusion of Western theory is not seen as a legitimation of the indigenization exercise but rather a recognition that all civilizations must be considered as sources of not only data but theory as well.

Pitfalls of the term 'indigenization'

An important reason for the indifference or even hostility towards the various indigenization of social sciences projects around the world has to do with the term indigenization itself. The term indigenization has its pitfalls. There is a pernicious rhetoric that is a property of 'indigenization'.

First of all, the term carries with it the notion of indigeny which itself has been mutilated to some degree (Benjamin 1995). Indigeny refers to concrete place, not abstractly defined states and provinces. Forms of consociation based on indigeny are 'bound up in the physical and biotic details' of the place of abode (ibid.: 3–4). The term indigeny, then, connotes insularity and closeness. The adjective, indigenous, is equally unattractive because it connotes tribality, ethnicity, native status or race (ibid.: 2–3).

Second, it has been argued by Syed Hussein Alatas that the term indigenization assumes that there is a local or indigenous social scientific tradition as a base from which to construct original theories, which is generally not the case.[1]

Third, there is the view that indigenization implies that Western knowledge is universal and that it simply needs to be localized or domesticated and that there is nothing endogenous to be contributed to the social sciences.[2]

Fourth, another reason for negative reactions to the term indigenization has to do with the way it has been used in political discourse. For example, during his rule in South Korea, Park Chung-Hee had referred to the indigenization of democracy, to justify authoritarian rule with a Confucian basis.[3]

The aforementioned refer not to logical or conceptual problems of the idea of indigenization but rather to rhetorical properties of the term. For strategic reasons, some may choose to distance themselves from the term but not from the ideas couched in it and the programmatic action encouraged by it.

Prospects for the successful indigenization of anthropology

Obstacles to the indigenization of anthropology and the other social sciences are varied, but there are at least two which are universal. One concerns the structure of academic dependency and the other the cultural environment of academic discourse.

The structure of academic dependency is illustrated by the relative availability of Euro-American funding for research, the generally greater prestige attached to publishing in American and British journals, the higher premium placed on a Western university education and a number of other indicators. There is also the question of the intellectual dependency on ideas. For example, it will be found that the social sciences in former British colonies are likely to be dominated by Anglo-Saxon theoretical traditions.

Such a context that is presented by the structure of academic dependency is not conducive to the indigenization of the social sciences. But what are the possibilities of academic dependency reversal? Eades' account of where Japanese academics publish provides an example of a line of action. Most scholarly publications in the social sciences and humanities in Japan appear in in-house university journals, working paper series, monograph series and other occasional publications. What is very revealing about the Japanese case is that there does not appear to be any discrimination against these in-house publications when it comes to the evaluation of academic staff for promotion (Eades, Chapter 4, in this volume). Such a practice would auger well for the indigenization of the social sciences, as it lessens reliance on European or American standards that may not be appropriate and it works towards the upgrading of local publication capabilities. It also frees academics from being tied to themes and research agendas that are determined by the contents of American and European publications.

But even if some inroads are made towards dismantling the structure of academic dependency, in the final analysis what must change is the intellectual culture in Asia and Africa. By this is meant consciousness of the problem of mental captivity and the irrelevance of an uncritically applied social science. Conscientizing can only take place through the various media of intellectual socialization, including the schools, universities and other institutions of higher learning. For example, a more universalistic approach to the teaching of sociological theory would have to raise the question as to whether sociological theory was to be found in pre-modern, non-European areas. There is also the matter of teaching the context of the rise of sociological theory, which is not only defined by the series of political revolutions in Europe since the seventeenth century or the industrial revolution, but also by colonization and the emergence of Eurocentrism. This in term would imply changes in the way sociological theory is taught. For example, there would be more emphasis on Marx and Weber's Orientalist and Eurocentric dimensions.

In line with the view that indigenization and universalization are one and the same thing, indigenizers of knowledge do not wish to discard Western social sciences, but wish to open up the possibilities for indigenous philosophies, epistemologies and histories to become bases on knowledge. Without indigenization projects throughout the world, it is one set of indigenous (Western) discourse that dominates.

Evans suggests that what is needed in Asia is not an indigenous or indigenized anthropology 'but an anthropology that is more self-consciously and sensitively internationalised' (Evans, Chapter 2, in this volume). This is in fact what has been proposed by the vast majority of proponents of indigenization. They conceive of indigenization as not the rejection of Western social sciences, but the selective adaptation of it to local needs. The acceptance, rejection or extension of knowledge from the West is not based on the grounds of origin but rather on criteria of relevance that are established as a result of consciousness of the problems of academic imperialism, mental captivity and uncritical imitation. The call to indigenization is simultaneously a call to the universalization of the social sciences. This call generally accepts the notion of social science as a universal discourse which is constituted by various civilizational or cultural expressions all contributing to the understanding of the human condition. To the extent that the internationalization of the social sciences requires a plurality of philosophical and cultural expressions, the indigenization of social science projects around the world must be seen as adding to the hitherto dominant Euro-American voice.

Acknowledgement

I wish to thank Dr Hsu for translating and explaining the meaning of some passages in his article for me.

Notes

1 Syed Hussein Alatas, personal communication, Manila, 29 May 1996.
2 Zeus Salazar, personal communication, Manila, 1 June 1996.
3 Kim Kyong-Dong, personal communication, Seoul, 21 June 1996.

References

Alatas, Syed Farid (1993) 'On the indigenization of academic discourse', *Alternatives*, 18(3): 307–38.

——(1995) 'Dependency, rhetorics and the transnational flow of ideas in the social sciences', Paper presented at the Goethe-Institute International Seminar on Cultural and Social Dimensions of Market Expansion, Labuan, 16–17 October.

——(1998) 'Western theories, East Asian realities and the social sciences', in Su-Hoon Lee (ed.), *Sociology in East Asia and Its Struggle for Creativity*, International Sociological Association Pre-Congress Volumes, Social Knowledge: Heritage, Challenges, Perspectives, Maria-Luz Moran (general editor).

Alatas, Syed Hussein (1956) 'Some fundamental problems of colonialism', *Eastern World*, November.

——(1969) 'Academic imperialism', Lecture delivered to the History Society, University of Singapore, 26 September.

——(1972) 'The captive mind in development studies', *International Social Science Journal*, 34(1): 9–25.

——(1974) 'The captive mind and creative development', *International Social Science Journal*, 36(4): 691–9.

——(1981) 'Social aspects of endogenous intellectual creativity: the problem of obstacles – guidelines for research', in A. Abdel-Malek and A.N. Pandeya (eds), *Intellectual Creativity in Endogenous Culture*, Tokyo: United Nations University.

Al-'Azm, Sadiq Jalal (1984) 'Orientalism and orientalism in reverse', in John Rothschild (ed.), *Forbidden Agendas: Intolerance and Defiance in the Middle East*, London: Al Saqi Books, pp. 349–76.

Al-e Ahmad, Jalal (n.d.) *Gharbzadegi (Weststruckness)*, Tehran: Ravaq Press.

Altbach, Philip G. (1977) 'Servitude of the mind? Education, dependency, and neocolonialism', *Teachers College Record*, 79(2): 187–204.

Altbach, Philip G. and Selvaratnam, Viswanathan Selvaratnam (eds) (1989) *From Dependence to Autonomy: The Development of Asian Universities*, Dordrecht: Kluwer Academic Publishers.

Atal, Yogesh (1981) 'The call for indigenization', *International Social Science Journal*, 33(1): 189–97.

Bachtiar, Harsja (1984) 'Indonesia', in *Social Sciences in Asia and the Pacific*, Paris: UNESCO, pp. 249–80.

Bell, Morag (1994) 'Images, myths and alternative geographies of the Third World', in Derek Gregory, Ron Martin and G. Smith (eds), *Human Geography: Society, Space and Social Science*, London: Macmillan, pp. 174–99.

Benjamin, Geoffrey (1995) 'The sociology of indigeny', Paper presented at the Second ASEAN Inter-University Seminar on Social Development, Cebu City, The Philippines, 28–30 November.

Bennagen, P.L. (1980) 'The Asianization of anthropology', *Asian Studies*, 18: 1–26.

Boehmer, Elleke (1995) *Colonial and Postcolonial Literature*, Oxford: Oxford University Press.

Cesaire, Aime (1972) *Discourse on Colonialism*, New York: Monthly Review.

Chee, Stephen (1984) 'Malaysia', in *Social Sciences in Asia and the Pacific*, Paris: UNESCO, pp. 296–323.

Dube, S.C. (1984) 'India', in *Social Sciences in Asia and the Pacific*, Paris: UNESCO, pp. 229–48.

Enriquez, Virgilio G. (1994) 'Towards cross-cultural knowledge through cross-indigenous methods and perspective', in Teresita B. Obusan and Angelina R. Enriquez (eds), *Pamamaraan: Indigenous Knowledge and Evolving Research Paradigms*, Quezon City: Asian Center, University of the Philippines, pp. 19–31.

Fahim, Hussein (1970) 'Indigenous anthropolgy in non-Western countries', *Current Anthropology*, 20(2): 397.

Fahim, Hussein and Katherine Helmer (1980) 'Indigenous anthropology in non-Western countries: a further elaboration', *Current Anthropology*, 21(5): 644–50.

Fanon, Frantz (1968) *The Wretched of the Earth*, New York: Grove Press.

Fei Hsiao-t'ung [Fei Xiaotong] (1947/1979) 'The growth of Chinese sociology', in Fei Hsiao-t'ung (ed.), *The Dilemma of a Chinese Intellectual*, James P. Gough (select. and trans.), White Plains, Armonk, NY: M.E. Sharpe.

Feliciano, Gloria D. (1984) 'Philippines', in *Social Sciences in Asia and the Pacific*, Paris: UNESCO, pp. 468–501.

Freire, Paulo (1970) *Pedagogy of the Oppressed*, New York: Seabury Press.

Garreau, Frederick H. (1985) 'The multinational version of social science with emphasis upon the discipline of sociology', *Current Sociology*, 33(3): 1–169.

Gellner, Ernest (1981) *Muslim Society*, Cambridge: Cambridge University Press.

Hettne, Björn (1991) *The Voice of the Third World: Currents in Development Thinking*, Studies on Developing Countries No. 134, Budapest: Institute for World Economics of the Hungarian Academy of Sciences.

Hsu, C.K. (1991) 'The formation and transformation of a research paradigm: a revisit of Prof. Chen Shao-Hsing's Article', *Chinese Journal of Sociology*, 15: 29–40 [in Chinese].

Hsu, Leonard Shih-Lien (1931) 'The sociological movement in China', *Pacific Affairs*, 4(4): 283–307.

Huang, Lucy Jen (1987) 'The status of sociology in People's Republic of China', *International Review of Modern Sociology*, 17: 111–36.

Hudson, B. (1977) 'The new geography and the new imperialism, 1870–1918', *Antipode*, 9: 12–19.

Illich, Ivan D. (1973) *Deschooling Society*, Harmondsworth: Penguin.

Ben Jelloun, Taher (1974) 'Décolonisation de la Sociologie au Maghreb: utilité et risques d'une fonction critique,' *Le Monde Diplomatique*, August.

Karim, A.K. Nazmul (1984) 'Bangladesh', in *Social Sciences in Asia and the Pacific*, Paris: UNESCO, pp. 79–92.

Khatibi, M. (1967) *Bilan de la Sociologie au Maroc*, Rabat: Publications de l'Association pour la Recherche en Sciences Humaines.

Kuwayama, Takami and Jan van Bremen (1997) 'Kuwayama – van Bremen debate: native anthropologists – with special reference to Japanese studies inside and outside Japan', *Japan Anthropology Workshop Newsletter*, pp. 52–69.

Kyi, Khin Maung (1984) 'Burma', in *Social Sciences in Asia and the Pacific*, Paris: UNESCO, pp. 93–141.

Lee Chong-Bum (1979) 'Prolegomenon to the indigenization of public administration', *Social Science Journal*, 6: 7–26.

Lie, John (1996) 'Sociology of contemporary Japan', *Current Sociology*, 44(1): 1–95.

Memmi, Albert (1965) *The Colonizer and the Colonized*, Boston, MA: Beacon.

Pertierra, R. (forthcoming) 'Culture, social science and the Philippine Nation State', *Asian Journal of Social Science*, 33(3).

Rahimi, Wali Mohammad (1984) 'Afghanistan', in *Social Sciences in Asia and the Pacific*, Paris: UNESCO, pp. 21–51.

Rana, Ratna S.J.B. (1984) 'Nepal', in *Social Sciences in Asia and the Pacific*, Paris: UNESCO, pp. 354–73.

Roy, Rammohun (1906) *The English Works of Raja Rammohun Roy*, Allahabad.

Saberwal, Satish (1968) 'The problem', *Seminar*, 112: 10–13.

Said, Edward (1979) *Orientalism*, New York: Vintage Books.

——(1990) 'Third World intellectuals and metropolitan culture', *Raritan*, 9(3): 27–50.

Sarkar, Benoy Kumar (1937/1985) *The Positive Background of Hindu Sociology*, Delhi: Motilal Banarsidass [First edition published in 1937 in Allahabad, reprinted in Delhi in 1985].

Shin Yong-Ha (1994) 'Suggestions for the development of a creative Korean sociology', in *Korean Sociology in the 21st Century*, Korean Sociological Association, Seoul: Moon-Hak-Kwa Ji-Seong-Sa, 1994, pp. 15–30 [in Korean].

Siddiqui, K. (n.d.) *The Islamic Movement: A Systems Approach*, Tehran: Bunyad Be'that.

Sinha, Vineeta (1998) 'Socio-cultural theory and colonial encounters: the discourse on indigenizing anthropology in India', Manuscript, Department of Sociology, National University of Singapore.

Taylor, Peter J. (1993) 'Full circle or new meaning for global', in R.J. Johnston (ed.), *The Challenge for Geography: A Changing World, A Changing Discipline*, Oxford: Blackwell, pp. 181–97.

Watanuki, Joji (1984) 'Japan', in *Social Sciences in Asia and the Pacific*, Paris: UNESCO, pp. 281–95.

Zawiah Yahya (1994) *Resisting Colonialist Discourse*, Bangi: Penerbit Universiti Kebangsaan Malaysia.

Zghlal, Abdelkader and Karoui, Hachmi (1973) 'Decolonization and social science research: the case of Tunisia', *Middle East Studies Association Bulletin*, 7(3): 11–27.

Index